Ford Mustang Automotive Repair Manual

by J H Haynes
Member of the Guild of Motoring Writers
Bruce Gilmour
and Marcus S Daniels

Models covered:
All Mustang V8 models

ISBN 0 85696 357 7

© Haynes North America, Inc. 1979
With permission from J. H. Haynes & Co. Ltd.

Printed in the USA

(6D4 - 36048)
(357)

ABCDE
FGHIJ
K

3

Haynes Publishing Group
Sparkford Nr Yeovil
Somerset BA22 7JJ England

Haynes North America, Inc.
861 Lawrence Drive
Newbury Park
California 91320 USA

Acknowledgements

Thanks are due to the Ford Motor Company in the USA for the supply of technical information and certain illustrations.

Special thanks are also due to all those people at Sparkford and in the USA who helped in the production of this Manual. Particularly, these are Brian Horsfall and Les Brazier who carried out the mechanical work and took the photographs respectively, Pete Ward who edited the text and Stanley Randolf who planned the page layout.

About this manual

Its aims

The aim of this Manual is to help you get the best value from your car. It can do so in several ways. It can help you decide what work must be done (even should you choose to get it done by a repair station), provide information on routine maintenance and servicing, and give a logical course of action and diagnosis when random faults occur. However, it is hoped that you will use the Manual by tackling the work yourself. On simpler jobs it may even be quicker than booking the car into a repair station, and going there twice to leave and collect it. Perhaps most important, a lot of money can be saved by avoiding the costs the garage must charge to cover its labor and overheads.

The manual has drawings and descriptions to show the function of the various components so that their layout can be understood. Then the tasks are described and photographed in a step-by-step sequence so that even a novice can do the work.

Its arrangement

The Manual is divided into twelve Chapters, each covering a logical sub-division of the vehicle. The Chapters are each divided into Sections, numbered with single figures, eg 5; and the Sections into paragraphs (or sub-sections), with decimal numbers following on from the Section they are in, eg 5.1, 5.2, 5.3 etc.

It is freely illustrated, especially in those parts where there is a detailed sequence of operations to be carried out. There are two forms of illustration: figures and photographs. The figures are numbered in sequence with decimal numbers, according to their position in the Chapter: eg Fig. 6.4 is the 4th drawing/illustration in Chapter 6. Photographs are numbered (either individually or in related groups) the same as the Section or sub-section of the text where the operation they show is described.

There is an alphabetical index at the back of the manual as well as a contents list at the front.

References to the 'left' 'right' of the vehicle are in the sense of a person in the driver's seat facing forwards.

Whilst every care is taken to ensure that the information in this manual is correct no liability can be accepted by the authors or publishers for loss, damage or injury caused by any errors in, or omissions from, the information given.

Introduction to the Ford Mustang

The original Mustang design was created by Ford's chief stylist Joseph Oros and when the finished car was introduced to the market in April 1964 it caused even more interest and excitement amongst the American motoring fraternity than its predecessor the Thunderbird.

With its racy and definitely masculine appearance, the low price tag and not least the excellent choice of name, the Mustang was a phenomenal success. In fact, by 1966, the sales figures were nearing the two million figure.

When first introduced, the Mustang was available with an option of four engine capacities. For the owner with good gas mileage uppermost in mind, Ford offered the 170 cu in or 200 cu in six-cylinder engines, while the 260 cu in and 289 cu in V8 engines were available to the customer whose prime consideration was acceleration. For those who required even more power beneath the hood, a tuned version of the 289 cu in engine was obtainable which developed 271 brake horsepower at 6000 rpm.

Beneath the attractive bodyshell the mechanical layout of the Mustang was quite conventional, comprising a front-mounted engine driving the rear wheels via the transmission unit, driveshaft and differential unit. A choice of either three- or four-speed manual transmission, or three-speed automatic transmission was offered. Front suspension on all models is the independent coil spring and wishbone type, while the rear axle is located on leaf springs. Telescopic shock absorbers are fitted all round.

For 1967 / 1968 the larger capacity 302 and 390 V8 engines became optional and these were followed by the powerful 427, 428 and Boss 429 engines. Inevitably, as engines got larger, so the body size increased until it could no longer be described as a compact sports car. Because it had lost the original Mustang individuality, sales inevitable dropped and in 1974 Ford launched the Mustang Series II.

Contents

1966 Mustang Convertible, 289 cu in

1967 Mustang Hardtop

1971 Mustang Sports Roof

1972 Mustang Hardtop

Buying spare parts
and vehicle identification numbers

Buying spare parts

Replacement parts are available from many sources, which generally fall into one of two categories – authorized dealer parts departments and independent retail auto parts stores. Our advice concerning these parts is as follows:

Retail auto parts stores: Good auto parts stores will stock frequently needed components which wear out relatively fast, such as clutch components, exhaust systems, brake parts, tune-up parts, etc. These stores often supply new or reconditioned parts on an exchange basis, which can save a considerable amount of money. Discount auto parts stores are often very good places to buy materials and parts needed for general vehicle maintenance such as oil, grease, filters, spark plugs, belts, touch-up paint, bulbs, etc. They also usually sell tools and general accessories, have convenient hours, charge lower prices and can often be found not far from home.

Authorized dealer parts department: This is the best source for parts which are unique to the vehicle and not generally available elsewhere (such as major engine parts, transmission parts, trim pieces, etc.).

Warranty information: If the vehicle is still covered under warranty, be sure that any replacement parts purchased – regardless of the source – do not invalidate the warranty!

To be sure of obtaining the correct parts, have engine and chassis numbers available and, if possible, take the old parts along for positive identification.

Vehicle identification numbers

Modifications are a continuing and unpublicized process in car manufacture. Spare parts catalogs and lists are compiled on a numerical basis, the individual vehicle numbers being essential to correctly identify the component required.

A vehicle identification decal is located on the rear edge of the left hand door on all Mustang models. The decal gives the vehicle serial number and coded information regarding the engine, transmission and bodywork. Refer to the accompanying examples showing the type of decals used and a key to the coding.

A vehicle safety certification label is attached to the rear face of the left hand door on later models only. This gives the Gross Vehicle Weight Rating (GVWR) and the Gross Axle Weight Rating (GAWR) for that particular car.

The engine number on all models prior to 1968 is stamped on the left side of the cylinder block. On 1968 and later models the engine number is stamped on a metal tag adjacent to the ignition coil.

The transmission number is stamped on a small metal plate which is riveted to the right side of the transmission casing.

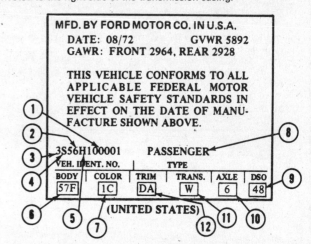

Vehicle identification/safety certification decal (later models)

1 Consecutive unit no.
2 Body serial code
3 Model year code
4 Assembly plant code
5 Engine code
6 Body type code
7 Color code
8 Vehicle type
9 District - special equipment
10 Rear axle code
11 Transmission code
12 Trim code

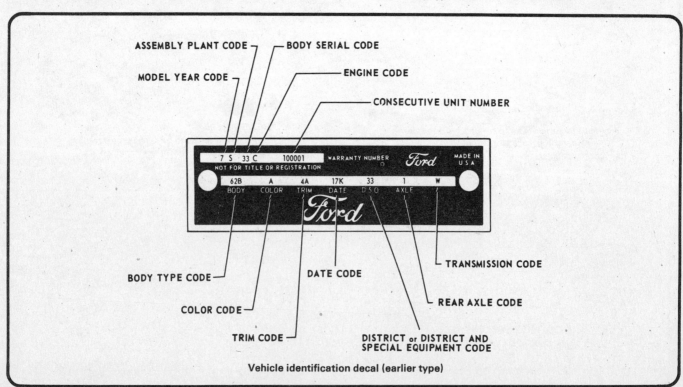

Vehicle identification decal (earlier type)

Jacking and Towing

Jacking points

To change a wheel in an emergency, use the jack supplied with the car. Ensure that the roadwheel nuts are released before jacking up the car and make sure that the top of the jack is fully engaged with the body cutout, and that the base of the jack is standing on a firm surface.

The jack supplied with the vehicle is not suitable for use when raising the vehicle for maintenance or repair operations. For this work, use a trolley, hydraulic or screw type jack located under the front crossmember, bodyframe side-members or rear axle casing, as illustrated. Always supplement the jack with jack stands or blocks before crawling beneath the car.

Towing points

If your vehicle is being towed, make sure that the tow rope is attached to the front crossmember. If the vehicle is equipped with automatic transmission, the distance towed must not exceed 15 miles (24 km), nor the speed 30 mph (48 km/h), otherwise serious damage to the transmission may result. If these limits are likely to be exceeded, disconnect and remove the propeller shaft.

If you are towing another vehicle, attach the tow rope to the spring mounting bracket at the axle tube.

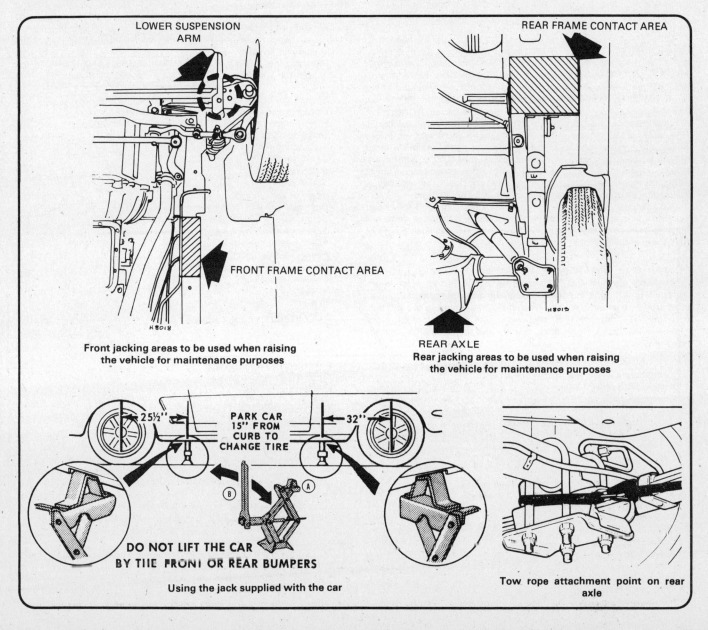

LOWER SUSPENSION ARM

FRONT FRAME CONTACT AREA

Front jacking areas to be used when raising the vehicle for maintenance purposes

REAR FRAME CONTACT AREA

REAR AXLE

Rear jacking areas to be used when raising the vehicle for maintenance purposes

25½"   PARK CAR 15" FROM CURB TO CHANGE TIRE   32"

B   A

DO NOT LIFT THE CAR BY THE FRONT OR REAR BUMPERS

Using the jack supplied with the car

Tow rope attachment point on rear axle

Tools and working facilities

Introduction

A selection of good tools is a fundamental requirement for anyone contemplating the maintenance and repair of a car. For the owner who does not possess any, their purchase will prove a considerable expense, offsetting some of the savings made by doing-it-yourself. However, provided that the tools purchased are of good quality, they will last for many years and prove an extremely worthwhile investment.

To help the average owner to decide which tools are needed to carry out the various tasks detailed in this Manual, we have compiled three lists of tools under the following headings: *Maintenance and minor repair*, *Repair and overhaul*, and *Special*. The newcomer to practical mechanics should start off with the *Maintenance and minor repair* tool kit and confine himself to the simpler jobs around the car. Then, as his confidence and experience grow, he can undertake more difficult tasks, buying extra tools as, and when, they are needed. In this way, a *Maintenance and minor repair* tool kit can be built-up into a *Repair and overhaul* tool kit over a considerable period of time without any major cash outlays. The experienced do-it-yourselfer will have a tool kit good enough for most repair and overhaul procedures and will add tools from the *Special* category when he feels the expense is justified by the amount of use to which these tools will be put.

It is obviously not possible to cover the subject of tools fully here. For those who wish to learn more about tools and their use there is a book entitled *How to Choose and Use Car Tools* available from the publishers of this Manual.

Maintenance and minor repair tool kit

The tools given in this list should be considered as a minimum requirement if routine maintenance, servicing and minor repair operations are to be undertaken. We recommend the purchase of combination wrenches (ring one end, open-ended the other); although more expensive than open-ended ones, they do give the advantages of both types of wrench.

Combination wrenches - $\frac{3}{8}$ to $\frac{11}{16}$ in AF
Adjustable wrench - 9 inch
Engine oil pan/transmission/rear axle drain plug key (where applicable)
Spark plug wrench (with rubber insert)
Spark plug gap adjustment tool
Set of feeler gauges
Brake adjuster wrench (where applicable)
Brake bleed nipple wrench
Screwdriver - 4 in long x $\frac{1}{4}$ in dia (flat blade)
Screwdriver - 4 in long x $\frac{1}{4}$ in dia (cross blade)
Combination pliers - 6 inch
Hacksaw, junior
Tire pump
Tire pressure gauge
Grease gun
Oil can
Fine emery cloth (1 sheet)
Wire brush (small)
Funnel (medium size)

Repair and overhaul tool kit

These tools are virtually essential for anyone undertaking any major repairs to a car, and are additional to those given in the *Maintenance and minor repair* list. Included in this list is a comprehensive set of sockets. Although these are expensive they will be found invaluable as they are so versatile - particularly if various drives are included in the set. We recommend the $\frac{1}{2}$ in square-drive type, as this can be used with most proprietary torque wrenches. If you cannot afford a socket set, even bought piecemeal, then inexpensive tubular box wrenches are a useful alternative.

The tools in this list will occasionally need to be supplemented by tools from the *Special* list.

Sockets (or box wrenches) to cover range $\frac{1}{4}$ $1\frac{1}{8}$ in AF
Reversible ratchet drive (for use with sockets)
Extension piece, 10 inch (for use with sockets)
Universal joint (for use with sockets)
Torque wrench (for use with sockets)
Self-grip wrench - 8 inch
Ball pein hammer
Soft-faced hammer, plastic or rubber
Screwdriver - 6 in long x $\frac{5}{16}$ in dia (flat blade)
Screwdriver - 2 in long x $\frac{5}{16}$ in square (flat blade)
Screwdriver - $1\frac{1}{2}$ in long x $\frac{1}{4}$ in dia (cross blade)
Screwdriver - 3 in long x $\frac{1}{8}$ in dia (electricians)
Pliers - electricians side cutters
Pliers - needle nosed
Pliers - snap-ring (internal and external)
Cold chisel - $\frac{1}{2}$ inch
Scriber
Scraper
Centre punch
Pin punch
Hacksaw
Valve grinding tool
Steel rule/straight edge
Allen keys
Selection of files
Wire brush (large)
Jack stands
Jack (strong scissor or hydraulic type)

Special tools

The tools in this list are those which are not used regularly, are expensive to buy, or which need to be used in accordance with their manufacturers' instructions. Unless relatively difficult mechanical jobs are undertaken frequently, it will not be economic to buy many of these tools. Where this is the case, you could consider clubbing together with friends (or an automobile club) to make a joint purchase, or borrowing the tools against a deposit from a local repair station or tool hire specialist.

The following list contains only those tools and instruments freely available to the public, and not those special tools produced by the vehicle manufacturer specifically for its dealer network. You will find occasional references to these manufacturers' special tools in the text of this Manual. Generally, an alternative method of doing the job without the vehicle manufacturer's special tool is given. However, sometimes, there is no alternative to using them. Where this is the case and the relevant tool cannot be bought or borrowed you will have to entrust the work to a franchised dealer.

Valve spring compressor
Piston ring compressor
Balljoint separator
Universal hub/bearing puller
Impact screwdriver
Micrometer and/or vernier gauge
Carburetor flow balancing device (where applicable)
Dial gauge
Stroboscopic timing light
Dwell angle meter/tachometer
Universal electrical multi-meter
Cylinder compression gauge
Lifting tackle
Trolley jack
Light with extension lead

Buying tools

For practically all tools, a tool factor is the best source since he will have a very comprehensive range compared with the average garage or accessory shop. Having said that, accessory shops often offer excellent quality tools at discount prices, so it pays to shop around.

Remember, you don't have to buy the most expensive items on the shelf, but it is always advisable to steer clear of the very cheap tools. There are plenty of good tools around at reasonable prices, so ask the proprietor or manager of the shop for advice before making a purchase.

Working facilities

Not to be forgotten when discussing tools, is the workshop itself. If anything more than routine maintenance is to be carried out, some form of suitable working area becomes essential.

It is appreciated that many an owner mechanic is forced by circumstances to remove an engine or similar item, without the benefit of a garage or workshop. Having done this, any repairs should always be done under the cover of a roof.

Wherever possible, any dismantling should be done on a clean flat workbench or table at a suitable working height.

Any workbench needs a vise: one with a jaw opening of 4 in (100 mm) is suitable for most jobs. As mentioned previously, some clean dry storage space is also required for tools, as well as the lubricants, cleaning fluids, touch-up paints and so on which become necessary.

Another item which may be required, and which has a much more general usage, is an electric drill with a chuck capacity of at least $\frac{5}{16}$ in (8 mm). This, together with a good range of twist drills, is virtually essential for fitting accessories such as wing mirrors and reversing lights.

Last, but not least, always keep a supply of old newspapers and clean, lint-free rags available, and try to keep any working area as clean as possible.

Care and maintenance of tools

Having purchased a reasonable tool kit, it is necessary to keep the tools in a clean serviceable condition. After use, always wipe off any dirt, grease and metal particles using a clean, dry cloth, before putting the tools away. Never leave them lying around after they have been used. A simple tool rack on the garage or workshop wall, for items such as screwdrivers and pliers is a good idea. Store all normal wrenches and sockets in a metal box. Any measuring instruments, gauges, meters, etc, must be carefully stored where they cannot be damaged or become rusty.

Take a little care when tools are used. Hammer heads inevitably become marked and screwdrivers lose the keen edge on their blades from time to time. A little timely attention with emery cloth or a file will soon restore items like this to a good serviceable finish.

Wrench jaw gap comparison table

Jaw gap (in)	Wrench size
0·250	$\frac{1}{4}$ in AF
0·275	7 mm AF
0·312	$\frac{5}{16}$ in AF
0·315	8 mm AF
0·340	$\frac{11}{32}$ in AF; $\frac{1}{8}$ in Whitworth
0·354	9 mm AF
0·375	$\frac{3}{8}$ in AF
0·393	10 mm AF
0·433	11 mm AF
0·437	$\frac{7}{16}$ in AF
0·445	$\frac{3}{16}$ in Whitworth; $\frac{1}{4}$ in BSF
0·472	12 mm AF
0·500	$\frac{1}{2}$ in AF
0·512	13 mm AF
0·525	$\frac{1}{4}$ in Whitworth; $\frac{5}{16}$ in BSF
0·551	14 mm AF
0·562	$\frac{9}{16}$ in AF
0·590	15 mm AF
0·600	$\frac{5}{16}$ in Whitworth; $\frac{3}{8}$ in BSF
0·625	$\frac{5}{8}$ in AF
0·629	16 mm AF
0·669	17 mm AF
0·687	$\frac{11}{16}$ in AF
0·708	18 mm AF
0·710	$\frac{3}{8}$ in Whitworth; $\frac{7}{16}$ in BSF
0·748	19 mm AF
0·750	$\frac{3}{4}$ in AF
0·812	$\frac{13}{16}$ in AF
0·820	$\frac{7}{16}$ in Whitworth; $\frac{1}{2}$ in BSF
0·866	22 mm AF
0·875	$\frac{7}{8}$ in AF
0·920	$\frac{1}{2}$ in Whitworth; $\frac{9}{16}$ in BSF
0·937	$\frac{15}{16}$ in AF
0·944	24 mm AF
1·000	1 in AF
1·010	$\frac{9}{16}$ in Whitworth; $\frac{5}{8}$ in BSF
1·023	26 mm AF
1·062	$1\frac{1}{16}$ in AF; 27 mm AF
1·100	$\frac{5}{8}$ in Whitworth; $\frac{11}{16}$ in BSF
1·125	$1\frac{1}{8}$ in AF
1·181	30 mm AF
1·200	$\frac{11}{16}$ in Whitworth; $\frac{3}{4}$ in BSF
1·250	$1\frac{1}{4}$ in AF
1·259	32 mm AF
1·300	$\frac{3}{4}$ in Whitworth; $\frac{7}{8}$ in BSF
1·312	$1\frac{5}{16}$ in AF
1·390	$\frac{13}{16}$ in Whitworth; $\frac{15}{16}$ in BSF
1·417	36 mm AF
1·437	$1\frac{7}{16}$ in AF
1·480	$\frac{7}{8}$ in Whitworth; 1 in BSF
1·500	$1\frac{1}{2}$ in AF
1·574	40 mm AF; $\frac{15}{16}$ in Whitworth
1·614	41 mm AF
1·625	$1\frac{5}{8}$ in AF
1·670	1 in Whitworth; $1\frac{1}{8}$ in BSF
1·687	$1\frac{11}{16}$ in AF
1·811	46 mm AF
1·812	$1\frac{13}{16}$ in AF
1·860	$1\frac{1}{8}$ in Whitworth; $1\frac{1}{4}$ in BSF
1·875	$1\frac{7}{8}$ in AF
1·968	50 mm AF
2·000	2 in AF
2·050	$1\frac{1}{4}$ in Whitworth; $1\frac{3}{8}$ in BSF
2·165	55 mm AF
2·362	60 mm AF

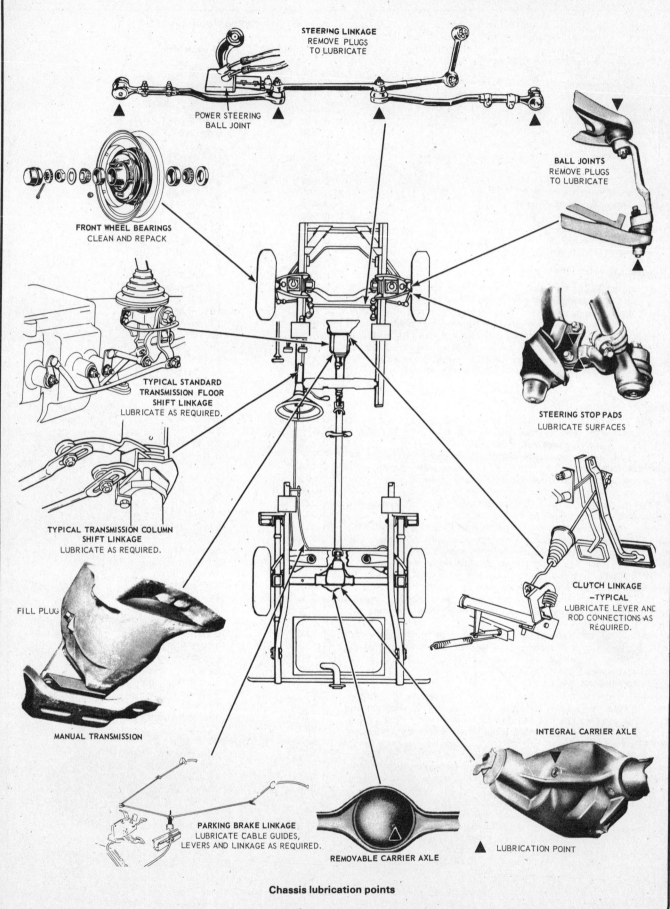

STEERING LINKAGE
REMOVE PLUGS
TO LUBRICATE

POWER STEERING
BALL JOINT

BALL JOINTS
REMOVE PLUGS
TO LUBRICATE

FRONT WHEEL BEARINGS
CLEAN AND REPACK

TYPICAL STANDARD
TRANSMISSION FLOOR
SHIFT LINKAGE
LUBRICATE AS REQUIRED.

STEERING STOP PADS
LUBRICATE SURFACES

TYPICAL TRANSMISSION COLUMN
SHIFT LINKAGE
LUBRICATE AS REQUIRED.

FILL PLUG

CLUTCH LINKAGE
–TYPICAL
LUBRICATE LEVER AND
ROD CONNECTIONS AS
REQUIRED.

MANUAL TRANSMISSION

INTEGRAL CARRIER AXLE

PARKING BRAKE LINKAGE
LUBRICATE CABLE GUIDES,
LEVERS AND LINKAGE AS REQUIRED.

REMOVABLE CARRIER AXLE

▲ LUBRICATION POINT

Chassis lubrication points

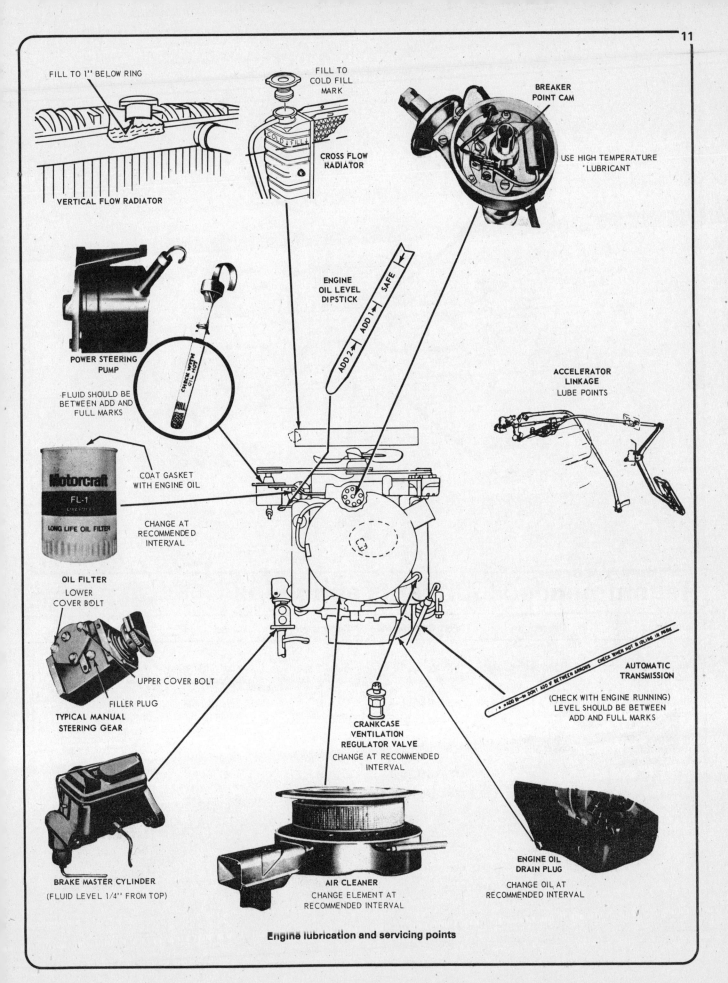

FILL TO 1" BELOW RING

VERTICAL FLOW RADIATOR

FILL TO COLD FILL MARK

CROSS FLOW RADIATOR

BREAKER POINT CAM

USE HIGH TEMPERATURE LUBRICANT

POWER STEERING PUMP

FLUID SHOULD BE BETWEEN ADD AND FULL MARKS

CHECK WHEN OIL HOT

FULL

ENGINE OIL LEVEL DIPSTICK

SAFE

ADD 1

ADD 2

ACCELERATOR LINKAGE LUBE POINTS

Motorcraft FL-1 LONG LIFE OIL FILTER

COAT GASKET WITH ENGINE OIL

CHANGE AT RECOMMENDED INTERVAL

OIL FILTER

LOWER COVER BOLT

UPPER COVER BOLT

FILLER PLUG

TYPICAL MANUAL STEERING GEAR

BRAKE MASTER CYLINDER

(FLUID LEVEL 1/4" FROM TOP)

CRANKCASE VENTILATION REGULATOR VALVE

CHANGE AT RECOMMENDED INTERVAL

AIR CLEANER

CHANGE ELEMENT AT RECOMMENDED INTERVAL

ADD IF BELOW DON'T ADD IF BETWEEN ARROWS CHECK WHEN HOT & IDLING IN PARK

AUTOMATIC TRANSMISSION

(CHECK WITH ENGINE RUNNING) LEVEL SHOULD BE BETWEEN ADD AND FULL MARKS

ENGINE OIL DRAIN PLUG

CHANGE OIL AT RECOMMENDED INTERVAL

Engine lubrication and servicing points

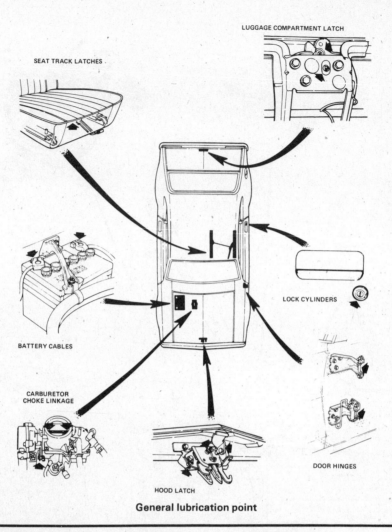

SEAT TRACK LATCHES

LUGGAGE COMPARTMENT LATCH

BATTERY CABLES

LOCK CYLINDERS

CARBURETOR CHOKE LINKAGE

HOOD LATCH

DOOR HINGES

General lubrication point

Recommended lubricants and fluids

Component	Description	Ford Specification	Component	Description	Ford Specification
Hinges, hinge check and pivots	Polyethylene grease	ESB-M1C106-B	Automatic transmission	Ford automatic transmission fluid	ESW-M2C33-F Type F
Brake master cylinder	Heavy duty brake fluid	ESA-M6C25-A	Manual transmission	Ford manual transmisstion oil	ESW-M2C83-B or ESP-M2C83-C
Front suspension balljoints, front wheel bearings and clutch linkage	balljoint and multi-purpose grease	ESA-M1C75-B	Engine	Engine oil*	ESE-M2C101-C
Hood latch and auxiliary catch	Polyethylene grease	ESB-M1C106-B	Engine coolant	Ford cooling system fluid	ESE-M97B18-C
Lock cylinders	Lock lubricant	ESB-M2C20-A	Steering gear housing (manual and power)	Hypoid gear oil	ESW-M2C105-A
			Power steering pump reservoir	Power steering fluid	ESW-M2C128-B
			Door weatherstrip	Silicone lubricant	ESR-M1314-A
Rear axle: Conventional	Hypoid gear oil	ESW-M2C105-A			
Traction-Lok	Hypoid gear oil	ESW-M2C119-A			

Note engine oil of a viscosity suitable for the ambient temperature must be used. Consult the operates handbook supplied with the car.

Routine maintenance

Introduction

The Routine Maintenance instructions are basically those recommended by the vehicle manufacturer. They are supplemented by additional maintenance tasks proven to be necessary.

It must be emphasised that if any part of the engine or its ancillary equipment involved with emission control is disturbed, cleaned or adjusted the car must be taken to the local Ford dealer for checking to ensure that it still meets legal requirements.

Tasks in the maintenance instructions marked with an asterisk (*) must be entrusted to a Ford dealer.

Radiator filler cap (cross-flow type)

Every 250 miles (400 km), weekly or before a long journey

Check tyre pressures (when cold)
Examine tyres for wear and damage
Check steering for smooth and accurate operation
Check brake reservoir fluid level. If this has fallen noticeably, check for fluid leakage
Check for satisfactory brake operation
Check operation of all lights
Check operation of windscreen wipers and washers
Check that the horn operates
Check that all instruments and gauges are operating
Check the engine oil level; top-up if necessary
Check radiator coolant level (photo)
Check battery electrolyte level

Every 3000 miles (5000 km) or 3 months

The following maintenance items must be carried out at this mileage/time interval if the car is being operated in severe conditions. These are considered to be:

(a) *Outside temperature remains below 10°F (–12.2°C) for 60 days or more and most trips are less than 10 miles*
(b) *If a trailer having a total weight of more than 2000 lb is towed over long distances*
(c) *Extended periods of idling or low speed operation*

Complete the checks in the weekly inspection plus the following:
Change the engine oil
Install a new oil filter (photo)

For normal car operation these service items may be carried out at 6000 miles (10 000 km) or 6 month intervals

Location of engine oil filter

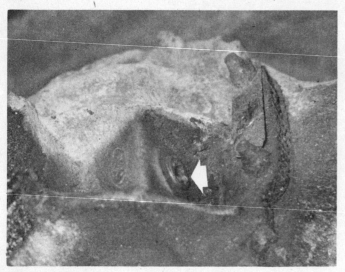

Rear axle filler plug

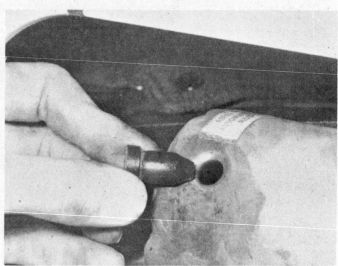

Checking the hood pump fluid level (convertibles only)

Every 6000 miles (10 000 km) or 6 months, whichever occurs first

Change engine oil and filter
Check transmission fluid levels (photo)
Check brake fluid level
Adjust clutch pedal free-play, if necessary
*Check fuel deceleration valve if so equipped
*Adjust engine idle speed and mixture
Check the torque of intake manifold bolts
Lubricate exhaust control valve if so equipped
Check operation of throttle and choke linkage
Renew fuel filter
Check all drivebelt tensions
Check fluid level of hood hydraulic pump reservoir (photo)

Every 12 000 miles (20 000 km) or 12 months, whichever occurs first

Adjust engine valve clearances
Check carburetor air cleaner element
Renew all spark plugs
Inspect spark plug leads
*Check spark control systems and delay valve
*Check EGR system and delay valve
Check condition of coolant
Inspect all drivebelts for wear and install new ones if necessary
*Inspect evaporative emission canister (if so equipped)
Check the torque of all engine-driven accessory mounting bolts
Check front suspension and steering linkage for abnormal slackness or damaged seals
*Adjust automatic transmission bands
Inspect exhaust system and heat shields for corrosion or damage

Every 18 000 miles (30 000 km) or 18 months, whichever occurs first

Inspect distributor cap and rotor
Check tightness of rear spring mountings

Every 24 000 miles (40 000 km) or 2 years, whichever occurs first

Dismantle, lubricate and adjust front wheel bearings
Renew crankcase filter in air cleaner
Renew air cleaner element
Inspect filler cap and fuel line for deterioration or leakage
*Check thermactor system if so equipped
Check cooling system hoses for leakage
Inspect disc pads and rear brake lining for wear
Inspect all brake hoses and lines

Every 30 000 miles (50 000 km) or 30 months, whichever occurs first

Lubricate front suspension and steering linkage
Drain and refill automatic transmission fluid
Renew coolant
Examine all brake hoses and pipes, and renew if necessary
Check wheel cylinders and master cylinder for leaks, and renew seals where necessary
Renew brake fluid

Chapter 1 Engine

Contents

1

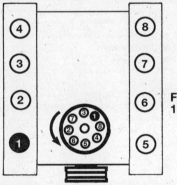

351
Firing order
1-3-7-2-6-5-4-8

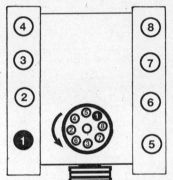

All others
Firing order
1-5-4-2-6-3-7-8

Cylinder location and
distributor rotation

Specifications

Engine (general)

Engine types .... V8, overhead valve

Engine capacities .... 260, 289, 302, 351, 390, 427, 428 and 429 cu in

Engine data (260 cu in)

Compression ratio .... 8.8 : 1

Bore .... 3.80 in (96.5 mm)

Stroke .... 2.87 in (72.8 mm)

Firing order .... 1, 5, 4, 2, 6, 3, 7, 8 (No. 1 cylinder on right-hand bank, nearest radiator)

Oil pressure (hot) .... 35 to 60 lbf/in^2

Pistons
Diameter:
   Color coded red .... 3.7976 to 3.7982 in (96.45 to 97.47 mm)
   Color coded blue .... 3.7988 to 3.7994 in (96.48 to 96.50 mm)
Piston-to-cylinder bore clearance .... 0.0021 to 0.0039 in (0.053 to 0.099 mm)

Piston rings
Ring side clearance:
    Top ring . . . .   0.0019 to 0.0036 in (0.048 to 0.091 mm)
    Second ring . . . .   0.001 to 0.004 in (0.025 to 0.101 mm)
    Oil ring . . . .   Snug fit
Ring gap:
    Top ring . . . .   0.010 to 0.032 in (0.254 to 0.812 mm)
    Second ring . . . .   0.010 to 0.032 in (0.254 to 0.812 mm)
    Oil ring . . . .   0.015 to 0.067 in (0.381 to 1.701 mm)

Crankshaft
Main bearing journal diameter . . . .   2.2482 – 2.2490 in (57.104 – 57.124 mm)
Connecting rod journal diameter . . . .   2.1228 – 2.1236 in (53.919 – 53.939 mm)

Engine data (289 cu in)

Compression ratio . . . .   9.3 : 1

Bore . . . .   4.00 in (101.6 mm)

Stroke . . . .   2.870 in (72.8 mm)

Firing order . . . .   1, 5, 4, 2, 6, 3, 7, 8 (No. 1 cylinder on right-hand bank, nearest radiator)

Oil pressure (hot) . . . .   35 to 60 lbf/in^2

Pistons
Diameter:
    Color coded red . . . .   3.9984 to 3.9990 in (101.55 to 101.57 mm)
    Color coded blue . . . .   3.9996 to 4.0002 in (101.58 to 101.60 mm)
Piston-to-cylinder bore clearance . . . .   0.0018 to 0.0026 in (0.045 to 0.066 mm)

Pistons rings
Ring side clearance:
    Top ring . . . .   0.0019 to 0.0036 in (0.048 to 0.091 mm)
    Second ring . . . .   0.002 to 0.004 in (0.050 to 0.101 mm)
    Oil ring . . . .   Snug fit
Ring gap:
    Top ring . . . .   0.010 to 0.020 in (0.254 to 0.508 mm)
    Second ring . . . .   0.010 to 0.020 in (0.254 to 0.508 mm)
    Oil ring . . . .   0.015 to 0.055 in (0.381 to 1.397 mm)

Crankshaft
Main bearing journal diameter . . . .   2.2482 to 2.2490 in (57.10 to 57.12 mm)
Connecting rod journal diameter . . . .   2.1228 to 2.1236 in (53.91 to 53.93 mm)

Engine data (302 cu in)

Compression ratio . . . .   8.0 : 1 (10.5 : 1 Boss)

Bore . . . .   4.0 in (101.6 mm)

Stroke . . . .   3.0 in (76.0 mm)

Firing order . . . .   1, 5, 4, 2, 6, 3, 7, 8 (No. 1 cylinder on right-hand bank, nearest radiator)

Oil pressure (hot) . . . .   40 to 60 lbf/in^2

Pistons (standard 302 engine)
Diameter:
    Color coded red . . . .   4.0004 to 4.0052 in (101.61 to 101.73 mm)
    Color coded blue . . . .   3.9996 to 4.0002 in (101.58 to 101.60 mm)
Piston-to-cylinder bore clearance . . . .   0.0018 to 0.0026 in (0.045 to 0.066 mm)

Pistons (Boss 302 engine)
Diameter:
    Color coded red . . . .   3.9968 to 3.9974 in (101.51 to 101.53 mm)
    Color coded blue . . . .   3.9980 to 3.9986 in (101.54 to 101.56 mm)
Piston-to-cylinder bore clearance . . . .   0.0034 to 0.0042 in (0.086 to 0.106 mm)

Piston rings (all 302 engines)
Ring side clearance:
    Top ring . . . .   0.002 to 0.004 in (0.050 to 0.101 mm)
    Second ring . . . .   0.002 to 0.004 in (0.050 to 0.101 mm)
    Oil ring . . . .   Snug fit

Ring gap:
    Top ring . . . . 0.010 to 0.020 in (0.254 to 0.508 mm)
    Second ring . . . . 0.010 to 0.020 in (0.254 to 0.508 mm)
    Oil ring . . . . 0.015 to 0.069 in (0.381 to 1.752 mm)

Crankshaft
Main bearing journal diameter . . . . 2.2482 to 2.2490 in (57.10 to 57.12 mm)
Connecting rod journal diameter . . . . 2.1228 – 2.1236 in (53.91 – 53.93 mm)
Connecting rod journal diameter (Boss engine) . . . . 2.1222 – 2.1230 in (53.90 – 53.92 mm)

Engine data (351 cu in)

Compression ratio . . . . 9.5 : 1 (10.7 : 1 C-type)

Bore . . . . 4.0 in (101.6 mm)

Stroke . . . . 3.5 in (88.9 mm)

Firing order . . . . 1, 3, 7, 2, 6, 5, 4, 8 (No. 1 cylinder on right-hand bank, nearest radiator)

Oil pressure (hot) . . . . 45 to 75 lbf in²

Pistons
Diameter:
    Color coded red . . . . 3.9978 to 3.9984 in (101.54 to 101.55 mm)
    Colour coded blue . . . . 3.9990 to 3.9960 in (101.57 to 101.49 mm)
Piston-to-cylinder bore clearance . . . . 0.0018 to 0.0026 in (0.045 to 0.066 mm)

Piston rings
Ring side clearance:
    Top ring . . . . 0.002 to 0.004 in (0.050 to 0.101 mm)
    Second ring . . . . 0.002 to 0.004 in (0.050 to 0.101 mm)
    Oil ring . . . . Snug fit
Ring gap:
    Top ring . . . . 0.010 to 0.020 in (0.254 to 0.508 mm)
    Second ring . . . . 0.010 to 0.020 in (0.254 to 0.508 mm)
    Oil ring . . . . 0.015 to 0.069 in (0.381 to 1.752 mm)

Crankshaft
Main bearing journal diameter (351 W) . . . . 2.9994 to 3.0002 in (76.18 to 76.20 mm)
Main bearing journal diameter (351 C) . . . . 2.7484 to 2.7492 in (69.80 to 69.82 mm)
Connecting rod journal diameter . . . . 2.3103 to 2.3111 in (58.68 to 58.70 mm)

Engine data (390 cu in)

Compression ratio . . . . 10.5 : 1

Bore . . . . 4.050 in (102.87 mm)

Stroke . . . . 3.784 in (96.11 mm)

Firing order . . . . 1, 5, 4, 2, 6, 3, 7, 8 (No. 1 cylinder on right-hand bank, nearest radiator)

Oil pressure . . . . 35 to 60 lbf/in²

Pistons
Diameter:
    Color coded red . . . . 4.0484 to 4.0490 in (102.82 to 102.84 mm)
    Color coded blue . . . . 4.0496 to 4.0502 in (102.85 to 102.87 mm)
Piston-to-cylinder bore clearance . . . . 0.0015 to 0.0023 in (0.038 to 0.058 mm)

Piston rings
Ring side clearance:
    Top ring . . . . 0.002 to 0.004 in (0.050 to 0.101 mm)
    Second ring . . . . 0.002 to 0.004 in (0.050 to 0.101 mm)
    Oil ring . . . . Snug fit
Ring gap:
    Top ring . . . . 0.010 to 0.020 in (0.254 to 0.508 mm)
    Second ring . . . . 0.010 to 0.020 in (0.254 to 0.508 mm)
    Oil ring . . . . 0.015 to 0.055 in (0.001 to 1.097 mm)

Crankshaft
Main bearing journal diameter . . . . 2.7484 to 2.7492 in (69.80 to 69.82 mm)
Connecting rod journal diameter . . . . 2.4380 to 2.4388 in (61.92 to 61.94 mm)

Engine data (427 cu in)

Compression ratio .... 10.9 : 1

Bore .... 4.236 in (107.59 mm)

Stroke .... 3.781 in (96.03 mm)

Firing order .... 1, 5, 4, 2, 6, 3, 7, 8 (No. 1 cylinder on right-hand bank nearest radiator)

Oil pressure .... 35 to 60 lbf/in²

Pistons
Diameter:
   Color coded red .... 4.2298 to 4.2299 in (107.43 to 107.44 mm)
   Color coded blue .... 4.2305 to 4.2311 in (107.45 to 107.46 mm)
Piston-to-cylinder bore clearance .... 0.0030 to 0.0038 in (0.076 to 0.096 mm)

Piston rings
Ring side clearance:
   Top ring .... 0.0024 to 0.0041 in (0.060 to 0.104 mm)
   Second ring .... 0.0020 to 0.0040 in (0.050 to 0.101 mm)
   Oil ring .... Snug fit
Ring gap:
   Top ring .... 0.010 to 0.031 in (0.254 to 0.787 mm)
   Second ring .... 0.010 to 0.020 in (0.254 to 0.508 mm)
   Oil ring .... 0.015 to 0.066 in (0.381 to 1.676 mm)

Crankshaft
Main bearing journal diameter .... 2.7484 to 2.7492 in (69.80 to 69.82 mm)
Connecting rod journal diameter .... 2.4380 to 2.4388 in (61.92 to 61.94 mm)

Engine data (428 cu in)

Compression ratio .... 10.6 : 1

Bore .... 4.130 in (104.90 mm)

Stroke .... 3.984 in (101.19 mm)

Firing order .... 1, 5, 4, 2, 6, 3, 7, 8 (No. 1 cylinder on right-hand bank, nearest radiator)

Oil pressure .... 35 to 60 lbf/in²

Pistons
Diameter:
   Color coded red .... 4.1284 to 4.1290 in (104.86 to 104.48 mm)
   Color coded blue .... 4.1296 to 4.1302 in (104.89 to 104.90 mm)
Piston-to-cylinder bore clearance .... 0.0015 to 0.0023 in (0.038 to 0.058 mm)

Piston rings
Ring side clearance:
   Top ring .... 0.002 to 0.004 in (0.050 to 0.101 mm)
   Second ring .... 0.002 to 0.004 in (0.050 to 0.101 mm)
   Oil ring .... Snug fit
Ring gap:
   Top ring .... 0.010 to 0.020 in (0.254 to 0.508 mm)
   Second ring .... 0.010 to 0.020 in (0.254 to 0.508 mm)
   Oil ring .... 0.015 to 0.035 in (0.381 to 0.889 mm)

Crankshaft
Main bearing journal diameter .... 2.7484 to 2.7492 in (69.80 to 69.82 mm)
Connecting rod journal diameter .... 2.4380 to 2.4388 in (61.92 to 61.94 mm)

Engine data (429 cu in)

Compression ratio .... 10.5 : 1

Bore .... 4.360 in (110.74 mm)

Stroke .... 3.590 in (91.18 mm)

Firing order .... 1, 5, 4, 2, 6, 3, 7, 8 (No. 1 cylinder on right-hand bank, nearest radiator)

Oil pressure .... 45 to 60 lbf/in²

Pistons
Diameter:
    Color coded red . . . .   4.3569 to 4.3575 in (110.66 to 110.68 mm)
    Color coded blue . . . .   4.3581 to 4.3587 in (110.69 to 110.71 mm)

Piston rings
Ring side clearance:
    Top ring . . . .   0.002 to 0.004 in (0.050 to 0.101 mm)
    Second ring . . . .   0.002 to 0.004 in (0.050 to 0.101 mm)
    Oil ring . . . .   Snug fit
Ring gap:
    Top ring . . . .   0.010 to 0.020 in (0.254 to 0.508 mm)
    Second ring . . . .   0.010 to 0.020 in (0.254 to 0.508 mm)
    Oil ring . . . .   0.010 to 0.035 in (0.254 to 0.889 mm)

Crankshaft
Main bearing journal diameter . . . .   2.9994 to 3.0002 in (76.18 to 76.20 mm)
Connecting rod journal diameter . . . .   2.4992 to 2.5000 in (63.47 to 63.50 mm)

Lubrication
Engine oil capacity . . . .   5 US qts/4 Imp qts (including 1 qt filter capacity)

Engine oil type . . . .   Multigrade

Torque wrench settings

	lbf ft	kgf m
Cylinder head bolts:		
260, 289, 302 cu in	65 to 70	8.9 to 9.7
390, 428 cu in	80 to 90	11 to 12.4
351 cu in	95 to 100	13 to 13.8
429 cu in	130 to 140	18 to 19.3
429 cu in Boss	90 to 95	12.4 to 13
Connecting rod bearing bolts:		
260, 289, 302 cu in	19 to 24	2.6 to 3.3
302 cu in HP	40 to 45	5.5 to 6.2
351, 390, 429 cu in	40 to 45	5.5 to 6.2
429 cu in Boss	85 to 90	11.7 to 12.4
428 cu in	53 to 58	7.3 to 8
Main bearing bolts:		
260, 289, 302 cu in	60 to 70	8.2 to 9.7
302 cu in boss (outer bolts)	35 to 40	4.8 to 5.5
351, 390, 427, 428, 429 cu in		
1/2-13 bolts	95 to 105	13 to 14.5
3/8-16 bolts (outer bolts on four-bolt main blocks)	35 to 45	4.8 to 6.2
429 cu in Boss	70 to 80	9.7 to 11
Crankshaft pulley bolts:		
All engine types	70 to 90	9.7 to 12.4
Flywheel bolts:		
All engine types	75 to 85	10.3 to 11.7
Exhaust manifold bolts:		
260, 289, 302 cu in	15 to 20	2 to 2.8
351, 390, 427, 428 cu in	18 to 24	2.5 to 3.3
429 cu in	28 to 33	3.9 to 4.5
Intake manifold bolts:		
260, 289, 302 cu in	20 to 22	2.8 to 3
351 cu in	23 to 25	3.2 to 3.4
390, 427, 428 cu in	32 to 35	4.4 to 4.8
429 cu in	25 to 30	3.4 to 4.1

1 General description

The engines covered in this Chapter comprise the 260, 289, 302, 351, 390, 427, 428 and 429 cu in V8 units. Also covered are the Boss variants of the 302, 351 and 429 cu in engines and the Cleveland 351 cu in version.

All the above engines are similar in basic design having two banks of four cylinders set in a V-configuration. The cylinder bores are machined directly into the cast iron cylinder block which is integral with the crankcase. The one-piece crankshaft is supported within the crankcase on five renewable shell-type bearings.

The valve gear is actuated by a five-bearing camshaft located in the center of the cylinder banks, and is chain-driven from a sprocket on the front of the crankshaft. A gear on the front of the camshaft drives the distributor which in turn drives the oil pump via an intermediate shaft.

The most widely used engines are the 260, 289, 302 and 351 cu in units. These are very compact motors incorporating stud-mounted valve rockers, hydraulic valve lifters and wedge-shaped combustion chambers. The 260 cu in version was dropped from production in 1965 and the 289 cu in was last used in the Mustang in 1968.

In 1967 the 390 cu in engine became available and the following year saw the introduction of the still larger 427 and 428 cu in Cobra Jet units. 1969 saw the introduction of the special Boss version of the 302 cu in engine. This is basically the 302 unit fitted with cylinder heads from the 351 Cleveland engine. It was built to qualify for sedan racing purposes and had a limited production. It was later replaced by a high-performance Boss version of the 351 Cleveland engine.

In 1969/70 a limited number of Mustangs were equipped with the powerful Boss 429 cu in unit. This unique engine features specially modified combustion chambers with oversize valves and ports. The valve rockers operate on individual shafts and the aluminium cylinder heads use O-rings and chevron seals in place of head gaskets. Each of the main bearing caps is secured by four bolts.

Fig. 1.1 302 engine; 260 and 289 engines are similar

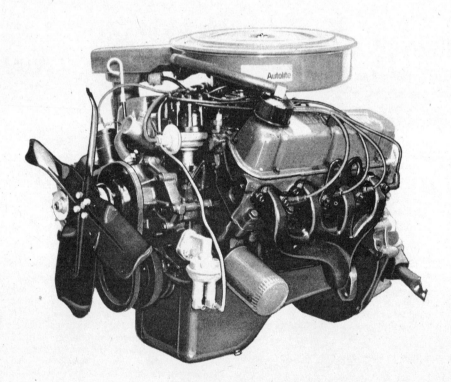

Fig. 1.2 351 engine

Fig. 1.3 390 engine with thermactor pump; 427 and 428 engines are similar

1

Fig. 1.4 429 engine

2 Major operations with engine installed

The following major operations may be carried out without taking the engine from the car:

    (a) *Removal and installation of the cylinder heads*
    (b) *Removal and installation of the timing gear*
    (c) *Removal and installation of the front engine mountings*
    (d) *Removal and installation of the rear mounting*
    (e) *Removal and installation of the camshaft*
    (f) *Removal and installation of the oil pan*
    (g) *Removal and installation of the connecting rod bearings*
    (h) *Removal and installation of the pistons and connecting rods*
    (i) *Removal and installation of the oil pump*

3 Major operations with engine removed

Although it would be possible to carry out some of the following operations with the engine installed if the transmission and clutch were removed, it is deemed inadvisable:

    (a) *Removal and installation of the flywheel*
    (b) *Removal and installation of the rear main bearing oil seal*
    (c) *Removal and installation of the crankshaft and crankshaft main bearings*

4 Methods of engine removal

The engine may be lifted out together with the transmission or separated from the transmission and lifted out by itself. If the transmission is left attached the disadvantage is that the engine has to be tilted to a very steep angle to get it out, particularly when automatic transmission is installed. Unless both the engine and transmission are being repaired or overhauled together, there is no other reason for removing them as a unit.

5 Engine – removal without transmission

This task takes about three hours. It is essential to have a good hoist. If an inspection pit is not available, two axle stands will also be required. In the later stages, when the engine is being separated from the transmission and lifted, the assistance of another person is most useful.

1 Open the hood.
2 Place a container of suitable size under the radiator and one under the engine, and drain the cooling system, as described in Chapter 2. Do not drain the water in the garage or the place where the engine is to be removed if receptacles are not at hand to catch the water.
3 Place a container of 8 US quarts (4 liters) capacity under the oil pan and remove the drain plug. Let the oil drain for 10 minutes and then install the plug.
4 Place old blankets over the fenders and across the cowl to prevent damage to the paintwork.
5 Using a pencil, mark the outline of the hinges on the hood.
6 Undo and remove the four nuts, washers and bolt plates that secure the hinges to the hood. It is easier if two assistants are available so that the hood can be supported whilst the hinges are being released.
7 Carefully lift the hood away from the car and place it against a wall out of the way.
8 Disconnect both battery terminals, release the battery clamp and lift out the battery.
9 Refer to Chapter 3 and remove the air cleaner and intake duct assembly.
10 Slacken the clips that secure the upper and lower radiator hoses; carefully remove the hoses.
11 On cars equipped with automatic transmission, disconnect the oil cooler lines at the radiator and plug the ends to prevent dirt ingress.
12 Remove the radiator and shroud as described in Chapter 2.
13 If air-conditioning is installed, unbolt the compressor and position it out of the way without disconnecting the refrigerant hoses. Unbolt

the refrigerant radiator and position it forward out of the way. *Do not disconnect the refrigerant hoses.*
14 Detach the terminal connector at the rear of the alternator. Slacken the mounting bolts and push the alternator towards the engine. Lift away the fanbelt. Remove the alternator mounting bolts and lift away the alternator. **Note**: *On cars fitted with a power steering and thermactor pump, the drivebelts for these units will have to be removed first (refer to Chapter 2).*
15 Remove the alternator bracket securing bolts and spring washer, and lift away the bracket and ground cable from the side of the cylinder block.
16 On some 428 Cobra Jet engines and all 429 Super Cobra Jet, Boss 302 and Boss 429 engines, disconnect the inlet and outlet pipes from the engine oil cooler, remove the retaining bracket and lift out the cooler assembly.
17 Remove the cooling fan and drivebelt pulley (refer to Chapter 2 if necessary).
18 Slacken the heater hose clips at the inlet manifold and water pump unions, detach the hoses.
19 Remove the engine ground cable securing bolt from the engine and move the ground cable to one side.
20 Disconnect the main fuel line from the inlet side of the fuel pump and plug the end of the line to prevent syphoning of gasoline.
21 Detach the accelerator cable or linkage at the carburetor installation and inlet manifold. Further information will be found in Chapter 3.
22 When an automatic transmission is installed, disconnect the downshift linkage.
23 Make a note of the cable connections to the ignition coil, water temperature sender unit and detach from the terminals. Also release the oil pressure gauge pressure pipe.
24 Detach the vacuum hose to the brake servo unit (where applicable) from the inlet manifold.
25 Disconnect the emission control pipes and electrical connections from the carburetor and inlet manifold.
26 Remove the two hoses and electrical connector from the choke thermostat housing.
27 Undo and remove the nuts that secure each exhaust downpipe to the exhaust manifolds, release the clamp plates and move the downpipes to the side of the engine compartment.
28 Chock the rear wheels, jack up the front of the car and support on firmly based axle stands. To give better access, remove the front wheels.
29 Make a note of the cable connections to the starter motor. Detach the cables from the starter motor terminals.
30 Undo and remove the bolts and spring washers that secure the starter motor to the engine. Lift away the starter motor.
31 Undo and remove the engine front mounting through-bolts at the insulator (Fig. 1.5).

Automatic transmission

32 Undo and remove the bolts and spring washers that secure the converter inspection cover to the housing. Lift away the inspection cover.

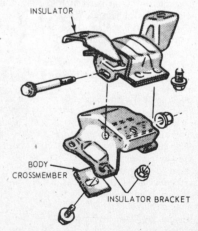

Fig. 1.5 Front engine mounting bracket – typical (Sec. 9)

33 Undo and remove the bolts that secure the torque converter to the flywheel/adaptor plate. It will be necessary to rotate the crankshaft using a large wrench on the crankshaft pulley securing bolt.
34 Undo and remove the converter housing-to-engine block securing bolts and spring washers. **Note:** *The upper converter housing bolts are accessible through plugged holes in the floor pan.*
35 Detach the downshift rod from its bracket.

Manual transmission

36 Pull back the clutch release arm rubber boot, if applicable. Slacken the locknut and adjustment nut. Detach the inner cable from the release arm and withdraw the cable assembly.
37 Undo and remove the bolts and spring washers securing the clutch bellhousing to the engine.

All models

38 Install the wheels and lower the front of the car.
39 Wrap rope slings around the exhaust manifolds or, if chains are to be used, mount brackets on the exhaust manifold and then attach the chain hooks to the brackets. Take up the slack.
40 Place a jack under the transmission unit to support its weight.
41 Check that all cables and controls have been detached and are safely tucked out of the way.
42 Raise the engine slightly and then draw it forward. When automatic transmission is installed, make sure that the torque converter remains attached to the transmission unit.
43 Continue lifting the engine taking care that the backplate does not foul the bodywork (photo).
44 With the engine away from the engine compartment, lower to the ground or bench and suitably support so that it does not roll over.

5.43 Hoisting out the engine

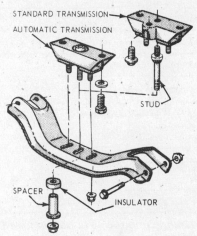

Fig. 1.6 Rear transmission support member (Sec. 9)

6 Engine – removal with manual transmission attached

1 Proceed exactly as described in Section 5 up to and including paragraph 21, then 23 through 31, and finally paragraph 36.
2 Unscrew the transmission drain plug and allow the oil to drain away for five minutes. Install the drain plug.
3 Disconnect the gearshift rods from the transmission shift levers. If four-speed transmission is installed, remove the bolts securing the shift control bracket to the extension housing (see Chapter 6).
4 Support the weight of the transmission using a small jack located adjacent to the drain plug.
5 Undo and remove the center bolt which locates the transmission extension housing into the support member. Then, making sure that the transmission support jack is firmly in position, undo and remove the two bolts and washers that secure the crossmember to the underside of the body. Lift away the crossmember (Fig. 1.6).
6 Remove the muffler inlet pipe bracket-to-housing bolt.
7 With the crossmember removed it is now an easy task to disconnect the speedometer cable from the transmission by removing the clamp bolt and withdrawing the cable.
8 Detach the back-up lamp cable connector at its snap connector.
9 Wrap rope slings around the exhaust manifolds or if chains are to be used, mount brackets on the exhaust manifold and then attach the chain hooks to the brackets. Take up the slack.
10 Check that all cables and controls have been detached and are safely tucked out of the way.
11 With the jack under the transmission still in position start lifting and at the same time, once the front mountings have been cleared, move the engine forward until the propeller shaft is withdrawn from the end of the transmission. Support the shaft on a wooden block.
12 Due to the fact that the transmission is attached, the engine will have to be lifted out at a much steeper angle than for removing the engine on its own. As the weight is more towards the rear, it will be fairly easy to achieve the necessary angle.
13 Continue to raise the engine and move it forward at the necessary angle. At this stage the forward edge of the clutch bellhousing is likely to catch against the front crossmember and the tail of the transmission will need raising until the whole unit is forward and clear of it.
14 Finally the whole unit will rise clear and, if the maximum height of the lifting tackle has been reached, it will be necessary to swing the unit so that the tail can be lifted clear whilst the hoist is moved away or the car lowered from its axle stands and pushed from under the unit.
15 The whole unit should be lowered to the ground (or bench) as soon as possible, and the transmission may then be separated from the engine.

7 Engine – removal with automatic transmission attached

It is recommended that the engine should not be removed whilst still attached to the automatic transmission, because of the weight involved. If it is necessary to remove both units refer to Chapter 6 and remove the transmission unit first. Then remove the engine as described in Section 5 but disregard information on detachment from the transmission unit.

8 Engine dismantling – general

1 Ideally, the engine should be mounted on a proper stand for overhaul but it is anticipated that most owners have a strong bench on which to place it instead. If a sufficiently large strong bench is not available then the work can be done at ground level. It is essential, however, that some form of substantial wooden surface is available. Timber should be at least $\frac{3}{4}$ inch thick, otherwise the weight of the engine will cause projections to punch holes straight through it.
2 It will save a great deal of time later if the exterior of the engine is thoroughly cleaned down before any dismantling begins. This can be done by using kerosene and a stiff brush or more easily, by the use of a proprietary solvent which can be brushed on and then the dirt swilled off with a water jet. This will dispose of all the heavy grime and grit once and for all so that later cleaning of individual components will be a relatively clean process and the kerosene bath will not become contaminated with abrasive metal.

1

3   As the engine is stripped down, clean each part as it comes off. Try to avoid immersing parts with oilways in kerosene, as pockets of liquid could remain and cause oil dilution in the critical first few revolutions after reassembly. Clean oilways with pipe cleaners or, preferably, an air jet.

4   Where possible, avoid damaging gaskets on removal, especially if new ones have not been obtained. They can be used as patterns if new ones have to be specially cut.

5   It is helpful to obtain a few blocks of wood to support the engine whilst it is in the process of being dismantled. Start dismantling at the top of the engine and then turn the block over and deal with the oil pan and crankshaft etc., afterwards.

6   Nuts and bolts should be re-installed in their locations where possible to avoid confusion later. As an alternative keep each group of nuts and bolts (all the timing gear cover bolts for example) together in a jar or can.

7   Many items dismantled must be re-installed in the same position, if they are not being renewed. These include valves, rocker arms, valve lifters, pistons, pushrods, bearings and connecting rods. Some of these are marked on assembly to avoid any possibility of mix-up during overhaul. Others are not, and it is a great help if adequate preparation is made in advance to classify these parts. Suitably labelled cardboard boxes or trays should be used. The time spent in this preparation will be amply repaid later.

9   Engine ancillaries – removal

Before beginning a complete overhaul, or if the engine is being exchanged for a works reconditioned unit, the following items should be removed:

Fuel system components:
Carburetor
Intake and exhaust manifolds
Fuel pump
Fuel lines

Ignition system components:
Spark plugs
Distributor
Coil

Electrical system components (if not removed already):
Alternator and mounting brackets
Starter motor

Cooling system components:
Fan and fan pulley
Water pump, thermostat housing and thermostat
Water temperature sender unit

Engine:
Crankcase ventilation tube
Oil filter element
Oil pressure sender unit
Oil level dipstick
Oil filler cap
Engine mounting brackets

Clutch:
Clutch pressure plate assembly
Clutch friction plate assembly

Optional equipment:
Air-conditioning compressor
Power steering pump
Thermactor pump

10 Cylinder heads – removal with engine in car

1   For safety reasons disconnect the battery.
2   Remove the air cleaner from the carburetor installation, as described in Chapter 3.

3   Disconnect the accelerator linkage from the carburetor.
4   Refer to Chapter 2 and drain the cooling system.
5   Detach the HT leads from the spark plugs, release the distributor cap securing clips and remove the distributor cap.
6   Slacken the clips and disconnect the hose from the water pump to the water outlet.
7   Detach the vacuum pipe from the distributor body and carburetor installation.
8   Refer to Figs. 1.7, 1.8, 1.9, 1.10, 1.11, 1.12 and remove the carburetor and intake manifold assembly. This will necessitate removal of the distributor.
9   Remove the two rocker covers by undoing and removing the securing screws and lifting away together with their respective gaskets.
10 On cars equipped with air-conditioning, remove the mounting bolts and drivebelt, and position the compressor out of the way.
Caution: *Do not disconnect the refrigerant lines. If there is not enough slack in the refrigerant pipes to enable the compressor to be positioned out-of-the-way, the air-conditioning system will have to be drained by a trained serviceman before the pipes can be disconnected. Under no circumstances should this task be attempted by the home mechanic.*
11 If power steering is installed, remove the hydraulic pump and bracket and tie the pump out of the way taking care not to spill the fluid from the reservoir.
12 Remove the alternator mounting bracket, the ignition coil and the air cleaner inlet duct from the right-hand cylinder head.
13 On cars equipped with the thermactor exhaust control system, remove the air pump and mounting bracket, and disconnect the hoses from each cylinder head manifold.
14 On all engines except the 390, 427, 428 and Boss 429, slacken the rocker arm stud nuts just enough to enable the rocker arms to be rotated to one side.
15 In the case of the 390, 427, 428 and Boss 429 engines, remove the nuts securing the rocker shaft pedestals to the cylinder heads and carefully lift off the rocker arms, shafts and pedestals. Retain them in their correct sequence to ensure that they are re-installed in their original positions.
16 Lift out the pushrods and keep them in the correct order of removal to ensure that they are re-installed in their original positions.

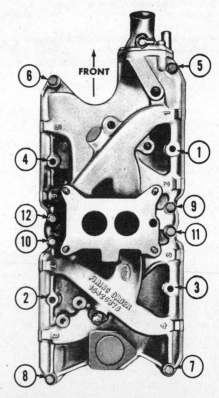

Fig. 1.7 Correct slackening and tightening sequence of intake manifold bolts – 260, 289 and 302 engines (Sec. 9)

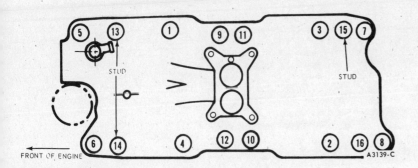

Fig. 1.8 Correct slackening and tightening sequence of intake manifold bolts – 351W engine (Sec. 9)

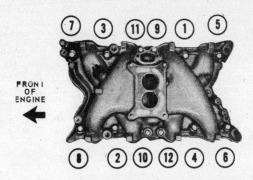

Fig. 1.9 Correct slackening and tightening sequence of intake manifold bolts – 351 Cleveland engine (Sec. 9)

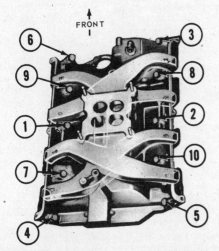

Fig. 1.10 Correct slackening and tightening sequence of intake manifold bolts – 390, 427 and 428 engines (Sec. 9)

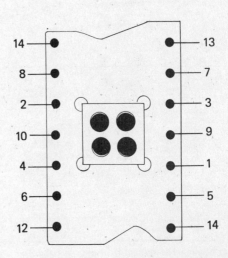

Fig. 1.11 Correct slackening and tightening sequence of intake manifold bolts – Boss 429 engine (Sec. 9)

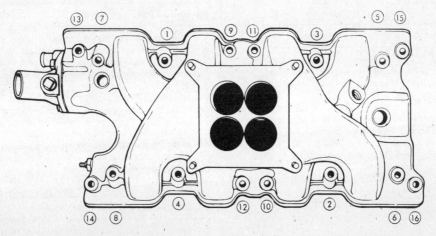

Fig. 1.12 Correct slackening and tightening sequence of intake manifold bolts – Boss 302 engine (Sec. 9)

17 Detach the exhaust downpipes from the exhaust manifolds. On the 351W and 427 engines it will be necessary to unbolt the exhaust manifolds from the cylinder heads and tie them out of the way.

18 Taking each cylinder head in turn, slacken the holding down bolts in the order shown in Fig. 1.13. When all are free of tension remove all the bolts.

19 On occasions the heads may have stuck to the head gasket and cylinder block, in which case if pulling up on the exhaust manifolds does not free them they should be struck smartly with a soft faced

hammer in order to break the joints. *Do not try to pry them off with a blade of any description or damage will be caused to the faces of the head or block, or both.*

20 With the help of an assistant, lift off the cylinder heads, remove them from the car and place them on the workbench. Remove the exhaust manifolds if still attached to the cylinder heads.

21 Remove the cylinder head gaskets; new ones will be required for reassembly.

Fig. 1.13 Correct sequence for slackening and tightening the cylinder head bolts – all engines (Sec. 10)

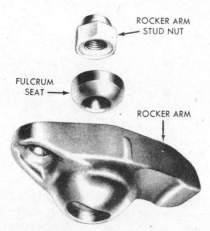

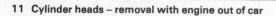

Fig. 1.14 Rocker arm and retaining nut (Sec. 12)

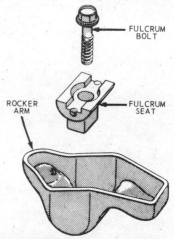

Fig. 1.15 Bolt-type rocker arm (Sec. 12)

11 Cylinder heads – removal with engine out of car

Follow the sequence given in Section 10, paragraph 5 through 21, disregarding information on parts mentioned that have been previously removed.

12 Cylinder heads – dismantling of valves and springs

1   On engines equipped with stud-mounted rockers, remove the rocker arm retaining nuts and lift off the fulcrum seats and rocker arms. Note that on some engines the rocker arms are retained by a bolt, and oil deflectors are installed (see Figs. 1.14 and 1.15).

2   Lay the cylinder head on its side and using a proper valve spring compressor place the U-shaped end over the spring retainer and the screw on the valve head so as to compress the spring.

3   Sometimes the retainer will stick, in which case the end of the compressor over the spring should be tapped with a hammer to release the retainer from the locks (collets).

4   As the spring is compressed, two tapered locks will be exposed and should be taken from the recess in the retainer.

5   When the compressor is released the spring may be removed from the valve. Lift off the retainer, spring and oil seal. Withdraw the valve from the cylinder head.

6   It is essential that the valves, springs, retainers, locks and seals are all kept in order so that they may be re-installed in their original positions.

13 Valve rocker shaft assembly – dismantling

1   On engines equipped with shaft-mounted rockers, the shafts and rockers should be dismantled, cleaned and inspected for wear.

2   With the rocker shaft on the bench, remove the cotter pins from each end of the shaft.

3   Referring to Fig. 1.16, withdraw the washers, rocker arms, supports and springs from the shaft. Keep all the components in the correct order of removal so that they can be re-installed in their original positions.

14 Valve lifters – removal

1   The valve lifters may now be removed from the cylinder block by pushing them up from the camshaft (which can be revolved if necessary to raise the valve lifters) and lifting them out. **Note:** *With the engine in the car a magnet may be required to withdraw them, (see Fig. 1.17).*

2   If necessary the pushrod bearing caps in each valve lifter can be taken out by first extracting the retaining snap-ring.

3   Make sure that all the valve lifters are kept in order so that they may be replaced in their original locations.

4   Note that certain high performance versions of the Mustang engines are equipped with solid (non-hydraulic) valve lifters and these obviously cannot be dismantled.

15 Crankshaft damper – removal

1   Undo the retaining bolts and remove the pulley wheel from the front of the damper.

2   Remove the bolt and washer locating the damper to the front of the crankshaft. The damper is keyed to the crankshaft and must be drawn off with a proper sprocket puller. Attempts to lever it off with long bladed articles such as screwdrivers or tire levers are not suitable in this case because the timing cover behind the damper is a light and relatively fragile casting. Any pressure against it could certainly crack it and possibly make a hole in it.

3   The damper may be removed with the engine in the car but it will be necessary to remove the radiator, and drivebelts.

4   Recover the Woodruff key from the crankshaft nose.

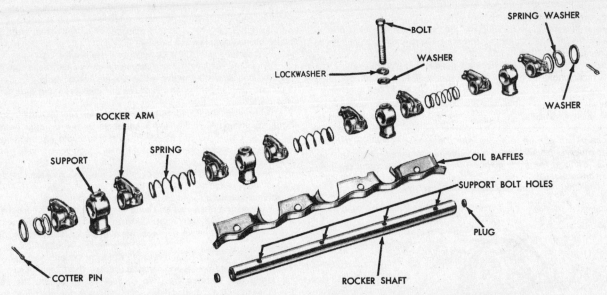

Fig. 1.16 Shaft-mounted rocker assembly used on the 390, 427, 428 and Boss 429 engines (Sec. 13)

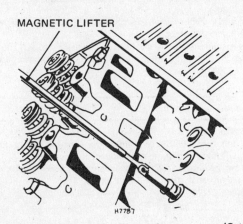

Fig. 1.17 Removing a valve lifter using a magnet (Sec. 14)

16 Flywheel – removal

1   Remove the clutch assembly as described in Chapter 5.
2   The flywheel is held in position to the crankshaft by six bolts and a locating dowel.
3   Remove the six bolts, taking care to support the weight of the flywheel as they are slackened off in case it slips off the flange. Remove it carefully, taking care not to damage the mating surfaces on the crankshaft and flywheel.

17 Oil pan – removal

1   With the engine removed from the car, first make sure that all the oil is drained.
2   With the engine inverted remove the retaining bolts and lift away the oil pan. If it is stuck, carefully insert a knife blade in the gasket joint and work it along to break the seal. After removing the oil pan, discard the gasket.
3   If the oil pan is to be removed with the engine in the car, refer to the appropriate sub-section following.

260, 289, 302 and 351 engines through 1970
4   Remove the oil level dipstick. Jack-up the front of the car, support it on axle stands and drain the engine oil into a suitable container.
5   Remove the front stabilizer bar as described in Chapter 11.
6   Disconnect the starter cable and remove the starter motor.
7   On models fitted with the 351C engine, remove the two bolts

securing the No 2 crossmember and lift away the crossmember.
8   Remove the oil pan securing bolts and lower the oil pan as far as possible. If the oil pump obstructs the removal of the oil pan, unbolt the pump from inside the crankcase. Allow it to drop into the oil pan and withdraw the oil pan complete with pump. It may be necessary to rotate the crankshaft to provide sufficient clearance for removal of the oil pan.

390, 427, 428, 429 and 1971/1973 302 and 351
9   Remove the oil level dipstick. Jack-up the front of the car, support it on axle-stands and drain the engine oil into a suitable container.
10 Remove the front stabilizer bar as described in Chapter 11.
11 If the radiator is equipped with a fan shroud, detach it from the radiator and position it over the fan.
12 Remove the nuts and lockwashers securing the front engine mountings to the support brackets.
13 If the car is equipped with automatic transmission, disconnect the oil cooler lines from the radiator.
14 Place a flat block of wood beneath the front of the oil pan to prevent damage, and using a floor jack raise the engine approximately $1\frac{1}{4}$ in (31 mm). Insert a 1 in (25 mm) block of wood between the engine mountings and crossmember and remove the jack.
15 Remove the oil pan securing bolts and lower the pan as far as possible. Remove the inlet tube and filter screen from the oil pump.
16 Rotate the crankshaft to provide clearance if necessary and withdraw the oil pan.
17 Remove the oil pan gasket. A new one must be obtained for reassembly.

18 Front cover – removal

1   With the engine out of the car, remove the oil pan, and crankshaft damper.
2   Undo and remove the water pump retaining bolts and lift the water pump from the front cover. It may be necessary to tap it with a soft-faced hammer if a jointing compound has been used.
3   Undo and remove the front cover securing bolts and lift away. If it is stuck, carry out the instructions in paragraph 2. Remove the front cover gasket.
4   If the engine is still in the car it will be necessary to remove the front oil pan bolts which run through the timing cover. It will also be necessary to remove the fanbelt, crankshaft damper and fuel pump.

19 Timing chain and sprockets – removal

1   Remove the front timing chain cover as described in the previous Section and withdraw the oil slinger from the front of the crankshaft.

2   Undo the camshaft sprocket securing bolt and remove the fuel pump eccentric from the sprocket.
3   Using a suitable puller, withdraw the crankshaft sprocket and, if necessary, the camshaft sprocket; remove both sprockets and chain as a complete assembly, (Fig. 1.18).
4   Recover the Woodruff key from the groove in the crankshaft.
5   To test the chain for wear, refer to Section 38 of this Chapter.

20 Camshaft – removal

The camshaft can be removed with the engine in the car. (Should camshaft renewal be necessary it will probably be necessary to overhaul other parts of the engine too. If this is the case engine removal should be considered).
1   Refer to Chapter 2 and remove the radiator.

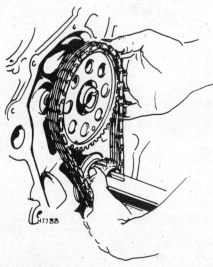

Fig. 1.18 Withdrawing the timing chain and sprockets (Sec. 19)

2   Detach the spark plug leads from the spark plugs, release the cap securing clips and place the cap to one side.
3   Detach the distributor vacuum line and then remove the distributor as described in Chapter 4.
4   Remove the alternator as described in Chapter 10.
5   Undo and remove the screws that secure each rocker cover to the cylinder heads. Lift away the rocker covers and gaskets.
6   Refer to Chapter 3 and remove the inlet manifold and carburetor installation.
7   On engines equipped with shaft-mounted rocker arms, remove the bolts securing the rocker shaft supports to the cylinder heads. This should be done in a progressive manner to avoid straining the shaft. Lift away the rocker shaft assemblies noting on which head each shaft was installed.
8   On engines equipped with stud-mounted rockers, slacken the rocker arm retaining nuts (bolts on some engines) just enough to enable the rocker arms to be rotated to one side.
9   Remove the pushrods and note the location from where they came and also which way up. Keep them in order and the right way up by pushing them through a piece of stiff paper with valve numbers marked.
10   Refer to Section 18 and remove the front cover.
11   Refer to Section 19 and remove the camshaft timing gear.
12   Undo and remove the two screws which secure the camshaft thrust plate to the cylinder block face. Lift away the plate and spacer.
13   Using a magnet, recover the valve lifters from the 'Vee' in the cylinder block. Keep them in order as they must be re-installed in their original positions.
14   If any valve lifters cannot be removed, retain in their maximum height positions with clips.
15   The camshaft may now be drawn forwards through the cylinder block. Take care that the sharp edges of the cams do not damage the bearings.

21 Oil pump – removal

1   Refer to Section 17 and remove the oil pan.
2   Undo and remove the two bolts that secure the pump to the crankcase. Lift away the pump and recover the gasket.
3   The long hexagonal section driveshaft will come out with the pump. This is driven by the distributor shaft.

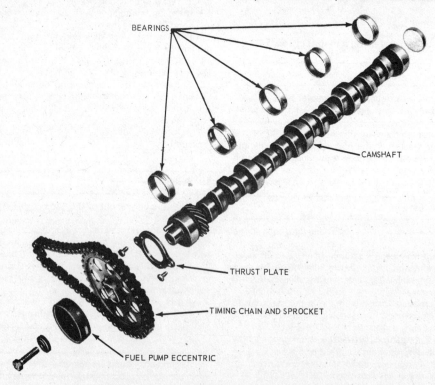

Fig. 1.19 Camshaft and associated components (Sec. 20)

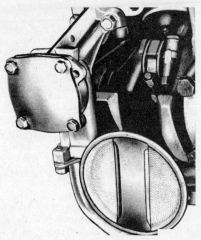

Fig. 1.20 Location of oil pump – typical (Sec. 21)

22 Pistons, connecting rods and bearings – removal

1   Pistons and connecting rods may be removed with the engine in the car, provided the oil pan and cylinder heads are first removed. The bearing shells may be removed with the heads on.
2   Slacken the two nuts holding each bearing cap to the connecting rod. Use a good quality socket wrench for this work. A ring wrench may be used for removal but not for installation which calls for a special torque wrench. Having slackened the nuts two or three turns tap the caps to dislodge them from the connecting rods. Completely remove the nuts and lift away the end caps.
3   Each bearing cap normally has the cylinder number etched on one end as does the connecting rod. However, this must be verified and if in doubt the cap should be marked with a dab of paint or punch mark to ensure that its relationship with the connecting rod and its numerical position in the cylinder block is not altered.
4   The piston and connecting rod may then be pushed out of the top of each cylinder.
5   The connecting rod bearing shells can be removed from the connecting rod and cap by sliding them round in the direction of the notch at the end of the shell and lifting them out. If they are not being renewed it is vital they are not interchanged – either between pistons or between cap and connecting rod.

23 Piston rings – removal

1   Remove the pistons from the engine.
2   The rings come off over the top of the pistons. Starting with the top one, lift one end of the ring out of the groove and gradually ease it out all the way round. With the second and third rings an old feeler blade is useful for sliding them over the other grooves. However, as rings are only normally removed if they are going to be renewed it should not matter if breakages occur.

24 Piston pin – removal

The piston pins need removing if the pistons are being renewed. New pistons are supplied with new pins for fitting to the existing connecting rods. The piston pin is semi-floating – that is, it is a tight shrink fit with the connecting rod and a moving fit in the piston. To press it out requires considerable force and under usual circumstances a proper press and special tools are essential, otherwise piston damage will occur. If damage to the pistons does not matter, then the pins may be pressed out using suitable diameter pieces of rod and tube between the jaws of a vise. However, this is not recommended as the connecting rods might be damaged also. It is recommended that piston pins and pistons are removed from, and refitted to, connecting rods, by a dealer with the necessary facilities.

25 Crankshaft rear oil seal – renewal

1   It is possible to remove the crankshaft rear oil seal with the engine in or out of the car. Where the engine is being completely removed, refer to Section 26 and remove the crankshaft. Remove the two halves of the seal from the upper rear main bearing and cap.
2   To remove the seal with the engine still in the car, drain the engine oil, and remove the oil pan and pump as described in Section 17.
3   Undo the two bolts and carefully pry the rear main bearing cap from the crankshaft. Remove the oil seal from the cap and, if a locating pin is fitted in the bottom of the groove in the cap, drive it out using a pin punch.
4   Slacken all the main bearing cap bolts to enable the crankshaft to drop down slightly, *but* **not** *more than $\frac{1}{32}$ in (0·8 mm).*
5   Using a piece of brass rod, push one end of the upper half of the oil seal upwards to rotate it around the crankshaft. When the other end of the seal is protruding sufficiently, grip it with a pair of pliers and carefully pull it out while continuing to push on the other end with the rod. Great care must be taken not to scratch the crankshaft oil seal surface.
6   Clean out the oil seal grooves in the cylinder block and cap using a suitable solvent.
7   Soak the new rubber seals in clean engine oil prior to installation.
8   Install the upper half of the seal in the cylinder block with the inner lip facing towards the front of the engine (see Fig. 1.33). Slide the seal around the crankshaft until $\frac{3}{8}$ in (9 mm) protrudes from the base of the block.
9   Repeat the procedure for the lower half of the seal, allowing an equal amount of the seal to protrude beyond the opposite seal of the bearing cap, (see Fig. 1.33).
10 Install the rear bearing cap and seal ensuring that the protruding ends of the seals correctly enter the respective grooves. Apply a bead of sealer to the rear corners of the block and sides of the cap as shown in Fig. 1.34.
11 Tighten all the main bearing cap bolts to the specified torque wrench setting.
12 Fit new oil pan seals and gaskets, and install the oil pump and oil pan as described in Sections 45 and 47 respectively.

26 Main bearings and crankshaft – removal

1   The engine should be removed from the car and the oil pan, cylinder heads, timing gears and pistons removed.
2   With a good quality socket wrench undo the bolts holding the five main bearing caps.
3   When all the bolts are removed lift out the caps. If they should be tight, tap the sides gently with a piece of wood or soft mallet to dislodge them.
4   On some engines the main bearing caps are marked from 1 to 5. However, if they are not, identify the location of each cap with paint marks or light center punch marks to ensure correct reassembly.
5   Lift out the crankshaft from the cylinder block taking care not to scratch the journals.
6   Slide out the bearing shells from the cylinder block and bearing caps, noting that the center shells also function as thrust bearings.

27 Lubrication and crankcase ventilation systems – description

The oil pump is located on the crankcase and is driven from the distributor by a hexagonal driveshaft. An oil pressure relief valve is incorporated in the pump body. Oil under pressure is directed via a full-flow filter to the main, connecting rod and camshaft bearings and to the hydraulic valve lifters, (where applicable) pushrods and rocker arms.

A drilling in the front cylinder block face enables oil to pass through to the timing chain and sprocket.

Oil from the valve gear drains down over the camshaft lobes and distributor drivegear before passing back into the oil pan.

The cylinder bores are lubricated by a squirt of oil from a drilling in each connecting rod. The piston pins are lubricated continuously by the oil mist thrown up inside the crankcase.

The crankcase has a positive ventilation (PCV) system. Instead of

1

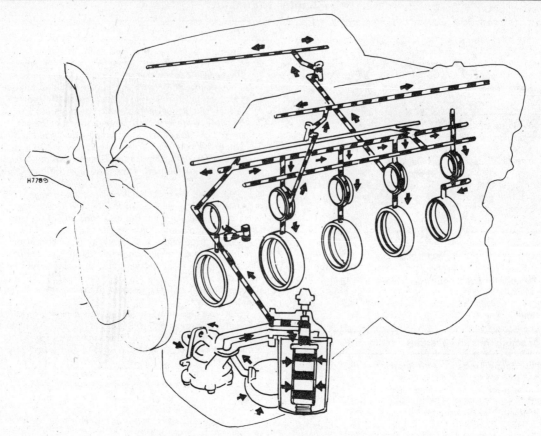

Fig. 1.21 Engine lubrication system – typical (Sec. 27)

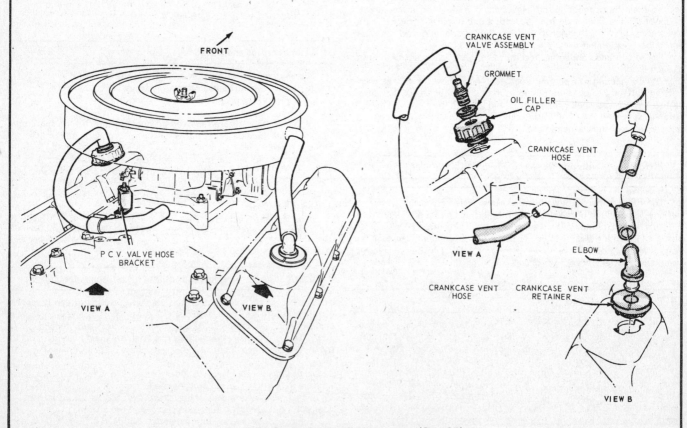

FRONT

P.C.V. VALVE HOSE BRACKET

VIEW A

VIEW B

CRANKCASE VENT VALVE ASSEMBLY

GROMMET

OIL FILLER CAP

CRANKCASE VENT HOSE

VIEW A

CRANKCASE VENT HOSE

ELBOW

CRANKCASE VENT RETAINER

VIEW B

Fig. 1.22 Crankcase ventilation system (Sec. 27)

allowing engine fumes to escape into the atmosphere they are drawn back into the engine via a hose and vent valve connected between the oil filler cap on the left-hand rocker cover and the carburetor intake flange. A second hose connects the air cleaner to the right-hand rocker cover (see Fig. 1.22).

28 Oil filter – removal and installation

The oil filter is a complete throwaway cartridge screwed into the left-hand side of the engine block. Simply unscrew the old unit, clean the seating on the block and screw the new one in, taking care not to cross the thread. Continue until the sealing ring just touches the block face. Then tighten one half turn. Always run the engine and check for signs of leaks after installation.

29 Engine components – examination for wear

When the engine has been stripped down and all parts properly cleaned, decisions have to be made as to what needs renewal and the following sections tell the examiner what to look for. In any borderline case it is always best to decide in favour of a new part. Even if a part may still be serviceable its life will have been reduced by wear and the degree of trouble needed to renew it in the future must be taken into consideration. However, these things are relative and it depends on whether a quick 'survival' job is being done or whether the car as a whole is being regarded as having many thousands of miles of useful and economical life remaining.

30 Crankshaft – examination and renovation

1   Look at the eight main bearing journals and the eight crankpins; if there are any scratches or score marks then the shaft will need grinding. Such conditions will nearly always be accompanied by similar deterioration in the matching bearing shells.
2   Each bearing journal should also be round and can be checked with a micrometer of caliper gauge around the periphery at several points. If there is more than 0.0004 in (0.01 mm) of ovality regrinding is necessary.
3   A main Ford agent or motor engineering specialist will be able to decide to what extent regrinding is necessary and also supply the special under-size shell bearings to match whatever may need grinding off the journals.
4   Before taking the crankshaft for regrinding, check also the cylinder bores and pistons as it may be more convenient to have the engineering operations performed at the same time by the same engineer.

31 Crankshaft (main) bearings and connecting rod bearings – examination and renovation

1   With careful servicing and regular oil and filter changes, bearings will last for a very long time but they can still fail for unforeseen reasons. With connecting rod bearings the indications are a regular rhythmic loud knocking from the crankcase, the frequency depending on engine speed. It is particularly noticeable when the engine is under load. This symptom is accompanied by a fall in oil pressure although this is not normally noticeable unless an oil pressure gauge is fitted. Main bearing failure is usually indicated by serious vibration, particularly at higher engine revolutions, accompanied by a more significant drop in oil pressure and a 'rumbling' noise.
2   Bearing shells in good condition have bearing surfaces with a smooth, even, matt silver/gray color all over. Worn bearings will show patches of a different color where the bearing metal has worn away and exposed the underlay. Damaged bearings will be pitted or scored. It is nearly always well worthwhile fitting new shells as their cost is relatively low. If the crankshaft is in good condition it is merely a question of obtaining another set of standard size. A reground cranks as will need new bearing shells as a matter of course.

32 Cylinder bores – examination and renovation

1   A new cylinder is perfectly round and the walls parallel throughout

COAT GASKET WITH ENGINE OIL

Fig. 1.23 Installing a new oil filter (Sec. 27)

its length. The action of the pistons tends to wear the walls at right angles to the gudgeon pin due to side thrust. This wear takes place principally on that section of the cylinder swept by the piston rings.
2   It is possible to get an indication of bore wear by removing the cylinder heads with the engine still in the car. With the piston down in the bore first signs of wear can be seen and felt just below the top of the bore where the top piston ring reaches and there will be a noticeable lip. If there is no lip it is fairly reasonable to expect that bore wear is low and any lack of compression or excessive oil consumption is due to worn or broken piston rings or pistons (see next Section).
3   If it is possible to obtain a bore measuring micrometer, measure the bore in the thrust plane below the lip and again at the bottom of the cylinder in the same plane. If the difference is more than 0.010 in (0.254 mm) then a rebore is necessary. Similarly, a difference of 0.005 in (0.127 mm) or more across the bore diameter is a sign of ovality calling for a rebore.
4   Any bore which is significantly scratched or scored will need reboring. This symptom usually indicates that the piston or rings are damaged in that cylinder. In the event of only one cylinder being in need of reboring it will still be necessary for all eight to be bored and supplied with new oversize pistons and rings. Your Ford dealer or local engineering specialist will be able to rebore and obtain the necessary matched pistons. If the crankshaft is undergoing regrinding it is a good idea to let the same firm renovate and reassemble the crankshaft and pistons to the block. A reputable firm normally gives a guarantee for such work. In cases where engines have been rebored already to their maximum, new cylinder liners are available which may be installed. In such cases the same reboring processes have to be followed and the services of a specialist engineering firm are required.

33 Pistons and piston rings – examination and renovation

1   Worn pistons and rings can usually be diagnosed when the symptoms of excessive oil consumption and low compression occur and are sometimes, though not always, assocated with worn cylinder bores. Compression testers that screw into the spark plug holes are available and these can indicate where low compression is occurring. Wear usually accelerates the more it is left so when the symptoms occur, early action can possibly save the expense of a rebore.
2   Another symptom of piston wear is piston slap – a knocking noise from the crankcase not to be confused with connecting rod bearing failure. It can be heard clearly at low engine speed when there is no load (idling for example) and the engine is cold, and is much less audible when the engine speed increases. Piston wear usually occurs in the skirt or lower end of the piston and is indicated by vertical

streaks in the worn area which is always on the thrust side. It can also be seen where the skirt thickness is different.

3   Piston ring wear can be checked by first removing the rings from the pistons, as described in Section 23. Then place the rings in the cylinder bores from the top, pushing them down about 1.5 inches (38 mm) with the head of a piston (from which the rings have been removed) so that they rest square in the cylinder. Then measure the gap the ends of the ring with a feeler gauge. If the gap on any of the rings exceeds the dimensions given in the Specifications, they should be renewed (Fig. 1.24).

4   The groove in which the rings locate in the piston can also become enlarged due to wear. The side clearance between the rings and piston should not exceed the dimensions given in the Specifications, (Fig. 1.25).

5   However, it is rare that a piston is only worn in the ring groove and the need to renew them for this fault alone is hardly ever encountered.

34 Connecting rods and piston pins – examination and renovation

1   Piston pins are a shrink-fit into the connecting rods. Neither of these components would normally need renewal unless the pistons were being changed, in which case the new pistons would automatically be supplied with new pins.

2   Connecting rods are not subject to wear but in extreme circumstances such as engine seizure, they could be distorted. Such conditions may be visually apparent but where doubt exists they should be changed. The bearing caps should also be examined for indications of filing down which may have been attempted in the mistaken idea that bearing slackness could be remedied in this way. If there are such signs then the connecting rods should be renewed.

35 Camshaft and camshaft bearings – examination and renovation

1   The camshaft bearing bushes should be examined for signs of scoring and pitting. If they need renewal they will have to be dealt with professionally as, although it may be relatively easy to remove the old bushes, the correct fitting of new ones requires special tools. If they are not fitted evenly and square from the very start they can be distorted, thus causing localised wear in a very short time. See your Ford dealer or local engineering specialist for this work.

2   The camshaft itself may show signs of wear on the bearing journals, cam lobes or the skew gear. The main decision to take is what degree of wear justifies renewal, which is costly. Any signs of scoring or damage to the bearing journals must be rectified and, as undersize bearing bushes are not supplied, the journals cannot be reground. Renewal of the whole camshaft is the only solution. Similarly, excessive wear on the skew gear which can be seen where the distributor driveshaft teeth mesh, will mean renewal of the whole camshaft.

3   The cam lobes themselves may show signs of ridging or pitting on the high points. If the ridging is light then it may be possible to smooth it out with fine emery. The cam lobes, however, are surface hardened and once this is penetrated wear will be very rapid thereafter. The cams are also offset and tapered to cause the valve lifters to rotate – thus ensuring that wear is even – so do not mistake this condition for wear.

36 Valve lifters – examination and renovation

1   The faces of the valve lifters which bear on the camshaft should show no signs of pitting, scoring or other forms of wear. They should also not be a loose fit in their housing. Wear is only normally encountered at very high mileages or in cases of neglected engine lubrication. Renew if necessary.

2   Although it is possible to dismantle the hydraulic valve lifters by removing the spring clips and tapping out the valve assembly, it is not worthwhile fitting new components to an old valve body and the best policy is to renew all the valve lifters whenever a major engine overhaul is carried out.

Fig. 1.24 Checking a piston ring gap (Sec. 33)

Fig. 1.25 Checking the piston rings side clearance (Sec. 33)

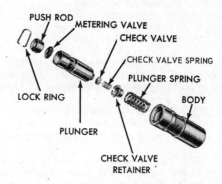

Fig. 1.26 Type 1 hydraulic valve lifter (Sec. 35)

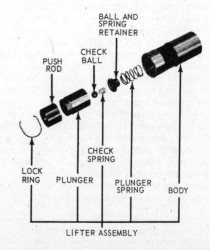

Fig. 1.27 Type 2 hydraulic valve lifter (Sec. 35)

37 Valves and valve seats – examination and renovation

1   With the valves removed from the cylinder heads examine the heads for signs of cracking, burning away and pitting of the edge where it seats in the port. The seats of the valves in the cylinder head should also be examined for the same signs. Usually it is the valve that deteriorates first but if a bad valve is not rectified the seat will suffer and this is more difficult to repair.

2   Providing the valve heads and seats are not cracked or badly pitted, minor burn marks and blemishes can be ground out using carborundum paste. This may be done by placing a smear of carborundum paste on the edge of the valve and, using a suction-type valve holder, grinding the valve in-situ. This is done with a semi-rotary action, twisting the handle of the valve holder between the hands and lifting it occasionally to redistribute the paste. Use a coarse paste to start with and finish with a fine paste. As soon as a matt gray unbroken line appears on both the valve and the seat, the valve is 'ground-in'. All traces of carbon should also be cleaned from the head and the neck of the valve stem. A wire brush mounted in a power drill is a quick and effective way of doing this.

4   Another form of valve wear can occur on the stem where it runs in the guide in the cylinder head. This can be detected by trying to rock the valve from side-to-side. If there is any movement at all it is an indication that the valve stem or guide is worn. Check the stem first with a micrometer at points all along and around its length; if they are not within the specified size, new valves will probably solve the problem. If the guides are worn, however, they will need reboring for oversize valves or for installing guide inserts. The valve seats will also need recutting to ensure they are concentric with the stems. This work should be given to your Ford dealer or local engineering works.

5   When all valve grinding is completed it is essential that every trace of grinding paste is removed from the valves and ports in the cylinder head. This should be done with thorough washing in gasoline or kerosene and blowing out with a jet of air. If particles of carborundum paste should work their way into the engine they would cause havoc with bearings or cylinder walls.

6   The Boss 429 engine is equipped with aluminium cylinder heads and the valve seats are a shrink-fit in the head. If the seats are beyond renovation, the cylinder head(s) should be given to your Ford dealer or local engineering works who will be able to remove the old seats and install new ones.

38 Timing chain and sprockets – examination and renovation

1   Examine the sprocket teeth for excessive wear and renew if necessary.

2   Check the timing chain for wear and slackness in the pins and links. As a guide, temporarily install the chain and sprockets, and rotate the crankshaft so that one side of the chain is under tension. Now check that the maximum possible sideways movement of the slack side of the chain does not exceed $\frac{1}{2}$ in (12.5 mm).

3   If any doubt exists regarding the condition of the chain the most sensible policy is to renew it.

39 Flywheel ring gear – examination and renovation

1   If the ring gear is badly worn or has missing teeth it should be renewed. The old ring can be removed from the flywheel by cutting a notch between two teeth with a hacksaw and then splitting it with a cold chisel.

2   To install a new ring gear requires heating the ring to 400°F (204°C). This can be done by polishing four equally spaced sections of the gear, laying it on a suitable heat resistant surface (such as fire bricks) and heating it evenly with a blow lamp or torch until the polished areas turn a light yellow tint. Do not overheat or the hard wearing properties will be lost. The gear has a chamfered inner edge which should go against the shoulder when put on the flywheel. When hot enough place the gear in position quickly, tapping it home if necessary, and let it cool naturally without quenching in any way.

40 Oil pump – overhaul

1   The oil pump maintains a pressure of around 45-60 lbf/in². An oil pressure gauge is fitted to give earlier warning of falling oil pressures

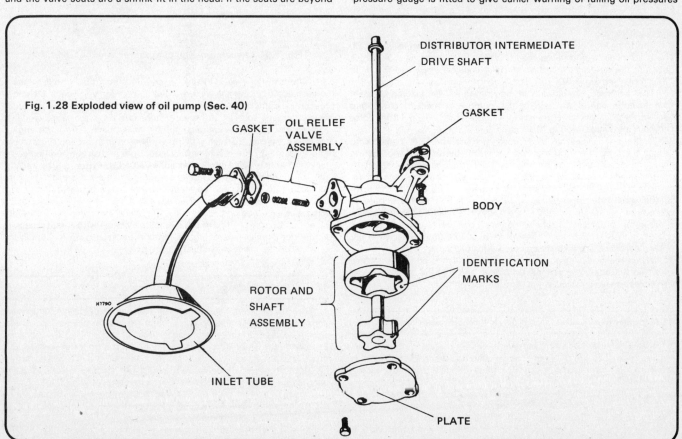

Fig. 1.28 Exploded view of oil pump (Sec. 40)

DISTRIBUTOR INTERMEDIATE DRIVE SHAFT

GASKET

OIL RELIEF VALVE ASSEMBLY

GASKET

BODY

IDENTIFICATION MARKS

ROTOR AND SHAFT ASSEMBLY

INLET TUBE

PLATE

Fig. 1.29 Checking the oil pump inner rotor lobe clearance (Sec. 40)

Fig. 1.30 Checking the clearance between the outer rotor and oil pump housing (Sec. 40)

Fig. 1.31 Checking the oil pump rotor endfloat (Sec. 40)

due to overheating or general wear.

2   At a major engine overhaul it is as well to check the pump and exchange it for a reconditioned unit if necessary. The efficient operation of the oil pump depends on the finely machined tolerances between the moving parts of the rotor and the body, and reconditioning of these is generally not within the competence of the non-specialist owner.

3   To dismantle the pump, first remove it from the engine, as described in Section 21.

4   Remove the two bolts securing the inlet tube and filter to the pump body; remove the inlet tube and relief valve components which will be released.

5   Remove the four bolts securing the rotor end plate, and lift off the plate.

6   The necessary clearances may now be checked using a machined straight-edge (a good steel rule) and a feeler gauge.

7   On bi-rotor type pumps the critical clearances are between the lobes of the center rotor and convex faces of the outer rotor, between the outer rotor and the pump body, and between both rotors and the end cover plate.

8   The rotor lobe clearances may be checked as shown in Fig. 1.29. The clearances should not exceed 0.006 in (0.15 mm). The clearance between the outer rotor and pump body should not exceed 0.010 in (0.25 mm). See Fig. 1.30.

9   The endfloat clearance can be measured by placing a steel straight-edge across the end of the pump and measuring the gap between the rotors and the straight-edge. The gap on either rotor should not exceed 0.005 in (0.13 mm). See Fig. 1.31.

10   If the only excessive clearances are endfloat it is possible to reduce them by removing the rotors from the pump body and lapping away the face of the body on a flat bed until the necessary clearances are obtained. It must be emphasised, however, that the face of the body must remain perfectly flat and square to the axis of the rotor spindle otherwise the clearances will not be equal and the end cover will not be a pressure-tight fit to the body. It is worth trying, of course, if the pump is in need of renewal anyway, but unless done properly it could seriously jeopardise the rest of an overhaul. Any variations in the other clearances should be overcome with an exchange unit.

11   When reassembling the pump and installing the end cover, make sure that the interior is scrupulously clean and that the pressure relief valve parts are assembled in the correct positions.

41 Cylinder heads and piston crowns – decarbonization

1   When cylinder heads are removed either in the course of an overhaul, or for inspection of bores or valve condition when the engine is in the car, it is normal to remove all carbon deposits from the piston crowns and heads.

2   This is best done with a cup-shaped wire brush and an electric drill and is fairly straightforward when the engine is dismantled and the pistons removed. Sometimes hard spots of carbon are not easily removed except by a scraper. When cleaning the pistons with a scraper take care not to damage the surface of the piston in any way.

3   When the engine is in the car certain precautions must be taken when decarbonizing the piston crowns, in order to prevent dislodged pieces of carbon falling into the interior of the engine which could cause damage to cylinder bores, pistons and rings – or if allowed into the water passages – damage to the water pump. Turn the engine, therefore, so that the piston being worked on is at the top of its stroke and then mask off the adjacent cylinder bore and all surrounding water jacket channels with paper and adhesive tape. Press grease into the gap all round the piston to keep carbon particles out and then scrape all carbon away by hand carefully. Do not use a power drill and wire brush when the engine is in the car as it will be virtually impossible to keep all the carbon dust clear of the engine. When completed, carefully clear out the grease round the rim of the piston with a matchstick or something similar – bringing any carbon particles with it. Repeat the process on the other seven piston crowns.

42 Rocker gear – examination and renovation

1   The rocker arms should be examined for signs of excessive wear and, on engines equipped with shaft-mounted rockers, the shafts should be checked for possible distortion.

2   Check the shaft for straightness by rolling it on a flat surface. It is most unlikely that it will deviate from normal, but if it does, then a judicious attempt may be made to straighten it. If this is not successful purchase a new shaft. The surface of the shaft should be free from any worn ridges caused by the rocker arms. If any wear is evident renew the rocker shaft. Wear is likely to have occurred only if the rocker shaft oil holes have become blocked.

3   Check the rocker arms for wear of the rocker bushes, for wear at the rocker arm face which bears on the valve stem, and for wear of the

adjusting ball-ended screws. Wear in the rocker arm bush can be checked by gripping the rocker arm tip and holding the rocker arm in place on the shaft, noting if there is any lateral rocker arm shake. If any shake is present, and the arm is loose on the shaft, remedial action must be taken. It is recommended that any worn rocker arm be taken to the local Ford dealer or automobile engineering works to have the old bush drawn out and a new one installed.

4   Check the tip of the rocker arm where it bears on the valve head, for cracking or serious wear on the case-hardening. If none is present the rocker arm may be re-installed. Check the pushrods for straightness by rolling them on a flat surface.

43 Engine reassembly – general

1   All components of the engine must be cleaned of oil sludge and old gaskets, and the working areas should also be clear and clean. In addition to the normal range of good quality socket wrenches and general tools which are essential, the following must be available before reassembly begins:
   (a) Complete set of new gaskets
   (b) Supply of clean rags
   (c) Clean oil can full of new engine oil
   (d) Torque wrench
   (e) All new spare parts as necessary

44 Engine reassembly – camshaft and crankshaft

1   Insert the camshaft carefully into the block, taking care not to let any of the cam lobes damage the bearing bushes (photo).
2   Install the camshaft thrust plate and secure it with the two screws. These screws must be tightened firmly (photo).
3   Ensure that the crankcase is thoroughly clean and that all oilways are clear. A thin twist drill is useful for clearing the oilways, or if possible they may be blown out with compressed air. Treat the crankshaft in the same fashion, and then inject engine oil into the oilways.

4   Select the halves of the five main bearing shells that have the oil slots and grooves and position them into the crankcase bearing housings (photo). Ensure that the notches in the ends of the shells are correctly located in the cut-outs in the housings.
5   Note that the center main bearing shells have flanges, which act as thrust washers. These are available in various thicknesses in order to be able to set the crankshaft endfloat.
6   Push the upper half of the crankshaft oil seal into the recess at the rear of the crankcase (photo). For further information on installing the rear crankshaft oil seal refer to Section 25.
7   Lubricate the crankshaft journals with engine oil and carefully lower the crankshaft into position (photo).
8   Place the lower (plain) shells into the main bearing caps (photo).
9   Push the lower half of the crankshaft oil seal into the recess in the rear main bearing cap (photo).
10   Position the rear and center main bearing caps over the crankshaft and temporarily tighten the retaining bolts (photos).
11   Check the crankshaft endfloat using feeler gauges (photo). If the endfloat is not within 0.004 to 0.008 in (0.1 to 0.2 mm) the crankshaft should be removed and the center thrust bearings replaced with ones of the necessary thickness to achieve this tolerance.
12   When the crankshaft endfloat is correct, install all the main bearing caps and retaining bolts. Note that the bearing caps should be marked with a number from 1 to 5 and an arrow to ensure that they are installed in the correct position (photo).
13   Finally, tighten the main bearing cap bolts to the specified torque wrench setting (photo). **Note**: *On certain Boss-type engines the main bearing caps are secured by four bolts and these must be tightened in a diagonal sequence.*

45 Engine reassembly – pistons, connecting rods and oil pump

1   The subsequent paragraphs on assembly assume that all the checks described in Sections 33 and 34 have been carried out. Also the engine has been partially assembled as described in Section 44.
2   The assembly of new pistons to connecting rods should have been

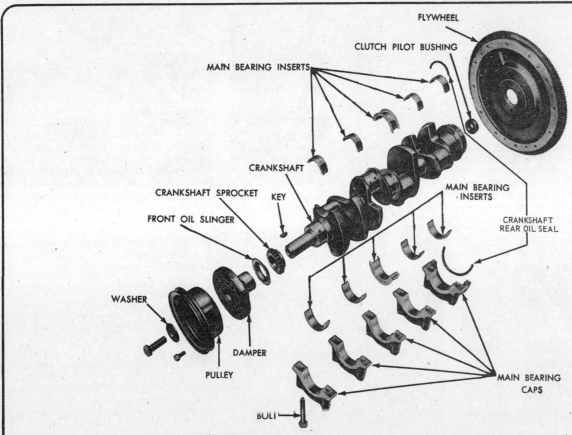

Fig. 1.32 Exploded view of crankshaft and associated components (Sec. 44)

44.1 Installing the camshaft

44.2 Installing the camshaft thrust plate

44.4 Installation of center main bearing shell

44.6 Installation of rear main bearing and oil seal

44.7 Lowering the crankshaft into the cylinder block

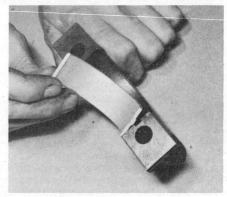
44.8 Installing a shell bearing into a main bearing cap

44.9 Oil seal recess in rear main bearing cap

44.10A Installing the rear main bearing cap ...

44.10B ... followed by the center main bearing cap

44.11 Checking the crankshaft endfloat

44.12 Identification mark on main bearing cap

44.13 Tightening the main bearing cap bolts

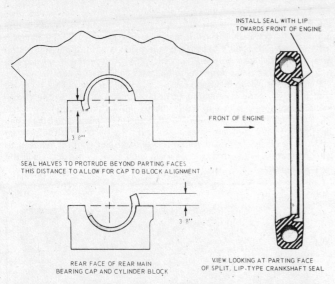

INSTALL SEAL WITH LIP
TOWARDS FRONT OF ENGINE

FRONT OF ENGINE

3 8"

SEAL HALVES TO PROTRUDE BEYOND PARTING FACES
THIS DISTANCE TO ALLOW FOR CAP TO BLOCK ALIGNMENT

3 8"

REAR FACE OF REAR MAIN
BEARING CAP AND CYLINDER BLOCK

VIEW LOOKING AT PARTING FACE
OF SPLIT, LIP-TYPE CRANKSHAFT SEAL

Fig. 1.33 Method of installing crankshaft rear oil seal (Sec. 44)

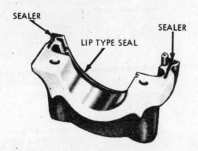

SEALER

SEALER

LIP TYPE SEAL

Fig. 1.34 Applying sealer to rear main bearing caps (Sec. 44)

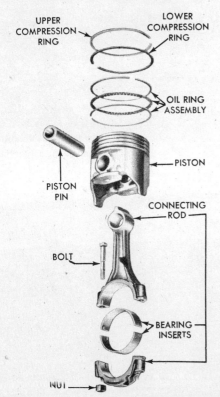

UPPER
COMPRESSION
RING

LOWER
COMPRESSION
RING

OIL RING
ASSEMBLY

PISTON

PISTON
PIN

CONNECTING
ROD

BOLT

BEARING
INSERTS

NUT

Fig. 1.35 Piston and connecting rod assembly – typical (Sec. 45)

carried out as detailed in Section 24. The new pistons should be supplied with rings already installed.

3   If new rings are being installed to existing pistons, make sure that each ring groove in the piston is completely cleaned of carbon deposits. This is done most easily by breaking one of the old rings and using the sharp end as a scraper. Be careful not to remove any metal from the groove by mistake!

4   The end-gap of the new piston rings – three for each piston – must be checked in the cylinder bores as described in Section 33.

5   The minimum gap for all three rings must be within Specifications. If the gap is too small, one end of the ring must be filed to increase the gap. To do this the ring should be gripped in a vise between two thin pieces of soft metal in such a way that only the end to be filed is gripped and so that it only protrudes above the jaws of the vise a very small distance. This will eliminate the possibility of bending and breaking the ring while filing the end. Use a thin, fine file and proceed in easy stages – checking the gap by replacing the ring in the bore until the necessary minimum gap is correct. This must be done with every ring, checking each one in the bore to which it will eventually be fitted. To avoid mistakes it is best to complete one set of rings at a time, and replace the piston in the cylinder bore before proceeding to the next.

6   To install the rings on to the pistons calls for patience and care if breakages are to be avoided. The three rings for each piston must all be fitted over the crown, so obviously the first one to go on is the slotted oil control ring. Hold the ring over the top of the piston and spread the ends just enough to get it around the circumference. Then, with the fingers ease it down, keeping it parallel to the ring grooves by 'walking' the ring ends alternately down the piston. Being wider than the compression rings no difficulty should be encountered in getting it over the first two grooves in the piston.

7   The lower compression ring, which goes on next, must only be fitted one way up. It is marked *TOP* to indicate its upper face.

8   Start installing this ring by spreading the ends to get it located over the top of the piston.

9   The lower compression ring has to be guided over the top ring groove and this can be done by using a suitably cut piece of tin which can be placed so as to cover the top groove under the ends of the ring.

10 Alternatively, a feeler blade may be slid around under the ring to guide it into its groove.

11 The top ring may be installed either way up as it is barrel faced.

12 With the rings installed, the piston/connecting rod assembly is ready for installing in the cylinder.

13 Each connecting rod and bearing cap should have been marked on removal, but in any case the cylinder number is etched lightly on the end of the cap and connecting rod alongside (photo).

14 The connecting rod and bearing caps are numbered from 1 to 4 in the right bank of the cylinder block and from 5 to 8 in the left bank with the lower number commencing at the front of the block. The numbered side of the rod and cap must face toward the outside of the cylinder block and the notch in the top of the piston must face toward

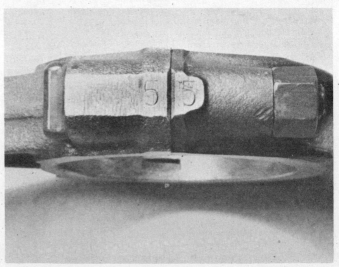

45.13 Identification numbers on connecting rod and bearing cap

1

the front of the engine. On 351 HO engines the arrow on top of the piston must face inboard (see Figs. 1.36 and 1.37 and photo).

IMPORTANT: *One side of the bearing cap and connecting rod is chamfered and this must be positioned toward the crank pin thrust face of the crankshaft to allow for the small radius between the journal and web (photo).*

15 Before installing the pistons, position the three rings around each piston so that the gaps are spaced from each other as shown in Fig. 1.38.

16 Clean the cylinder bores using a clean piece of lint-free cloth, and lubricate the bores with some engine oil.

17 Install a new shell bearing half into the first connecting rod ensuring the oil feed hole in the shell lines up with the hole in the connecting rod (photo).

18 Push the piston into the cylinder bore (the correct way round) until the oil control ring abuts the face of the block. Then, using a piston ring compressor contract the rings and tap the piston into the cylinder (photo). Take great care to be sure that a ring is not trapped on the top edge of the cylinder bore and when tapping the piston in do not use any force. If this is not done the rings could easily be broken.

19 When the piston has been fully located in the bore push it down so that the end of the connecting rod seats on the journal on the crankshaft. Make sure the journal is well lubricated with engine oil.

20 Maintaining absolute cleanliness all the time, install the other shell bearing half into the cap, once again with the notches in the bearing and cap lined up (photo). Lubricate it with engine oil and install it to the connecting rod so that the holes in the cap fit to the dowels in the connecting rod.

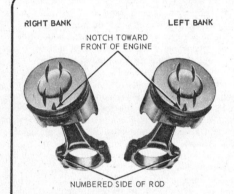

Fig. 1.36 Correct positioning of pistons and connecting rods (Sec. 45)

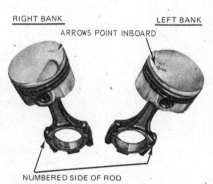

Fig. 1.37 Correct positioning of pistons and connecting rods used in type 351 HO engines (Sec. 45)

45.14A Notches in piston crown must face towards the front of the engine ...

45.14B ... and the chamfered side of the connecting rod and bearing cap must face the radius between the crankshaft journal and web

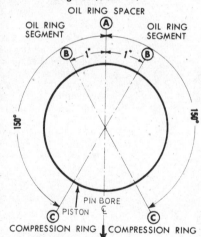

Fig. 1.38 Spacing the piston ring gaps (Sec. 45)

45.17 Installing a bearing shell on a connecting rod

45.18 Tapping a piston into the cylinder block

Fig. 1.39 Tapping a piston into the bore (Sec. 45)

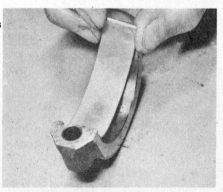

45.20 Installing a shell bearing into a connecting rod cap

21 Install all pistons and connecting rods in a similar manner and do not make any mistakes locating the correct number piston in the correct bore.

22 When all the connecting rod caps are correctly installed, tighten the securing nuts to the specified torque wrench setting (photo).

23 Before installing the oil pump, prime it by filling the inlet port with engine oil and rotating the driveshaft to distribute it.

24 Install the hexagonal driveshaft into the pump body noting that the end with the spring washer must be furthest away from the pump.

25 Carefully install the driveshaft and pump into the block ensuring that the end of the shaft is correctly entered into the distributor aperture (photo).

26 Secure the pump in place with the two retaining bolts, and install the filter and pipe assembly (photo).

46 Engine reassembly – timing chain and timing cover

1 Install the spacer onto the end of the camshaft ensuring that the slot is correctly located over the dowel (photo).

2 Rotate the camshaft so that the dowel is facing downward and then rotate the crankshaft so that the keyway in the front end of the crankshaft is facing upward in line with the camshaft dowel. **Note:** *If the task is being carried out with the engine in the vehicle and the distributor has not been removed, lift off the distributor cap and check that the rotor is pointing toward the No. 1 cylinder spark plug lead position. If it is not, rotate the camshaft 180°.*

3 Lay the camshaft and crankshaft sprockets on the bench so that the single dot on the camshaft sprocket perimeter is directly opposite the mark on the crankshaft sprocket. Maintain them in this position and install the timing chain around both sprockets.

4 Carefully install both sprockets and the chain onto the camshaft and crankshaft, and tap them onto the dowel and keyway respectively.

5 Now make a careful check to ensure that the timing marks are still correctly aligned (photo and Fig. 1.40).

6 Position the fuel pump eccentric on the camshaft dowel and secure it with the washer and bolt, (photo). Tighten the bolt to the specified torque wrench setting.

45.22 Tightening the connecting rod nuts

45.25 Installing the oil pump and driveshaft

45.26 Installing the oil pump inlet pipe and filter

1

46.1 Installing the camshaft spacer

46.5 Alignment of camshaft and crankshaft sprocket timing marks

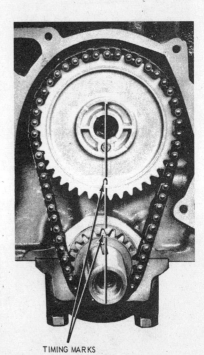
TIMING MARKS

Fig. 1.40 Correct alignment of camshaft and crankshaft timing marks (Sec. 46)

46.6 Installing the fuel pump operating eccentric

46.7 Location of crankshaft oil thrower

46.8 Installing the timing cover oil seal

46.9 Lowering the timing cover into position

46.10 Installation of the crankshaft damper

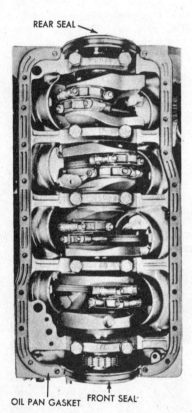

REAR SEAL

OIL PAN GASKET   FRONT SEAL

Fig. 1.41 Location of oil pan gaskets and seals — typical (Sec. 47)

47.3 Correct interlocking of oil pan seals and gaskets

47.7 Flywheel in position on the crankshaft

47.8 Installing the flywheel retaining bolts

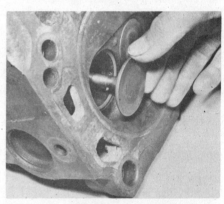

48.2 Inserting the valves in the cylinder head

48.3 Location of valve stem seal

48.5 Installing the valve retainer

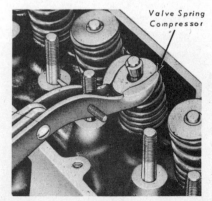

Valve Spring Compressor

Fig. 1.42 Compressing a valve spring (Sec. 48)

7 Place the oil thrower in position on the end of the crankshaft (photo).

8 Install a new seal in the timing cover aperture ensuring it is the correct way round (photo). Tap it fully home using a flat block of wood.

9 Select the front cover gasket and using a suitable sealing compound position it on the engine front plate and offer up the cover (photo).

10 Place the front cover bolts in position and screw them up loosely. Then install the crankshaft damper onto the keyway of the crankshaft (photo). See that the boss of the damper is lubricated where the oil seal runs.

11 The installation of the crankshaft damper, before tightening the cover bolts, centralises the seal to the damper. The bolts holding the cover may then be tightened to the specified torque setting.

47 Engine reassembly – rear plate, crankshaft damper, oil pan and flywheel

1 If the engine rear plate has been removed it should now be installed. Make sure that both metal faces are quite clean before installation. No gasket is used.

2 Install the bolt and washer which locate the crankshaft damper, block the crankshaft with a piece of wood against the side of the crankcase and tighten the bolt to the specified torque setting.

3 Clean all traces of old gasket which may remain from the oil pan joint faces and cover the faces of both the crankcase and pan with jointing compound. The oil pan gasket is in four sections which dovetail together and these should be carefully positioned and the joints interlocked (photo).

4 The engine is then ready for the oil pan to be installed.

5 Clean the interior of the pan thoroughly, apply jointing compound to the joint edge and place it in position.

6 Install all the oil pan bolts and tighten them evenly.

7 The flywheel may now be installed. Make sure that the mating flanges are clean and free from burrs, and line up the bolt holes correctly (photo).

8 Offer up the spacer (where applicable) and screw in the six retaining bolts. Tighten them evenly to the specified torque wrench setting (photo).

48 Engine reassembly – valve gear, cylinder heads, and intake manifold

1 When the cylinder heads have been decarbonized and the valves ground in as described in Sections 37 and 41, the cylinder heads may be reassembled. If the valves have been removed as described in Section 12 there will be no confusion as to which valve belongs in which position.

2 Make sure all traces of carbon and grinding paste have been removed, lubricate the valve stem with engine oil and place it in the appropriate guide (photo). It will then protrude through the top of the cylinder head.

3 Install a new seal cup over the valve stem (photo).

4 Place the valve spring over the valve stem. Note that on some engines a spacer is fitted between the spring and cylinder head.

5 Install the circular retainer over the spring with the protruding center boss retainer downward (photo).

6 Using a proper valve spring compressor tool, compress the spring down the valve stem sufficiently far to enable the two halves of the locks (collets) to be installed into the groove in the valve stem. If necessary the locks should be smeared with grease to keep them in position. The spring compressor may then be released. Watch to ensure that the locks stay together in position as the retainer comes past them. If the retainer is a little off-center it may force one lock out of its groove in which case the spring must be recompressed and the lock repositioned. When the compressor is finally released, tap the head of the valve stem with a soft mallet to make sure the valve assembly is securely held in position.

7 Stand the engine the right way up on the bench and install the valve lifters if they have been removed from the block. If these have been kept in order on removal, as suggested, it will be a simple matter to install them (photo).

Installing the cylinder heads (standard engines)

8 Make sure that the cylinder head and block faces are clean and free from grease or oil, and place the new head gasket in position. To ensure correct location the word *FRONT* is usually marked on the upper side of the gasket (photos).

9 Carefully place the cylinder heads in position on the block (photo).

10 Make sure the cylinder head bolts are clean and lightly oiled, and install them. Nip them all down lightly and then tighten them in the sequence shown in Fig. 1.13. The bolts should be tightened down to progressive torque loadings – all to 50 lbf ft (6.9 kgf m) then all to 60 lbf ft (8.30 kgf m), and finally to the specified torque wrench setting.

11 Now install the pushrods into position, making sure that they are installed the same way up as they came out and according to the original valve position. This will not be difficult if they have been kept in order (photo).

Installing the cylinder heads (Boss 429 engine)

The Boss 429 engines use special seals and gaskets in place of the conventional cylinder head gasket and the following procedure must be used when installing the cylinder heads.

12 Thoroughly clean the cylinder head and block mating surfaces with a clean piece of cloth soaked in chlorathane.

13 Coat the upper end of the cylinder head and block with a silicone rubber primer such as Dow Corning A-4094. Coat the gasket counterbores in the cylinder head with a quick drying adhesive sealer to prevent the gasket dropping out when the head is lifted into position.

14 Install four of the combustion chamber gaskets in the counterbores ensuring the tabs are seated down.

15 Install four of the $\frac{1}{4}$ in (6 mm) gaskets into the cylinder head counterbores with the stepped side facing up.

16 Install seventeen of the $\frac{1}{2}$ in (12 mm) gaskets into the cylinder head counterbores with the stepped side facing up.

17 Apply a continuous strip of sealant along the top edge of the cylinder head.

18 Install a steel rod of suitable diameter into one of the bolt holes in each end of the cylinder block. These will act as guides when lowering the head into position. Ensure that the rods are long enough to be withdrawn after the head is in place.

19 Carefully lower the cylinder head into position over the guide pins.

48.7 Inserting a hydraulic valve lifter into the block

48.8A Cylinder head gasket in position

48.8B The word FRONT ensures correct positioning of the cylinder head gaskets

48.9 Cylinder heads positioned on block

48.11 Inserting the pushrods

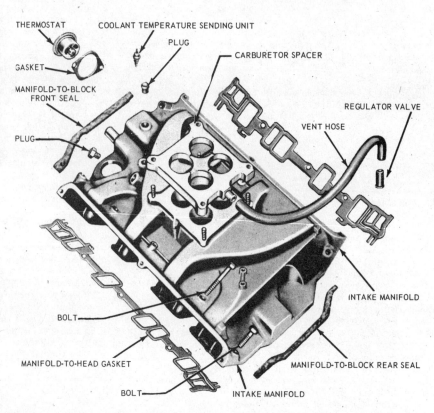

Fig. 1.43 Location of inlet manifold gaskets – typical (Sec. 48)

Make sure that none of the gaskets drop out of the head.

20 Screw in eight of the cylinder head bolts and washers but do not tighten them fully at this stage.

21 Remove the two guide rods and install the remaining two cylinder head bolts.

22 Tighten the bolts in sequence to an initial torque wrench setting of 60 lbf ft (8.28 kgf m). Next, torque tighten them to 80 lbf ft (11.0 kgf m); finally, torque tighten them to 90/95 lbf ft (12.4/13.1 kgf m).

23 Repeat the above procedures with the other cylinder head.

24 Install the pushrods as described in paragraph 12 of this Section.

All engines

25 On engines with stud-mounted rockers, position the rocker arms over the pushrods and valve stems, and carefully tighten the retaining nuts (bolts on some engines) just enough to retain the pushrods in their correct positions.

26 In the case of shaft-mounted rockers, lubricate the shafts with clean engine oil and reassemble the rockers, springs and pedestals onto the shafts in the correct order (see Fig. 1.16).

27 Install the rockers and shafts to the cylinder heads, and tighten down the retaining bolts progressively to avoid distortion of the shafts. Tighten the bolts to a torque wrench setting of 40/45 lbf ft (5.5/6.2 kgf m).

28 The valve clearances must be adjusted either now or at a later stage as described in the following Section.

29 To install the inlet manifold, first ensure that the cylinder head faces are clean and then lightly coat them with a suitable jointing compound.

30 Carefully stick the gaskets in place ensuring that the small front and rear pieces are interlocked with the two main gaskets (photo).

31 Lower the intake manifold carefully into place and check that none of the gaskets have been pushed out of position (photo).

32 Insert the intake manifold securing bolts. Note that some of the bolts are longer than others and care must be taken to ensure that they are installed in the correct hole.

33 Tighten the intake manifold bolts progressively in the appropriate sequence shown in Figs. 1.7, 1.8, 1.9, 1.10, 1.11, or 1.12. Finally tighten them to the specified torque wrench setting.

49 Valve lash – adjustment

1 With the exception of certain high-performance versions of the V8 engines which include the Boss 302, 351 and 429 series, all standard engines are equipped with hydraulic valve lifters. These automatically compensate for valve gear wear and once the initial clearance has been correctly set no further adjustment will be required until a considerable mileage has been covered.

2 The 390, 427 and 428 engines are fitted with shaft-mounted rocker arms which are non-adjustable. The correct clearance is obtained by installing a longer or shorter push rod as necessary. These are available in increments of 0.060 in (1.5 mm) and can be obtained from your Ford dealer.

3 Some of the early 302 cu in engines are equipped with adjustable rockers but all later V8 engines have positive-stop rocker mounting studs. On the former type the correct valve clearance is obtained by screwing the rocker arm locknut up or down as necessary, while on the latter type the nut is screwed right down until it stops. If the clearance is then found to be outside the specified limits, a longer or shorter pushrod must be installed, as necessary. These are obtainable from your Ford dealer.

4 The later positive-stop type rocker stud can be identified by the fact that the plain section of the stud nearest the cylinder head is larger in diameter than the threaded portion.

5 Before commencing adjustment, ensure that the rocker arm locknuts are in good condition and the fulcrum spacer slides easily on the rocker studs.

6 On the earlier 302 cu in engines with adjustable rocker arms, proceed by rotating the crankshaft until No 1 piston is at TDC (top dead center) of the compression stroke. This can be ascertained by removing the spark plug and with a finger placed over the hole, rotating the crankshaft until pressure is felt. This indicates the piston is rising on the compression stroke. Continue to rotate the crankshaft until the timing pointer on the front cover is aligned with the TDC mark on the crankshaft damper (photo).

7 Push down the No 1 cylinder rocker arms so that the pushrod forces the valve lifter down into the completely collapsed position.

48.30 Correct positioning of intake manifold gaskets

48.31 Installation of intake manifold

49.6 Alignment of pointer and TDC mark on crankshaft damper

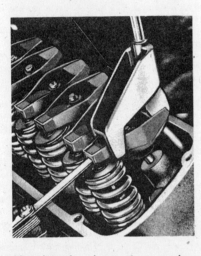

Fig. 1.44 Checking the valve clearances on engine equipped with hydraulic lifters. Note that the special tool shown is not essential for this task (Sec. 49)

49.9 Setting the valve clearances on earlier engines equipped with adjustable stud-mounted rocker arms

8   Using feeler gauges, check that the clearance between the rocker arm and valve stem is within the limits given at the end of this Section.

9   Adjust the clearances as necessary by turning the rocker arm retaining nut up or down using a socket wrench (photo).

10 When the No 1 cylinder valve clearances are correct, rotate the crankshaft until the next piston is at the TDC position of the compression stroke and adjust the valve clearances as described for No 1 cylinder. Continue to adjust the remaining valve clearances following the appropriate firing order sequence given in the engine Specifications.

11 On later engines with the positive-stop rocker arm studs, the piston must be set to the TDC position as described previously and then the rocker arm nut must be screwed down fully and tightened to a torque wrench setting of 18 to 20 lbf ft (2.4 to 2.5 kgf m). Push the rocker arm down so that the valve lifter is in the fully collapsed position and check the clearance between the rocker arm and valve stem using feeler gauges.

12 If the clearance is not within the specified dimensions, the pushrod must be replaced with an oversize or undersize one as appropriate.

13 The valve clearances on engines with shaft-mounted rockers are also adjusted by using undersize or oversize pushrods. **Note:** *When obtaining replacement pushrods, always take the old pushrod along to your Ford dealer to ensure that the new rod is the size required.*

14 *Solid valve lifters.* The valve clearances on engines equipped with solid valve lifters are adjusted by means of a set screw and locknut on the pushrod end of the rocker arm.

15 With the exception of the Boss 429 engines, final valve adjustment should only be carried out with the engine hot. However, for initial start-up purposes following an engine overhaul, the valve clearances can be set cold and then re-checked after the engine has been started and warmed up. The valve clearances on the Boss 429

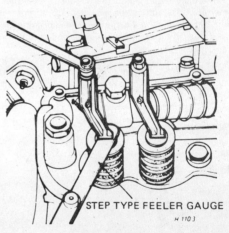

Fig. 1.45 Adjusting the valve clearances on engines equipped with solid valve lifters (Sec. 49)

should only be adjusted when the engine is cold.

16 Begin by rotating the engine until the No 1 piston is at TDC on the firing stroke as described previously and check the No 1 cylinder valve clearances using feeler gauges. If the clearances are not within the specified dimensions given at the end of this Section, slacken the locknut and turn the set screw in or out to decrease or increase the gap as required. Tighten the locknut and re-check the clearance.

17 Rotate the crankshaft 90° until the next piston is at TDC on the

firing stroke and adjust the valve clearances as described. Continue to adjust the remaining valve clearances following the appropriate firing order sequence in the engine Specifications.

Valve clearances (hydraulic lifters)

Engine (cu in)	Minimum	Maximum
260 and 289	0.082 in (2.08 mm)	0.152 in (3.86 mm)
302	0.067 in (1.70 mm)	0.167 in (4.24 mm)
351	0.083 in (2.10 mm)	0.183 in (4.64 mm)
390, 427 and 428	0.100 in (2.54 mm)	0.200 in (5.08 mm)
429	0.075 in (1.90 mm)	0.175 in (4.44 mm)

Valve clearances (solid lifters)

Engine (cu in)	Intake	Exhaust
289 HP	0.018 in (0.45 mm)	0.018 in (0.45 mm)
302 Boss	0.025 in (0.63 mm)	0.025 in (0.63 mm)
351 Boss and HO	0.025 in (0.63 mm)	0.025 in (0.63 mm)
429 Boss	0.013 in (0.33 mm)	0.013 in (0.33 mm)
429 SCJ	0.019 in (0.48 mm)	0.019 in (0.48 mm)

50 Engine reassembly – installing ancillary components

1   The exhaust manifolds are best installed before putting the engine back into the car as they provide very useful holds if the engine has to be manhandled at all. Note that no gaskets are used on the exhaust manifolds.
2   Install each manifold, tighten the bolts evenly and bend over the locking tabs (photos).
3   The ancillary engine components must be installed and the method of doing this is detailed in the appropriate Chapters. Section 9 of this Chapter gives a list of the items involved. When this has been done the engine is ready to be put back in the car.
4   For details on how to install the distributor and the method of ignition timing, refer to Chapter 4.

51 Engine installation – without transmission

1   The engine must be positioned suitably so that the sling used can be easily attached and the lifting tackle hooked on. Position the engine the right way round in front of the car and then raise it so that it may be brought into position over the car, or the car rolled into position underneath it.
2   The transmission should be jacked up to its approximately normal position.
3   Lower the engine steadily into the engine compartment, keeping all ancillary wires, pipes and cables well clear of the sides. It is best to have a second person guiding the engine while it is being lowered.
4   The tricky part is finally mating the engine to the transmission;

which involves locating the transmission input shaft into the clutch housing and flywheel. Provided that the clutch friction plate has been centered correctly as described in Chapter 5, there should be little difficulty. Grease the splines of the input shaft first. It may be necessary to rock the engine from side to side in order to get the engine fully home. Under no circumstances let any strain be imparted onto the input shaft. This could occur if the shaft was not fully located and the engine was raised or lowered more than the amount required for very slight adjustment of position.
5   As soon as the engine is fully up to the clutch housing, install the bolts holding the two together.
6   Now finally lower the engine onto its mounting brackets at the front, and install and tighten the nuts, and washers.
7   Re-connect all electrical connections, the fuel lines and carburetor linkages, cooling system hoses and radiator in the reverse order to that described in Section 5.
8   Reconnect the clutch cable as described in Chapter 5, install the exhaust pipes and reconnect them to the manifold extensions, install the plate covering the lower half of the clutch housing and remove the supporting jack.
9   Fill the engine with fresh oil and refill the radiator with coolant.

52 Engine installation – with manual transmission

1   The transmission should be installed in the engine, taking the same precautions regarding the input shaft as mentioned in Section 50.
2   The general principles of lifting the engine/transmission assembly are the same as for the engine alone but the transmission will tilt everything to a much steeper angle. Installation will certainly require the assistance of a second person.
3   Lift the transmission end of the unit into the engine compartment (unless you are fortunate enough to have a hoist with a very high lift) and then lower and guide the unit down. One of the first things to be done is to reconnect the propeller shaft into the transmission rear extension casing so someone should be ready to lift and guide the propeller shaft into position as soon as the transmission is near enough. This cannot be done after the unit has been lowered beyond a certain position.
4   If a trolley jack is available this is the time to place it under the transmission so that as the engine is lowered further the rear end can be supported and raised as necessary – at the same time being able to roll back as required. Without such a jack, support the rear in such a way that it can slide if possible. In any case the transmission will have to be jacked and held up in position when the unit nears its final position.
5   Locate the front mounting brackets on the locating bolts as described in Section 50.

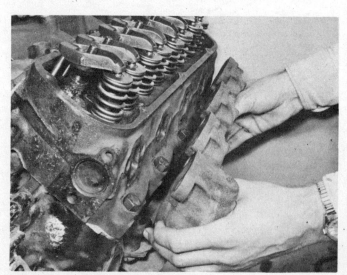

50.2A Installing the exhaust manifolds

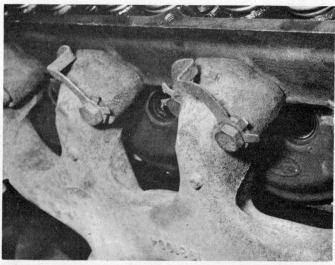

50.2B Do not forget the locking tabs when installing the manifold retaining bolts

6 Install the speedometer drive cable with the transmission drive socket and install the snap-ring and bolt. This *must* be done before the transmission supporting crossmember is in place.

7 Jack up the rear of the transmission and position the crossmember to the bodyframe. Then install and tighten down the two retaining bolts and the center bolt to the transmission extension.

8 Install the transmission remote control shift lever and housing as described in Chapter 6.

9 Reconnect the clutch cable and adjust as described in Chapter 5 and reconnect the back-up light wire. The final connections should then be made as described in Section 51 and in addition to the engine lubricant and coolant, the transmission should also be refilled with fresh oil.

53 Engine – initial start-up after overhaul or major repair

1 Make sure that the battery is fully charged and that all lubricants, coolants and fuel are replenished.

2 If the fuel system has been dismantled it will require several revolutions of the engine on the starter motor to get the fuel up to the carburetor. It will help if the spark plugs are removed and the engine turned over on the starter motor. This will ensure that the carburetor is primed with fuel and also that oil is circulated around the engine prior to starting.

3 As soon as the engine fires and runs, keep it going at a fast idle only (no faster) and bring it up to normal working temperature.

4 As the engine warms up there will be odd smells and some smoke from parts getting hot and burning off oil deposits. The signs to look for are leaks of oil or water which will be obvious if serious. Check also the clamp connections of the exhaust pipes to the manifolds as these do not always 'find' their exact gas-tight position until warmth and vibration have acted on them and it is almost certain that they need tightening further. This should be done, of course, with the engine stopped.

5 When the running temperature has been reached adjust the idling speed as described in Chapter 3.

6 Stop the engine and wait a few minutes to see if any lubricant or coolant is dripping out when the engine is stationary.

7 Road test the car to check that the timing is correct and giving the necessary smoothness and power. Do not race the engine – if new bearings and/or pistons and rings have been installed it should be treated as a new engine and run-in at reduced speed for 500 miles (800 km).

54 Fault diagnosis – engine

Symptom	Reason/s
Engine will not turn over when starter switch is operated	Flat battery Bad battery connections Bad connections at solenoid switch and/or starter motor Starter motor jammed Defective solenoid Starter motor defective
Engine turns over normally but fails to fire and run	No spark at plugs No fuel reaching engine Too much fuel reaching the engine (flooding)
Engine starts but runs unevenly and misfires	Ignition and/or fuel system faults Incorrect valve clearances Burnt out valves Blown cylinder head gasket Worn piston rings or cylinder bores
Lack of power	Ignition and/or fuel system faults Incorrect valve clearances Burnt out valves Blown cylinder head gasket Worn piston rings or cylinder bores
Excessive oil consumption	Oil leaks from crankshaft rear oil seal, timing cover gasket and oil seal, rocker cover gasket, oil filter gasket, oil pan gasket, oil pan plug washer. Worn piston rings or cylinder bores, resulting in oil being burnt by engine – smoky exhaust is an indication Worn valve guides and/or defective valve stem seals - smoke blowing out from the rocker cover vents is an indication
Excessive mechanical noise from engine	Wrong valve-to-rocker clearances (solid lifters) Worn crankshaft bearings Worn cylinders (piston slap) Worn timing chain and/or sprocket

Note 1: *When investigating starting and uneven running faults do not be tempted into snap-diagnosis. Start from the beginning of the check procedure and follow it through. It will take less time in the long run. Poor performance from an engine in terms of power and economy is not normally diagnosed quickly. In any event the ignition and fuel systems must be checked first before assuming any further investigation needs to be made.*

Note 2: *On engines equipped with hydraulic valve lifters, a mechanical tapping noise may be heard on initial start up. However, as the engine oil pressure rises, the valve lifters will expand and the noise should cease. If it does not, the valve lifters should be checked for correct operation.*

Chapter 2 Cooling system

Contents

Specifications

System type . . . . Pressurized, assisted by pump and fan

Thermostat
Type . . . . Wax-filled
Location . . . . Front of intake manifold
Opening temperature . . . . 188° to 195° F (86° to 91° C)
Fully open . . . . 212° to 215° F (100° to 101° C)

Radiator
Type . . . . Vertical-flow or cross-flow, depending on model
Pressure cap setting . . . . 13 lbf/in² (0.91 kgf/cm²)

Water pump
Type . . . . Centrifugal impeller type
Drivebelt tension . . . . Approximately 0.5 in (13 mm) of movement at midpoint of longest
span of belt

Cooling system capacities
260 cu in . . . . 15 US quarts (14 liters)
289 cu in . . . . 15 US quarts (14 liters)
302 cu in . . . . 15 US quarts (14 liters)
351 cu in . . . . 16 US quarts (15 liters)
390 cu in . . . . 20.5 US quarts (19.5 liters)
427 cu in . . . . 20.5 US quarts (19.5 liters)
428 cu in . . . . 19.5 US quarts (18.5 liters)
429 cu in . . . . 18.5 US quarts (17.5 liters)

Torque wrench settings

	lbf ft	kgf m
Fan-to-pulley hub	12 to 18	1.6 to 2.5
Water pump bolts	20 to 25	2.8 to 3.5
Alternator pivot bolts	40 to 50	6.0 to 7.0
Thermostat housing bolts	12 to 15	1.6 to 2.1

1 General description

The cooling system on all models comprises a radiator connected to the engine by top and bottom water hoses, a belt-driven fan and water pump, and a thermostat. Small bore hoses transfer water to the heater and automatic choke control unit.

The intake manifold is water-heated and on some models the fan incorporates a temperature-controlled fluid coupling which reduces power absorption and fan noise.

The cooling system is pressurized to enable a higher operating temperature to be maintained without boiling. If the water pressure within the system rises above the preset limit of the radiator cap, (see Specifications) the spring-loaded valve within the cap opens and allows the excess water to pass along an overflow pipe, thus relieving the pressure. It is therefore important to ensure that the cap has the correct pressure setting stamped on the top and that the spring and sealing washer are in good condition.

In operation, cold water in the bottom of the radiator circulates up the lower radiator hose to the water pump where it is pushed round the water passages in the cylinder block, helping to keep the cylinder bores and pistons cool. The water then travels up to the intake manifold and cylinder heads, and circulates round the combustion spaces and valve seats absorbing more heat.

Either a cross-flow or down-flow radiator may be installed depending on the model and year of manufacture. The cross-flow type has a header tank on each side of the radiator and the water flows horizontally between the two tanks. The down-flow type has tanks at the top and bottom of the radiator, and the water flows vertically through the connecting tubes within the radiator core.

The thermostat is located on the front of the intake manifold and its function is to restrict the flow of water between the radiator and the engine to provide fast warm-up until the normal operating temperature is reached.

2 Cooling system – draining

1   If the engine is cold, remove the filler cap from the radiator by turning the cap counterclockwise. If the engine is hot, then turn the filler cap very slightly until pressure in the system has had time to be released. Use a rag over the cap to protect your hand from escaping steam. If, with the engine very hot, the cap is released suddenly, the drop in pressure can result in the water boiling. With the pressure released the cap can be removed.

2   If antifreeze is used in the cooling system, drain it into a bowl having a capacity of at least that of the cooling system, for re-use.

3   Open the drain plug located at the base of the radiator, or remove the bottom radiator hose. Also remove the engine drain plugs located on either side of the cylinder block. If the heater has a water control valve, open it to drain the heat exchanger.

4   When the water has finished running, probe the drain plug orifices with a short piece of wire to dislodge any particles of rust or sediment which may be causing a blockage.

3 Cooling system – flushing

1   In time the cooling system will gradually lose its efficiency as the radiator becomes choked with rust, scale deposits from the water, and other sediment. To clean the system out, remove the radiator filler cap and drain plug and leave a hose running in the filler cap neck for ten to fifteen minutes.

2   In very bad cases the radiator should be reverse-flushed. This can be done with the radiator in position. The cylinder block plug is removed and a hose with a suitable tapered adaptor placed in the drain plug hole. Water under pressure is then forced through the radiator and out of the header tank filler cap neck. It is recommended that some polythene sheeting is placed over the engine to stop water finding its way into the electrical system.

3   The hose should now be removed and placed in the radiator cap filler neck, and the radiator washed out in the usual manner.

4 Cooling system – filling

1   Install the cylinder block and radiator drain plugs.

2   Fill the system slowly to ensure that no air lock develops. If the heater has a water control valve, check that it is open (control at hot), otherwise an airlock may form in the heater. The best type of water to use in the cooling system is rain water, mixed in the correct proportion with the recommended antifreeze/rust inhibitor solution (see Section 15). On the down-flow type radiator the level of coolant must be $\frac{3}{4}$ to $1\frac{1}{2}$ in (20 to 35 mm) below the filler neck, while the cross-flow type radiator must be filled to the *cold fill* mark (see Fig. 2.4). Overfilling will

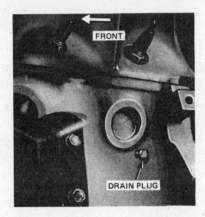

Fig. 2.1 Cylinder block drain plug (one each side) (Sec. 2)

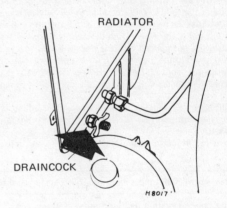

Fig. 2.2 Location of radiator drain tap (Sec. 2)

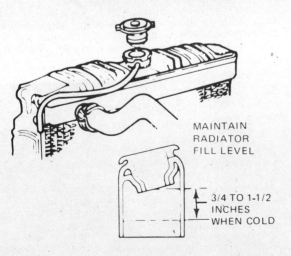

Fig. 2.3 Coolant level for down-flow type radiators (Sec. 4)

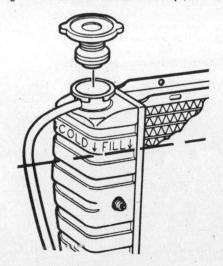

Fig. 2.4 Coolant level for cross-flow type radiators (Sec. 4)

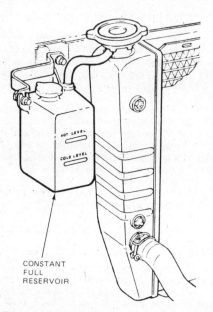

Fig. 2.5 Later type radiator overflow reservoir (Sec. 4)

merely result in wastage which is especially to be avoided when antifreeze is in use.

3   It is usually found that air locks develop in the heater radiator so the system should be vented during refilling by detaching the heater supply hose from the elbow connection on the water outlet housing.

4   Pour coolant into the radiator filler neck whilst the end of the heater supply hose is held at the elbow connection height. When a constant stream of water flows from the supply hose quickly install the hose. If venting is not carried out it is possible for the engine to overheat. Should the engine overheat for no apparent reason then the system should be vented before seeking other causes. On some models a bleed nipple is incorporated in the coolant hose which runs at the rear of the engine.

5   After filling the system run the engine with the filler cap off until normal operating temperature is reached. Check the coolant level and refill if necessary.

6   Install the radiator cap and turn it clockwise to lock it in position.

5   Radiator – removal, inspection, cleaning and installation

1   Drain the cooling system as described in Section 2.

2   Slacken the two clips which hold the top and bottom radiator hoses on the radiator and carefully pull off the two hoses.

3   Where applicable, remove radiator upper splash shield and disconnect the hose from the automatic transmission oil cooler. Plug the ends of the hoses to prevent fluid loss and ingress of dirt.

4   Undo and remove the four bolts that secure the radiator shroud to the radiator side panels and move the shroud over the fan blades. This

is only applicable when a shroud is installed (photo).

5   Undo and remove the four bolts that secure the radiator to the front panel. The radiator may now be lifted upwards and away from the engine compartment. The fragile matrix must not be touched by the fan blades as it is easily punctured (photo).

6   Lift the radiator shroud from over the fan blades and remove from the engine compartment.

7   With the radiator away from the car, any leaks can be soldered or repaired with a suitable proprietary substance. Clean out the inside of the radiator by flushing as described in this Chapter. When the radiator is out of the car it is advantageous to turn it upside down and reverse flush. Clean the exterior of the radiator by carefully using a compressed air jet or a strong jet of water to clear away any road dirt, bugs etc.

8   Inspect the radiator hoses for cracks, internal or external perishing, and damage by overtightening of the securing clips. Also inspect the overflow pipe. Renew the hoses if suspect. Examine the radiator hose clips and renew them if they are rusted or distorted.

9   The drain plug and washer should be renewed if there has been any leakage.

10 Installation of the radiator is the reverse sequence to removal. After refilling the system run the engine and check for leaks.

11 If a transmission oil cooler is installed, check the hoses for leaks and top-up the fluid level, if necessary.

6   Thermostat – removal and installation

1   Partially drain the cooling system, as described in Section 2.

2   Slacken the top radiator hose to the thermostat housing and remove the hose.

3   Undo and remove the two bolts and spring washers that secure the thermostat housing to the intake manifold.

4   Carefully lift the thermostat housing away from the intake manifold. Recover the joint washer adhering to either the housing or intake manifold (photo).

5   Withdraw the thermostat, making a note of which way round it is fitted (photo).

6   Install the thermostat using the reverse procedure to removal.

7   Always ensure that the thermostat housing and intake manifold mating faces are clean and flat. If the thermostat housing is badly corroded install a new housing. Always use a new gasket. Tighten the two securing bolts to the specified torque.

7   Thermostat – testing

1   Remove the thermostat, as described in the previous Section.

2   Test the thermostat for correct functioning by suspending it on a string in a saucepan of cold water together with a thermometer. Heat the water and note the temperature at which the thermostat begins to open. This should be as given in the Specifications. Continue heating the water until the thermostat is fully open. Then let it cool down naturally.

3   If the thermostat does not fully open in boiling water, or does not close down as the water cools, then it must be discarded and a new one installed. Should the thermostat be stuck open when cold, this will usually be apparent when removing it from the housing.

5.4 Removing the radiator cowl securing bolts

5.5 Lifting out the radiator

6.4 Removing the thermostat housing

6.5 Location of thermostat

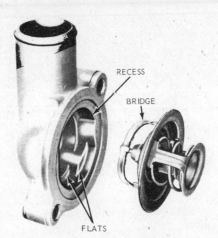

Fig. 2.6 Correct location of thermostat (Sec. 6)

Fig. 2.7 Viscous drive cooling fan (Sec. 10)

8 Water pump – removal and installation

1 Drain the cooling system, as described in Section 2.
2 Remove the radiator and shroud, as described in Section 5.
3 Loosen the alternator adjusting bolts and remove the drivebelt. If an air-conditioning pump is installed the alternator and mounting bracket will have to be removed completely.
4 Remove the fan and pulley from the pump.
5 Unscrew and remove the bolts and washers that secure the water pump assembly. Note the location of the bolts as they are of different lengths.
6 Lift away the water pump assembly. Recover the gasket if not stuck to the casting. If necessary also remove the thermostat housing from the water pump.
7 Before installing the water pump assembly, remove all traces of the old gasket and sealing compound from the front cover and water pump assembly.
8 Carefully apply a sealer to both sides of a new gasket and accurately position on the water pump.
9 Hold the water pump in position and screw in two bolts and washers, so retaining it to the front cover.
10 Remove all gasket material from the thermostat housing mating faces. Apply a sealer to both sides of the new gasket and position it on the water pump. Secure in position with the two bolts and washers.
11 Install all remaining securing bolts and washers ensuring they are located in their original positions. Tighten in a diagonal and progressive manner to the correct torque wrench settings (see Specifications).
12 Install the fan, drivebelt(s) and radiator; then refill the cooling system.

9 Water pump – overhaul

Water pump failure will be indicated by coolant leakage, noisy operation and/or excess movement of the drive spindle. If any of these faults are present a replacement pump must be obtained from a Ford dealer as it is not practical or even economical to attempt repairing a worn-out unit.

10 Viscous cooling fan – removal and installation

1 Remove the radiator, as described in Section 5.
2 Slacken the fan belt and remove the bolts securing the fan drive clutch to the water pump hub.
3 Remove the fan drive clutch and fan as a complete assembly.
4 Remove the retaining bolts and separate the drive clutch from the fan.
5 The viscous clutch assembly is not repairable and if faulty should be replaced with a new clutch unit.
6 Install the fan and clutch using the reverse of the removal procedure.

11 Drivebelts – inspection and adjusting

1 The number of drivebelts on the car will depend on which extras are installed, ie air-conditioning compressor, power steering pump and thermactor pump (photo).
2 Periodically the belts should be checked for correct tension and wear. Use a flashlight and examine the inside surface of the belts for cracks and if in evidence renew the belt(s).
3 The alternator belt tension is adjusted by slackening the two lower pivot bolts and top slide bolt, and moving the alternator in the required direction (photo).
4 Power steering and thermactor pump drivebelts are adjusted by slackening the slot bolts and screwing the adjusting bolts in or out to achieve the required belt tension. The slot bolts are then tightened (see Fig. 2.9). Note: *On some earlier models the power steering and thermactor pump drivebelts are adjusted by slackening the mounting bolts on the pump bracket and carefully levering the pump away from the engine (see Fig. 2.10 and photo).*
5 When an air-conditioning pump is installed the drivebelt tension is controlled by an idler pulley; this has a single pivot bolt and an adjusting bolt located behind the pulley.
6 To get the belts adjusted correctly the car should be taken to a Ford dealer who will have a special belt tensioning tool. However the home mechanic can obtain approximately the correct tension by adjusting the belt(s) until there is about $\frac{1}{2}$ in (13 mm) of movement midway between the pulleys (see Fig. 2.12).

11.1 Layout of engine driven accessories and drivebelts – typical

11.3 Alternator top pivot mounting

PIVOT BOLT
PULLEYS
ADJUSTING BOLT
DRIVE BELT

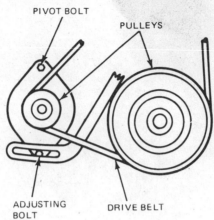

11.4 Earlier type power steering pump mounting bracket

Fig. 2.8 Pivot bolt and slide adjustment – typical (Sec. 11)

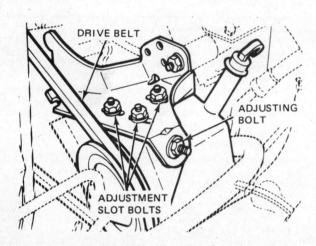

DRIVE BELT
ADJUSTING BOLT
ADJUSTMENT SLOT BOLTS

Fig. 2.9 Power steering pump adjustment – later models (Sec. 11)

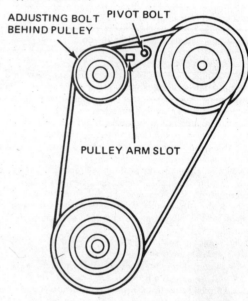

ADJUSTING BOLT BEHIND PULLEY   PIVOT BOLT
PULLEY ARM SLOT

Fig. 2.11 Air-conditioning pump idler pulley adjustment – typical (Sec. 11)

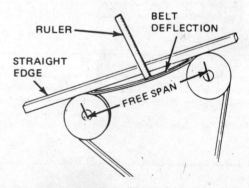

ADJUSTING AND MOUNTING BOLTS
PUMP COVER PLATE
POWER STEERING PUMP

Fig. 2.10 Power steering pump adjustment – earlier models (Sec. 11)

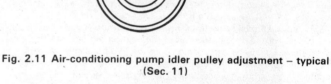

RULER   BELT DEFLECTION
STRAIGHT EDGE   FREE SPAN

Fig. 2.12 Method of checking drivebelt adjustment (Sec. 11)

12 Drivebelts – removal and installation

1   To remove a drivebelt, slacken the relevant accessory pivot and adjusting bolts and move it in towards the engine as far as possible. Remove the belt by lifting it over the pulley, rotating the pulley at the same time. **Note**: *If air conditioning and/or power steering pumps are installed* these drivebelts will have to be removed prior to the removal of the alternator/fan belt.

2   Install the drivebelt(s) using the reverse sequence to removal. If a new belt is installed the engine should be run for 10 minutes then switched off and the belt tension re-checked.

3   On some engines the fan is driven by twin belts and these should always be renewed as a pair.

13 Temperature gauge – fault diagnosis

1 If the temperature gauge fails to work, either the gauge, the sender unit, the wiring or the connections are at fault.
2 It is not possible to repair the gauge or the sender unit and they must be replaced by new units if at fault.
3 First check that the wiring connections are sound. Check the wiring for breaks using an ohmmeter. The sender unit and gauge should be tested by substitution.

14 Temperature gauge and sender unit – removal and installation

1 Information on the removal of the gauge will be found in Chapter 10.
2 The sender unit is screwed into the left-hand side of the cylinder block. To remove the unit, disconnect the wire connector and unscrew the unit with a suitable wrench.
3 Install the sender unit using the reverse procedure to removal.

15 Antifreeze and corrosion inhibitors

1 In circumstances where it is likely that the temperature will drop below freezing it is essential that some of the water is drained and an adequate amount of ethylene glycol antifreeze is added to the cooling system. If antifreeze is not used, it is essential to use a corrosion inhibitor in the cooling system in the proportion recommended by the inhibitor manufacturer.
2 Any antifreeze of good quality can be used. Never use an antifreeze with an alcohol base as evaporation is too high.
3 Most antifreeze with an anti-corrosion additive can be left in the cooling system for up to two years, but after six months it is advisable to have the specific gravity of the coolant checked at your local repair station and thereafter once every three months.
4 The table below gives the proportion of antifreeze and degree of protection:

Antifreeze	Commences to freeze		Frozen solid	
%	°C	°F	°C	°F
25	-13	9	-26	-15
33⅓	-19	-2	-36	-33
50	-36	-33	-48	-53

Note: *Never use antifreeze in the windscreen washer reservoir as it will cause damage to the paintwork.*

16 Fault diagnosis – cooling system

Symptom	Reason/s
Overheating	Insufficient water in cooling system Fan belt slipping (accompanied by a shrieking noise on rapid engine acceleration) Radiator core blocked or radiator grille restricted Bottom water hose collapsed, impeding flow Thermostat not opening properly Ignition advance and retard incorrectly set (accompanied by loss of power, and perhaps misfiring) Carburetor incorrectly adjusted (mixture too lean) Exhaust system partially blocked Oil level in oil pan too low Blown cylinder head gasket (water/steam being forced down the radiator overflow pipe under pressure) Engine not yet broken-in Brakes binding
Underheating	Thermostat jammed open Incorrect thermostat installed allowing premature opening of valve Thermostat missing
Loss of cooling water	Loose clips on water hoses Top, bottom or by-pass water hoses perished and leaking Radiator core leaking Thermostat gasket leaking Radiator pressure cap spring worn or seal ineffective Blown cylinder head gasket/s (pressure in system forcing water/steam down overflow pipe) Cylinder wall or head cracked

2

Chapter 3 Fuel, exhaust and emission control systems

Contents

Specifications

Fuel pump

Type	Mechanical, single-action

Delivery pressure:
1965 thru 69	4.5 to 5.5 lbf/in^2 (0.31 – 0.38 kgf/cm^2)
1970 thru 73	5.5 to 6.5 lbf/in^2 (0.38 – 0.45 kgf/cm^2)
With 429 Boss engine	6 to 8 lbf/in^2 (0.42 – 0.56 kgf/cm^2)

Fuel tank capacity

	US gal	litre
1965 thru 68	16	60.56
1969	20	75.7
1970	22	83.27
1971	20	75.7
1972 thru 73	19.5	73.8

Fuel filter . . . . In-line, disposable

Air cleaner . . . . Disposable element

Carburetors

2-barrel type	Autolite 2100, Autolite 2100D or Motorcraft 2100D
4-barrel type	Autolite 4300, Autolite 4300D, Motorcraft 4300D, Holley 4150C or Rochester Quadrajet 4MV

Autolite 2100 carburetors (all dimensions in inches)

Carburetor No 9510	C8AF – BD	C9AF – A	C9ZF – B	C9ZF – A
Throttle bore diameter	1.56	1.56	1.68	1.68
Venturi diameter	1.08	1.08	1.23	1.23
Fuel level (wet) $\pm \frac{1}{64}$	$\frac{3}{4}$	$\frac{3}{4}$	$\frac{7}{8}$	$\frac{7}{8}$
Float setting (dry) $\pm \frac{1}{32}$	$\frac{3}{8}$	$\frac{3}{8}$	$\frac{31}{64}$	$\frac{9}{16}$
Main jet	48F	48F	54F	54F
Power valve identification	Green	Green	Green	Plain
Pump rod position	No 3	No 2	No 3	No 3

	C8AF-BD	C9AF-A	C9ZF-B	C9ZF-A
Choke system:				
Bi-metal identification	TN	TO	TW	TW
Cap setting	2 – rich	Index	2 – rich	1 – rich
Pulldown setting ($\pm$ 0.010)	0.130	0.120	0.120	0.150
Fast idle cam clearance	0.110	0.110	0.110	0.130
Dashpot adjustment ($\pm \frac{1}{64}$)	$\frac{1}{8}$	$\frac{1}{8}$	–	$\frac{7}{64}$
Idle speed:				
Curb idle rpm	650	550	550	650
Fast idle rpm – kickdown step	1400	1600	1600	1300

Autolite 2100D carburetors (all dimensions in inches)

Carburetor No 9510

	DOAF-C	DOAF-D	DOAF-E	DOAF-F
Transmission	Manual	Auto	Manual	Auto
Throttle bore diameter	1.56	1.56	1.68	1.68
Venturi diameter	1.08	1.08	1.23	1.23
Fuel level (wet) $\pm \frac{1}{32}$	$\frac{13}{16}$	$\frac{13}{16}$	$\frac{13}{16}$	$\frac{13}{16}$
Float setting (dry) $\pm \frac{1}{32}$	$\frac{7}{16}$	$\frac{7}{16}$	$\frac{7}{16}$	$\frac{7}{16}$
Main jet	48F	48F	54F	55F
Power valve identification	Plain	Green	Red	Red
Pump rod position	No 3	No 2	No 3	No 4
Choke system:				
Bi-metal identification	TN	TW	TW	TW
Cap setting	1 – rich	1 – rich	2 – lean	2 – lean
Pulldown setting ($\pm$ 0.010)	0.150	0.150	0.230	0.200
Fast idle cam clearance	0.130	0.130	0.190	0.170
Dashpot adjustment ($\pm \frac{1}{64}$)	–	$\frac{1}{8}$	–	$\frac{1}{8}$
Idle speed:				
Curb idle rpm	800/500*	575	700/500*	575
Fast idle rpm – kickdown step	1400	1500	1300	1600

*Higher idle speed with throttle solenoid energized/lower idle speed with throttle solenoid de-energized

Carburetor No 9510

	D1AF-DA	D1OF-PA	D1ZF-SA	D1OF-RA
Transmission	Auto	Manual	Auto	Auto (California only)
Throttle bore diameter	1.56	1.68	1.68	1.68
Venturi diameter	1.08	1.23	1.23	1.23
Fuel level (wet) $\pm \frac{1}{32}$	$\frac{13}{16}$	$\frac{13}{16}$	$\frac{13}{16}$	$\frac{13}{16}$
Float setting (dry) $\pm \frac{1}{32}$	$\frac{7}{16}$	$\frac{7}{16}$	$\frac{7}{16}$	$\frac{7}{16}$
Main jet	47F	61F	54F	54F
Power valve identification	Plain	Green	Red	Red
Pump rod position	No 3	No 3	No 3	No 3
Choke system:				
Bi-metal identification	TB5	TB5	TB4	TB4
Cap setting	1 – rich	Index	1 – rich	1 – rich
Pulldown setting ($\pm$ 0.010)	0.170	0.230	0.200	0.200
Fast idle cam clearance	0.150	0.190	0.170	0.170
Idle speed:				
Curb idle rpm*	600/500	700/500	600/500	600/500
Fast idle rpm – kickdown step	1400	1500	1500	1500

*Higher idle speed with throttle solenoid energized / lower idle speed with throttle solenoid de-energized

Carburetor No 9510

	D2OF-KA, -KB	D2AF-HA, -HB, -HC	D2ZF-LA	D2OF-UB
Transmission	Manual	Auto	Manual	Auto
Throttle bore diameter	1.56	1.56	1.68	1.68
Venturi diameter	1.08	1.08	1.21	1.21
Fuel level (wet) $\pm \frac{1}{16}$	$\frac{13}{16}$	$\frac{13}{16}$	$\frac{13}{16}$	$\frac{13}{16}$
Float setting (dry) $\pm \frac{1}{16}$	$\frac{7}{16}$	$\frac{7}{16}$	$\frac{7}{16}$	$\frac{7}{16}$
Main jet	48F	48F	61F	54F
Power valve identification	Yellow	Green	Green	Green
Pump rod position	2A	2A	3A	3A
Choke system:				
Bi-metal identification	TY	TX	TX	TX
Cap setting	1 – rich	1 – rich	1 – rich	1 – rich
Pulldown setting ($\pm$ 0.010)	0.140	0.150	0.240	0.190
Fast idle cam clearance	0.130	0.130	0.210	0.160
Idle CO (%)	0.5	0.19	0.5	0.5
Dashpot adjustment ($\pm \frac{1}{64}$)	–	$\frac{1}{8}$	–	–
Idle speed:				
Curb idle rpm*	800/500	600/500**	750/500	575/500***
Fast idle rpm – kickdown step	1400	1400	1100	1500

*Higher idle speed with throttle solenoid energized / lower idle speed with throttle solenoid de-energized.
**Without solenoid: 575   ***California: 625/500

3

Motorcraft 2100D carburetors *(all dimensions in inches)*

Carburetor No 9510	D3GF-BB	D3OF-EA	D3AF-DC	D3AF-PA
Transmission	Manual	Auto	Auto	Auto
Throttle bore diameter	1.56	1.56	1.68	1.68
Venturi diameter	1.08	1.08	1.21	1.21
Fuel level (wet) $\pm \frac{1}{16}$	$\frac{13}{16}$	$\frac{13}{16}$	$\frac{13}{16}$	$\frac{13}{16}$
Float setting (dry) $\pm \frac{1}{16}$	$\frac{7}{16}$	$\frac{7}{16}$	$\frac{7}{16}$	$\frac{7}{16}$
Main jet	47F	49F	54F	55F
Power valve identification	Brown	Black	Black	Black
Pump rod position	2A	2A	3	3
Electric choke system:				
Bi-metal identification	2 A/B B4	2 A/B B4	2 A/B B4	2 A/B B4
Cap setting	3 – rich	3 – rich	3 – rich	3 – rich
Pulldown setting			Refer to text	
Fast idle cam clearance			Refer to text	
Idle speed:				
Curb idle rpm			Refer to engine decal	
Fast idle rpm – kickdown	1250	1400	1500	1500
Idle CO (%) – California	0.2	0.2	0.2	–
– Other	0.5	0.5	0.5	–

Holley 4150C carburetors *(all dimensions in inches)*

Carburetor No 9510	C9AF-M	C9AF-N	D00F-S
Transmission	Manual	Auto	Manual
Throttle bore diameter – Primary	1.69	1.69	1.69
– Secondary	1.69	1.69	1.69
Venturi diameter – Primary	1.38	1.38	1.38
– Secondary	1.44	1.44	1.34
Fuel level		Lower edge of sight plug	
Dry float setting		Parallel with float bowl floor (bowl inverted)	
Main jet – Primary	66	66	64
– Secondary	79	79	82
Choke system:			
Bi-metal identification	GTI	GTA	Manual
Choke setting	2 – rich	1 – rich	–
Pulldown setting	0.30	0.30	–
Fast idle cam setting	0.060	0.080	–
Pump cam position	No 2	No 2	No 2
Pump override clearance	0.015	0.015	0.015
Dashpot adjustment	0.100	0.100	–
Idle speed:			
Curb idle rpm	700	650	700/500*
Fast idle rpm	1350**	1550**	2200***

**Kickdown or second step of cam   ***Highest stop of cam
*Higher idle speed with throttle solenoid energized / lower idle speed with throttle solenoid de-energized

Carburetor No 9510	DOZF-AA	DOZF-AB	DOZF-AC	DOZF-AD
Transmission	Manual	Auto	Manual	Auto
Throttle bore diameter – Primary	1.69	1.69	1.69	1.69
– Secondary	1.69	1.69	1.69	1.69
Venturi diameter – Primary	1.38	1.38	1.38	1.38
– Secondary	1.34	1.34	1.34	1.34
Fuel level			Lower edge of sight plug	
Dry float setting			Parallel with float bowl floor (bowl inverted)	
Main jet – Primary	66	66	66	66
– Secondary	79	79	79	79
Choke system	Manual	Manual	Manual	Manual
Pump cam position	No 2	No 2	No 2	No 2
Pump override clearance	0.015	0.015	0.015	0.015
Dashpot adjustment	0.140	0.200	–	–
Idle speed:				
Curb idle rpm	725	675	725/500*	675/500*
Fast idle rpm – highest step of cam	1900	2100	1900	2100

*Higher idle speed with throttle solenoid energized / lower speed with throttle solenoid de-energized

Carburetor No 9510	D1ZF-VA	D1ZF-YA	D1ZF-XA
Transmission	Manual	Manual	Auto
Throttle bore diameter – Primary	1.69	1.69	1.69
– Secondary	1.69	1.69	1.69
Venturi diameter – Primary	1.38	1.38	1.38
– Secondary	1.44	1.44	1.44
Fuel level		Lower edge of sight plug	
Dry float setting		Parallel with float bowl floor (bowl inverted)	
Main jet – Primary	71	71	70
– Secondary	82	83	83

	D1ZF-VA	D1ZF–YA	D1ZF-XA
Choke system	Manual	Auto	Auto
Bi-metal identification	–	GTI	GTA
Cap setting	–	2 – rich	2 – rich
Fast idle cam clearance		$\frac{3}{32}$	$\frac{3}{32}$
Pump cam position	No 2	No 2	No 2
Pump override clearance	0.015	0.015	0.015
Dashpot adjustment	$\frac{1}{8}$	$\frac{7}{64}$	–
Idle speed:			
Curb idle rpm	825	700	650/500*
Fast idle – highest step of cam	2100	2200	2400
Idle CO (%)	0.5	0.3	0.2

Higher idle speed with throttle solenoid energized / lower idle speed with throttle solenoid de-energized

Autolite 4300 carburetors (all dimensions in inches)

Carburetor No 9510	C9ZF-D	C9ZF-F	C9ZF-C	C9ZF-E
Transmission	Auto	Auto	Manual	Manual
Throttle bore diameter – Primary	1.437	1.562	1.437	1.562
– Secondary	1.562	1.687	1.562	1.687
Venturi diameter – Primary	1.00	1.250	1.00	1.250
Float setting ($\pm \frac{1}{32}$)	$\frac{13}{16}$	$\frac{13}{16}$	$\frac{13}{16}$	$\frac{13}{16}$
Supplemental valve setting ($\pm \frac{1}{64}$)	$\frac{1}{16}$	$\frac{1}{16}$	$\frac{1}{16}$	$\frac{1}{16}$
Main jet – Primary	48F	62F	49F	63F
– Secondary	0.120	0.128	0.120	0.128
Pump lever position	No 2	No 3	No 2	No 3
Choke system:				
Bi-metal identification	EX	EY	EY	EOB
Cap setting	1 – lean	1 – lean	2 – lean	Index
Pulldown setting (± 0.010)	0.160	0.250	0.170	0.230
Fast idle cam setting ± 0.010)	0.100	0.230	0.130	0.210
Dashpot adjustment	–	–	$\frac{3}{32}$	$\frac{1}{8}$
Idle speed:				
Curb idle rpm	575	550	675	700
Fast idle rpm	1400	1400	1250	1300

Carburetor No 9510	D00F-Z-AB	D00F-Y-AC	DI0F-EA	DI0F-AAA
Transmission	Manual	Auto	Manual	Auto
Throttle bore diameter – Primary	1.56	1.56	1.56	1.56
Secondary	1.69	1.69	1.69	1.69
Venturi diameter – Primary	1.25	1.25	1.25	1.25
Float setting ($\pm \frac{1}{32}$)	$\frac{13}{16}$	$\frac{13}{16}$	$\frac{13}{16}$	$\frac{13}{16}$
Supplemental valve setting ($\pm \frac{1}{64}$)	$\frac{1}{16}$	$\frac{1}{16}$	$\frac{1}{16}$	$\frac{1}{16}$
Main jet – Primary	61F	62F	61F	62F
– Secondary	0.128	0.128	0.116	0.116
Pump lever position	No 2	No 2	No 2	No 2
Choke system:				
Bi-metal identification	4TY	4TX	4TY	4TX
Cap setting	Index	Index	Index	Index
Pulldown setting	0.180	0.200	0.180	0.200
Fast idle cam setting	0.160	0.180	0.160	0.180
Dashpot adjustment	–	0.080	–	–
Idle speed:				
Curb idle rpm	800/500*	600	825/500*	625/500
Fast idle rpm	1250	1400	1250	1400
Idle CO (%)	–	–	1.1	0.5

Higher idle speed with throttle solenoid energized / lower idle speed with throttle solenoid de-energized

Autolite 4300D carburetors (all dimensions in inches)

Carburetor No 5910	D2ZF-GA	D2ZF-AA	D2ZF-BB	D2ZF-DA
Transmission	Manual	Manual	Auto	Auto
Throttle bore diameter – Primary	1.56	1.56	1.56	1.56
– Secondary	1.96	1.96	1.96	1.96
Venturi diameter	1.25	1.25	1.25	1.25
Float setting ($\pm \frac{1}{32}$)	$\frac{13}{16}$	$\frac{13}{16}$	$\frac{13}{16}$	$\frac{13}{16}$
Supplemental valve setting ($\pm \frac{1}{64}$)	0.030	0.030	0.030	0.030
Main jet – Primary	61F	61F	61F	61F
Secondary metering rod identification	4 ring	3 ring	3 ring	3 ring
Pump lever position	No 1	No 1	No 1	No 1
Choke system:				
Bi-metal identification	4TY	4TY	4TX	4TX
Cap setting	Index	Index	Index	Index
Pulldown setting	0.200	0.200	0.200	0.200
Fast idle cam setting	0.180	0.180	0.200	0.200
Idle speed:				
Curb idle rpm*	1000/500	1000/500	700/500	800/500
Fast idle rpm	1200	1200	1200	1200

	D2ZF-GA	D2ZF-AA	D2ZF-BB	D2ZF-DA
Idle CO (%)	–	0.5	0.5	0.5

Higher idle speed with throttle solenoid energized / lower idle speed with throttle solenoid de-energized

Motorcraft 4300D carburetors (all dimensions in inches)

Carburetor No 9510

	D3ZF-AC	D3ZF-BC	D3ZF-DC	D3ZF-LA	D3ZF-MA
Transmission	Manual	Auto	Manual	Manual	Auto
Throttle bore diameter – Primary	1.56	1.56	1.56	1.56	1.56
– Secondary	1.96	1.96	1.96	1.96	1.96
Venturi diameter	1.25	1.25	1.25	1.25	1.25
Float setting ($\pm \frac{1}{32}$)	$\frac{13}{16}$	$\frac{13}{16}$	$\frac{13}{16}$	$\frac{13}{16}$	$\frac{13}{16}$
Supplemental valve setting ($\pm \frac{1}{64}$)	0.030	0.030	0.030	0.030	0.030
Metering jet – Primary/Secondary	63F	62F	62F	60F	63F
Secondary metering rod identification	1 ring	1 ring	1 ring	3 rings	3 rings
Pump lever position	No 1	No 1	No 1	No 1	No 1
Electric choke system:					
Bi-metal identification	4TOB	4TD	4TH	4AP	4AP
Cap setting	Index	1NR	Index	Index	Index
Pulldown setting	0.180	0.170	0.180	0.170	0.180
Fast idle cam setting	0.180	0.170	0.180	0.170	0.180
Idle speed:					
Curb idle rpm			Refer to engine decal		
Fast idle rpm – kickdown	1750	1750	2000	1300	1300
Idle CO (%) – California	0.2	0.2	0.2	0.2	0.2
– Other	0.5	0.6	0.6	0.6	0.6

Rochester Quadrajet 4MV carburetors (all dimensions in inches)

Carburetor No 9510

	DOOF–A	DOOF-E
Transmission	Manual	Auto
Throttle bore diameter – Primary	$1\frac{3}{8}$	$1\frac{3}{8}$
– Secondary	$2\frac{1}{4}$	$2\frac{1}{4}$
Venturi diameter	$1\frac{3}{32}$	$1\frac{3}{32}$
Adjustments:		
Float level	$\frac{11}{32}$	$\frac{11}{32}$
Pump rod location	Outboard	Outboard
Air valve dashpot	0.030	0.030
Pulldown vacuum break	0.140	0.190
Cam clearance (choke rod)	0.130	0.166
Unloader (dechoke)	0.300	0.300
Air valve lockout	0.015	0.015
Curb idle rpm	700	650/500*
Fast idle rpm (second step of cam)	1800	2000
Idle CO (%)	0.3	0.3

Higher idle speed with throttle solenoid energized / lower idle speed with throttle solenoid de-energized

1 General description

The carburetors fitted to Mustang V8 engines are of the downdraft two- or four-barrel type, which are capable of supplying the correct air-/fuel mixture under all operating conditions. Both the primary and secondary venturis are provided with throttle valves.

The fuel system comprises a fuel tank at the rear of the car, an in-line disposable fuel filter and a mechanically-operated fuel pump mounted on the left side of the cylinder front cover. The pump draws gasoline from the tank and delivers it to the carburetor. The gasoline level in the carburetor is controlled by a float-operated needle valve. Gasoline flows past the needle valve until the float rises to a predetermined level and closes the needle valve. The fuel pump then freewheels under slight back pressure until the gasoline level drops in the carburetor float chamber and the needle valve opens.

Various arrangements of the emission control systems are used to control the amount of air pollution caused by the emission of carbon monoxide, hydro-carbons and oxides of nitrogen produced by the engine. Three types of emission control systems are used (though not on all models); these are crankcase emission control, exhaust emission control and fuel evaporation control. Further information will be found in the relevant Sections of this Chapter. **Note:** *Before starting any work on the fuel system refer to Section 2.*

2 US Federal Regulations – emission control

The fuel system has been modified (according to year and model) so that the car will comply with the US Federal Regulations covering emission of hydrocarbons and carbon monoxide. To achieve this the ignition system must be accurately set using special equipment (see Chapter 4) before any attempt is made to adjust the carburetor or its controls. Thereafter the fuel system may be reset but once again special equipment must be used. The information contained in this Chapter is given to assist the reader to clean and/overhaul the various components but, when completed, the car must be taken to the local Ford dealer for final adjustments to be made. Failure to do this will probably mean that the car does not comply with the regulations.

3 Air cleaner and duct systems – general description

Temperature-operated type

The temperature-operated system has a thermostatically controlled valve plate within the duct. When the engine is cold the thermostat maintains the valve plate in the raised position and air is drawn into the air cleaner via a shroud tube. This ensures more efficient fuel atomisation as the engine warms up. When the engine has reached its normal operating temperature the thermostat closes the plate valve and cool air is drawn into the air cleaner (see Fig 3.1).

Vacuum-operated type

On the vacuum-operated system the plate valve is controlled by the inlet manifold vacuum. When the engine is cold, heated air is ducted by the heat stove tube into the air cleaner, but as the engine warms up cold air is progressively mixed with this warm air to maintain a carburetor air temperature of 105 to 130°F (40.5 to 76.8°C). At high ambient temperatures the hot air intake is closed off completely. The mixing of air is regulated by a vacuum-operated motor on the air cleaner inlet duct, which is controlled by a bi-metal temperature sensor.

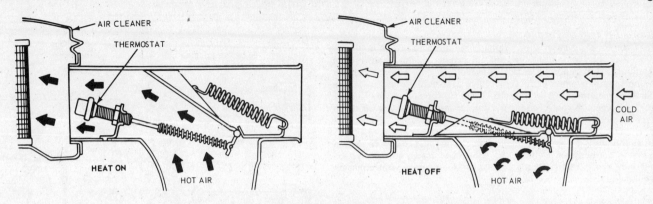

Fig. 3.1 Temperature-operated duct and valve assembly – operation (Sec. 3)

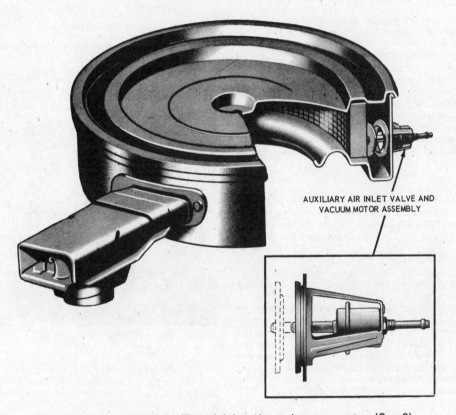

Fig. 3.2 Air cleaner with auxiliary air inlet valve and vacuum motors (Sec. 3)

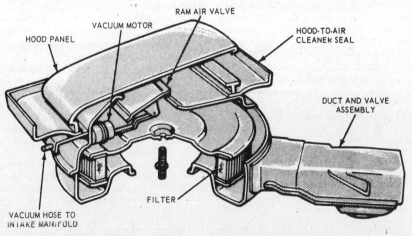

Fig. 3.3 428 Cobra Jet ram air cleaner assembly (Sec. 3)

3

Cobra Jet ram air intake

The ram air system allows outside air to be forced through the functional hood scoop and into the air cleaner during open throttle conditions. During normal engine operation, air enters the air cleaner through the conventional duct and valve assembly. When the intake manifold vacuum drops to 4 in (101 mm) Hg (open throttle or heavy load) the vacuum motor opens the ram air valve, allowing air to be forced directly into the air cleaner from the hood air scoop. (Fig. 3.3)

On all models it is important that the air cleaner duct and valve system operates correctly as it affects the exhaust emission control system and may result in the failure of the car to meet Federal emission regulations.

4   Air cleaner duct and valve assembly – testing

Temperature-operated type

1   With a cold engine and under-hood temperature of less than 100°F (37.8°C), the valve plate should be in the *Heat On* position (see Fig. 3.1).
2   If the plate is not in the *Heat On* position check for sticking or binding of the valve plate, and correct if necessary.
3   To check the thermostat, remove the duct assembly and immerse it in water so that the thermostat capsule is covered with water. Raise the water temperature to 100°F (37.8°C) and check that the valve plate is in the *Heat On* position.
4   Raise the water temperature to 135°F (57.2°C) and check that the valve plate is in the *Heat Off* position.
5   If the valve plate does not operate as specified, the duct and valve assembly must be renewed.

Vacuum-operated type

6   Check that the duct valve is open when the engine is switched off. Start the engine and check that the valve closes when idling (except where the engine is hot). If this fails to happen check for disconnected or leaking vacuum lines and for correct operation of the bi-metal sensor (see Fig. 3.4).
7   Open and close the throttle rapidly. The valve should open during throttle opening. If this does not happen check the valve for binding.
8   The bi-metal switch can be checked by subjecting it to heated air (eg a hair dryer) or removing it and immersing it in water heated to 80°F (26.7°C). Only slight movement of the bi-metal is necessary to unseat the bleed valve.
9   To check the vacuum motor, start the engine and check that the vacuum motor plate is fully closed. Disconnect the vacuum hose and check that the plate is in the fully open position. If this does not happen check for binding of the plate and motor rod, and for vacuum from the motor. If there is no binding and there is no vacuum from the motor the vacuum motor is faulty and must be renewed.

Ram air intake

10   Check that the valve is open with the engine switched off or the vacuum hose disconnected. With the engine idling the ram air valve should be closed. If this does not happen check for valve binding, vacuum leaks or a disconnected vacuum line, and rectify as necessary. If the system still does not function correctly renew the vacuum motor.

5   Air cleaner and filter element – removal and installation

1   Disconnect the vacuum hose from the vacuum motor (where applicable), and the crankcase ventilation hose from the air cleaner.
2   Remove the wingnut attaching the air cleaner to the carburetor and lift off the air cleaner and duct assembly.
3   Remove the air cleaner top cover and take out the filter element (photo).
4   Installation is the reverse of the removal procedure, using new gaskets as necessary. On ram air systems check the hood-to-air cleaner seal for all-round contact.

6   Fuel pump – description

1   The fuel pump is located on the left side of the front cover of the

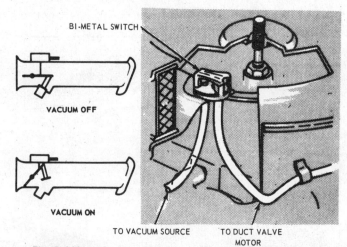

BI-METAL SWITCH

VACUUM OFF

VACUUM ON

TO VACUUM SOURCE   TO DUCT VALVE
                                                MOTOR

Fig. 3.4 Vacuum-operated duct and valve assembly (Sec. 4)

5.3 Air cleaner with top cover removed

engine, and is operated by an eccentric on the front of the camshaft.
2   The pump is a sealed unit and cannot be repaired. If it develops a fault it must be discarded and a new pump installed.

7   Fuel pump – removal and installation

1   Remove the inlet and outlet pipes at the pump and plug the ends to stop fuel loss, or dirt finding its way into the system (photo).
2   Undo and remove the two bolts and spring washers that secure the pump to the front cover.
3   Lift away the fuel pump and gasket.
4   Installation of the fuel pump is the reverse sequence to removal but there are several additional points that should be noted:
   (a)   Tighten the pump securing bolts to the specified torque.
   (b)   Before reconnecting the pipe from the fuel tank to the pump inlet, move the end to a position lower than the fuel tank so that fuel can syphon out. Quickly connect the pipe to the pump inlet.
   (c)   Disconnect the pipe at the carburetor and turn the engine over until gasoline issues from the open end. Quickly connect the pipe to the carburetor union. This last operation will help to prime the pump.

8   Fuel pump – testing

Assuming that the fuel lines and unions are in good condition and

7.1 Disconnecting the fuel lines at the fuel pump

that there are no leaks anywhere, check the performance of the fuel pump in the following manner. Disconnect the fuel pipe at the carburetor inlet union, and the high tension lead to the coil and, with a suitable container or large rag in position to catch the ejected fuel, turn the engine over. A good spurt of gasoline should emerge from the end of the pipe every second revolution. **CAUTION:** *Do not carry out this test when the engine is hot.*

9 Fuel filter – renewal

1   Initially remove the carburetor air cleaner.
2   Loosen the fuel line clips at the filter, pull off the fuel lines and discard the clips. On later models, unscrew the filter from the carburetor.
3   Install the new filter using new clips, start the engine and check for fuel leaks **Note**: *If the new filter shows the direction of fuel flow, take care that it is installed the correct way round.*
4   Install the air cleaner.

10 Carburetion – warning

1   Before making any adjustment or alteration to the carburetor or emission control systems the owner is advised to make himself aware of any Federal, State or Provincial laws which may be contravened by making any such adjustment or alteration.
2   Setting dimensions and specifications are given in this Chapter where relevant to adjustment procedures. Where these differ from those given on the engine tune-up decal (if so equipped) the decal information should be assumed to be correct.
3   Where the use of special test equipment is called up (eg, exhaust gas CO analyzer, etc), and this equipment is not available, any setting or calibration should be regarded as a temporary measure only and should be rechecked by a suitably equipped Ford dealer or carburetion/emission control specialist at the earliest opportunity.
4   Before attempting any carburetor adjustments, first ascertain that the following items are serviceable or correctly set:

    (a)   All vacuum hoses and connections
    (b)   Ignition system
    (c)   Spark plugs
    (d)   Ignition initial advance

5   If satisfactory adjustment cannot be obtained check the following points:

    (a)   Carburetor fuel level
    (b)   Crankcase ventilation system
    (c)   Valve clearances
    (d)   Engine compression
    (e)   Idle mixture.

11 Carburetor – general description

The following two- and four-barrel carburetors are used on Mustangs with V8 engines. Both types are of downdraft design with automatic choke:

Two-barrel type
    Autolite 2100 2-V
    Autolite 2100D 2-V
    Motorcraft 2100D 2-V

Four-barrel type
    Autolite 4300 4-V
    Autolite 4300D 4-V
    Motorcraft 4300D 4-V
    Holley 4150C 4-V
    Rochester Quadrajet 4MV

Type 2100 carburetor (Autolite and Motorcraft)
The carburetor has two main assemblies; these are the air horn and the main body. The air horn assembly contains the choke plate and the internal vents for the fuel bowl.
The throttle plate, the accelerating pump assembly, the power valve assembly and the fuel bowl are in the main body; the automatic choke housing is attached to the main body. Each bore contains a main and a booster venturi, main fuel discharge, accelerating pump discharge, idle fuel discharge and a throttle plate.
The Autolite 2100D 2-V has a two-piece fast idle lever and the crankcase emission hose connection is incorporated in the main body.
The Motorcraft 2100D has an electric choke system consisting of a choke cap, thermostatic spring, a bi-metal temperature sensing switch and a ceramic heater. The choke is powered from the center tap of the alternator (see Fig. 3.10). At temperatures below 60°F (15.6°C) the switch is open; at above 60°F the switch closes and current is supplied to the ceramic heater. As the heater warms, it causes the thermostat spring to pull the choke plates open within $1\frac{1}{2}$ minutes.

Type 4300 (Autolite and Motorcraft)
The carburetor has three main assemblies; these are the air horn, main body and throttle body.
The main (primary) fuel system has booster-type venturis cast integral with the air horn and the main venturis are cast integral with the main body. The secondary throttle plates are mechanically operated from the primary linkage.
The secondary air valve plates are located above the secondary bore. Secondary fuel supply is controlled by metering rods which are attached to the air valve plates. A single fuel bowl supplies both the primary and secondary systems. The accelerating pump is located in the fuel bowl.
The automatic choke system is a bi-metal thermostatic type which operates when the under-hood temperature is below 60°F (15.6°C).
The Motorcraft 4300D carburetor has an electric choke system which is the same as that on the Motorcraft 2300D carburetor described previously.

Type 4150C (Holley)
The fuel inlet system contains an external fuel distribution tube which passes fuel from the primary fuel inlet to the secondary fuel inlet. The primary fuel bowl is vented during curb and off-idle engine operation through a vent valve, actuated by a lever on the throttle shaft.
The primary stage of the carburetor contains a fuel bowl, fuel bowl vent, metering block and an accelerating pump. The primary power valve is located in the primary metering block. The primary bores each contain a primary and booster venturi, main fuel discharge nozzle, throttle plate and an idle fuel passage. The choke plate, mounted on the air horn, is controlled by an automatic choke mechanism.
The secondary stage contains the secondary fuel bowl, metering block and throttle operating diaphragm assemblies. The secondary bores each contain a primary and booster venturi, a transfer system, a main secondary fuel discharge nozzle and a throttle plate.

Rochester Quadrajet 4MV
The Quadrajet carburetor has two stages of operation. The primary side has a triple venturi set-up equipped with plain tube nozzles.

3

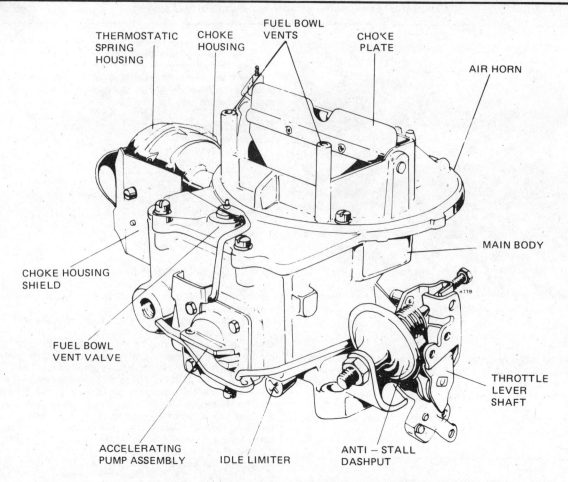

THERMOSTATIC SPRING HOUSING

CHOKE HOUSING

FUEL BOWL VENTS

CHOKE PLATE

AIR HORN

MAIN BODY

CHOKE HOUSING SHIELD

FUEL BOWL VENT VALVE

THROTTLE LEVER SHAFT

ACCELERATING PUMP ASSEMBLY

IDLE LIMITER

ANTI — STALL DASHPUT

Fig. 3.5 Autolite 2100 carburetor – left front ¾ view (Sec. 10)

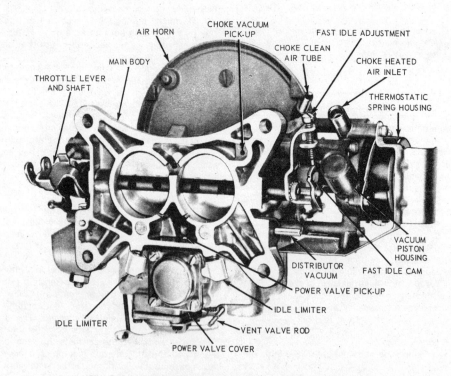

AIR HORN

CHOKE VACUUM PICK-UP

FAST IDLE ADJUSTMENT

CHOKE CLEAN AIR TUBE

CHOKE HEATED AIR INLET

MAIN BODY

THERMOSTATIC SPRING HOUSING

THROTTLE LEVER AND SHAFT

VACUUM PISTON HOUSING

DISTRIBUTOR VACUUM

FAST IDLE CAM

POWER VALVE PICK-UP

IDLE LIMITER

IDLE LIMITER

VENT VALVE ROD

POWER VALVE COVER

Fig. 3.6 Autolite 2100 carburetor – bottom view (Sec. 10)

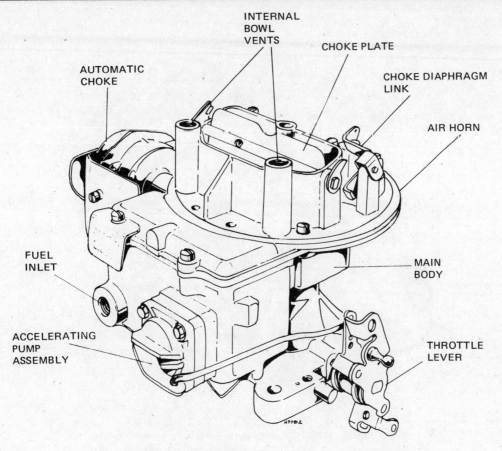

INTERNAL BOWL VENTS

CHOKE PLATE

AUTOMATIC CHOKE

CHOKE DIAPHRAGM LINK

AIR HORN

FUEL INLET

MAIN BODY

ACCELERATING PUMP ASSEMBLY

THROTTLE LEVER

Fig. 3.7 Autolite 2100D carburetor – left front ¾ view (Sec. 10)

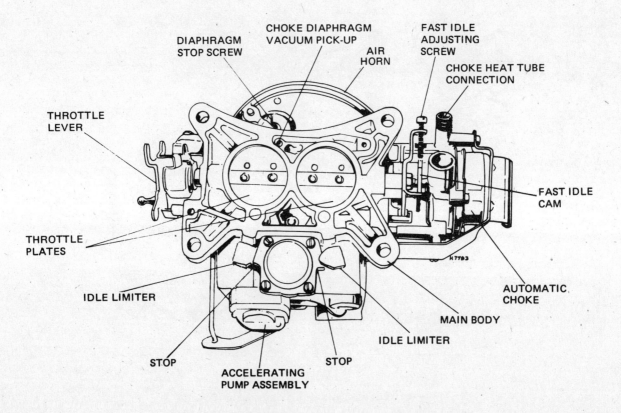

DIAPHRAGM STOP SCREW

CHOKE DIAPHRAGM VACUUM PICK-UP

AIR HORN

FAST IDLE ADJUSTING SCREW

CHOKE HEAT TUBE CONNECTION

THROTTLE LEVER

FAST IDLE CAM

THROTTLE PLATES

IDLE LIMITER

AUTOMATIC CHOKE

MAIN BODY

IDLE LIMITER

STOP

STOP

ACCELERATING PUMP ASSEMBLY

Fig. 3.8 Autolite 2100D carburetor – bottom view (Sec. 10)

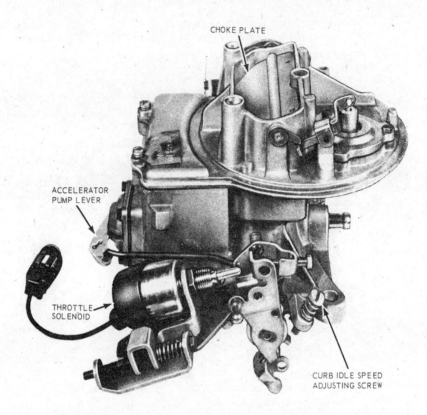

CHOKE PLATE

ACCELERATOR
PUMP LEVER

THROTTLE
SOLENOID

CURB IDLE SPEED
ADJUSTING SCREW

Fig. 3.9 Motorcraft 2100D carburetor – left front ¾ view (Sec. 10)

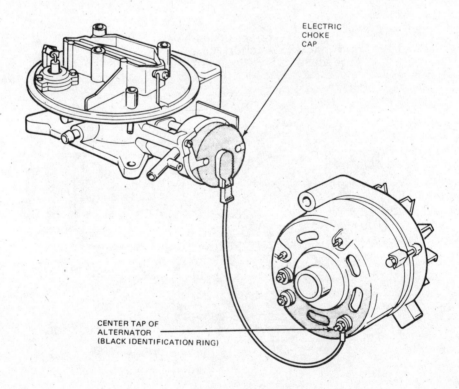

ELECTRIC
CHOKE
CAP

CENTER TAP OF
ALTERNATOR
(BLACK IDENTIFICATION RING)

Fig. 3.10 Electric choke wiring connections (Sec. 10)

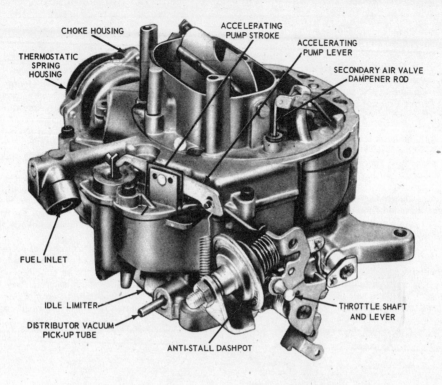

CHOKE HOUSING

THERMOSTATIC SPRING HOUSING

ACCELERATING PUMP STROKE

ACCELERATING PUMP LEVER

SECONDARY AIR VALVE DAMPENER ROD

FUEL INLET

IDLE LIMITER

DISTRIBUTOR VACUUM PICK-UP TUBE

THROTTLE SHAFT AND LEVER

ANTI-STALL DASHPOT

Fig. 3.11 Autolite 4300 carburetor – left front ¾ view (Sec. 10)

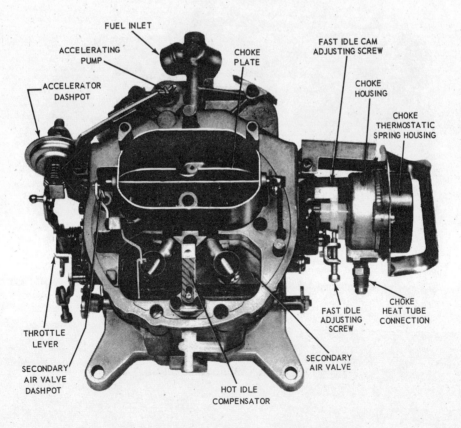

FUEL INLET

ACCELERATING PUMP

ACCELERATOR DASHPOT

CHOKE PLATE

FAST IDLE CAM ADJUSTING SCREW

CHOKE HOUSING

CHOKE THERMOSTATIC SPRING HOUSING

THROTTLE LEVER

SECONDARY AIR VALVE DASHPOT

HOT IDLE COMPENSATOR

FAST IDLE ADJUSTING SCREW

SECONDARY AIR VALVE

CHOKE HEAT TUBE CONNECTION

Fig. 3.12 Autolite 4300 carburetor – top view (Sec. 10)

3

Operation is similar to most carburetors using the venturi principle. The triple venturi stack-up, plus the small primary bores, result in more stable and finer fuel control during idle and part-throttle operation. During off-idle and part-throttle, fuel metering is achieved with tapered metering rods operating in specially designed jets, positioned by a manifold-vacuum-responsive piston.

The secondary side has two bores. These, added to the primary, supply enough air to meet engine requirements. The air valve is used in the secondary side for metering control and supplements the primary bores to meet air and fuel requirements of the engine.

The secondary air valve mechanically operates tapered metering rods, which move in orifice plates, so that fuel flow from the secondary nozzles is controlled in direct proportion to air flowing through the secondary bores.

The primary side of the carburetor has six operating systems; these are float, idle, main metering, power, pump and choke. The secondary side has one main metering system. All metering systems receive fuel from the one float bowl.

Solenoid throttle positioner

A solenoid throttle positioner assembly is incorporated on certain versions of the different types of carburetor to prevent dieseling (running-on) after the ignition has been switched off, by allowing the throttle plates to close beyond the point required for idling.

12 Carburetor adjustments – general

The method of adjusting the two- and four-barrel carburetors is basically the same for both types. To identify the location of the adjusting screws and components for each type of carburetor reference should be made to the appropriate illustrations which accompanies the text.

After adjustments have been carried out, the car must be taken to a Ford service station for final checking to ensure that the exhaust emission is within the limits specified by Federal Regulations.

13 Curb idle speed and fuel mixture – adjustment

1   Apply the parking brake and chock the road wheels.
2   Check the choke and throttle linkage for freedom of movement and adjust if necessary.
3   To enable the carburetor to be set correctly it will be necessary to attach a tachometer unless the car is already so equipped.
4   Where applicable set the air conditioning to *Off*.
5   Set the automatic transmission to *Park*, or manual transmission in *Neutral*, then run the engine at normal operating temperature. Check that the choke plates are in the fully open position.

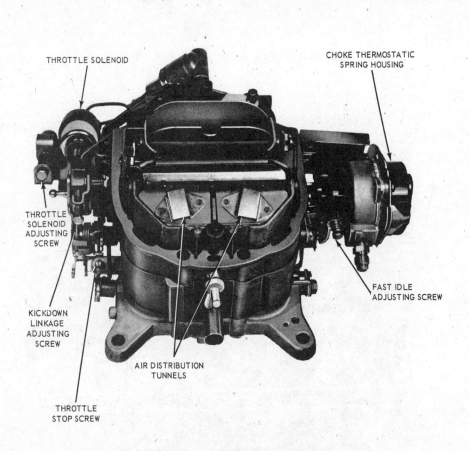

Fig. 3.13 Motorcraft 4300D carburetor (Sec. 10)

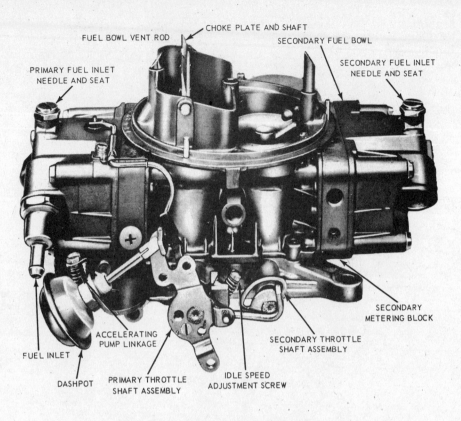

FUEL BOWL VENT ROD
CHOKE PLATE AND SHAFT
SECONDARY FUEL BOWL
SECONDARY FUEL INLET NEEDLE AND SEAT
PRIMARY FUEL INLET NEEDLE AND SEAT
ACCELERATING PUMP LINKAGE
FUEL INLET
DASHPOT
PRIMARY THROTTLE SHAFT ASSEMBLY
IDLE SPEED ADJUSTMENT SCREW
SECONDARY THROTTLE SHAFT ASSEMBLY
SECONDARY METERING BLOCK

Fig. 3.14 Holley 4150C carburetor – left side view (Sec. 10)

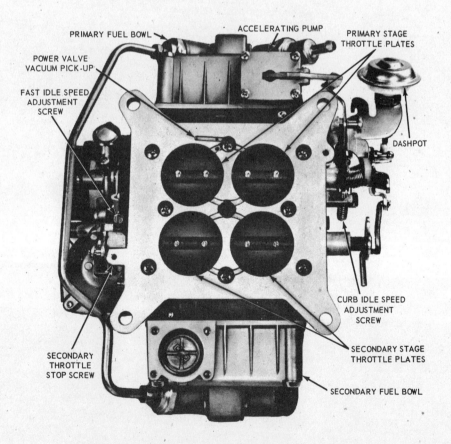

PRIMARY FUEL BOWL
ACCELERATING PUMP
PRIMARY STAGE THROTTLE PLATES
POWER VALVE VACUUM PICK-UP
FAST IDLE SPEED ADJUSTMENT SCREW
DASHPOT
SECONDARY THROTTLE STOP SCREW
CURB IDLE SPEED ADJUSTMENT SCREW
SECONDARY STAGE THROTTLE PLATES
SECONDARY FUEL BOWL

3

Fig. 3.15 Holley 4150C carburetor – bottom view (Sec. 10)

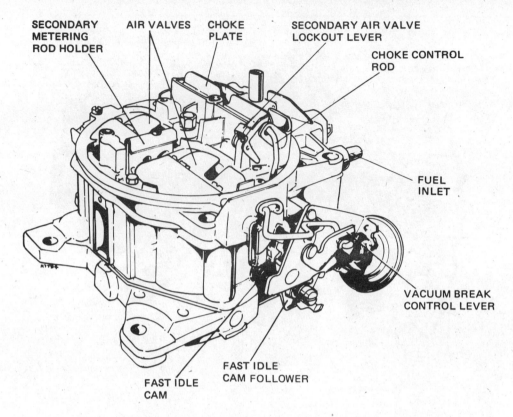

SECONDARY METERING ROD HOLDER

AIR VALVES

CHOKE PLATE

SECONDARY AIR VALVE LOCKOUT LEVER

CHOKE CONTROL ROD

FUEL INLET

VACUUM BREAK CONTROL LEVER

FAST IDLE CAM FOLLOWER

FAST IDLE CAM

Fig. 3.16 Rochester Quadrajet 4MV carburetor – right rear view (Sec. 10)

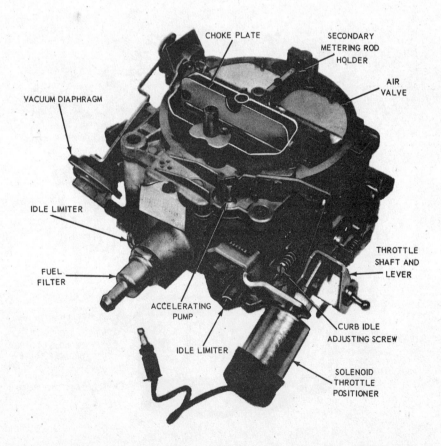

CHOKE PLATE

SECONDARY METERING ROD HOLDER

AIR VALVE

VACUUM DIAPHRAGM

IDLE LIMITER

FUEL FILTER

THROTTLE SHAFT AND LEVER

ACCELERATING PUMP

CURB IDLE ADJUSTING SCREW

IDLE LIMITER

SOLENOID THROTTLE POSITIONER

Fig. 3.17 Rochester Quadrajet 4MV carburetor – left front view (Sec. 10)

6 On cars with automatic transmission place the selector lever in *Drive* position.

7 Adjust the curb idle screw in or out to obtain the specified curb idle speed. If it is not possible to adjust the idle speed with the air cleaner in position, remove it, make the adjustment, then install the air cleaner again and recheck the idle speed.

8 Where a throttle solenoid is fitted, turn the solenoid adjusting screw, located in the solenoid mounting bracket, to obtain the specified curb idle speed. Disconnect the solenoid wire at the connector near the wiring harness then adjust the curb idle screw to obtain the specified idle speed. Connect the solenoid wire and open the throttle slightly by hand. The solenoid plunger will remain in the extended position as long as the ignition is *On* and the solenoid is energized.

9 Turn the idle mixture screws within the range of the limiting caps to obtain the smoothest idle possible. Where the idle mixture is too rich, indicated by a sooty exhaust smoke and the engine hunting,

rotate the screws clockwise. Where the mixture is too lean, indicated by the engine speed tending to increase then decrease, and possibly a 'hollow' exhaust note, rotate the screws counterclockwise.

10 Reset the idle speed after the mixture is satisfactorily adjusted.

11 If the idle mixture cannot be set satisfactorily within the range of the limiting caps, pull off the caps and adjust the mixture screws but re-install the caps afterwards. In case it is not possible to obtain a satisfactory setting, rotate each screw in turn, counting the exact number of turns to just seal it, then back off the same number of turns. This will give a datum point from which adjustment can commence. Both screws can be expected to be the same number of turns from the seat when correctly set, after which the limiting cap must be re-installed.

12 On completion of *any* idle mixture adjustment, ensure that the setting is checked by a Ford dealer or carburetor/emission control specialist at the earliest opportunity.

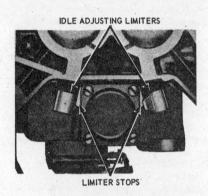

Fig. 3.18 Idle fuel mixture adjusting limiters – 2100D carburetor (Sec. 13)

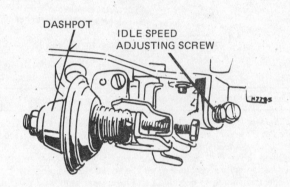

Fig. 3.19 Curb idle speed adjusting screw – 2100D carburetor (Sec. 13)

Fig. 3.20 Idle fuel mixture adjusting limiters – 4300D carburetor (Sec. 13)

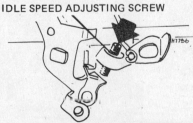

Fig. 3.21 Curb idle speed adjusting screw – 4300D carburetor (Sec. 13)

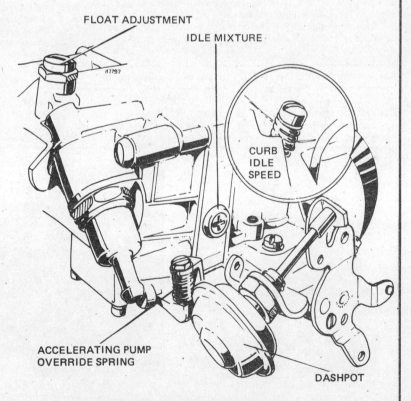

Fig. 3.22 Holley 4150C carburetor adjustments (Sec. 13)

3

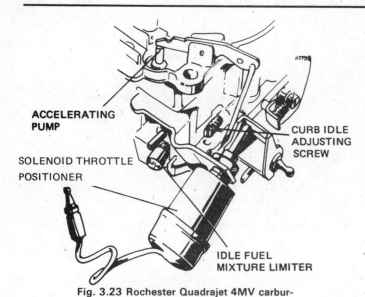

ACCELERATING
PUMP

CURB IDLE
ADJUSTING
SCREW

SOLENOID THROTTLE
POSITIONER

IDLE FUEL
MIXTURE LIMITER

Fig. 3.23 Rochester Quadrajet 4MV carburetor (Sec. 13)

14 Fast idle speed – adjustment

The fast idle speed adjusting screw contacts one edge of the fast idle cam. The cam permits a faster engine idle speed for smoother running when the engine is cold during choke operation.

1   Check that the curb idle speed and mixture are adjusted to specification before setting the fast idle speed (see Section 13).
2   Run the engine to normal operating temperature and remove the air cleaner.
3   Connect a tachometer, if necessary.
4   Manually rotate the fast idle cam until the fast idle adjusting screw rests on the specified step of the cam.
5   Turn the fast idle adjusting screw inward or outward, as required, to obtain the specified fast idle speed.
6   Switch off the engine, disconnect the tachometer (where applicable) and re-install the air cleaner.

15 Autolite and Motorcraft 2100 carburetors – adjustments

Automatic choke thermostatic spring housing

1   Remove the air cleaner assembly, and the heater hose and mounting bracket (where applicable) from the carburetor.

2   Loosen the thermostatic spring housing clamp securing screws.
3   Set the spring housing to the specified index mark, (see Specifications at the beginning of this Chapter). Turning the housing clockwise will give a leaner mixture (Fig. 3.26).
4   Install the heater hose and mounting bracket, and the air cleaner assembly.

Anti-stall dashpot (if installed)

5   With the engine at normal operating temperature, and the idle speed and mixture properly adjusted, loosen the dashpot locknut.
6   Hold the throttle in the closed position and depress the plunger with a screwdriver, then measure the clearance between the throttle lever and the plunger (Fig. 3.27).
7   Turn the dashpot in the direction required to obtain the specified clearance between the tip of the plunger and the throttle lever.
8   Tighten the locknut and then recheck the adjustment.

Accelerating pump stroke setting

9   The accelerating pump stroke should not be altered from the specified setting. If it has been altered, or after repair, set the stroke as follows.
10   The primary throttle shaft lever (overtravel lever) has 4 holes and the accelerating pump link has 2 holes (see Fig. 3.28) to control the pump stroke.
11   Release the operating rod from the retaining clip by pressing the tab end of the clip toward the rod, and at the same time press the rod away from the clip.
12   Position the clip over the specified hole in the overtravel lever. Press the ends of the clip together and insert the operating rod through the clip and the overtravel lever. Release the clip to engage the rod.

Choke plate pulldown – Autolite carburetor

13   Remove the air cleaner.
14   With the engine at normal operating temperature, loosen the choke thermostatic spring housing securing screw and set the housing 90° in the rich direction (counterclockwise).
15   Disconnect the heater hose from the choke housing.
16   Turn the fast idle adjusting screw outward one full turn.
17   Start the engine, then check for the specified clearance by inserting a drill, of the appropriate diameter, between the lower edge of the choke plate and the air horn wall, (see Fig. 3.29).
18   Adjust the clearance, if necessary, by turning the diaphragm stop-screw, clockwise to decrease or counterclockwise to increase the clearance.
19   Reconnect the heater hose and set the choke thermostatic spring housing to specification. Adjust the fast idle speed (see Section 14).

Choke plate pulldown – Motorcraft carburetor

20   Carry out the procedure described in paragraphs 13 through 17 for Autolite carburetors.
21   Because the choke plate pulldown is set in production by means of

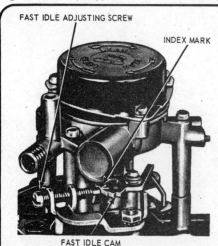

FAST IDLE ADJUSTING SCREW

INDEX MARK

FAST IDLE CAM

Fig. 3.24 Fast idle speed adjustment –
2100D carburetor (Sec. 14)

FAST IDLE CAM
ADJUSTING SCREW

FAST IDLE
CAM

FAST IDLE SPEED
ADJUSTING SCREW

Fig. 3.25 Fast idle speed adjustment –
4300D carburetor (Sec. 14)

THERMOSTATIC SPRING HOUSING INDEX MARK

CHOKE
HOUSING
INDEX MARK

Fig. 3.26 Automatic choke thermostatic
spring housing adjustment (2100 carburetor) (Sec. 15)

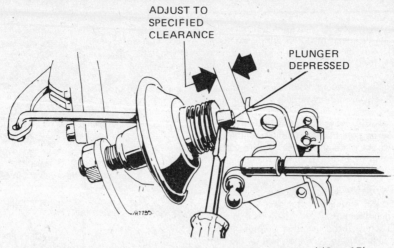

Fig. 3.27 Anti-stall dashpot adjustment (2100 carburetor) (Sec. 15)

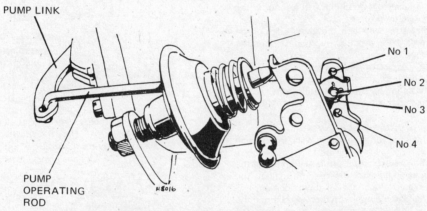

Fig. 3.28 Accelerator pump stroke adjustment (2100 carburetor) (Sec. 15)

3

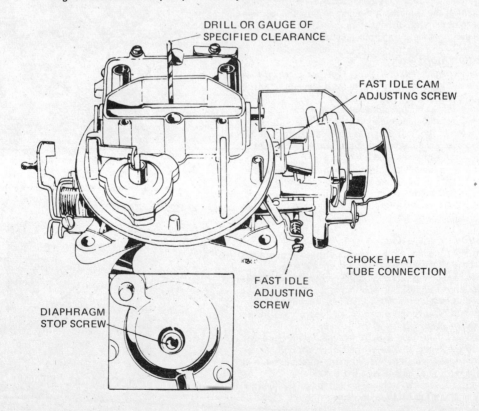

Fig. 3.29 Checking the choke plate pulldown clearance (2100 carburetor) (Sec. 15)

an air/fuel meter, no specific clearance is indicated for pulldown adjustment. If there is an indication of lean mixture during cold starting, decrease the clearance between the choke plate and the air horn wall by 0.02 in (0.5 mm) by turning the diaphragm stop screw clockwise.

22 If an overrich condition is indicated during cold starting, increase the pulldown clearance by 0.02 in (0.5 mm) by turning the diaphragm stop screw counterclockwise.

23 If further adjustment is necessary always make the adjustments in steps of 0.02 in (0.5 mm). If the original pulldown adjustment is lost, set the clearance between the choke plate and the air horn to 0.16 in (4.0 mm); then adjust as required in steps of 0.02 in (0.5 mm).

24 Carry out the procedures described in paragraph 19.

Fast idle cam clearance – Autolite carburetors

25 Loosen the choke thermostatic spring housing securing screws and set the housing 90° in the rich direction.

26 Position the fast idle speed screw at the kickdown step of the fast idle cam. The kickdown step is identified by a 'V' stamped on the cam (see Fig. 3.30).

27 On 351-C and 400 engines, a two-piece fast idle is used to provide clearance between the lever and manifold, and a tang on the top lever will align with the V-mark on the cam.

28 Check for the specified clearance between the lower edge of the choke plate and the air horn wall, using a drill of appropriate diameter to determine the clearance.

29 To adjust, turn the fast idle cam clearance adjusting screw clockwise to increase and counterclockwise to decrease the clearance.

30 Set the choke thermostatic spring housing to specifications, adjust the dashpot (where applicable), and the idle speed and fuel mixture.

Fast idle cam clearance – Motorcraft carburetor

31 Rotate the choke thermostatic spring housing 90° in the rich direction.

32 Position the fast idle speed screw or lever on the high step of the cam, then depress the choke pulldown diaphragm against the diaphragm stop screw to place the choke in the pulldown position.

33 While holding the choke pulldown diaphragm depressed, open the throttle slightly and allow the fast idle cam to fall, then close the throttle and check the position of the fast idle cam or lever. The screw should contact the cam at the V-mark on the cam. Adjust the fast idle cam adjusting screw to obtain the correct setting.

34 Reset the choke thermostatic spring housing to specifications.

Fuel level float adjustment – dry

This is a preliminary adjustment made after repair or overhaul with the carburetor off the engine. Final adjustment (set) is made after the carburetor is installed on the engine.

35 With the air horn removed, the float raised and the fuel inlet needle seated, check the distance between the top surface of the main body casting and the top of the float. Depress the float tab to seat the fuel inlet needle. Take the measurement near the center of the float at the point $\frac{1}{8}$ in from the free end of the float.

36 If a float level gauge is used, place the gauge in the corner of the enlarged end section of the fuel bowl (see Fig. 3.31). The gauge should touch the float near the end, but not on the end radius.

37 Adjust, if necessary, by bending the tab on the float to obtain the specified setting.

Fuel level float adjustment – wet

38 With the car on level ground and the engine at normal operating temperature, remove the air cleaner assembly and anchor screw.

39 Remove the air horn securing screws and the carburetor identification tag. Leave the air horn and gasket in position.

40 Start the engine and let it idle for a few minutes, then rotate the air horn out of the way and remove the gasket to provide access to the float assembly.

41 While the engine is idling, use a depth gauge to measure the distance from the top machined surface of the carburetor body to the level of the fuel in the fuel bowl. The measurement must be made at least $\frac{1}{4}$ in away from any vertical surface (see Fig. 3.32).

42 Before making any adjustment, stop the engine for safety reasons. To adjust the fuel level, bend the float tab upwards to raise the level or downwards to lower it.

43 When checking the level after each adjustment, allow the engine to idle for a few minutes to stabilize the fuel level. Check the fuel level

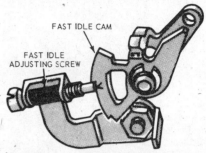

CONVENTIONAL ONE - PIECE FAST IDLE LEVER

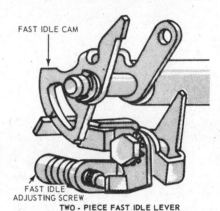

TWO - PIECE FAST IDLE LEVER FOR 351-C ENGINE

Fig. 3.30 Fast idle levers – Autolite 2100D carburetor (Sec. 15)

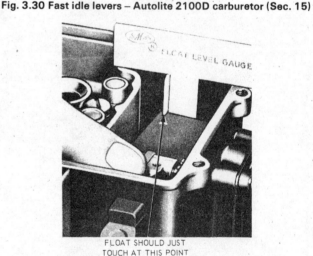

FLOAT SHOULD JUST TOUCH AT THIS POINT

Fig. 3.31 Fuel level float adjustment (dry) (Sec. 15)

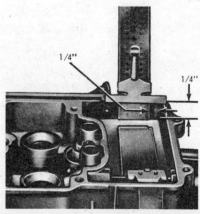

Fig. 3.32 Fuel level float adjustment (wet) (Sec. 15)

after each adjustment until the specified level is obtained.

44 Install the air horn and identification tag using a new gasket. Install the air cleaner anchor screw.

45 Check the idle speed and fuel mixture adjustment, and also the dashpot setting (where applicable).

46 Install the air cleaner assembly.

16 Autolite and Motorcraft 4300 carburetors – adjustments

Automatic choke thermostatic spring housing

1 The procedure is the same as described for 2100-type carburetors (see Section 15).

Anti-stall dashpot (if installed)

2 The procedure is the same as described for 2100-type carburetors (see Section 15).

Accelerating pump stroke setting

3 The procedure is the same as described for 2100-type carburetors (see Section 15).

Choke plate pulldown

4 Remove the air cleaner and the choke thermostatic spring housing.

5 Bend a wire gauge of 0.036 in diameter at a 90° angle approximately $\frac{1}{8}$ in from one end. Block the throttle about half open so that the fast idle cam does not contact the fast idle adjustment screw, then insert the bent end of the wire gauge between the lower edge of the piston slot and the upper edge of the right-hand slot in the choke housing (see Fig. 3.33).

6 Pull the choke piston lever counterclockwise until the gauge is snug in the piston slot. Check the choke plate clearance (pulldown) between the lower edge of the choke plate and the wall of the air horn.

7 To adjust, if necessary, loosen the hexagon-head screw (left-hand thread) on the choke plate shaft and pry the link away from the tapered shaft.

8 Insert a drill, 0.010 in less than the specified clearance, between the lower edge of the choke plate and the wall of the air horn. Hold the plate against the drill and with the choke piston snug against the 0.036 in wire gauge tighten the hexagon-head screw in the choke plate shaft. The 0.010 in drill is used to allow for tolerances in the linkage. Use a drill of diameter equal to the specified clearance for final checking.

9 Install the choke thermostatic spring housing and the air cleaner.

Fast idle cam clearance adjustment

10 Rotate the spring housing counterclockwise 90° past the index mark alignment point.

11 Position the fast idle speed adjusting screw on the kickdown (center) step of the fast idle cam and check the clearance between the lower edge of the choke plate and the air horn wall. Turn the fast idle cam adjusting screw inward to increase, or outward to decrease, the clearance (see Fig. 3.33).

12 Set the thermostatic choke housing to the specified index mark and tighten the securing screws.

13 Check the idle speed, fuel mixture and dashpot (where applicable) adjustments.

Fuel level float and auxiliary (supplemental) valve setting

14 Fabricate a float gauge and bending tool, to the dimensions as shown in Fig. 3.34, for checking the parallel setting of the dual pontoons.

15 Adjust the gauge to the specified height and fit it on the air horn as shown in Fig. 3.35.

16 Check the alignment and clearance of the pontoons to the gauge. Both pontoons should just touch the gauge. Align the pontoons, if necessary by slightly twisting them.

17 Float clearance is adjusted by bending the primary needle tab, downward to raise the float and upward to lower it, using the bending tool.

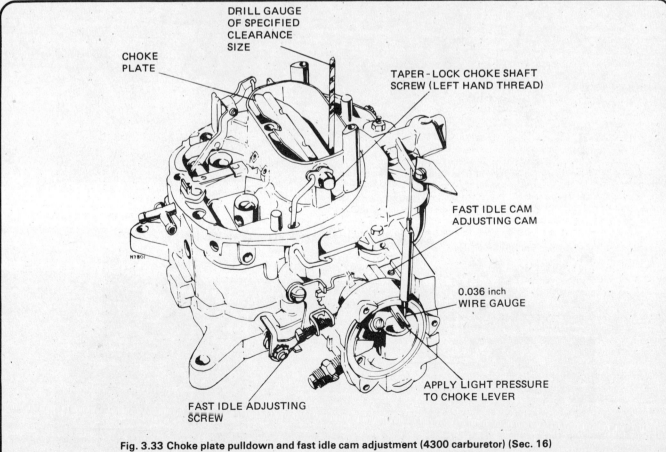

Fig. 3.33 Choke plate pulldown and fast idle cam adjustment (4300 carburetor) (Sec. 16)

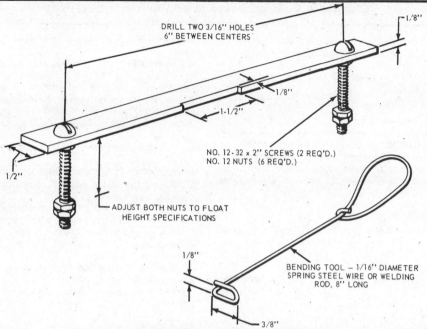

DRILL TWO 3/16" HOLES
6" BETWEEN CENTERS

1/8"

1/8"

1-1/2"

NO. 12-32 x 2" SCREWS (2 REQ'D.)
NO. 12 NUTS (6 REQ'D.)

1/2"

ADJUST BOTH NUTS TO FLOAT
HEIGHT SPECIFICATIONS

1/8"

BENDING TOOL — 1/16" DIAMETER
SPRING STEEL WIRE OR WELDING
ROD, 8" LONG

3/8"

Fig. 3.34 Float gauge and bending tool (Sec. 16)

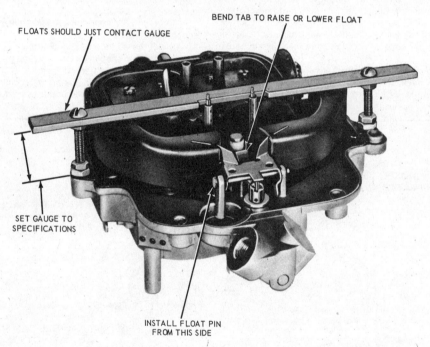

BEND TAB TO RAISE OR LOWER FLOAT

FLOATS SHOULD JUST CONTACT GAUGE

SET GAUGE TO
SPECIFICATIONS

INSTALL FLOAT PIN
FROM THIS SIDE

Fig. 3.35 Float setting (4300 carburetor) (Sec. 16)

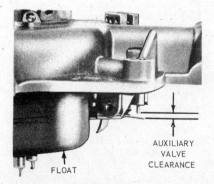

AUXILIARY
VALVE
CLEARANCE

FLOAT

**Fig. 3.36 Checking the auxiliary valve clearance (4300 carbur-
etor) (Sec. 16)**

0.015"

**Fig. 3.37 Adjusting the accelerating pump override clearance
(Holley 4150C carburetor) (Sec. 17)**

18 Check the auxiliary valve clearance (see Fig. 3.36). If necessary, adjust by bending the auxiliary valve and float tab, as required, with the bending tool (Fig. 3.34).

17 Holley 4150C carburetor – adjustments

Automatic choke thermostatic spring housing
1   The procedure is the same as described for the Autolite 2100 carburetor (see Section 15).

Anti-stall dashpot
2   The procedure is the same as described for the Autolite 2100 carburetor (see Section 15).

Accelerating pump override clearance
3   With the primary throttle plates in the wide open position, use a feeler gauge to check that the clearance between the pump operating lever adjusting screw head and the pump arm, when the pump arm is fully depressed manually, is to specification (see Fig. 3.37).
4   Adjust, if necessary, by turning the adjusting screw in to increase, or out to decrease, the clearance. One half turn of the adjusting screw is equal to 0.015 in.

Choke plate clearance and fast idle cam adjustment
5   Remove the choke thermostatic housing cap.
6   Hold the choke plate fully closed and measure the distance between the flat of the fast idle cam and the choke housing mounting post (see Fig. 3.38). If necessary straighten or bend the choke rod to obtain the specified clearance.
7   Bend a 0.036 in wire at a 90° angle approximately $\frac{3}{32}$ in from one end. Insert the bent end between the lower edge of the piston slot and the upper edge of the slot in the choke housing (Fig. 3.39). Open the throttle lever to about $\frac{1}{3}$ throttle and rotate the choke lever counterclockwise so that the bent end of the wire is held in the housing slot by the piston slot with light pressure applied to the choke lever. Measure the clearance between the air horn and the lower edge of the choke plate. Adjust, if necessary, by bending the adjusting tab on the choke lever to obtain the specified clearance.
8   Install the choke thermostatic housing cap and set the cap notch to specification.
9   Connect a tachometer to the engine and, with the engine at normal operating temperature, set the fast idle screw on the kickdown or second high step of the fast idle cam.
10 Install the choke thermostatic housing cap.

Fuel level float adjustment – dry
11 As a preliminary adjustment, after repair or overhaul, adjust the float so that the center of the float is an equal distance from the top and bottom of the fuel bowl (see Fig. 3.40).

Fuel level float adjustment – wet
12 With the car on a level surface and the engine at normal operating temperature, check the fuel level in each fuel bowl separately. Remove the air cleaner.
13 Place a suitable container below the fuel level sight plug to collect any spillage of fuel. Remove the fuel level sight plug and check that the fuel level is within $\frac{1}{16}$ in of the lower edge of the sight plug opening.
14 If the level is too high it should first be lowered below specification and then raised to the correct level. If the level is too low raise it to the specified level.
15 To lower the fuel level proceed as follows:
   (a) With the engine stopped, loosen the lock screw on top of the fuel bowl just enough to allow turning of the adjusting nut underneath (Fig. 3.41). **CAUTION**: Do not attempt to adjust the fuel level with the sight plug removed and the engine running as the pressure in the line will spray fuel out and present a fire hazard.
   (b) Turn the adjusting nut approximately $\frac{1}{2}$ turn in to lower the fuel level to below specification
   (c) Tighten the lock screw and install the fuel level sight plug. Start the engine. After the fuel level has stabilized stop the engine and check the fuel level at the sight plug opening. If it is above the specified limit repeat the previous steps, turning the adjusting nut sufficient to lower the fuel below the specified level

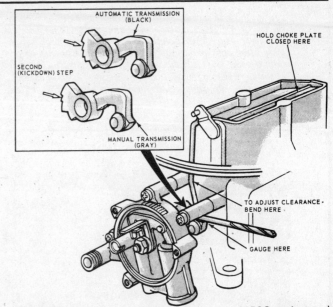

Fig. 3.38 Fast idle cam adjustment (Holley 4150C carburetor) (Sec. 17)

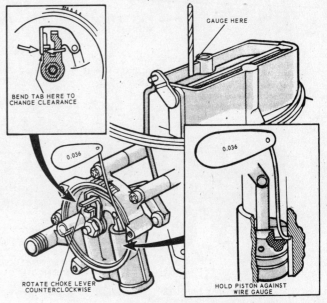

Fig. 3.39 Choke plate pulldown adjustment (Holley 4150C carburetor) (Sec. 17)

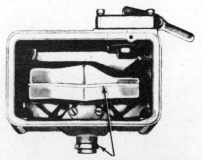

TURN ADJUSTING NUT UNTIL CENTER OF FLOAT IS AN EQUAL DISTANCE FROM TOP AND BOTTOM OF BOWL WITH FUEL BOWL INVERTED

Fig. 3.40 Float adjustment – dry (Holley 4150C carburetor) (Sec. 17)

3

(d) Loosen the lock screw and turn the adjusting nut out in increments of 1/6 turn or less until the correct fuel level is obtained. After each adjustment, tighten the lock screw, install the sight plug and start the engine. Run the engine until the fuel level is stabilized and then recheck the fuel level at the sight plug opening. Install the sight plug and gasket.

(e) Check the idle speed and fuel mixture adjustment, (see Section 13).

16 To raise the fuel level carry out the procedure in paragraph 15 (a), (d) and (e).

Secondary throttle plates

17 Hold the secondary plates closed.

18 Turn the secondary throttle shaft lever adjusting screw (stop screw) out until the secondary throttle plates stick in the throttle bores (Fig. 3.42).

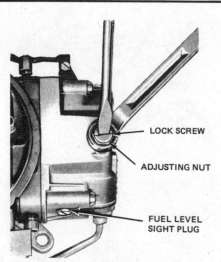

LOCK SCREW

ADJUSTING NUT

FUEL LEVEL SIGHT PLUG

Fig. 3.41 Fuel level float adjustment – wet (Holley 4150C carburetor) (Sec. 17)

CAM FOLLOWER ON HIGH STEP OF FAST IDLE CAM

PRIMARY THROTTLE VALVE CLOSED

AFTER SCREW MAKES CONTACT ON LEVER, TURN SCREW (2) TURNS TO ADJUST

Fig. 3.43 Pre-setting the fast idle screw (Rochester Quadrajet 4MV carburetor) (Sec. 18)

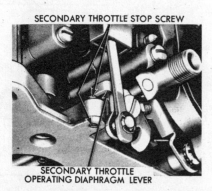

SECONDARY THROTTLE STOP SCREW

SECONDARY THROTTLE OPERATING DIAPHRAGM LEVER

Fig. 3.42 Adjusting the secondary throttle plate (Holley 4150C carburetor) (Sec. 17)

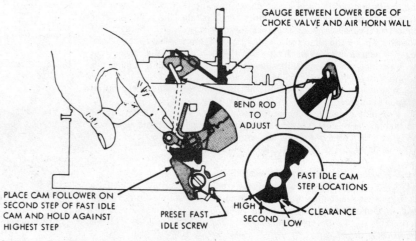

GAUGE BETWEEN LOWER EDGE OF CHOKE VALVE AND AIR HORN WALL

BEND ROD TO ADJUST

FAST IDLE CAM STEP LOCATIONS

HIGH SECOND LOW CLEARANCE

PLACE CAM FOLLOWER ON SECOND STEP OF FAST IDLE CAM AND HOLD AGAINST HIGHEST STEP

PRESET FAST IDLE SCREW

Fig. 3.44 Choke rod adjustment (Rochester Quadrajet 4MV carburetor) (Sec. 18)

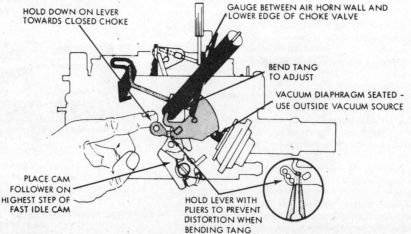

HOLD DOWN ON LEVER TOWARDS CLOSED CHOKE

GAUGE BETWEEN AIR HORN WALL AND LOWER EDGE OF CHOKE VALVE

BEND TANG TO ADJUST

VACUUM DIAPHRAGM SEATED – USE OUTSIDE VACUUM SOURCE

PLACE CAM FOLLOWER ON HIGHEST STEP OF FAST IDLE CAM

HOLD LEVER WITH PLIERS TO PREVENT DISTORTION WHEN BENDING TANG

Fig. 3.45 Vacuum break adjustment (Rochester Quadrajet 4MV carburetor) (Sec. 18)

19 Turn the screw in (clockwise) until the screw just contacts the secondary lever, then turn it a further $\frac{1}{2}$ turn clockwise.

18 Rochester Quadrajet 4MV carburetor – adjustments

Choke rod adjustment

1 Place the fast idle cam follower on the highest step of the fast idle cam (Fig. 3.43). Back-out the fast idle screw until the primary throttle plates are closed and the cam follower is away from the highest step of the cam. Now turn the fast idle screw inward until the cam follower just contacts the highest step of the cam, then from this point turn the screw two more complete turns. This presets the fast idle screw so that the following choke settings can be made accurately.
2 With the fast idle adjustment made, place the cam follower on the second step of the fast idle cam and against the rise to the highest step (Fig. 3.44). Rotate the choke plate towards the closed choke position by pushing counterclockwise on the vacuum break lever.
3 Check the clearance between the lower edge of the choke plate, at the choke lever end, and the air horn wall using a drill of suitable diameter. Adjust, if necessary, by bending the choke rod at the point shown in Fig. 3.44, to obtain the specified clearance.

Vacuum break adjustment

4 Seat the vacuum break diaphragm using an outside vacuum source.
5 Place the cam follower on the highest step of the fast idle cam (Fig. 3.45).
6 Rotate the vacuum break lever counterclockwise toward the closed choke until the vacuum break tang contacts the offset in the vacuum break dashpot rod.
7 With the choke rod in the bottom of the slot in the choke lever, check that the clearance between the lower edge of the choke plate and the air horn wall is to specification. Adjust if necessary by bending the vacuum break tang.

Air valve dashpot adjustment

8 Seat the vacuum break diaphragm using an outside vacuum source.
9 With the air valve completely closed and the diaphragm seated, check the clearance between the air valve dashpot rod and the air valve lever.
10 Adjust, if necessary, by bending the rod at the air valve end (Fig. 3.46).

Unloader adjustment

11 Use a rubber band or spring to hold the choke plate in the closed position, then open the primary throttle plates fully.
12 Check the clearance between the lower edge of the choke plates and the air horn wall, using a drill of the specified diameter as a gauge. The choke rod should be in the bottom of the slot when checking the setting.
13 Adjust, if necessary, by bending the tang on the fast idle lever to the rear to increase, and to the front to decrease the clearance.
14 Recheck the clearance after the carburetor is installed on the engine.

Fuel level float adjustment

15 Remove the air horn assembly.
16 Measure the distance from the top of the float bowl casting to the top of the float at the toe ($\frac{1}{16}$ in back from the toe on the float surface). When checking the adjustment, make sure that the float hinge pin is firmly seated and the float arm is held down against the float needle so that it is seated.
17 Adjust, if necessary, by bending the float pontoon up or down at the point shown in Fig. 3.47.
18 Install the air horn assembly using a new gasket.

19 Carburetor – removal and installation

1 Remove the air cleaner as described in Section 6.
2 Disconnect the fuel feed line from the carburetor.
3 Disconnect the electrical wiring and vacuum hoses from the carburetor.
4 Disconnect the control linkage from the carburetor (photo).

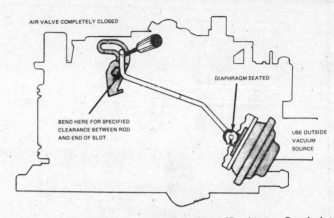

Fig. 3.46 Adjusting the air valve dashpot (Rochester Quadrajet 4MV carburetor) (Sec. 18)

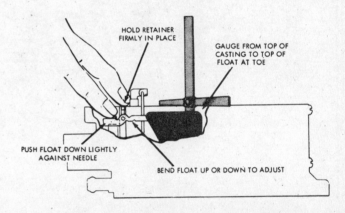

Fig. 3.47 Adjusting the float level (Rochester Quadrajet 4MV carburetor) (Sec. 18)

19.4 Carburetor throttle linkage – left-hand side

5 Partially drain the cooling system and disconnect the hoses from the choke housing.
6 Using suitably cranked ring/socket wrenches, remove the carburetor mounting nuts. Lift off the carburetor.
7 Installation of the carburetor is the reversal of the removal procedure. Always use a new flange gasket.

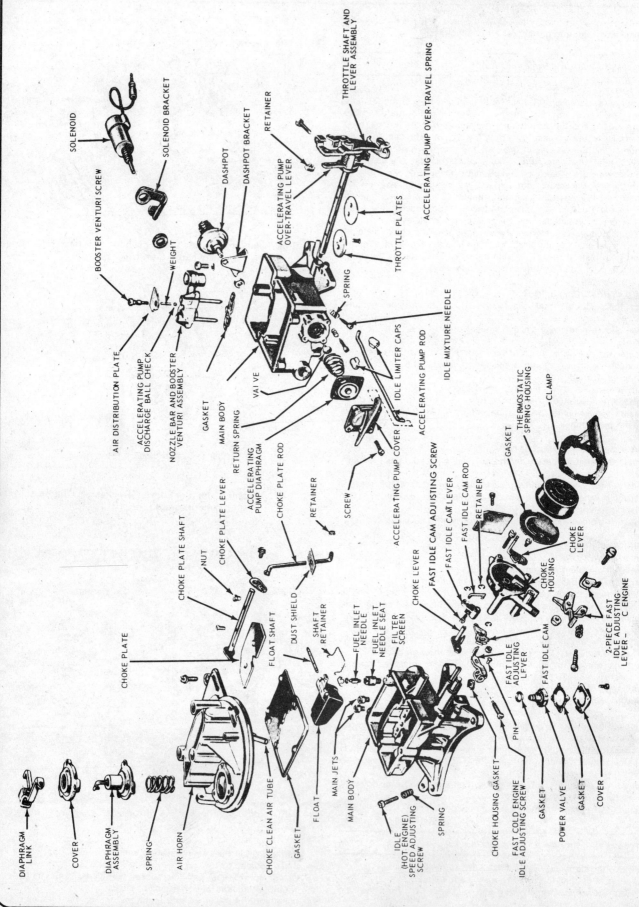

Fig. 3.48 Exploded view of Autolite 2100D carburetor (Sec. 21)

20 Carburetor – servicing (general)

1 As wear takes place in the carburetor an increase in fuel consumption and a falling-off in performance will be evident. When a carburetor requires major repair it is recommended that an exchange unit is purchased. Because of the high degree of precision involved and the necessity to renew the casing when wear takes place round spindles and other moving parts, this is one time when it is better to buy a replacement component rather than to rebuild the old one.

2 Repair kits are available for servicing carburetors and providing care is taken the carburetor can be serviced by following the instructions in Section 21, 22, 23 and 24, in conjunction with the exploded views in Fig. 3.48, 3.52, 3.54 and 3.57.

3 Efficient carburetion depends on careful cleaning to a great extent, therefore care must be taken to exclude all dirt, gum or water from the carburetor during servicing. Always make sure to have a clean area for dismantling and lay parts out separately to avoid similar-looking parts from getting mixed-up.

4 Never probe jets, fuel passages, or air bleeds with a wire, or similar, to clean them. Always blow them out with compressed air or air from a car tire pump. Use gasoline when cleaning the dismantled parts. Always use wrenches and screwdrivers of the correct size when dismantling the carburetor to avoid damage to jets and screws.

21 Carburetor (type 2100) – dismantling and reassembly

Refer to Fig. 3.48.

1 Remove the air cleaner anchor screw.

2 Remove the automatic choke control rod retainer.

3 Undo the air horn securing screws and remove the carburetor identification tag, air horn and gasket.

4 Loosen the securing screw and remove the choke control rod from the air horn. Slide the plastic dust seal out of the air horn.

5 Remove the choke diaphragm assembly (Fig. 3.49).

6 If it is necessary to remove the choke plate relieve the staking on the attaching screws, undo the screws and slide the plate off the shaft and out from the top of the air horn. Slide the shaft out of the air horn.

7 Remove the fast idle cam retainer.

8 Undo the thermostatic choke spring housing securing screws and remove the clamp, housing and gasket.

9 Remove the choke housing assembly retaining screws and lift off the choke housing and gasket; then remove the fast idle cam and rod from the fast idle cam lever.

10 Undo the choke lever retaining screw and remove the choke lever and fast idle cam lever from the choke housing.

11 Use a screwdriver to pry the float shaft retainer from the fuel inlet seat (Fig. 3.50) and lift out the float, float shaft retainer and fuel inlet needle assembly; then remove the retainer and float shaft from the float lever.

12 Remove the fuel inlet needle, seat, filter screen, and the main jets with a jet wrench.

13 Remove the booster venturi screw, air distribution plate, booster venturi and gasket. Invert the main body and collect the accelerating pump discharge weight and ball.

14 Remove the accelerating pump operating rod and retainer.

15 Undo the attaching screws and remove the accelerating pump cover, diaphragm assembly and spring (Fig. 3.51). If it is necessary to remove the elastomer valve, grasp it firmly and pull it out. If the valve is removed it must be discarded and a new valve fitted.

16 Remove the power valve cover and gasket, then using a box or socket wrench unscrew the power valve. Discard the power valve gasket.

17 Remove the idle fuel mixture adjusting screws and the springs, and then the limiters from the adjusting screws.

18 Undo the securing nut and remove the fast idle adjusting lever from the throttle shaft.

19 Remove the anti-stall dashpot or solenoid (if installed).

20 If it is necessary to remove the throttle plates, lightly scribe the throttle plates along the throttle shaft, and mark each plate and its corresponding bore with an identification mark, so that they can be reassembled in their original positions. Slide the throttle shaft out of the main body.

21 Reassembly is the reverse of the dismantling procedure. Use all the items in the repair kit. If the elastomer valve was removed,

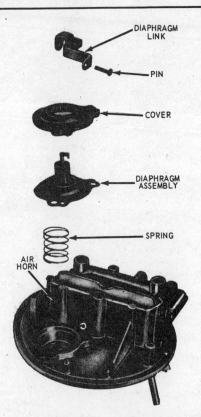

Fig. 3.49 Removing the choke diaphragm assembly (2100D carburetor) (Sec. 21)

Fig. 3.50 Using a screwdriver to remove the float shaft retainer (2100D carburetor) (Sec. 21)

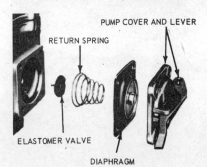

Fig. 3.51 Removing the accelerating pump assembly (2100D carburetor) (Sec. 21)

lubricate the tip of a new valve and insert the tip into the accelerator pump cavity center hole. Using a pair of needle-nosed pliers, grip the valve tip and pull the valve in until it seats in the pump cavity then cut off the tip forward of the retaining shoulder. Be sure to remove the cut off tip from the fuel bowl.

22 When installing the idle mixture adjusting screws, turn them in

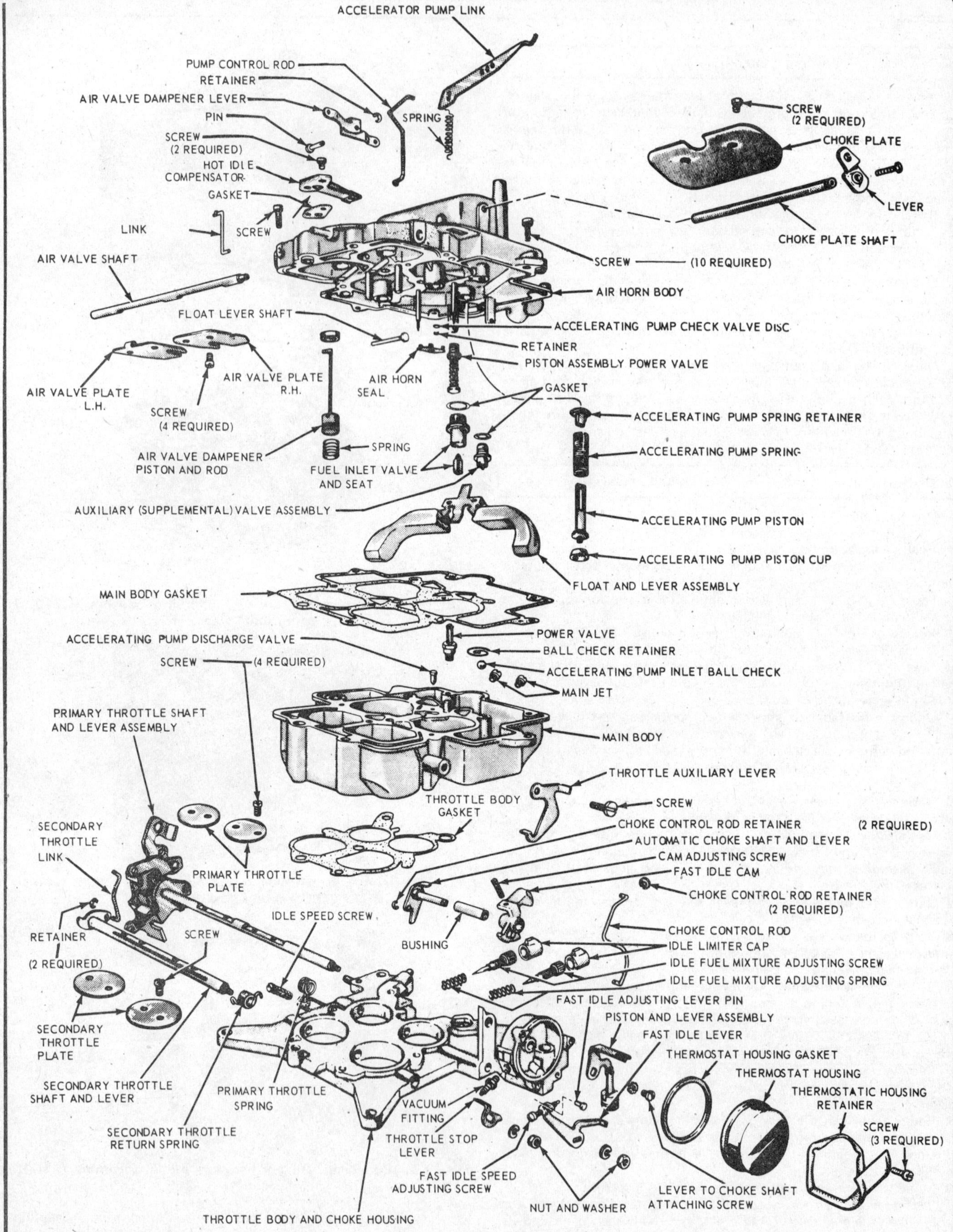

ACCELERATOR PUMP LINK

PUMP CONTROL ROD
RETAINER

AIR VALVE DAMPENER LEVER
PIN
SCREW
(2 REQUIRED)
HOT IDLE
COMPENSATOR
GASKET

SPRING

SCREW
(2 REQUIRED)

CHOKE PLATE

LEVER

CHOKE PLATE SHAFT

LINK
SCREW

AIR VALVE SHAFT

FLOAT LEVER SHAFT

SCREW (10 REQUIRED)

AIR HORN BODY

ACCELERATING PUMP CHECK VALVE DISC

RETAINER

PISTON ASSEMBLY POWER VALVE

AIR VALVE PLATE
L.H.

AIR VALVE PLATE
R.H.

SCREW
(4 REQUIRED)

AIR HORN
SEAL

GASKET

ACCELERATING PUMP SPRING RETAINER

ACCELERATING PUMP SPRING

SPRING

AIR VALVE DAMPENER
PISTON AND ROD

FUEL INLET VALVE
AND SEAT

ACCELERATING PUMP PISTON

ACCELERATING PUMP PISTON CUP

AUXILIARY (SUPPLEMENTAL) VALVE ASSEMBLY

FLOAT AND LEVER ASSEMBLY

MAIN BODY GASKET

ACCELERATING PUMP DISCHARGE VALVE

SCREW (4 REQUIRED)

POWER VALVE

BALL CHECK RETAINER

ACCELERATING PUMP INLET BALL CHECK

MAIN JET

PRIMARY THROTTLE SHAFT
AND LEVER ASSEMBLY

MAIN BODY

THROTTLE AUXILIARY LEVER

SCREW

SECONDARY
THROTTLE
LINK

PRIMARY THROTTLE
PLATE

THROTTLE BODY
GASKET

CHOKE CONTROL ROD RETAINER   (2 REQUIRED)

AUTOMATIC CHOKE SHAFT AND LEVER

CAM ADJUSTING SCREW

FAST IDLE CAM

CHOKE CONTROL ROD RETAINER
(2 REQUIRED)

CHOKE CONTROL ROD

IDLE LIMITER CAP

IDLE FUEL MIXTURE ADJUSTING SCREW

IDLE FUEL MIXTURE ADJUSTING SPRING

FAST IDLE ADJUSTING LEVER PIN

PISTON AND LEVER ASSEMBLY

FAST IDLE LEVER

THERMOSTAT HOUSING GASKET

THERMOSTAT HOUSING

THERMOSTATIC HOUSING
RETAINER

SCREW
(3 REQUIRED)

RETAINER
(2 REQUIRED)

SCREW

IDLE SPEED SCREW

BUSHING

SECONDARY
THROTTLE
PLATE

SECONDARY THROTTLE
SHAFT AND LEVER

SECONDARY THROTTLE
RETURN SPRING

PRIMARY THROTTLE
SPRING

VACUUM
FITTING

THROTTLE STOP
LEVER

FAST IDLE SPEED
ADJUSTING SCREW

THROTTLE BODY AND CHOKE HOUSING

NUT AND WASHER

LEVER TO CHOKE SHAFT
ATTACHING SCREW

Fig. 3.52 Exploded view of Autolite 4300 carburetor (Sec. 22)

until they are just seated then back them off $1\frac{1}{2}$ turns for an initial fuel mixture adjustment.

23 During assembly carry out the settings and adjustments described in Section 15.

22 Carburetor (type 4300) – dismantling and reassembly

Refer to Fig. 3.52

1 Remove the choke control rod retainer from the automatic choke lever and separate the rod from the lever.

2 Remove the accelerator pump spring and washer, then separate the pump rod from the lever.

3 Remove the air cleaner anchor stud and the air horn securing screws. Lift off the air horn.

4 Pull out the flot pin pivot and lift out the float assembly.

5 Remove the main and auxiliary (supplemental) fuel inlet valve seats and gaskets.

6 Remove the secondary air valve lever pivot pin and the rod from the dampener piston assembly and air valve plate, then remove the air valve dampener piston rod and spring.

7 If it is necessary to remove the secondary air valve plates or shaft, remove the attaching screws, lift out the plates and then slide the shaft out of the air horn.

8 Relieve the staking on the choke plate securing screws, remove the screws, lift out the choke plate, then slide the shaft out of the air horn.

9 Turn the main body upside down and collect the accelerating pump discharge needle (Fig. 3.53).

10 Using a socket wrench unscrew the power valve from the fuel bowl.

11 Remove the main metering jets from the fuel bowl.

12 Using long-nosed pliers, remove the accelerating pump inlet check ball retainer, then turn the body over and collect the check ball.

13 Remove the throttle body-to-main body attaching screws and separate the two castings.

Note: *Do not remove the idle mixture limiter caps or the mixture screws.*

14 Remove the choke housing cover screws, cover, gasket and thermostatic spring (photo).

15 Undo the choke piston lever retaining screw and remove the piston assembly.

16 Remove the secondary throttle lever-to-primary throttle connecting link retainers then lift away the link.

17 Relieve the staking on the throttle plate attaching screws, undo the screws and remove the plates.

18 Undo the nut from the secondary throttle shaft, then remove the lockout lever and slide the shaft and return spring out of the throttle body.

19 Undo the securing screw on the primary throttle shaft and remove the fast idle lever and adjusting screw. Slide the primary throttle shaft and lever assembly out of the throttle body.

20 Remove the retainer and slide the lever and springs off the primary throttle shaft.

21 Reassembly is the reverse of the dismantling procedure. Use all the items in the repair kit. During assembly carry out the settings and adjustments described in Section 16.

23 Carburetor (Holley 4150C) – dismantling and reassembly

Refer to Fig. 3.54
Primary fuel bowl and metering block

1 Disconnect the interconnecting fuel line at the primary and secondary fuel bowls. Undo the retaining screws and remove the primary fuel bowl and metering block. Discard the gaskets. Remove the baffle.

2 Remove the idle fuel mixture limiters and the idle adjusting screws.

3 Unscrew and remove the main jets (Fig. 3.55).

4 Unscrew the power valve with a socket wrench.

5 Remove the fuel level adjustment lock screw. Turn the adjustment nut counterclockwise and remove the locknut and gasket. Remove the fuel inlet needle and seat assembly, do not dismantle them as they are matched and are renewed as an assembly.

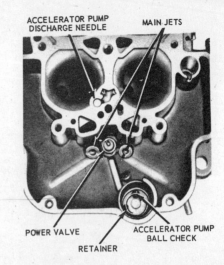

Fig. 3.53 Main body valves and jets (4300 carburetor) (Sec. 22)

22.14A Removing the choke housing cover and spring

22.14B Choke housing with gasket removed

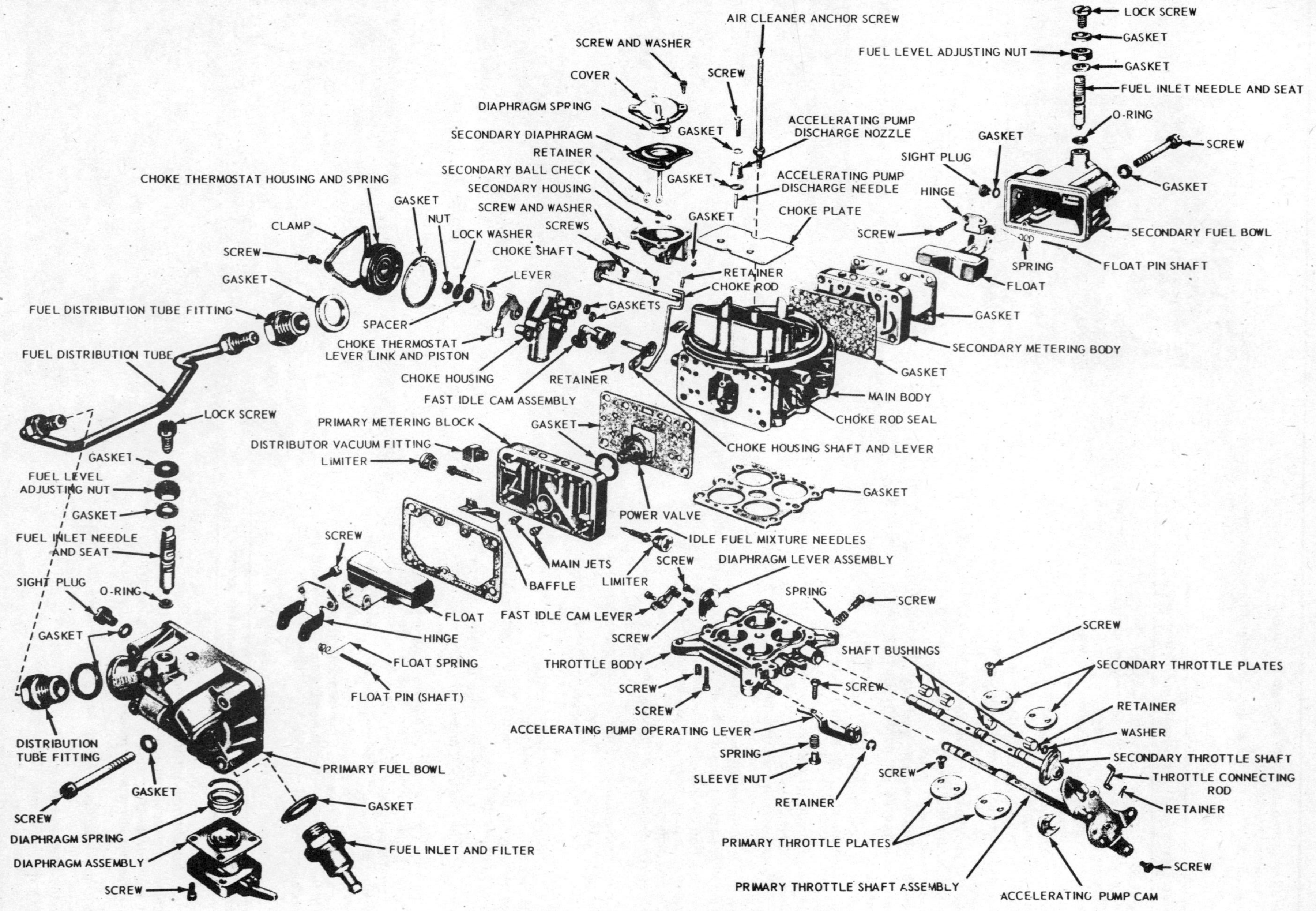

Fig. 3.54 Exploded view of Holley 4150C carburetor (Sec. 23)

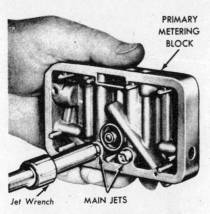

Fig. 3.55 Removing the main jets (Holley 4150C carburetor) (Sec. 23)

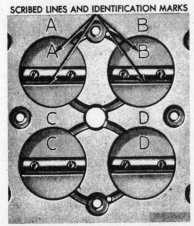

Fig. 3.56 Match mark the throttle plates (Sec. 23)

6   Undo the attaching screws and remove the float asembly, then slide the shaft out of the float assembly and collect the spring.
7   Remove the fuel level sight plug, fuel inlet fitting gasket and filter screen.
8   Remove the accelerator pump cover, diaphragm and spring.
9   Undo the retaining screw and remove the plug, spring and bracket from the vent rod.

Secondary fuel bowl and metering block
10   Remove the fuel bowl, metering block and gaskets. Dismantle the assembly by following the procedures described in paragraph 3 through 7.

Main body
11   Remove the air cleaner anchor stud and the secondary diaphragm operating rod-to-link retainer.
12   Remove the throttle body retaining screws and lift off the throttle body.
13   Remove the choke rod retainer, the thermostatic spring housing and then the choke housing.
14   Undo the choke housing shaft nut, then remove the lock washer, spacer, shaft, fast idle cam, and the choke piston and lever assembly.
15   Remove the choke rod and seal from the main body.
16   Relieve the staking on the securing screws and remove the choke plate, then slide the choke shaft and lever out of the air horn.
17   Remove the secondary diaphragm housing assembly and then the diaphragm housing cover; collect the spring, diaphragm and vacuum check ball from the housing.
18   Undo the attaching screw and lift the accelerating pump discharge nozzle out of the body. Invert the body and collect the pump discharge needle.

Throttle body
19   Remove the accelerator pump operating lever retainer.

20   Remove the secondary throttle connecting rod retainers and the connecting rod. Undo the securing screws and remove the secondary diaphragm lever and the fast idle cam lever.
21   Match-mark the throttle plates (see Fig. 3.56) then undo the retaining screws and remove the throttle plates.
22   Remove the primary throttle shaft return spring. Slide the primary throttle lever and shaft assembly out of the throttle body.
23   Slide the secondary throttle shaft out and remove the bushings from the shaft.
24   Reassembly is the reverse of the dismantling procedure. Use all the items in the repair kit. During assembly carry out the settings and adjustments described in Section 17.

24 Carburetor (Rochester Quadrajet 4MV) – dismantling and reassembly

Refer to Fig. 3.57

Air horn
1   Remove the retaining clips and disconnect the choke rod, pump rod and vacuum break rod.
2   Undo the attaching screw and lift the secondary metering rod holder and rods straight upward out of the air horn, then slide the secondary rods out of the holder.
3   Remove the nine securing screws (two are inside the air horn bore) and lift off the air horn.
4   Undo the attaching screws and remove the choke valve and shaft.
5   Remove the pump lever roll pin and pump lever.
6   Using a small diameter drift, drive the retaining roll pin out and remove the air valve lockout lever.
7   Undo the lock screw and remove the air valve spring fulcrum pin and then the air valve.
8   Undo the attaching screws and remove the four air valves from the shaft. Slide the air valve shaft out of the air horn, then remove the plastic metering rod cam.

Throttle body
9   Unscrew the pump rod from the primary throttle lever.
10   Remove the two idle limiters, and the idle mixture screws and springs.
11   Undo the attaching screw in the end of the primary throttle shaft and pull off the fast idle lever and fast idle cam follower lever.

Float bowl
12   Lift the pump plunger out of the pump well and remove the pump return spring.
13   Remove the plastic filler block over the float valve (Fig. 3.58).
14   Remove the power piston and the primary metering rods as an assembly by pushing down against spring tension and allowing the piston to snap back against the retainer until it pops out of the casting.
15   Disconnect the tension spring loops from the top of each primary metering rod then unscrew the rods from the hanger. Take care not to distort the tension springs or rods.
16   Lift the power piston spring out of the power piston cavity.
17   Pull upward on the hinge pin and remove the float assembly. The float needle and seat are a matched assembly and must be renewed as a set.
18   Remove the primary main metering jets. Do not remove the secondary metering discs; normal cleaning is all that is necessary.
19   Remove the pump discharge check ball retainer and steel check ball.
20   Lift the baffle plate from the secondary bores.
21   Remove the retaining screw and lift the choke bracket assembly from the float bowl.
22   Slide the fast idle cam off the bushing on the choke bracket.
23   Spread the retaining ears on the bracket next to the vacuum diaphragm, then slide the vacuum diaphragm assembly out of the bracket.
24   Reassembly is the reverse of the dismantling procedure. Use all the items in the repair kit. During assembly carry out the settings and adjustments described in Section 18. When installing the idle mixture needles and springs, turn them in until they are just seated and then back them off 1½ turns for an initial setting. Tighten the air horn securing screws in the sequence shown in Fig. 3.59.

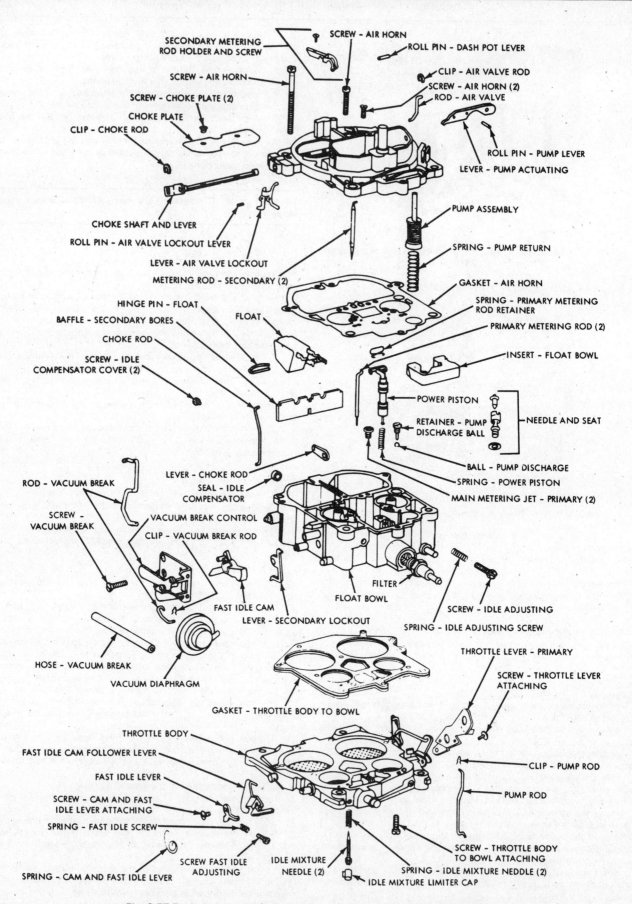

Fig. 3.57 Exploded view of Rochester Quadrajet 4MV carburetor (Sec. 24)

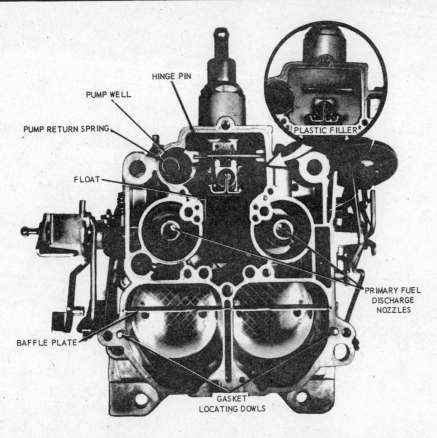

PUMP WELL
HINGE PIN
PUMP RETURN SPRING
PLASTIC FILLER
FLOAT
PRIMARY FUEL DISCHARGE NOZZLES
BAFFLE PLATE
GASKET LOCATING DOWLS

Fig. 3.58 Dismantling the float bowl (Rochester Quadrajet 4MV carburetor) (Sec. 24)

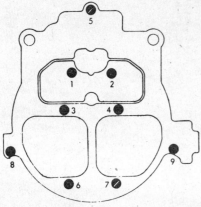

Fig. 3.59 Tightening sequence of air horn securing screws (Rochester Quadrajet 4MV carburetor) (Sec. 24)

25 Fuel tank – removal and installation

1   Disconnect the battery terminals.
2   Chock the front wheels, jack-up the rear of the car and support it on jack stands.
3   Remove the fuel tank drain plug and drain the fuel into a suitable container.
4   Disconnect the fuel gauge sender unit wiring from the sender unit, then loosen the hose clamp, slide the clamp forward and disconnect the fuel line from the sender unit.
5   Disconnect the fuel tank vent hose and the fuel evaporation emission control line (if installed).
6   Remove the spare tire from the luggage compartment to gain access to the fuel tank.
7   Remove the fuel tank filler neck securing screws, loosen the filler neck-to-hose clamps and remove the filler neck, gasket and hose.

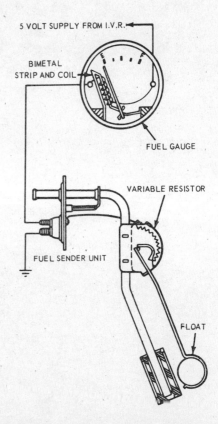

5 VOLT SUPPLY FROM I.V.R.
BIMETAL STRIP AND COIL
FUEL GAUGE
VARIABLE RESISTOR
FUEL SENDER UNIT
FLOAT

Fig. 3.60 Fuel level indicating system – schematic (Sec. 25)

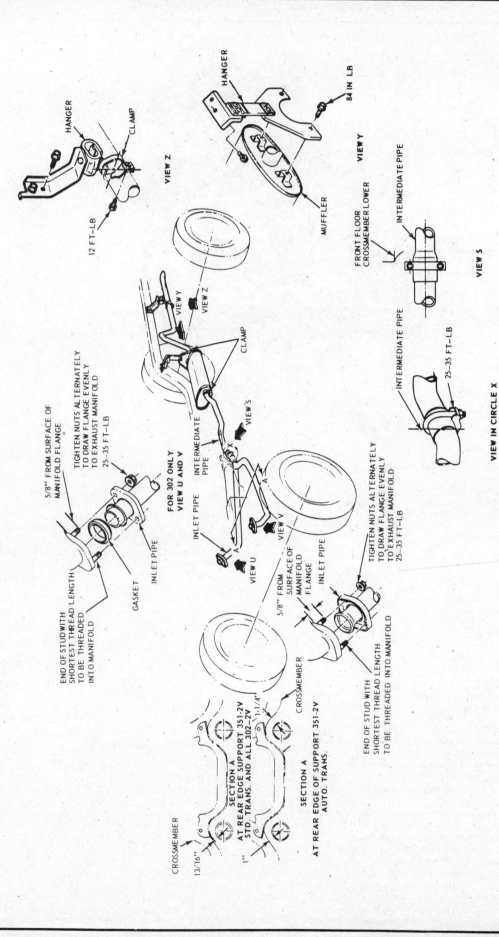

Fig. 3.61 Single exhaust system (Sec. 28)

8 Remove the fuel tank retaining screws and remove the fuel tank. Later models are secured by two support straps.
9 If it is necessary to remove the sender unit, this can be unscrewed from the tank using the appropriate Ford tool. Alternatively a suitable C-wrench or drift can probably be used, but great care should be taken that the flange is not damaged and that there is no danger from sparks if a hammer is used.
10 Installation is the reverse of the removal procedure. Use a new seal when installing the sender unit.

26 Fuel tank – cleaning and repair

1 With time it is likely that sediment will collect in the bottom of the fuel tank. Condensation, resulting in rust and other impurities, will usually be found in the fuel tank of any car more than three or four years old.
2 When the tank is removed it should be vigorously flushed out with hot water and detergent and, if facilities are available, steam cleaned.
3 Never weld, solder or bring a naked light close to an empty fuel tank, unless it has been cleaned as described in the previous paragraph, for at least two hours.

27 Downshift linkage (automatic transmission) – adjustment

1 Disconnect the throttle and downshift return springs.
2 Hold the carburetor throttle lever wide-open against the stop, with the transmission in full downshift against the stop.
3 Turn the adjustment screw on the carburetor kickdown lever to obtain a gap of 0.040 to 0.080 in (1 to 2 mm) between the carburetor lever and the adjusting screw.
4 Release the transmission and carburetor to the normal free position. Install the throttle and downshift return springs.

28 Exhaust system – description and renewal

Single and dual exhaust systems are used on the different models. The single system can consist of a single muffler exhaust system with or without a resonator, or a dual muffler exhaust system, without resonator. The dual exhaust system has two separate exhaust systems without resonators (Figs. 3.61 and 3.62).
1 The front pipes are secured to the manifold by means of flanges while the front and rear pipe sections are attached to the muffler and/or resonators by U-bolts and clamps. The complete system is attached to the underbody by brackets bolted to insulated hangers.
2 To conform to the current emission control regulations, later models are equipped with a catalytic converter located between the front pipe(s) and the muffler(s).
3 On all models a periodic check should be made on the exhaust system for excessive corrosion and leaks. Any faults should be rectified at once to avoid contravening the Emission Control laws, or enabling carbon monoxide fumes to enter the car.
4 Although the different exhaust system sections can be renewed separately it will usually be found that if one section is badly corroded the rest of the system will be approaching the same condition. Therefore the most sensible and safest policy is to renew the complete system.
5 When refitting a flange type joint always use a new gasket.
6 Models equipped with catalytic converter(s) are fitted with a heat shield which will have to be unbolted and removed prior to refitting the exhaust system.

29 Emission control systems – general description

To conform to the anti-pollution laws the Mustang range of models are equipped with various emission control devices. The specific controls installed on each car will depend on which State the car is sold in; the emission control information for individual cars is shown on a data plate inside the engine compartment. This Section describes the various emission controls that may be installed.
WARNING: *Before commencing any maintenance or testing of emission control systems the owner is advised to read Section 2 of this Chapter to avoid contravening the emission control regulations*

Improved combustion (IMCO) system
1 The main features of this system are covered by the design of the engine and carburetor, and therefore require no special information. However, an electrically assisted choke heater is used as an aid to fast choke release for better emission characteristics during engine warm-up.
2 The choke heater is a constant temperature, positive temperature coefficient (PTC) unit, energized from the alternator field (IND) terminal, and is energized when the engine is running.
3 Incorporated with the unit is a fast idle cam latch, which holds the cam on the high position until the choke heats up and the bi-metal latch backs off to allow the latch pin and fast idle cam to rotate to the normal run position.
4 An overcentre spring assists in closing the choke plate for initial starting of a cold engine in high ambient temperatures. This spring has no effect after initial choke pull-down occurs.

Positive crankcase ventilation (PCV) system
5 The PCV system operates by drawing in air and mixing it with the vapors which have escaped past the piston rings (blow-by vapors). This mixture is then drawn into the combustion chamber through an oil separator and PCV valve (Fig. 3.63).

Evaporative emission control
6 This system is designed to limit the emission of fuel vapors to the atmosphere. It comprises the fuel tank, pressure and vacuum sensitive fuel filler cap, a restrictor bleed orifice, a charcoal canister and the associated connecting lines (Fig. 3.64).
7 When the fuel tank is filled, vapors are discharged to the atmosphere through the filler tube, and a space between the inner filler tube and the outer neck. When fuel covers the filler control tube, vapors can no longer escape and a vapor lock is created by the orifice; therefore there can be no flow to the vapor charcoal canister.
8 When thermal expansion occurs in the fuel tank, vapor is forced through the orifice to the canister, where it is stored when the engine is not running and is drawn into the carburetor intake system as soon as the engine is started.

Exhaust gas recirculation (EGR) system
9 This system is designed to reintroduce small amounts of exhaust gas into the combustion cycle to reduce the generation of oxides of nitrogen (NOX). The amount of gas reintroduced is governed by engine vacuum and temperature.
10 The EGR valve is mounted on a spacer block between the carburetor and manifold. A venturi vacuum amplifier (VVA) is used to change the relatively weak vacuum signal in the carburetor throat to a strong signal for operation of the EGR valve (Fig. 3.65).
11 A relief valve is also used to modify the output EGR signal whenever venturi vacuum is equal to, or greater than, manifold vacuum. This allows the EGR valve to close at or near, wide open throttle, when maximum engine power is required.
12 The EGR/CSC (cold start cycle) regulates the distributor spark advance and EGR valve operation according to the engine coolant temperature, by sequentially switching the vacuum signals. When the coolant temperature is below 82°F (27.8°C), the EGR ported vacuum switch (PVS) admits carburetor EGR port vacuum (which occurs at approximately 2500 rpm) directly to the distributor advance diaphragm through the one-way check valve. At the same time the PVS shuts off the carburetor vacuum to the EGR valve.
13 When the engine coolant is 95°F (35°C) or above, the EGR/PVS directs carburetor vacuum to the EGR valve.
14 At temperatures between 82 and 95°F (27.8 and 35°C), the EGR/PVS may be closed, open or in the mid-position.
15 A spark delay valve (SDV) is incorporated in the system to delay the carburetor spark vacuum to the distributor diaphragm unit for a predetermined time. During acceleration, little or no vacuum is admitted to the distributor diaphragm unit until acceleration is completed because of the time delay of the SDV and the re-routing of the EGR port vacuum at temperatures above 95°F (32°C). The check valve blocks the vacuum signal from the SDV to the EGR/PVS, so that carburetor spark vacuum will not be dissipated at temperatures above 95°F (32°C) (Fig. 3.66).
16 The 235°F (113°C) PVS is not strictly part of the EGR system, but is connected to the distributor vacuum advance unit to prevent overheating while idling with a hot engine. At idle speeds, no vacuum is generated at either of the carburetor ports and the engine timing is

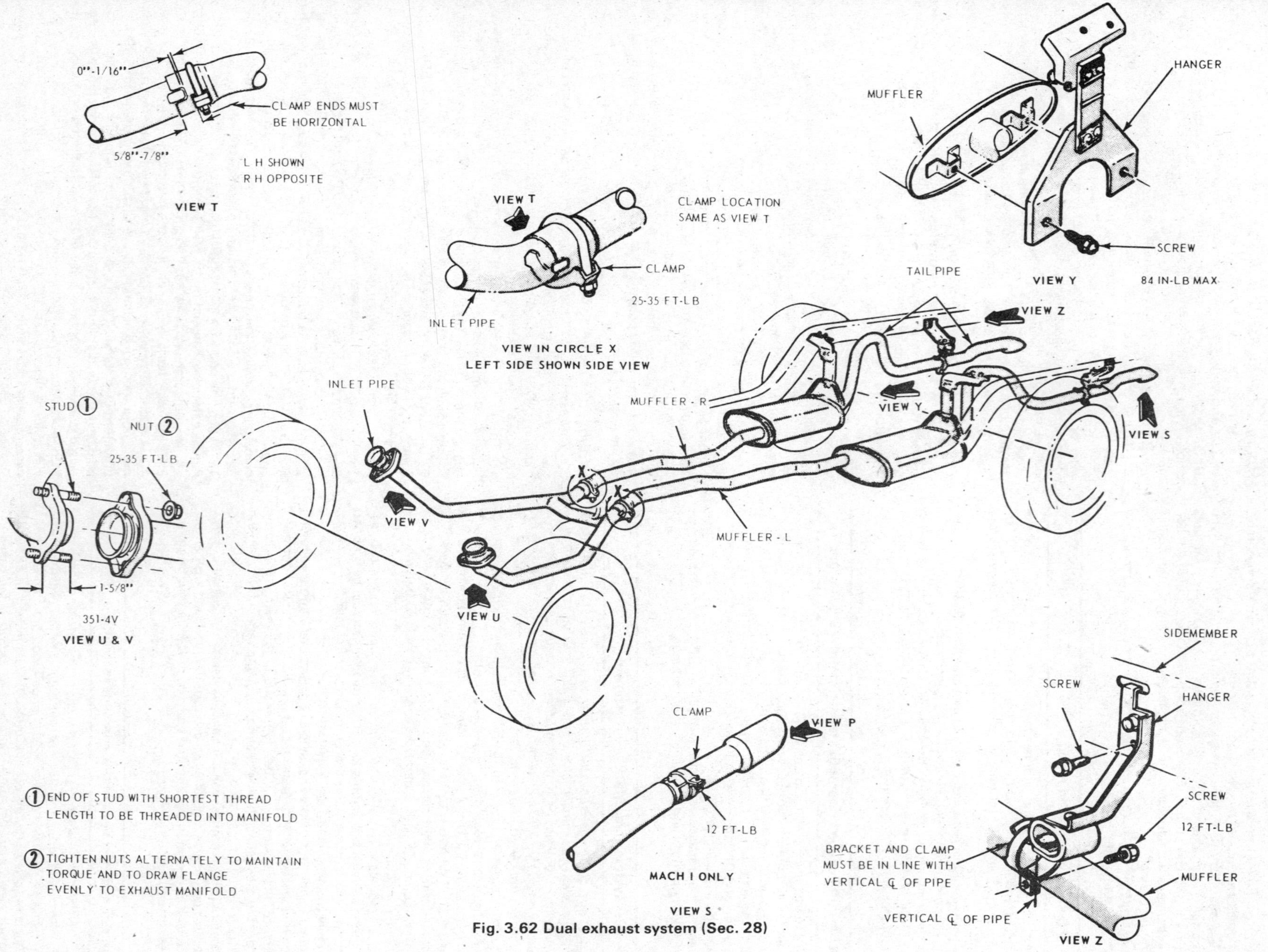

HANGER

SCREW

84 IN-LB MAX

MUFFLER

VIEW Y

VIEW Z

TAIL PIPE

CLAMP LOCATION
SAME AS VIEW T

CLAMP

25-35 FT-LB

VIEW T

INLET PIPE

VIEW IN CIRCLE X
LEFT SIDE SHOWN SIDE VIEW

MUFFLER - R

MUFFLER - L

VIEW S

VIEW Y

VIEW Z

VIEW V

INLET PIPE

VIEW U

CLAMP ENDS MUST
BE HORIZONTAL

L H SHOWN
R H OPPOSITE

VIEW T

0"-1/16"

5/8"-7/8"

STUD ①

NUT ②

25-35 FT-LB

1-5/8"

351-4V

VIEW U & V

SIDEMEMBER

HANGER

SCREW

12 FT-LB

MUFFLER

SCREW

VIEW Z

BRACKET AND CLAMP
MUST BE IN LINE WITH
VERTICAL ℄ OF PIPE

VERTICAL ℄ OF PIPE

VIEW P

CLAMP

12 FT-LB

MACH I ONLY

VIEW S

Fig. 3.62 Dual exhaust system (Sec. 28)

① END OF STUD WITH SHORTEST THREAD
LENGTH TO BE THREADED INTO MANIFOLD

② TIGHTEN NUTS ALTERNATELY TO MAINTAIN
TORQUE AND TO DRAW FLANGE
EVENLY TO EXHAUST MANIFOLD

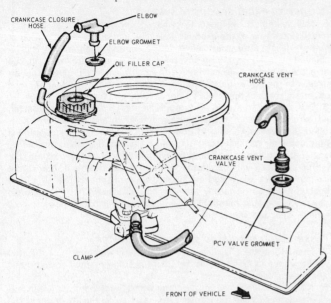

Fig. 3.63 Positive crankcase ventilation (PCV) system – typical (Sec. 29)

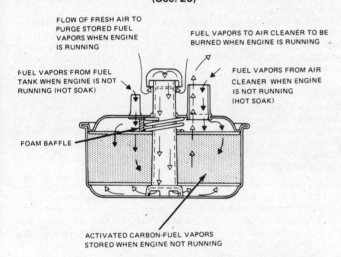

Fig. 3.64 Cross-section view of carbon canister (Sec. 29)

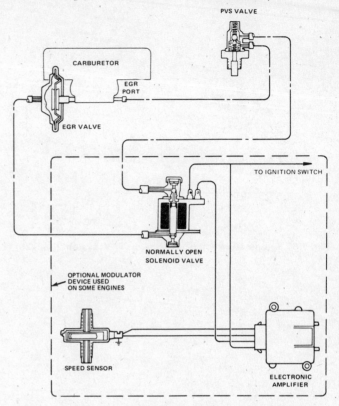

Fig. 3.65 Exhaust gas recirculation (EGR) system (Sec. 29)

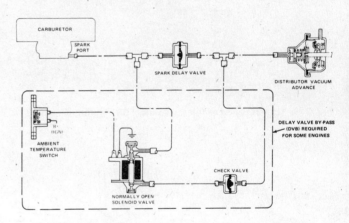

Fig. 3.66 Spark delay valve system (Sec. 29)

fully retarded. However, when the coolant temperature reaches 235°F (113°C) the PVS is actuated to admit intake manifold vacuum to the distributor advance diaphragm. The engine timing is thus advanced, idling speed is correspondingly increased and the engine temperature is lowered due to increased fan speed and coolant flow.

Catalytic converter

17 On some models a catalytic converter is incorporated upstream of the exhaust front muffler. The converter comprises a ceramic honeycomb-like core housed in a stainless steel pipe. The core is coated with a platinum and palladium catalyst which converts unburned carbon monoxide and hydrocarbons into carbon dioxide and water by a chemical reaction.

18 No special maintenance of the converter is required, but it can be damaged by the use of leaded fuels, engine misfiring, excessive richness of the carburetor mixture, incorrect operation of the Thermactor system or running out of gasoline.

Inlet air temperature regulation

19 Inlet air temperature regulation is accomplished by the use of a thermostatic air cleaner and duct system (see Section 3).

Temperature activated vacuum system (TAV)

20 An additional feature incorporated on some models is the temperature actuated vacuum (TAV) system. This is designed to select

either carburetor spark port vacuum or carburetor EGR port vacuum as a function of ambient air temperature. The selected vacuum source is used to control the distributor diaphragm unit (Fig. 3.67).

21 The system comprises an ambient temperature switch, a three-way solenoid valve, an external vacuum bleed and a latching relay.

22 The temperature switch activates the solenoid, which is open at temperatures below 49°F (9.5°C) and is closed above 60°F (15.6°C). Within this temperature range the solenoid valve may be open or closed.

23 Below 49°F (9.5°C) the system is inoperative and the distributor diaphragm receives carburetor spark port vacuum while the EGR valve receives EGR port vacuum.

24 When the temperature switch closes (above 60°F/15.6°C) the three-way solenoid valve is energized from the ignition switch and the carburetor EGR port vacuum is delivered to the distributor advance diaphragm as well as to the EGR valve. The latching relay is also energized by the temperature switch closing, and will remain energized until the ignition is switched off, regardless of the temperature switch being open or closed.

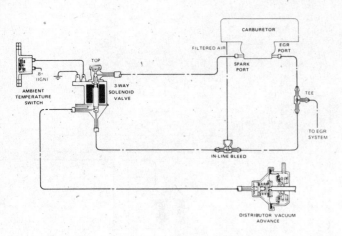

Fig. 3.67 Temperature activated vacuum (TAV) system (Sec. 29)

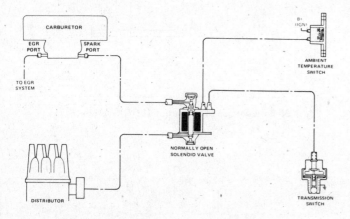

Fig. 3.68 Transmission regulated spark (TRS) system (Sec. 29)

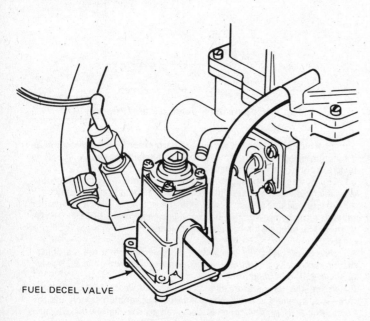

Fig. 3.69 Location of fuel decel valve (Sec. 29)

Thermactor exhaust control system

25 This system is designed to reduce the hydrocarbon and carbon monoxide content of the exhaust gases by continuing the oxidation of unburnt gases after they leave the combustion chamber. This is achieved by using an engine driven air pump to inject fresh air into the hot exhaust stream after it leaves the combustion chamber. This air mixes with the hot exhaust gases and promotes further oxidation, thus converting some of them into carbon dioxide and water.

26 The air pump draws in air through an impeller-type, centrifugal fan and exhausts it from the exhaust manifold through a vacuum controlled air bypass valve and check valve. Under normal conditions Thermactor air passes straight through the bypass valve, but during deceleration, when there is a high level of intake manifold vacuum, the diaphragm check valve operates to shut off the Thermactor air to the air supply check valve and exhausts it to atmosphere. The air supply check valve is a non-return valve which will allow Thermactor air to pass to the exhaust manifold but will not allow exhaust gases to flow in the reverse direction.

Transmission regulated spark (TRS) system

27 The TRS system is designed to eliminate vacuum (part throttle) spark advance in first and second gear for either manual or automatic transmission cars.

28 A transmission sensor determines when the transmission is in first or second gear. When the transmission is in one of the lower gears, the solenoid vacuum valve is closed preventing part-throttle spark vacuum from reaching the distributor diaphragm so that no part-throttle spark advance results.

29 This system results in insufficient spark advance at low ambient temperatures. To overcome this, an ambient temperature switch is installed in the system which overrides the transmission switch and re-establishes vacuum spark advance irrespective of which gear is engaged.

Deceleration valve

30 A deceleration valve is used to provide an enriched mixture when the engine is on overrun with the throttle closed. The valve screws into the intake manifold and has two vacuum outlet ports. When the engine decelerates a vacuum is applied to the control port and the valve opens and allows a fuel/air mixture to by-pass the carburetor and pass directly into the intake manifold (Fig. 3.69).

30 Emission control system – maintenance and testing

In view of the special test equipment and procedures there is little that can be done in the way of maintenance and testing for the emission control system. In the event of a suspected malfunction of the system, check the security and condition of all pneumatic and electrical connections then, where applicable, refer to the following paragraphs for further information.

Electrically assisted choke heater

1 The only test that can be carried out on this assembly, without special test equipment is a continuity check of the heater coil. If an ohmmeter is available, check for the specified resistance. If no ohmmeter is available, disconnect the stator lead from the choke cap terminal and connect it to one terminal of a 12V low wattage bulb (eg, instrument panel bulb). Ground the other terminal of the bulb and check that it illuminates when the engine is running. If it fails to illuminate, check the alternator output and the choke lead for continuity. If the bulb illuminates, disconnect the bulb ground terminal and reconnect it to the choke lead. If the bulb does not illuminate when the engine is warm, a faulty choke unit is indicated.

PCV system

2 Remove all the hoses and components of the system and clean them in kerosene or gasoline. Ensure that all hoses are free from any obstruction and are in a serviceable condition. Where applicable, similarly clean the crankcase breather cap and shake it dry. Install new parts as necessary, then install them on the car.

Carbon canister

3 The carbon canister is located in the engine compartment. To remove it, disconnect the two hoses, then undo the securing nuts and remove the canister and bracket. The canister installed on 1973

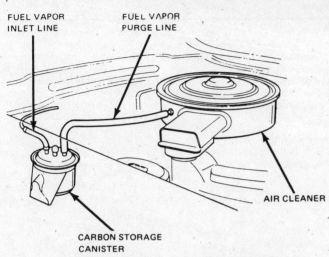

FUEL VAPOR INLET LINE

FUEL VAPOR PURGE LINE

AIR CLEANER

CARBON STORAGE CANISTER

Fig. 3.70 Location of carbon canister (Sec. 30)

models is larger than that used on earlier models and must not be replaced by the smaller size canister.

EGR system

4   The EGR valve can be removed for cleaning, but where it is damaged, corroded or extremely dirty it is preferable to install a new valve. If the valve is to be cleaned, check the orifice in the body is clear but take care not to enlarge it. If the valve can be dismantled, internal deposits can be removed with a small power-driven rotary wire brush. Deposits around the valve stem and disc can be removed by using a steel blade or shim approximately 0.028 in (0.7 mm) thick in a sawing motion around the stem shoulder at both sides of the disc. Clean the cavity and passages in the main body; ensure that the poppet wobbles, and moves axially before reassembly.

Thermactor system

5   Apart from checking the condition of the drivebelt and pipe connections, and checking the pump drivebelt tension, there is little that can be done without the use of special test equipment. Drivebelt tension should be checked by a Ford dealer with a special tensioning tool. However, this is approximately equal to $\frac{1}{2}$ in (13 mm) of belt movement between the longest pulley run under moderate hand pressure.

Deceleration valve system

6   Special equipment is required to carry out a complete test on the deceleration valve function and it is recommended that the car is taken to a Ford dealer.

---

31 Fault diagnosis – fuel system

Symptom	Reason/s
Excessive fuel consumption	Air cleaner choked or inlet duct system inoperative General leaks from fuel system Float chamber fuel level too high Rich mixture Dragging brakes Tires under-inflated Faulty choke operation

*May also be due to faulty condenser or advance/retard system in distributor OR an emission control system fault

Insufficient fuel delivery or weak mixture	Clogged fuel line or carburetor filter Fuel inlet needle valve stuck Faulty fuel pump Leaking pipe connections Leaking inlet manifold gasket Leaking carburetor mounting flange gasket Lean carburetor mixture setting

---

32 Fault diagnosis – emission control system

The following list is for guidance only, since a combination of faults may produce symptoms which are difficult to diagnose. It is therefore essential that a Ford dealer or emission control specialist is consulted in the event of problems occurring.

Symptom	Reason/s
Electrically assisted choke heater Long engine warm-up time	Faulty choke heater
PCV system Fumes escaping from engine	Clogged PCV valve Split or collapsed hoses
Evaporative control system Fuel odor or rough engine running	Choked carbon canister Stuck filler cap valve Split or collapsed hoses

Symptom	Reason/s

Thermactor system
Fume emission from exhaust

Air pump drivebelt incorrectly tensioned
Damaged air supply pipes
Split or collapsed sensing hoses
Defective air pump
Faulty pressure relief valve

EGR system
Rough idling

Faulty or dirty EGR valve
Split or collapsed hoses
Leaking valve gasket

Catalytic converter
Fume emission from exhaust

Damaged or clogged catalyst

Chapter 4 Ignition system

Contents

Specifications

Spark plugs

Make . . . .   Autolite (Motorcraft)
Type and gap:

Year and engine	Type	Gap
1965/66 – 260, 289, 289HP	BF-42	0.034 in (0.86 mm)
1967/68 – 289	BF-42	0.034 in (0.86 mm)
1967/68 – 302, 390, 427, 428	BF-32	0.034 in (0.86 mm)
1969 – 302, 351, 390	BF-42	0.034 in (0.86 mm)
1969 – 428	BF-32	0.034 in (0.86 mm)
1969 – 429 Boss	AF-32	0.035 in (0.88 mm)
1970 – 302-2V, 351-W2V, 429	BF-42	0.035 in (0.88 mm)
1970 – 302 Boss, 351-C4V	AF-32	0.035 in (0.88 mm)
1970 – 351-C2V	AF-42	0.035 in (0.88 mm)
1971/72 – 302, 351-W2V	BRF-42	0.034 in (0.86 mm)
1971/72 – 351-C4V, 351-CJ, 351 Boss, 351HO	ARF-42	0.034 in (0.86 mm)
1973 – 302, 351-W2V	BRF-42	0.034 in (0.86 mm)
1973 – 351C-2V, 351-4VCJ, 429-4V	ARF-42	0.034 in (0.86 mm)

Coil

Primary resistance . . . .   1.40 to 1.54 ohms (75°F)
Secondary resistance . . . .   7600 to 8800 ohms (75°F)
Primary circuit resistor . . . .   1.30 to 1.40 ohms (75°F)

Condenser

Capacity . . . .   0.21 to 0.25 mfd

Distributor

Type . . . .   Single or dual contact breaker
Automatic advance . . . .   Vacuum and centrifugal
Direction of rotation . . . .   Counterclockwise
Firing order:
    All except 351 engine . . . .   1 - 5 - 4 - 2 - 6 - 3 - 7 - 8
    351 engine . . . .   1 - 3 - 7 - 2 - 6 - 5 - 4 - 8

4

Characteristics

Engine	Points gap in (mm)	Dwell angle (degrees)	Initial timing (static) (degrees BTDC)	
			Manual	Auto
1965 – 260	0.015 (0.38)	27	4	4
1965 – 289	0.015 (0.38)	27	8	8
1965 – 289HP	0.020 (0.50)	27	10	–
1966 – 289	0.017 (0.43)	29	6	6
1966 – 289HP	0.020 (0.50)	31	12	–
1967 – 289	0.017 (0.43)	29	6	6
1967 – 289HP	0.020 (0.50)	32	12	12
1967 – 390	0.017 (0.43)	29	12	12
1968 – 289	0.021 (0.53)	27	6	6
1968 – 302, 390 (thermactor)	0.021 (0.53)	27	6	6
1968 – 302, 390	0.017 (0.43)	29	6	6
1968 – 390GT	0.016 (0.40)	29	6	6
1968 – 427, 428	0.017 (0.43)	29	–	6
1969 – 302	0.021 (0.53)	29	6	–
1969 – 302	0.017 (0.43)	27	–	6
1969 – 351	0.017 (0.43)	29	6	6
1969 – 390	0.017 (0.43)	29	6	–
1969 – 390	0.021 (0.53)	27	–	6
1969 – 428	0.021 (0.53)	27	6	–
1969 – 428	0.017 (0.43)	29	–	6
1969 – 429 Boss	0.020 (0.50)	30	10	10
1970 – 302	0.021 (0.53)	27	6	6
1970 – 302 Boss	0.020 (0.50)	32	16	–
1970 – 351C	0.021 (0.53)	27	6	6
1970 – 351W	0.021 (0.53)	27	10	10
1970 – 428	0.020 (0.50)	32	6	6
1970 – 429	0.021/0.017 (0.53/0.43)	27/29	10	10
1971 – 302, 351C, 351W, 351CS	0.021 (0.53)	27	6	6
1971 – 351 Boss	0.021/0.017 0.53/0.43	29/29	6	6
1971 – 429	0.020 (0.50)	28	10	10
1972 – 302, 351C	0.017 (0.43)	28	6	6
1972 – 351W	0.017 (0.43)	28	–	6
1972 – 351CJ	0.017 (0.43)	28	–	16
1972 – 351CJ	0.020 (0.50)	28	16	–
1972 – 351HO	0.020 (0.50)	28	10	–
1973 – 302, 351C2, 351C4	0.017 (0.43)	24 30	refer to decal in	
1973 – 351C4 (dual points)	0.020 (0.50)	32 35	engine compartment	

Torque wrench settings

Spark plugs:	lbf ft	kgf m
BF32, BF42, BRF42	15 to 20	2.07 to 2.76
AF32, AF42, ARF42	10 to 15	1.38 to 2.07

1 General description

In order that the engine can run correctly it is necessary for an electrical spark to ignite the fuel/air mixture in the combustion chamber at exactly the right moment in relation to engine speed and load. The ignition system is based on feeding low tension voltage from the battery to the coil where it is converted to high tension voltage. The high tension voltage is powerful enough to jump the spark plug gap in the cylinders many times a second under high compression pressures, providing that the system is in good condition and that all adjustments are correct.

The ignition system is divided into two circuits, low tension and high tension.

The low tension circuit (sometimes known as the primary) consists of the battery lead to the ignition switch, resistor lead from the ignition switch to the low tension or primary coil winding, positive terminal (+), and the lead from the low tension coil winding, negative terminal (-), to the contact breaker points and condenser in the distributor.

The high tension circuit consists of the high tension or secondary coil winding, the heavy ignition lead from the center of the coil to the center of the distributor cap, the rotor arm, the spark plug leads and spark plugs.

The system functions in the following manner. Low tension voltage is changed in the coil into high tension voltage by the opening of the contact breaker points in the low tension circuit. High tension voltage is then fed via the carbon brush in the center of the distributor cap to the rotor arm of the distributor, and each time it comes in line with one of the metal segments in the cap, which are connected to the spark plug leads, the opening of the contact breaker points causes the high tension voltage to build up, jump the gap from the rotor arm to the appropriate metal segment and so via the spark plug lead to the spark plug, where it finally jumps the spark plug gap before going to ground.

The ignition is advanced and retarded automatically, to ensure the spark occurs at just the right instant for the particular load at the prevailing engine speed.

The ignition advance is controlled both mechanically and by a vacuum-operated system. The mechanical governor comprises two weights, which move out from the distributor shaft as the engine speed rises due to centrifugal force. As they move outwards they rotate the cam relative to the distributor shaft, and so advance the spark. The weights are held in position by two light springs and it is the tension of the springs which is largely responsible for correct spark advancement.

The vacuum control consists of a diaphragm, one side of which is connected via a small bore tube to the carburetor, and the other side to the contact breaker plate. Depression in the inlet manifold and carburetor, which varies with the engine speed and throttle opening, causes the diaphragm to move, so moving the contact breaker plate, and advancing the spark. A spring within the vacuum unit returns the breaker plate to the normal position when the amount of manifold depression is reduced.

Some distributors are fitted with a dual diaphragm vacuum control unit.

The outer (primary) diaphragm senses carburetor vacuum just upstream of the throttle butterflies to advance ignition timing; the inner (secondary) diaphragm senses manifold vacuum. Therefore, when the manifold vacuum is high (eg during deceleration or idling) the secondary diaphragm retards the spark. As soon as the throttle is opened, the primary diaphragm takes control and causes the spark to advance. The purpose of this system is to decrease the emission of unburnt hydrocarbons at low throttle openings.

A dual contact breaker type distributor is fitted on high output engines to give a better high tension spark. On these models, the breaker plate is mounted on a ball bearing. Other than the dual points, these distributors are the same as the single contact breaker type.

2 Ignition system – servicing and Federal regulations

In order to conform to the Federal regulations which govern the emission of hydrocarbons and carbon monoxide from car exhaust systems, the engine, carburetion and ignition system have been suitably modified.

It is critically important that the ignition system is kept in good

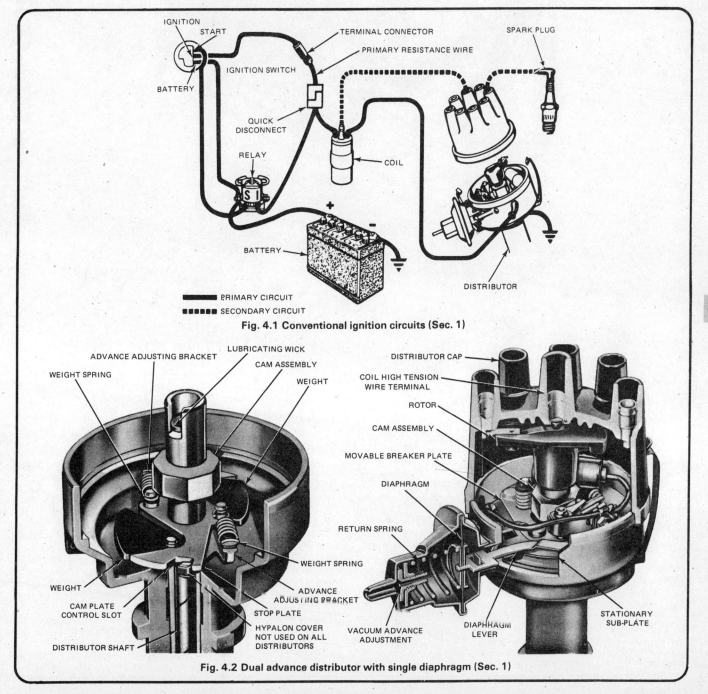

Fig. 4.1 Conventional ignition circuits (Sec. 1)

Fig. 4.2 Dual advance distributor with single diaphragm (Sec. 1)

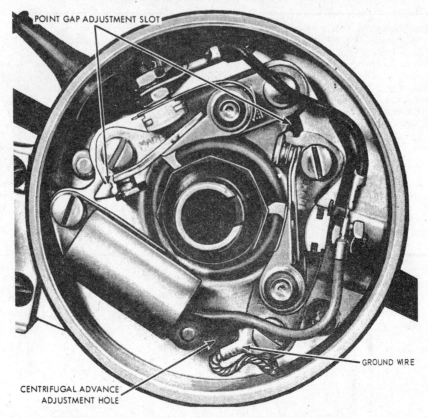

POINT GAP ADJUSTMENT SLOT

GROUND WIRE

CENTRIFUGAL ADVANCE
ADJUSTMENT HOLE

Fig. 4.3 Distributor with dual contact breaker points (Sec. 1)

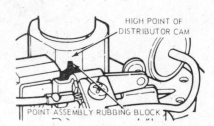

HIGH POINT OF
DISTRIBUTOR CAM

POINT ASSEMBLY RUBBING BLOCK

Fig. 4.5 Heel of breaker arm on highest
point of cam (Sec. 3)

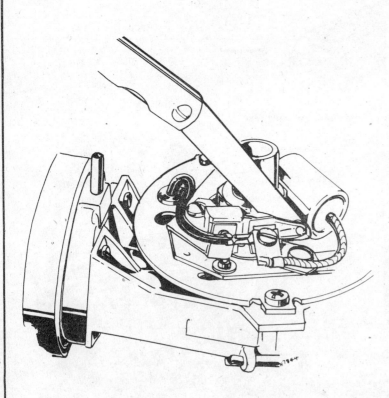

Fig. 4.4 Checking the contact breaker points gap (Sec. 3)

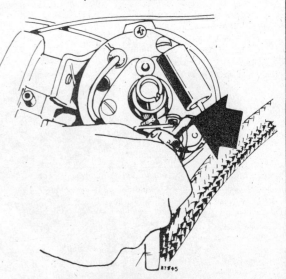

Fig. 4.6 Adjusting the breaker point gap
(Sec. 3)

operational order and to achieve this, accurate analytical equipment is needed to check and reset the distributor function. This will be found at your local dealer.

Information contained in this Chapter is supplied to enable the home mechanic to set the ignition system roughly so enabling starting of the engine. Thereafter the car must be taken to the local Ford dealer for final tuning. Failure to do this can result in heavy penalties.

3 Contact breaker points – adjustment

1   To adjust the contact breaker points to the correct gap, first release the two clips, securing the distributor cap to the distributor body, and lift away the cap. Clean the cap inside and out with a dry cloth. It is unlikely that the segments will be badly burnt or scored, but if they are the cap will have to be renewed.
2   Inspect the carbon brush contact located in the top of the cap to ensure that it is not broken and stands proud of the plastic surface.
3   Lift away the rotor arm and check the contact spring on the top of the rotor arm. It must be clean and have adequate tension to ensure good contact.
4   Gently pry the contact breaker points open to examine the condition of their faces. If they are rough, pitted or dirty it will be necessary to remove them for resurfacing, or for new points to be installed (see Section 5).
5   Presuming the points are satisfactory, or that they have been cleaned or renewed, measure the gap between the points with feeler gauges by turning the crankshaft until the heel of the breaker arm is on the highest point of the cam (Fig. 4.5). The gap should be as given in the Specifications.
6   If the gap varies from the specified amount slacken the contact plate securing screws.
7   Adjust the contact gap by inserting a screwdriver in the notched hole in the contact breaker plate. Turn clockwise to increase, and anticlockwise to decrease the gap. When the gap is correct, tighten the securing screws and check the gap again (see Fig. 4.6).
8   Install the rotor arm and distributor cap. Retain in position with the two clips.

4 Dwell angle – check and adjustment

Checking used points with a feeler gauge can result in an inaccurate gap setting, because of the roughness of the points, therefore it is better to check the dwell angle, if you have a dwell meter.
1   Connect the dwell meter according to the maker's instructions.
2   Start the engine and let it idle.
3   Read the dwell angle on the dwell meter and compare it against the figure given in Specifications at the beginning of this Chapter.
4   Switch off the engine.
5   If the dwell angle is below the specified figure, the breaker point gap is too large. If the dwell angle is above the specified figure, the breaker point gap is too small.
6   If necessary, adjust the breaker point gap as described in Section 3.
7   On dual breaker distributors, adjust the dwell on each set separately to get the specified combined dwell. Disconnect the wire to one set of points while adjusting the other or alternatively insert a piece of plastic between the points of one set to take it out of circuit.
8   Remove the dwell meter.

5 Contact breaker points – removal and installation

1   If the contact breaker points are burnt, pitted or badly worn they must be removed and renewed.
2   Lift off the rotor arm by pulling it straight up from the spindle.
3   Slacken the sheet metal screw that secures the condenser and low tension lead to the contact breaker point assembly. Slide out the forked ends of the lead terminals.
4   Undo and remove the two screws that secure the contact breaker points base plate to the distributor base plate. Lift away the points assembly.
5   To install the points is the reverse sequence to removal. Smear a trace of grease onto the cam to lubricate the moving point heel, and

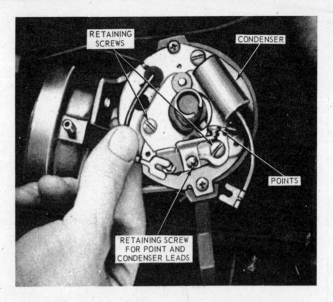

Fig. 4.7 Removing contact breaker points (Sec. 5)

then reset the gap, as described in Section 3 or 4.
6   Should the contact breaker points be badly worn, a new set must be installed. As an emergency measure clean the faces with fine emery paper folded over a thin steel rule. It is necessary to rub the points right down to the stage where all the pitting has disappeared. When the surfaces are flat a feeler gauge can be used to reset the gap.
7   Finally, install the rotor arm and distributor cap. Retain in position with the two clips.

6 Condenser – removal, testing and installation

1   The condenser is installed in parallel with the contact breaker points. If it develops a fault, it will cause ignition failure as the contact breaker points will be prevented from correctly interrupting the low tension circuit.
2   If the engine becomes very difficult to start, or begins to misfire and the breaker points show signs of excessive burning, then the condition of the condenser must be suspect. One further test can be made by separating the points by hand with the ignition switched on. If this is accompanied by a bright flash, it is indicative that the condenser has failed.
3   Without special test equipment the only safe way to diagnose condenser trouble is to replace a suspected unit with a new one and note if there is any improvement.
4   To remove the condenser from the distributor take off the distributor cap and rotor arm.
5   Slacken the nut holding the condenser lead and low tension lead to the contact breaker points. Slide out the forked terminal on the end of the condenser low tension lead. Undo and remove the condenser retaining screw and remove the condenser from the breaker plate.
6   To install the condenser, simply reverse the order of removal.

7 Distributor – lubrication

1   It is important that the distributor cam is lubricated with petroleum jelly or grease at 6000 miles (10 000 km) or 6 monthly intervals. Also the automatic timing control weights and cam spindle are lubricated with engine oil.
2   Great care should be taken not to use too much lubricant as any excess that finds its way onto the contact breaker points could cause burning and misfiring.
3   To gain access to the cam spindle, lift away the distributor cap and rotor arm. Apply no more than two drops of engine oil onto the felt pad. This will run down the spindle when the engine is hot and lubricate the bearings.
4   To lubricate the automatic timing control allow a few drops of oil

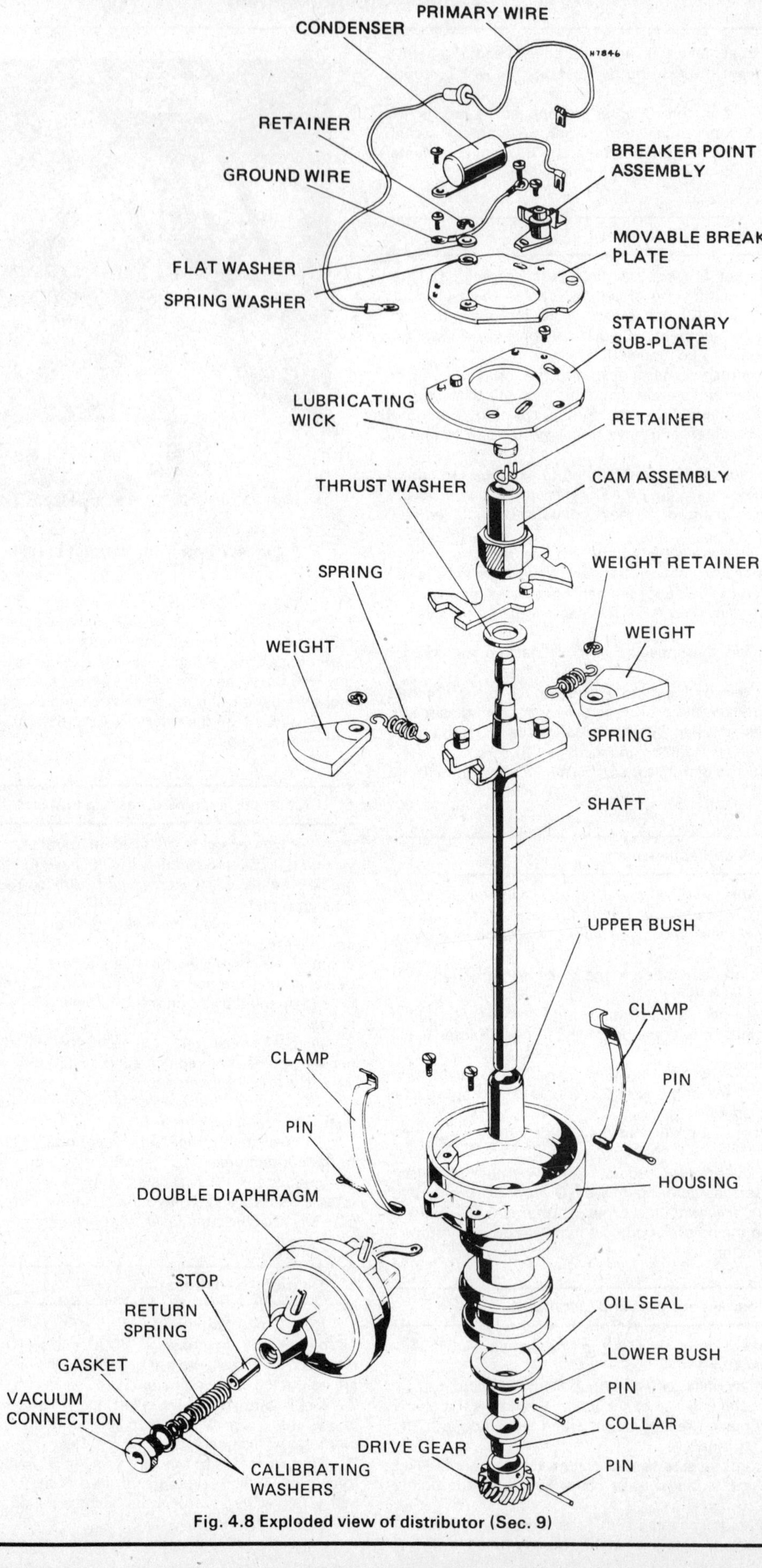

PRIMARY WIRE

CONDENSER

RETAINER

GROUND WIRE

BREAKER POINT
ASSEMBLY

MOVABLE BREAKER
PLATE

FLAT WASHER

SPRING WASHER

STATIONARY
SUB-PLATE

LUBRICATING
WICK

RETAINER

THRUST WASHER

CAM ASSEMBLY

SPRING

WEIGHT RETAINER

WEIGHT

WEIGHT

SPRING

SHAFT

UPPER BUSH

CLAMP

CLAMP

PIN

PIN

DOUBLE DIAPHRAGM

HOUSING

STOP

RETURN
SPRING

OIL SEAL

GASKET

LOWER BUSH

VACUUM
CONNECTION

PIN

COLLAR

DRIVE GEAR

PIN

CALIBRATING
WASHERS

Fig. 4.8 Exploded view of distributor (Sec. 9)

to pass through the holes in the contact breaker base plate through which the eight sided cam emerges. Apply not more than one drop of oil to the pivot post of the moving contact breaker point. Wipe away excess oil and install the rotor arm and distributor cap.

8 Distributor – removal and installation

1 Remove the air cleaner as described in Chapter 3.
2 Release the two spring clips, and remove the distributor cap and place it to one side.
3 Disconnect the primary wire from the coil and the vacuum advance line(s) at the distributor.
4 Scribe a mark on the distributor body and the cylinder block, to indicate the position of the distributor in the block, and also mark the position of the rotor on the top edge of the distributor body.
5 Remove the distributor clamp bolt and lift out the distributor.
Note: *Do not rotate the crankshaft while the distributor is removed or it will be necessary to time the engine as described in Section 13.*
6 To install the distributor insert it in the engine block, ensuring that the previously scribed marks are aligned and that the rotor is in exactly the same position it was in before the distributor was removed.
7 Install the clamp and securing bolt.
8 Reconnect the primary wire and the vacuum line(s).
9 Install the distributor cap and air cleaner.

9 Distributor – dismantling

1 Remove the condenser and contact breaker assembly, as described in Sections 5 and 6.
2 Using a small screwdriver, remove the C-clip retaining the vacuum advance link to the moveable breaker plate (not applicable with dual points).
3 Undo and remove the two screws retaining the vacuum advance unit and carefully remove the unit (with dual points, pull the unit straight out and tilt the link downward to unhook it).
4 Remove the retaining screws and lift out the breaker plate and sub-plate.
5 Mark one of the distributor centrifugal weight springs and its bracket. Also mark one of the weights and its pivot.
6 Carefully unhook and remove the weight springs.
7 Lift the lubricating wick from the cam assembly. Remove the spring clip retainer and lift the cam assembly off the distributor shaft. Remove the thrust washer.
8 Remove the retaining clip from the pivots and lift off the weights.

10 Distributor – inspection

1 Check the contact breaker points for wear, as described in Section 3. Check the distributor cap for signs of tracking indicated by a thin black line between the segments. Renew the cap if any signs of tracking are found.
2 If the metal portion of the rotor arm is badly burnt or loose, renew the arm. If only slightly burnt, clean the end with a fine file. Check that the contact spring has adequate pressure and the bearing surface is clean and in good condition.
3 Check that the carbon brush in the distributor cap is unbroken and stands proud of its holder.
4 Examine the centrifugal weights and pivots for wear and the advance springs for slackness. They can best be checked by comparing with new parts. If they are slack they must be renewed.
5 Check the points assembly for fit on the breaker plate, and the cam follower for wear.
6 Examine the fit of the spindle in the distributor body. If there is excessive side movement it will be necessary to either install a new bush or obtain a new distributor body.

11 Distributor – reassembly

1 Lubricate the weight pivots. Install the weights in the correct position (the marked weight on the marked pivot) and secure with the retaining clips.
2 Install the thrust washer on the shaft.

3 Lubricate the upper part of the distributor shaft and install the cam assembly. Ensure that the marked spring bracket on the cam assembly is near the marked spring bracket on the sub-plate.
4 Install the cam assembly retaining clip and the oil wick.
5 Install the weight springs with the marked spring attached to the marked bracket.
6 Install the plate assembly into the distributor body ensuring that the retaining screw holes line up. Install the retaining screws.
7 Position the vacuum advance unit on the distributor body (with dual points hook the diaphragm link in position) and install the spring clip that secures the diaphragm link to the moveable breaker plate (not dual points). Install the vacuum advance unit retaining screws.
8 Install the contact breaker points but do not tighten the securing screws.
9 Install the condenser and primary wire.
10 Adjust the contact breaker points as described in Section 3.

12 Spark plugs and HT leads

1 The correct functioning of the spark plugs is vital for the correct running and efficiency of the engine.
2 At intervals of 6000 miles the plugs should be removed, examined, cleaned, and if worn excessively, renewed. The condition of the spark plugs will also tell much about the overall condition of the engine (see illustration on page 99).
3 If the insulator nose of the spark plug is clean and white, with no deposits, this is indicative of a lean mixture, or too hot a plug. (A hot plug transfers heat away from the electrode slowly – a cold plug transfers it away quickly).
4 The plugs installed as standard are as listed in Specifications at the beginning of this Chapter. If the tip and insulator nose are covered with hard black looking deposits, then this is indicative that the mixture is too rich. Should the plug be black and oily, then it is likely that the engine is fairly worn, as well as the mixture being too rich.
5 If the insulator nose is covered with light tan to greyish brown deposits, then the mixture is correct and it is likely that the engine is in good condition.
6 If there are any traces of long brown tapering stains on the outside of the white portion of the plug, then the plug will have to be renewed, as this shows that there is a faulty joint between the plug body and the insulator, and compression is being allowed to leak away.
7 Plugs should be cleaned by a sand blasting machine, which will free them from carbon more thoroughly than cleaning by hand. The machine will also test the condition of the plugs under compression. Any plug that fails to spark at the recommended pressure should be renewed.
8 The spark plug gap is of considerable importance as, if it is too large or too small, the size of the spark and its efficiency will be seriously impaired. The spark plug gap should be set to the figure given in Specifications at the beginning of this Chapter.
9 To set it, measure the gap with a feeler gauge, and then bend open, or close, the outer plug electrode until the correct gap is achieved. The center electrode should never be bent as this may crack the insulator and cause plug failure if nothing worse.
10 When installing the plugs, remember to use new plug washers, and connect the leads from the distributor in the correct firing order.
11 The plug wires require no routine attention other than being kept clean and wiped over regularly.
12 At intervals of 6000 miles, however, pull the wires off the plugs and distributor one at a time and make sure no water has found its way onto the connections. Remove any corrosion from the brass ends, wipe the collars on top of the distributor, and reconnect the wires.

13 Initial (static) ignition timing

1 If the engine has been rotated with the distributor removed, it will be necessary to re-time the ignition.
2 Refer to the Specifications at the beginning of this Chapter for the initial advance (static) timing.
3 Turn the engine until No 1 piston is coming up to TDC on the compression stroke. This can be checked by removing No 1 spark plug and feeling the pressure being developed in the cylinder. If this check is not made it is all too easy to set the timing 180° out. The engine can most

easily be turned by engaging top gear and edging the car along (except automatic).

4   Continue turning the engine until the appropriate timing mark on the crankshaft pulley is in line with the pointer (Fig. 4.9).

5   Now, with the distributor and the rotor arm in the same position as was noted before removal, insert the distributor into its location. Note that the rotor arm rotates as the gears mesh. Lift out the distributor far enough to rotate the shaft one tooth at a time, lowering it home to check the direction of the rotor arm. When it points in the desired direction with assembly fully home, install the distributor clamp plate, bolt and washer. Do not fully tighten yet.

6   Gently turn the distributor body until the contact breaker points are just opening when the rotor is pointing to the contact in the distributor cap which is connected to No 1 spark plug. A convenient way is to put a mark on the outside of the distributor body in line with the segment in the cover, so that it shows when the cover is removed.

7   If this position cannot be reached, check that the drivegear has meshed on the correct tooth by lifting out the distributor once more. If necessary, rotate the driveshaft gear one tooth and try again.

8   Tighten the distributor body clamp enough to hold the distributor, but do not overtighten.

9   If a stroboscopic timing light is used for a final ignition check, clean the timing scale on the damper pulley and mark the specified degree line and the tip of the pointer with quick drying white paint or with chalk.

10 Disconnect the vacuum hose(s) from the vacuum unit and plug them with a pencil or similar item.

11 Run the engine to normal operating temperature and check that the idling speed is correct (see Chapter 3).

12 Connect the timing light between No 1 spark plug and the spark plug wire.

13 Start the engine and point the timing light at the white painted marks. They will appear stationary and if the timing is correct they will be in alignment.

14 If they are not directly opposite each other, adjust by loosening the distributor body clamp and turning the distributor housing as necessary to line-up the marks. The timing is advanced when the distributor is turned clockwise and retarded when turned counterclockwise. Tighten the clamp and recheck the timing.

15 If the engine speed is now increased the white mark on the pulley will move away from the fixed pointer, indicating that the centrifugal advance is operating. If the vacuum hose(s) are unplugged and reconnected to the vacuum unit the operation of the vacuum unit can be checked by revving up the engine and watching the timing marks.

16 Remove the timing light and reconnect the HT wire to the spark plug.

17 As a final check, take the car to a Ford service station which will have the proper equipment to correctly set the timing in relation to the fuel and emission control systems installed on the car, particularly on later models.

14 Distributor modulator – general

1   From 1970 some models are equipped with a distributor modulator system to reduce engine emissions by control of the distributor spark advance. It consists of four major components: a speed sensor, a thermal switch, an electronic control amplifier and a three-way solenoid valve controlling vacuum applied to the distributor.

2   When loss of engine performance and excessive fuel consumption is experienced with symptoms of retarded ignition timing, the modulator system must be checked. This is a job for a Ford service station with the necessary test equipment (Fig. 4.12).

15 Fault diagnosis – ignition system

By far the majority of breakdown and running troubles are caused by faults in the ignition system, either in the low tension or high tension circuits.

There are two main symptoms indicating faults. Either the engine will not start or fire, or the engine is difficult to start and misfires. If it is a regular misfire, (ie the engine is running on only six or seven cylinders), the fault is almost sure to be in the secondary or high tension circuit. If the misfiring is intermittent the fault could be in either the high or low tension circuits. If the car stops suddenly, or will

Fig. 4.9 Timing marks (Sec. 13)

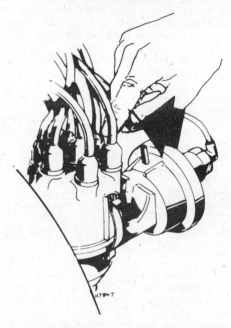

Fig. 4.10 Plugging the vacuum line (Sec. 13)

Fig. 4.11 Checking the timing with a timing light (Sec. 13)

not start at all, it is likely that the fault is in the low tension circuit. Loss of power and overheating, apart from faulty carburetion settings, are normally due to faults in the distributor or to incorrect ignition timing.

Engine fails to start

1   If the engine fails to start and the car was running normally when it was last used, first check there is fuel in the fuel tank. If the engine turns over normally on the starter motor and the battery is evidently

Common spark plug conditions

NORMAL
Symptoms: Brown to grayish-tan color and slight electrode wear. Correct heat range for engine and operating conditions.
Recommendation: When new spark plugs are installed, replace with plugs of the same heat range.

WORN
Symptoms: Rounded electrodes with a small amount of deposits on the firing end. Normal color. Causes hard starting in damp or cold weather and poor fuel economy.
Recommendation: Plugs have been left in the engine too long. Replace with new plugs of the same heat range. Follow the recommended maintenance schedule.

CARBON DEPOSITS
Symptoms: Dry sooty deposits indicate a rich mixture or weak ignition. Causes misfiring, hard starting and hesitation.
Recommendation: Make sure the plug has the correct heat range. Check for a clogged air filter or problem in the fuel system or engine management system. Also check for ignition system problems.

ASH DEPOSITS
Symptoms: Light brown deposits encrusted on the side or center electrodes or both. Derived from oil and/or fuel additives. Excessive amounts may mask the spark, causing misfiring and hesitation during acceleration.
Recommendation: If excessive deposits accumulate over a short time or low mileage, install new valve guide seals to prevent seepage of oil into the combustion chambers. Also try changing gasoline brands.

OIL DEPOSITS
Symptoms: Oily coating caused by poor oil control. Oil is leaking past worn valve guides or piston rings into the combustion chamber. Causes hard starting, misfiring and hesitation.
Recommendation: Correct the mechanical condition with necessary repairs and install new plugs.

GAP BRIDGING
Symptoms: Combustion deposits lodge between the electrodes. Heavy deposits accumulate and bridge the electrode gap. The plug ceases to fire, resulting in a dead cylinder.
Recommendation: Locate the faulty plug and remove the deposits from between the electrodes.

TOO HOT
Symptoms: Blistered, white insulator, eroded electrode and absence of deposits. Results in shortened plug life.
Recommendation: Check for the correct plug heat range, over-advanced ignition timing, lean fuel mixture, intake manifold vacuum leaks, sticking valves and insufficient engine cooling.

PREIGNITION
Symptoms: Melted electrodes. Insulators are white, but may be dirty due to misfiring or flying debris in the combustion chamber. Can lead to engine damage.
Recommendation: Check for the correct plug heat range, over-advanced ignition timing, lean fuel mixture, insufficient engine cooling and lack of lubrication.

HIGH SPEED GLAZING
Symptoms: Insulator has yellowish, glazed appearance. Indicates that combustion chamber temperatures have risen suddenly during hard acceleration. Normal deposits melt to form a conductive coating. Causes misfiring at high speeds.
Recommendation: Install new plugs. Consider using a colder plug if driving habits warrant.

DETONATION
Symptoms: Insulators may be cracked or chipped. Improper gap setting techniques can also result in a fractured insulator tip. Can lead to piston damage.
Recommendation: Make sure the fuel anti-knock values meet engine requirements. Use care when setting the gaps on new plugs. Avoid lugging the engine.

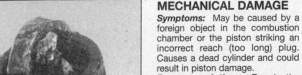

MECHANICAL DAMAGE
Symptoms: May be caused by a foreign object in the combustion chamber or the piston striking an incorrect reach (too long) plug. Causes a dead cylinder and could result in piston damage.
Recommendation: Repair the mechanical damage. Remove the foreign object from the engine and/or install the correct reach plug.

4

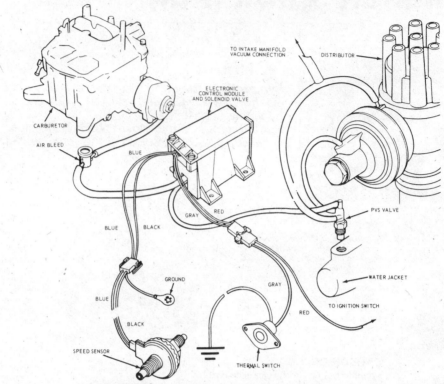

CARBURETOR

AIR BLEED

TO INTAKE MANIFOLD
VACUUM CONNECTION

DISTRIBUTOR

ELECTRONIC
CONTROL MODULE
AND SOLENOID VALVE

BLUE

BLUE   BLACK

GRAY   RED

PVS VALVE

BLUE

GROUND

GRAY

WATER JACKET

BLACK

RED

TO IGNITION SWITCH

SPEED SENSOR

THERMAL SWITCH

Fig. 4.12 Distributor modulator system – schematic (Sec. 14)

well charged, then the fault may be in either the high or low tension circuits. First check the HT circuit. **Note**: *If the battery is known to be fully charged, the ignition light comes on, and the starter motor fails to turn the engine* **check the tightness of the leads on the battery terminals** *and also the security of the ground lead at its* **connection to the body.** *It is quite common for the leads to have worked loose, even if they look and feel secure. If one of the battery terminal posts gets very hot when trying to work the starter motor, this is a sure indication of a faulty connection to that terminal.*

2   One of the most common reasons for bad starting is wet or damp spark plug leads and distributor cap. Remove the distributor cap. If condensation is visible internally dry the cap with a rag and also wipe over the leads. Install the cap.

3   If the engine still fails to start, check that voltage is reaching the plugs by disconnecting each plug lead in turn at the spark plug end, and holding the end of the cable about $\frac{3}{16}$ in (5 mm) away from the cylinder block. Spin the engine on the starter motor.

4   Sparking between the end of the cable and the block should be fairly strong with a strong regular blue spark. (Hold the lead with rubber glove or a thick dry cloth to avoid electric shocks). If voltage is reaching the plugs, remove them, and clean and regap them. The engine should now start.

5   If there is no spark at the plug leads, take off the HT leads from the center of the distributor cap and hold it to the block as before. Spin the engine on the starter once more. A rapid succession of blue sparks between the end of the lead and the block indicate that the coil is in order and that the distributor cap is cracked, the rotor arm is faulty, or the carbon brush in the top of the distributor cap is not making good contact with the spring on the rotor arm. Possibly, the points are in bad condition. Clean and reset them as described in Section 3.

6   If there are no sparks from the end of the lead from the coil, check the connections at the coil end of the lead. If it is in order start checking the low tension circuit.

7   Use a 12V voltmeter or a 12V bulb and two lengths of wire. With the ignition switched on and the points open, test between the low tension wire to the coil (it is marked 15 or +) and ground. No reading indicates a break in the supply from the ignition switch. Check the connections at the switch to see if any are loose. Reconnect them and the engine should run. A reading shows a faulty coil or condenser, or broken lead between the coil and the distributor.

8   Take the condenser wire off the points assembly and with the points open test between the moving point and ground. If there now is

a reading then the fault is in the condenser. Install a new one and the fault is cleared.

9   With no reading from the moving point to ground, take a reading between ground and the - or 1 terminal of the coil. A reading here shows a broken wire which will need to be renewed between the coil and distributor. No reading confirms that the coil has failed and must be renewed, after which the engine will run once more. Remember to reconnect the condenser wire to the points assembly. For these tests it is sufficient to separate the points with a piece of dry paper while testing with the points open.

Engine misfires

10   If the engine misfires regularly, run it at a fast idling speed. Pull off each of the plug caps in turn and listen to the note of the engine. Hold the plug cap in a dry cloth or rubber glove as additional protection against a shock from the HT supply.

11   No difference in engine running will be noticed when the lead from the defective circuit is removed. Removing the lead from one of the good cylinders will accentuate the misfire.

12   Remove it about $\frac{3}{16}$ in (5 mm) away from the block. Re-start the engine. If the sparking is fairly strong and regular, the fault must lie in the spark plug.

13   The plug may be loose, the insulation may be cracked, or the points may have burnt away giving too wide a gap for the spark to jump. Worse still, one of the points may have broken off. Either renew the plug, or clean it, reset the gap, and then test it.

14   If there is no spark at the end of the plug lead, or if it is weak and intermittent, check the ignition lead from the distributor to the plug. If the insulation is cracked or perished, renew the lead. Check the connections at the distributor cap.

15   If there is still no spark, examine the distributor cap carefully for tracking. This can be recognised by a very thin black line running between two or more electrodes, or between an electrode and some other part of the distributor. These lines are paths which now conduct electricity across the cap thus letting it run to ground. The only answer is a new distributor cap.

16   If the ignition timing is too far retarded, it should be noted that the engine will tend to overheat, and there will be a quite noticeable drop in power. If the engine is overheating and the power is down, and the ignition timing is correct, then the carburetor should be checked, as it is likely that this is where the fault lies.

Chapter 5 Clutch

Contents

Specifications

Type	Single dry disc

Clutch adjustments

Clutch pedal free-play (engine running)	0.875 to 1.125 in (22 to 28.5 mm)
Release lever rod adjusting nut-to-swivel sleeve clearance:	
1966	0.128 in (3.25 mm)
1967 through 68	0.206 in (5.23 mm)
1969 through 71, 390 and 428 engines	0.178 in (4.52 mm)
1969 through 71, all other engines	0.136 in (3.45 mm)
1972 through 73	0.194 in (4.92 mm)

Torque wrench settings

	lbf ft	kgf m
Flywheel housing-to-engine bolt	40 to 50	5.5 to 6.9
Pressure plate and cover assembly-to-flywheel bolt	12 to 20	1.6 to 2.7

1 General description

The centrifugal single dry disc type clutch, consisting of the clutch disc, pressure plate and clutch release bearing, is actuated by a pedal and mechanical linkage.

When the clutch pedal is in the engaged position, the clutch disc is clamped between the friction surface of the engine flywheel and the face of the clutch pressure plate by the pressure of the pressure plate springs, and thus drive from the engine is transmitted to the transmission through the clutch disc which is splined to the transmission input shaft. Friction lining material is riveted to the clutch disc and the splined hub is spring-cushioned to absorb transmission shocks.

When the clutch pedal is depressed the clutch release lever moves the release bearing against the clutch fingers, which in turn, moves the pressure plate away from the clutch disc, dis-engaging the clutch and disconnecting the drive to the transmission.

2 Clutch pedal free-play – adjustment

The clutch pedal adjustment must be checked whenever the clutch does not disengage or engage properly, or when new clutch parts are installed. Incorrect pedal free-play will result in clutch friction.

1965 models

1   Measure the amount of free-play at the clutch pedal; it should be between 0.875 in (22 mm) and 1.125 in (28.5 mm).
2   If necessary, adjust the clutch pedal-to-equalizer rod. To increase the amount of free-play, loosen the rear adjusting nut and tighten front nut. To reduce the free-play, loosen the front nut and tighten the rear nut.
3   After obtaining the specified free-play tighten both nuts against the trunnion.
4   Finally, check that the pedal free-play, with the engine running at 3000 rpm, is 0.50 in (12.7 mm). If necessary, re-adjust the clutch

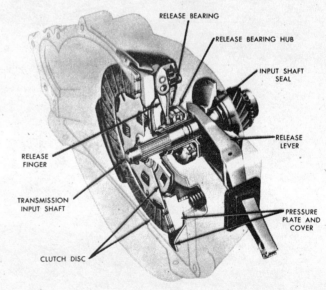

Fig. 5.1 Cutaway view of clutch assembly (Sec. 1)

pedal-to-equalizer rod to obtain the exact free-play of the clutch pedal.

1966 through 1973 models

5   Disconnect the clutch return spring from the release lever.
6   Loosen the release lever rod locknut and adjusting nut.
7   Move the clutch release lever rearward until the release bearing lightly contacts the clutch pressure plate release fingers.
8   Adjust the rod length until the rod seats in the release lever pocket.

5

9   Insert a feeler gauge between the adjusting nut and the swivel sleeve, then tighten the adjusting nut, finger-tight, against the gauge. The specified thickness of feeler gauge, according to model, is given in Specifications at the beginning of this Chapter.

10 Tighten the locknut against the adjusting nut, taking care not to disturb the adjustment.

11 Install the clutch return spring.

12 Operate the clutch pedal to actuate the clutch mechanism at least five times, then re-check the free-play setting with the specified feeler gauge. Re-adjust if necessary.

13 As a final check, measure the pedal free-play with the engine running at approximately 3000 rpm. If the pedal free-play is not at least 0.50 in (12.7 mm), re-adjust the pedal free-play. Failure to ensure this minimum amount of pedal free travel will result in premature release bearing and clutch failure.

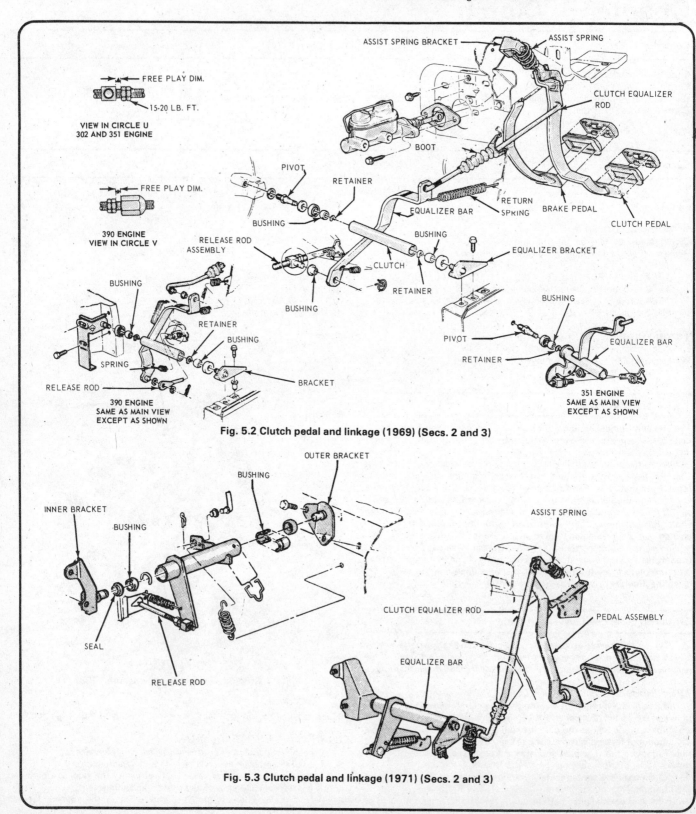

Fig. 5.2 Clutch pedal and linkage (1969) (Secs. 2 and 3)

Fig. 5.3 Clutch pedal and linkage (1971) (Secs. 2 and 3)

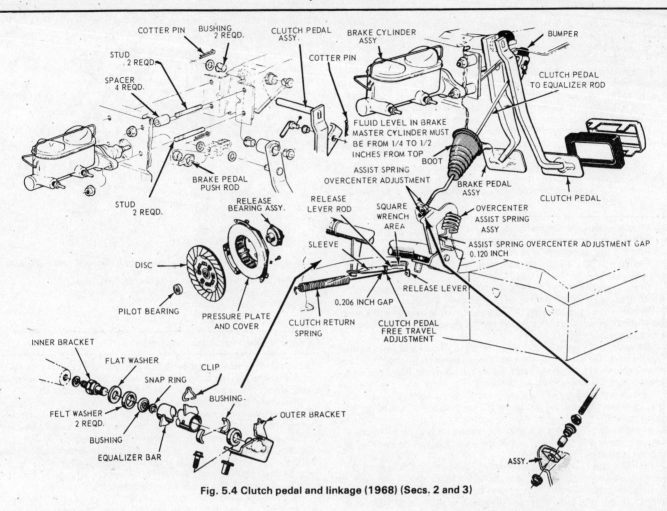

Fig. 5.4 Clutch pedal and linkage (1968) (Secs. 2 and 3)

3 Clutch pedal – removal and installation

Models through 1968

1 Depress the clutch pedal and insert a 0.25 in (6.3 mm) spacer in the assist spring adjustment gap.

2 Remove the equalizer rod-to-clutch pedal securing pin and disconnect the rod from the clutch pedal.

3 Disconnect the brake pedal pushrod from the brake pedal.

4 Remove the retaining clip from the end of the clutch pedal shaft, then remove the shaft, bushings, clutch pedal and brake pedal from the support.

5 Installation is the reverse of removal procedure. Lubricate the bushings with engine oil before assembly. Adjust the clutch pedal free-play as described in Section 2.

Models from 1969

6 Disconnect the battery ground cable.

7 Remove the steering column as described in Chapter 11.

8 Remove the two capscrews attaching the brake master cylinder or booster to the dash panel, then the two screws securing the pedal support bracket to the dash panel.

9 Working inside the car, disconnect the clutch pedal-to-equalizer rod at the clutch pedal by removing the retainer and bushing.

10 Secure the clutch pedal against the bumper stop with a small C-clamp.

11 Disconnect the stoplight switch at the connector.

12 Remove the switch retainer and slide the stoplight switch off the brake pedal pin just far enough for the switch outer hole to clear the pin. Now lower the switch away from the pin.

13 Remove the master cylinder pushrod, bushing and nylon washer from the brake pedal pin.

14 Remove the screw securing the pedal support bracket to the top

inner cowl bracket (see Fig. 5.5), and the two screws securing it to the dash panel.

15 Remove the two screws securing the pedal support bracket to the upper cowl brace, then lower it away from the steering column studs and remove it from the car.

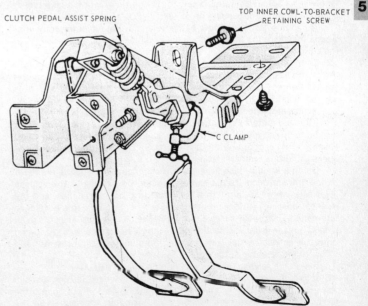

Fig. 5.5 Removing the clutch pedal (Sec. 3)

16 Mount the bracket in a vise and remove the small C-clamp, then slowly pivot the clutch pedal away from the bumper until the assist spring can be lifted from its seat (1969 through 1971 models).

17 On 1972/1973 models pivot the pedal away from the bumper until it comes to rest on the opposite flange on the brake pedal support bracket, then remove the forward bolt securing the assist spring bracket to the support. Using an adjustable wrench, hold the assist spring bracket and slowly pivot the bracket away from the spring until it can be lifted from its seat.

18 Remove the retaining clip from the clutch pedal shaft then withdraw the clutch pedal shaft assembly and bushings from the pedal support bracket.

19 Installation is the reverse of the removal procedure. Lubricate the bushings before installing them in the brake and clutch pedal assemblies. Adjust the clutch pedal free-play as described in Section 2.

4 Clutch – removal and installation

1 Remove the transmission as described in Chapter 6.

2 Disconnect the clutch release lever retaining spring from the release lever.

3 Disconnect the starter motor cable, then remove the starter motor attaching bolts and lift away the starter motor.

4 Remove the bolts securing the engine rear plate to the front lower part of the flywheel housing. Remove the flywheel housing lower cover (if so equipped).

5 Remove the flywheel housing securing bolts and move the housing back just far enough to clear the pressure plate, then move it to the right to free the pivot from the clutch equalizer bar. Take care not to disturb the linkage and assist spring.

6 Unscrew the six pressure plate cover securing bolts one turn at a time, to prevent distortion of the cover assembly, when releasing the spring tension.

7 If the same pressure plate and cover assembly is to be re-installed, mark the cover and flywheel so that the assembly can be installed in its original position.

8 Remove the clutch cover assembly and the clutch disc from the flywheel. Make a note of which way round the clutch disc is installed.

9 It is important that no oil or grease gets on the clutch disc friction linings, or the pressure plate and flywheel faces. It is advisable to handle the parts with clean hands and to wipe down the pressure plate and flywheel faces with a clean dry rag before installing the clutch cover assembly.

10 Place the clutch disc and pressure plate assembly in position on the flywheel. If the same assembly is being re-installed, align the matching marks made at removal, and install the securing bolts. Tighten the bolts alternately a few turns at a time until the clutch disc is gripped lightly but can still be moved.

11 The clutch disc must now be centered so that when the transmission is installed, the input shaft splines will pass through the splines in the clutch disc hub.

12 Centering can be carried out by inserting a screwdriver through the clutch assembly and moving the clutch disc as necessary to obtain correct centering. Alternatively, if an old input shaft is available, this can be used as an arbor to center the disc; this will eliminate all guesswork and achieve more accurate centering of the clutch disc.

13 After the clutch disc has been located correctly, tighten the securing bolts in an even and diagonal sequence to ensure the cover assembly is secured without distortion. Tighten the bolts to the specified torque wrench setting.

14 Using a lithium base grease, lightly lubricate the outside diameter of the transmission front bearing retainer, both sides of the release lever fork where it contacts the release bearing spring clips, and the release bearing surface that contacts the pressure plate release fingers. Fill the grease groove in the release bearing hub, then clean all excess grease from inside the bore, otherwise grease will be forced onto the splines by the transmission input shaft bearing retainer and will contaminate the clutch disc.

15 Install the release bearing and hub on the release lever.

16 Install the felt washer on the pivot in the flywheel housing and slip the pivot into the clutch equalizer shaft, taking care not to disturb the linkage; at the same time locate the housing on the dowels in the cylinder block. Install the securing bolts and tighten them to the specified torque.

17 Install the starter motor and connect the cable.

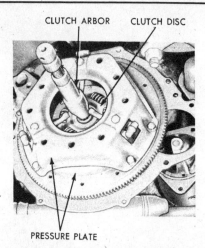

CLUTCH ARBOR   CLUTCH DISC

PRESSURE PLATE

Fig. 5.6 Centering the clutch disc using a special arbor (Sec. 4)

18 Install the transmission as described in Chapter 6.

19 Check and, if necessary, adjust the clutch pedal free-play as described in Section 2.

5 Clutch – inspection and renovation

1 Examine the machined faces of the flywheel and the pressure plate for scores, ridges or burn marks. Minor defects can be removed by machining. If badly scored or burnt, they must be renewed.

2 Check the wear on the clutch fingers; if there is a considerable difference in wear between the fingers, the excessively worn finger is binding and the pressure plate assembly must be renewed. Check the pressure plate for warpage using a steel rule as shown in Fig. 5.8.

3 Lubricate the pressure plate, with grease, between the driving lugs and the edges of the pressure plate openings as shown in Fig. 5.9. Depress the pressure plate fingers fully, apply the grease, and then move the fingers up and down until the grease is worked in.

4 Examine the clutch disc for worn or loose facings, distortion, loose nuts at the hub, and for broken springs. If any of these defects exist then the clutch disc must be renewed.

5 Wipe all oil and dirt off the release bearing; it is pre-lubricated and should not be cleaned with solvent. Inspect the bearing retainer for loose spring clips and rivets. Hold the bearing inner race and rotate the outer race. If it is rough or noisy, renew the bearing.

6 Pilot bush – renewal

1 If the pilot bush is worn or loose in the crankshaft bore it must be renewed.

2 The old bush can be removed by using a round bar that is a close fit in the bush. Fill the bush with grease and then drive the bar into the bush, this will hydraulically drive the bush out of the crankshaft bore.

3 Soak the new bush for at least half an hour in engine oil before installing it in the crankshaft bore.

4 Use a suitable diameter stepped mandrel which will ensure that the bush is not distorted or damaged when being driven in.

5 Wipe off all excess oil. Do not lubricate the bush with grease of any type.

7 Fault diagnosis – clutch

1 There are four main faults to which the clutch and release mechanism are prone. They may occur by themselves, or in conjunction with any of the other faults. They are clutch squeal, slip, spin and judder.

Clutch squeal

2 If on taking up the drive or when changing gear, the clutch squeals, this is indicative of a badly worn clutch release bearing.

3 As well as regular wear due to normal use, wear of the clutch release bearing is much accentuated if the clutch is ridden or held

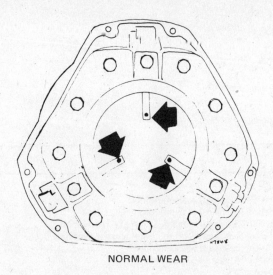

NORMAL WEAR

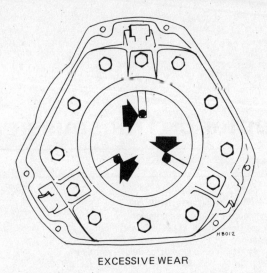

EXCESSIVE WEAR

Fig. 5.7 Checking the clutch fingers for wear (Sec. 5)

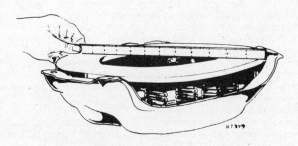

Fig. 5.8 Checking the pressure plate for warpage (Sec. 5)

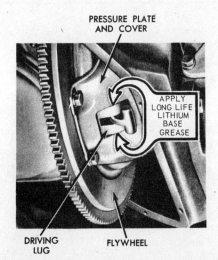

PRESSURE PLATE
AND COVER

APPLY
LONG LIFE
LITHIUM
BASE
GREASE

DRIVING
LUG

FLYWHEEL

Fig. 5.9 Pressure plate lubrication points (Sec. 5)

down for long periods in gear, with the engine running. To minimise wear of this component the car should always be taken out of gear at traffic lights and for similar traffic hold ups.

4   The clutch release bearing is not an expensive item but difficult to get at.

Clutch slip

5   Clutch slip is a self-evident condition which occurs when the clutch friction plate is badly worn, oil or grease have got onto the

flywheel or pressure plate faces, or the pressure plate itself is faulty.

6   The reason for clutch slip is that due to one of the faults above, there is insufficient pressure from the pressure plate, or insufficient friction from the friction plate to ensure solid drive.

7   If small amounts of oil get onto the clutch, they will be burnt off under the heat of the clutch engagement, and in the process, gradually darken the linings. Excessive oil on the clutch will burn off leaving a carbon deposit which can cause quite bad clutch slip, or fierceness, spin and judder.

8   If clutch slip is suspected, and confirmation of this condition is required, there are several tests which can be made.

9   With the engine in second or third gear and pulling lightly, sudden depression of the accelerator pedal may cause the engine to increase its speed without any increase in road speed. Easing off on the accelerator will then give a definite drop in engine speed without the car slowing.

10 In extreme cases of clutch slip the engine will race under normal acceleration conditions.

Clutch spin

11   Clutch spin is a condition which occurs when there is an obstruction in the clutch linkage, incorrect release bearing clearance, or oil may have partially burnt off the clutch lining and have left a resinous deposit which is causing the clutch disc to stick to the pressure plate or flywheel. The disc may also be sticking on the input shaft splines.

12 The reason for clutch spin is that due to any, or a combination of, the faults just listed, the clutch pressure plate is not completely freeing from the center plate even with the clutch pedal fully depressed.

13 If clutch spin is suspected, the condition can be confirmed by extreme difficulty in engaging first gear from rest, difficulty in changing gear, and very sudden take-up of the clutch drive at the fully depressed end of the clutch pedal travel as the clutch is released.

14 If the clutch linkage is checked and the clutch pedal free travel is correct, then the fault lies internally in the clutch and it will have to be removed for examination.

Clutch judder

15 Clutch judder is a self-evident condition which occurs when the transmission or engine mountings are loose or too flexible, when there is oil on the face of the clutch friction plate, or when the clutch pressure plate has been incorrectly adjusted.

16 The reason for clutch judder is due to one of the faults just listed, the clutch pressure plate is not freeing smoothly from the friction disc and is snatching.

17 Clutch judder normally occurs when the clutch pedal is released in first or reverse gears, and the whole car shudders as it moves forward or backward.

Chapter 6 Transmission

Contents

Specifications

Manual transmission

Number of gears

3-speed transmission	3 forward, 1 reverse
4-speed transmission	4 forward, 1 reverse

Type of gears . . . . Helical, constant mesh

Synchromesh . . . . All forward gears

Countergear endplay . . . . 0.004 to 0.018 in (0.10 to 0.45 mm)

Reverse idler gear endplay . . . . 0.004 to 0.018 in (0.10 to 0.45 mm)

Lubricant type . . . . Ford manual transmission lubricant (ESW-M2C83-B)

Refill capacity

3-speed transmission	3.5 US pts (1.7 litre)
4-speed transmission	4.0 US pts (1.9 litre)

Automatic transmission

Type . . . . C4, C6 or FMX

Lubricant type . . . . Automatic transmission fluid ESW-M2C33-F type F

Refill capacity (approx)

Type C4:	
302 cu in engines	9 US qt (8.5 litre)
351 cu in engines	10.25 US qt (9.6 litre)
Type C6	12.5 US qt (11.8 litre)
Type FMX	11.0 US qt (10.4 litre)

Torque wrench settings
Manual transmission

	lbf ft	kgf m
Input shaft bearing retainer bolt:		
3-speed transmission	30 to 36	4.1 to 4.9
4-speed transmission	19 to 25	2.6 to 3.4
Extension housing-to-case bolt	30 to 36	4.1 to 4.9
Cover-to-case bolt	20 to 25	2.7 to 3.4
Filler plug	10 to 20	1.3 to 2.7
Drain plug	20 to 30	2.7 to 4.1
Transmission-to-flywheel housing bolts	37 to 42	5.7 to 5.8
TRS switch	15 to 20	2.0 to 2.7
Lock-rod adjustment nut	10 to 20	1.3 to 2.7

Automatic transmission

	lbf ft	kgf m
Converter-to-flywheel nuts	23 to 28	3.2 to 3.8
Converter housing-to-case	28 to 40	3.8 to 5.5
Oil pan bolts	12 to 16	1.6 to 2.2
Converter cover-to-housing bolts	12 to 16	1.6 to 2.2
Transmission-to-engine bolts	23 to 33	2.2 to 4.5
Converter drain plug	15 to 28	2.0 to 3.8
Downshift lever-to-shaft	12 to 16	1.6 to 2.2
Band adjustment screw locknut	35 to 40	4.8 to 5.5

PART A – Manual transmission

1 General description

The manual transmission installed on models covered by this manual is a three or four forward speed and reverse type, with synchromesh action on all forward gears.

All forward gears are engaged through synchro hubs and rings to obtain a smooth, silent shift from one ratio to another. All forward gears on the output and input shafts are in constant mesh with their corresponding gears on the countershaft gear cluster, and are helical-cut to achieve quiet running.

The reverse gear, which is not synchronized, has straight-cut gear teeth and drives the first gear through an interposed sliding idler gear.

The gears are engaged inside the casing by means of the shift forks, shift rails, a detent mechanism and associated parts. The gears are selected by a floor-mounted shift lever. The system of interlocks and detents in the transmission case prevents the selection of more than one gear speed at the same time, and helps to hold any gear in the selected position.

From 1970 the 4-speed type transmission is fitted with a Hurst shifter control assembly which should not be dismantled. The only parts to be removed from it are the shift lever, shift lever handle, back-up light switch retainer and switch. It is protected from road splash by a rubber boot which fits tightly over the shifter mounting plate.

2 Transmission – removal and installation

1 When the transmission has to be removed from the car, it can be taken out from below without having to remove the engine. A considerable amount of working height is required beneath the car and ideally ramps or an inspection pit should be used. However, provided that suitable jacks and supports are available, the task can be accomplished without too much difficulty if the car is supported on jack stands.

2 Disconnect the battery ground lead.

3 Remove the transmission drain plug, (if so equipped), or lower extension housing bolt and drain the oil into a suitable container.

4 Disconnect the front of the driveshaft from the rear of the transmission, as described in Chapter 7, and tie the shaft out of the way.

5 Disconnect the speedometer cable from the extension housing.

6 Disconnect the TRS (transmission-regulated spark) switch, seat belt sensor and back-up light switches (if so equipped).

7 On three-speed transmissions, remove the gearshift selector assembly from the extension housing.

8 On four-speed transmissions, disconnect the parking brake cable from the equalizer lever and separate the lever from the crossmember. Remove the hairpin retainer securing the cable to the transmission rear support crossmember, then pull the cable assembly forward and out of

the crossmember. Disconnect the shift rods from the shift levers by removing the retaining clip, flat washer and spring washer. Remove the bolts that secure the shift linkage control bracket to the extension housing and tie the assembly out of the way.

9 Support the engine with a jack positioned under the rear of the engine, place a block of wood between the jack and the oil pan, and remove the extension housing-to-engine rear support attaching bolts.

10 Raise the rear of the engine high enough to take the weight from the crossmember. Remove the bolts retaining the crossmember to the frame side supports and withdraw the crossmember.

11 Support the transmission with a jack and remove the transmission-to-flywheel housing bolts.

12 Carefully move the transmission and supporting jack rearward until the input shaft is clear of the clutch housing; then lower the transmission to the ground.

13 Do not depress the clutch pedal while the transmission is removed. Before installing the transmission ensure that the clutch release lever and bearing are correctly located in the clutch housing.

14 Installation of the transmission is the reverse of the removal procedure. Apply a smear of grease on the input shaft splines. Take care not to put any strain on the input shaft, but note that it may be necessary to rotate the engine to align the clutch disc and input shaft splines. Don't forget to refill the transmission with the correct grade of oil.

3 Transmission (3-speed) – dismantling

1 Place the complete unit on a bench or table and ensure that you have the following tools available, in addition to the normal range of wrenches, etc.:
- (a) 2 pairs of snap ring pliers – 1 expanding and 1 contracting
- (b) Copper headed hammer, at least 2lb
- (c) Selection of steel and brass drifts
- (d) Suitable containers to hold small parts
- (e) Engineer's vise, securely mounted
- (f) Selection of steel tubing

2 Dismantling of the transmission without the foregoing equipment is not impossible, but will be very difficult. Read the whole of this Section before starting work.

3 Undo the capscrews securing the cover to the case, and remove the cover and gasket.

4 Remove the long spring and detent plug from the top left-hand side of the case. (Early models have a retaining screw: on later models the cover retains the spring).

5 Undo the capscrews attaching the extension housing to the case and remove the extension and gasket.

6 Undo the capscrews securing the front bearing retainer, and remove the retainer and gasket.

7 Remove the filler/level plug from the right-hand side of the case

6

Fig. 6.1 3-speed transmission (Sec. 1)

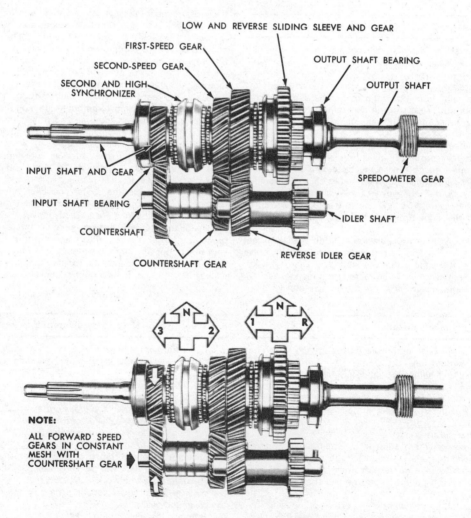

LOW AND REVERSE SLIDING SLEEVE AND GEAR

FIRST-SPEED GEAR

SECOND-SPEED GEAR

SECOND AND HIGH SYNCHRONIZER

OUTPUT SHAFT BEARING

OUTPUT SHAFT

INPUT SHAFT AND GEAR

INPUT SHAFT BEARING

COUNTERSHAFT

SPEEDOMETER GEAR

IDLER SHAFT

COUNTERSHAFT GEAR

REVERSE IDLER GEAR

NOTE:
ALL FORWARD SPEED GEARS IN CONSTANT MESH WITH COUNTERSHAFT GEAR

Fig. 6.2 Internal components and power flow (3-speed) (Sec. 1)

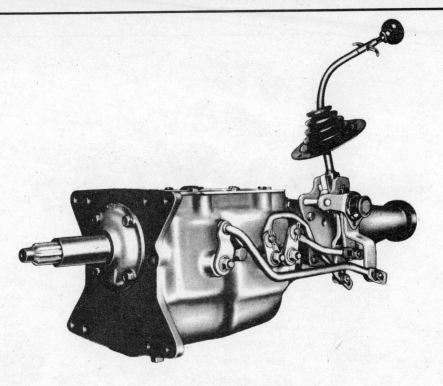

Fig. 6.3 4-speed transmission (Sec. 1)

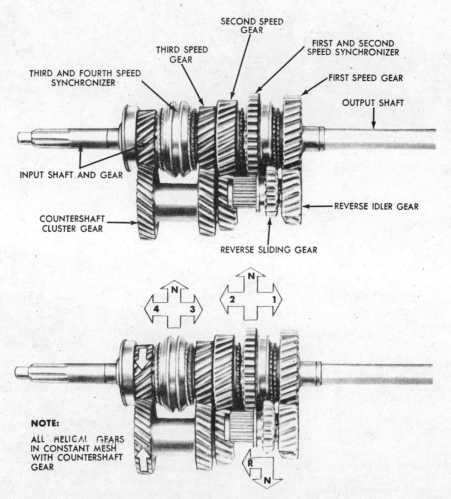

SECOND SPEED GEAR

THIRD SPEED GEAR

FIRST AND SECOND SPEED SYNCHRONIZER

THIRD AND FOURTH SPEED SYNCHRONIZER

FIRST SPEED GEAR

OUTPUT SHAFT

INPUT SHAFT AND GEAR

REVERSE IDLER GEAR

COUNTERSHAFT CLUSTER GEAR

REVERSE SLIDING GEAR

NOTE:
ALL HELICAL GEARS IN CONSTANT MESH WITH COUNTERSHAFT GEAR

Fig. 6.4 Internal components and power flow (4-speed) (Sec. 1)

6

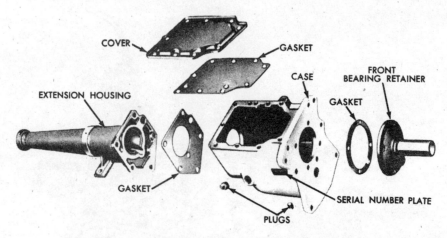

Fig. 6.5 Transmission case and associated parts (3-speed) (Sec. 3)

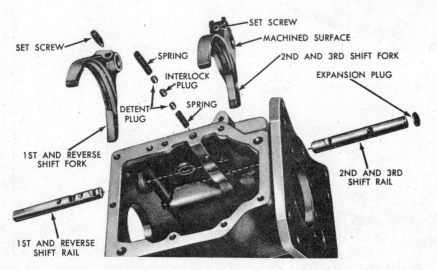

Fig. 6.6 Exploded view of shift rails and forks (3-speed) (Sec. 3)

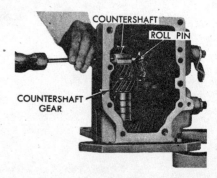

Fig. 6.7 Removing the countershaft roll pin
(3-speed) (Sec. 3)

Fig. 6.8 Removing the countershaft (3-speed) (Sec. 3)

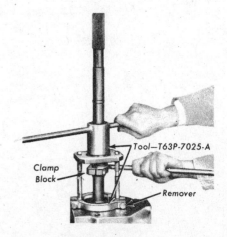

Fig. 6.9 Removing the output shaft bearing
(3-speed) (Sec. 3)

and, working through the plug opening, drive out the roll pin that secures the countershaft in the case, using a suitable sized drift (see Fig. 6.7).

8   Using a piece of tubing of slightly smaller diameter than the countershaft and about 1½ in shorter, drive the countershaft out of the rear of the casing, while supporting the countershaft gear cluster. Leave the tubing in the gear cluster to prevent the needle rollers from dropping out, and lower the countershaft gear cluster and thrust washers to the bottom of the case.

9   On some models, remove the snap-ring securing the speedometer drivegear on the output shaft. Slide the gear off the end of the shaft and remove the gear lock-ball from the shaft.

10   Remove the snap-ring retaining the rear bearing on the output shaft and, using two screwdrivers placed between the outer snap-ring and case, carefully lever the bearing out of the case and slide it off the end of the output shaft. If the bearing cannot be removed in this manner a special tool (No T63P-7025-A) (see Fig. 6.9) is available from Ford dealers.

11   Place both shift levers in the neutral (center) position. Remove the set-screw securing the 1st/reverse shift fork to the shift rail then slide

the rail out of the rear of the case.

12 Slide the 1st/reverse synchronizer forward as far as possible, then rotate the shift fork upward and lift it out of the case.

13 Push the 2nd/3rd speed shift fork rearward to the 2nd speed position to gain access to the retaining set-screw. Remove the set-screw from the fork then, using suitable pliers or grips, rotate the shift rail through 90° as shown in Fig. 6.10.

14 Lift the interlock plug out of the case with a magnet and then tap the rear end of the 2nd/3rd shift rail to remove the expansion plug from the front of the case. Withdraw the shift rail.

15 Remove the 2nd/3rd speed shift rail detent plug and spring from the case.

16 Pull the input shaft and bearing from the front of the case.

17 Rotate the 2nd/3rd speed shift fork upward and lift it from the case.

18 Carefully lift the output shaft assembly out through the top of the case.

19 Drive the reverse idler gear shaft out of the case and lift the reverse idler gear and two thrust washers from the case.

20 Lift the countershaft gear cluster, thrust washers, and dummy shaft from the case. If a dummy shaft was not used collect any needle bearings that may have fallen out of the gear cluster. **Note:** *There are 25 needle bearings in each end of the gear cluster.*

21 Remove the shift levers from the side of the case by undoing the securing nuts, withdrawing the levers and then sliding the shafts out of the case. Discard the O-ring seals.

22 Do not remove the TRS switch (if so equipped) from the case, unless the switch is damaged. Removal of the switch will damage the plastic sealing tape.

23 The dismantling of the input and output shaft assemblies is described in the following Sections.

---

4   Input shaft (3-speed) – dismantling

1   The only time the input shaft requires dismantling is when the bearing or shaft requires renewing.

2   With a pair of expanding snap-ring pliers, remove the small snap-ring which retains the bearing on the input shaft.

3   With a soft-headed hammer gently tap the bearing forward and then remove it from the shaft.

Fig. 6.10 Rotating the 2nd/3rd speed shaft rail (3-speed) (Sec. 3)

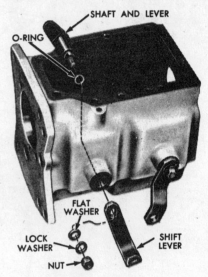

Fig. 6.11 Removing the shift levers and shafts (3-speed) (Sec. 3)

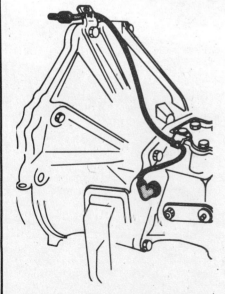

Fig. 6.12 Location of TRS switch on some models. (Sec. 3)

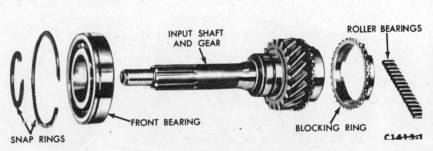

Fig. 6.13 Input shaft dismantled (Sec. 4)

5   Output shaft (3-speed) – dismantling

1   For dismantling, mount the plain section of the shaft in a vise with soft jaw-grips. As each component part is removed from the shaft make a note of its position and which way round it is installed, then place it on a clean sheet of paper in the order of removal.

2   Refer to Fig. 6.14. Remove the snap-ring from the front of the output shaft and slide the blocking rings, the synchronizer hub and 2nd gear off the shaft.

3   Remove the next snap-ring and the tabbed thrust washer, then slide the 1st gear and blocking ring off the shaft.

4   Now remove the next snap-ring and press the shaft out of the reverse gear and synchronizer sleeve assembly, (see Fig. 6.15). Do not attempt to remove the 1st/reverse synchronizer hub from the shaft by trying to hammer it or by prying it off with levers as this will probably cause damage to the synchronizer assembly.

5   When dismantling the synchro hubs and sleeves, first refer to Fig. 6.16 and 6.17, and etch or lightly punch alignment marks on each part.

6   Push the sleeves off the hubs and separate the inserts and insert springs, making a note which way round they are installed. Do not mix 1st/reverse synchro hub parts with those from the 2nd/3rd synchro hub assembly.

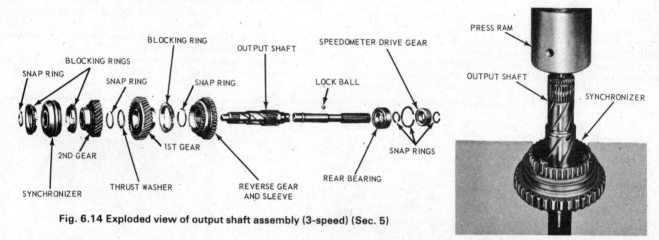

Fig. 6.14 Exploded view of output shaft assembly (3-speed) (Sec. 5)

Fig. 6.15 Removing 1st/reverse synchronizer (3-speed) (Sec. 5)

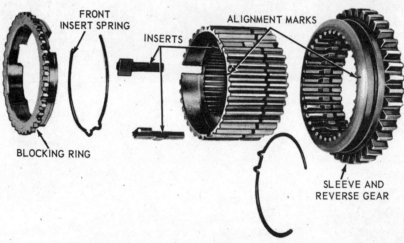

Fig. 6.16 Exploded view of 1st/reverse synchronizer (3-speed) (Sec. 5)

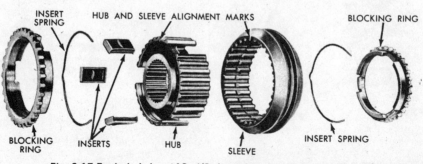

Fig. 6.17 Exploded view of 2nd/3rd synchronizer (3-speed) (Sec. 5)

6 Transmission (3-speed) – examination and renovation

1   Clean and then examine all the dismantled parts for general wear, distortion and damage.
2   Examine the gears for excessive wear and chipping of the teeth. Renew as necessary.
3   Examine the countershaft for signs of wear, where the countershaft gear cluster needle bearings run. If a small ridge can be felt at either end of the shaft it should be renewed.
4   The synchro blocking rings will probably be badly worn and it is false economy not to renew them. New rings will improve the smoothness and speed of shift considerably.
5   The needle roller bearings located between the nose of the output shaft and the annulus on the rear of the input shaft are also liable to wear and should be renewed.
6   Examine the condition of the two ball bearing assemblies, one on the input shaft and the one on the output shaft. Check them for noisy operation, looseness between the inner and outer races and for general wear. Normally they should be renewed on a transmission that is being rebuilt after a high mileage.
7   If the synchro hubs are worn it will be necessary to renew a complete assembly as the parts are not supplied separately.
8   If the bushing in the extension housing is worn it is recommended that you take the housing to your local Ford repair station to have the bushing renewed.
9   The oil seals in the extension housing, the input shaft bearing retainer and the selector lever O-ring seals should be renewed at each dismantling. Drive out the old seals with a drift. When installing new seals carefully tap the seals into place, using a piece of wood to spread the load evenly, so that they enter their housings squarely.
10 The only part of the output shaft that is likely to be worn is the part where it enters the input shaft. However, examine it thoroughly for any signs of scoring or picking-up, and if damage is apparent it should be renewed.

7 Input shaft (3-speed) – reassembly

1   When installing the bearing on the shaft ensure that the groove, cut in the outer periphery of the bearing, faces away from the gear. If the bearing is installed the wrong way round it will not be possible to fit the large snap-ring which retains the bearing in the housing.
2   Using the jaws of a vise as a support behind the bearing, tap the bearing squarely into place by striking the rear of the input shaft with a soft-faced hammer.
3   Install the snap-ring which retains the bearing in position on the input shaft.

8 Output shaft (3-speed) – reassembly

1   Assemble the synchro hubs. Position the insert spring in the hub of the 1st/reverse synchronizer. Make sure that the spring covers all the insert grooves. Start the hub on the sleeve until the index marks, made at dismantling, properly align. Position the three inserts in the hub, ensuring that the small end is on the inside of the hub, then slide the sleeve and reverse gear onto the hub.
2   Fit one insert spring into a groove of the 2nd/3rd synchro hub, ensuring that all three insert slots are fully covered, then with the index marks on the hub and sleeve aligned start the hub into the sleeve. Place the three inserts on top of the retaining spring and push the assembly together. Fit the remaining insert spring so that the spring ends cover the same slots as the other spring. Do not stagger the springs.
3   Before assembling the gears and synchro hub onto the output shaft lubricate the shaft machined surfaces and splines with fresh transmission oil.
4   Carefully press the reverse gear and synchronizer assembly onto the shaft, as shown in Fig. 6.18, then install the retaining snap-ring.
5   Install the blocking ring on the tapered surface of the 1st gear and slide the 1st gear onto the output shaft with the blocking ring facing toward the rear of the shaft. Rotate the gear as necessary to engage with the three notches in the blocking ring with the synchronizer inserts.

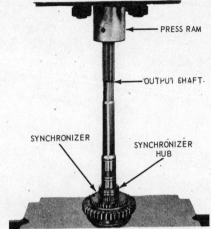

Fig. 6.18 Fitting the 1st/reverse synchronizer (3-speed) (Sec. 8)

6   Secure the 1st gear in position with the thrust washer and snap-ring.
7   Install the blocking ring onto the tapered surface of the 2nd gear. Slide the 2nd gear, with its blocking ring, onto the shaft, ensuring that the tapered side of the gear faces toward the front of the shaft.
8   Finally, slide the 2nd/3rd gear synchronizer onto the end of the shaft, and install the retaining snap-ring.

9 Transmission (3-speed) – reassembly

1   Lubricate the O-ring seals and install them on the shift lever shafts. Install the shafts in the case and position a shift lever on each shaft and secure them with a flat washer, lockwasher and nut.
2   Lubricate the reverse idler gear thrust surfaces in the case with a film of oil and install the two thrust washers in position. Hold the reverse idler gear in position and install the reverse idler shaft.
3   Measure the reverse idler gear endplay with a feeler gauge. If the endplay is not within the limits given in Specifications at the beginning of this Chapter, remove the thrust washers and install washers of a suitable thickness to obtain the specified endplay. When the endplay is within limits, install the retaining roll pin.
4   Smear some grease into each end of the countershaft gear and insert the 25 roller bearings and a thrust washer on each end of the gear. Install the dummy shaft, used at dismantling, inside the countershaft gear to keep the bearings in place.
5   Place the countershaft gear and dummy shaft assembly in the case. Place the case in a vertical position, align the gear bore and the thrust washers with the bores in the case, and install the countershaft.
6   Position the case horizontal and, using a feeler gauge, check the endplay of the countershaft gear. If the endplay is not within the limits given in Specifications at the beginning of this Chapter, replace the thrust washers with washers of the required thickness to obtain the specified endplay.
7   After ensuring that the endplay is within limits, install the dummy shaft in the countershaft gear and leave the countershaft gear in the bottom of the case until the input and output shafts have been installed.
8   Install the output shaft assembly into the case through the top of the case.
9   Install a new snap-ring in the groove round the rear bearing assembly and drive the bearing along the shaft until it enters the aperture in the rear of the case. Ensure that the groove in the bearing is

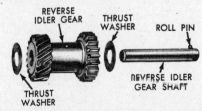

Fig. 6.19 Fitting the reverse idler gear and shaft (3-speed) (Sec. 9)

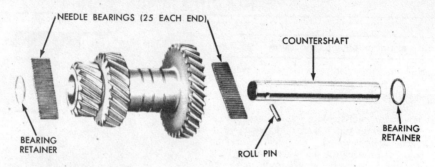

NEEDLE BEARINGS (25 EACH END)

COUNTERSHAFT

BEARING RETAINER

ROLL PIN

BEARING RETAINER

Fig. 6.20 Exploded view of countershaft gear (3-speed) (Sec. 9)

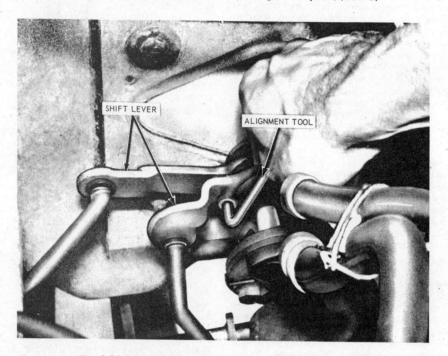

SHIFT LEVER

ALIGNMENT TOOL

Fig. 6.21 Adjusting the gearshift linkage (3-speed) (Sec. 10)

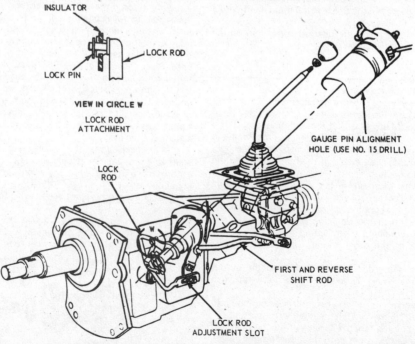

INSULATOR

LOCK ROD

LOCK PIN

VIEW IN CIRCLE W

LOCK ROD ATTACHMENT

GAUGE PIN ALIGNMENT HOLE (USE NO. 15 DRILL)

LOCK ROD

FIRST AND REVERSE SHIFT ROD

LOCK ROD ADJUSTMENT SLOT

Fig. 6.22 Gearshift linkage with lock-rod (later models) (Sec. 11)

toward the rear of the case.

10 Install a new retaining snap-ring on the output shaft.

11 Coat the bore of the input shaft with a thin film of grease and install the 15 roller bearings.

12 Install the input shaft, 3rd gear and synchro ring assembly through the front of the case, making sure that the end of the output shaft is correctly located in the roller bearing recess of the input shaft.

13 Install a new snap-ring in the front bearing groove and tap the bearing along the input shaft until it enters its housing in the case. Carefully tap the bearing fully home.

14 Position the 2nd/3rd gear shift fork on the 2nd/3rd gear synchro hub.

15 Install a detent plug spring and a plug in the case.

16 Push the 2nd/3rd gear synchro hub as far as possible toward the rear of the case (2nd speed position).

17 Align the hole in the shift fork with the case and push the 2nd/3rd gearshift rail in from the front of the case. It will be necessary to depress the detent plug to enable the rail to enter the bore. Push the rail inward until the detent plug engages the forward notch (second speed position).

18 Secure the fork with the set screw and then move the synchronizer to the neutral position.

19 Install the interlock plug in the case. When the 2nd/3rd gearshift rail in the neutral position, the top of the interlock plug will be slightly lower than the surface of the 1st/reverse shift rail bore.

20 Push the 1st/reverse synchronizer forward to the 1st speed position and install the 1st/reverse shift fork in the synchronizer groove. Rotate the shift fork into the correct position and push the 1st/reverse shift rail in from the rear of the case. Push the rail inward until the center notch (neutral) is in line with the detent bore.

21 Secure the fork to the rail with the set screw.

22 Install a new shift rail expansion plug in the front of the case, flush with or to 0.60 in (12 mm) below the face of the case to prevent interference with the clutch housing assembly.

23 Place the transmission case in a vertical position and working through the filler hole, align the bore of the countershaft gear and the thrust washers with the bore of case using a screwdriver or similar tool.

24 Insert the countershaft from the rear of the case and push the dummy shaft out of the countergear with the countershaft. Before the countershaft is completely inserted, ensure that the roll pin hole in the shaft is aligned with the hole in the case, then drive the countershaft into place and install the roll pin.

25 Check that the countershaft gear rotates smoothly.

26 Install a new front bearing retainer snap-ring onto the input shaft.

27 Install the input shaft bearing retainer and new gasket; ensure that the oil return slot is at the bottom of the case.

28 Apply gasket sealer to the bearing retainer bolts and tighten them to the specified torque.

29 Install the speedometer drivegear lock-ball into the hole in the output shaft, hold the ball in position and slide the drive gear over it. Secure with a snap-ring.

30 Coat a new extension housing gasket with sealer and position it on the case. Coat the threads of the attaching screws with sealer, install the extension housing to the case and tighten the securing screws to the specified torque.

31 Rotate the input shaft by hand and check that all the gears can be selected in turn and both shafts rotate smoothly.

32 Install the remaining detent plug and spring in the case. On early models install the retaining screw; on later models the spring is retained by the cover.

33 Coat a new cover gasket with sealer, install the top cover and tighten the capscrews to the specified torque.

34 Tighten the drain plug to the specified torque and install the filler/level plug temporarily.

10 Gear shift linkage (early 3-speed models) – adjustment

1 Loosen the three shift linkage adjusting nuts. Insert a 0.25 in (6.3 mm) diameter rod through the control bracket and lever alignment holes as shown in Fig. 6.21.

2 Tighten the three linkage adjustment nuts and remove the alignment rod.

3 Start the engine and shift the selector lever to each position to ensure that it operates freely.

11 Gearshift linkage (later 3-speed models) – adjustment

On models from 1970 a transmission lock-rod connects the lower steering column shift tube to the manual transmission reverse lever. It locks the transmission in reverse gear when the ignition switch is in the LOCK position. Adjustment can be carried out only when the shift control alignment is correct.

1 Place the hand shift lever in neutral. Loosen the lock-rod-to-lever nut.

2 Align the hole in the steering column socket casting with the column alignment mark (see Fig. 6.22), and insert a 0.18 in (4.5 mm) diameter pin. The column casting must not rotate with the pin in position.

3 Tighten the lock-rod adjustment nut to a torque of 10 to 20 lbf ft (1.3 to 2.7 kgf m).

4 Check for correct operation.

12 Transmission lock-rod – removal and installation

1 Disconnect the rod at the transmission lever.

2 Remove the retaining clip and pull the rod out of the grommet located in the lever attached to the steering column shift tube and lift away the rod.

3 Installation is the reverse of the removal procedure. Adjust the lock-rod as described in Section 11.

13 Transmission (4-speed) – dismantling

1 Refer to Section 3 and carry out the operations in paragraph 1 through 6.

2 Support the countershaft gear and, working from the front of the case, push the countershaft out of the rear of the case using a dummy shaft (refer to Section 3, para 8). Leave the dummy shaft in the gear cluster, to prevent the needle rollers from dropping out, and lower the countershaft gear to the bottom of the case.

3 Place the 1st/2nd gear shift lever and the reverse shift lever in the neutral position. Position the 3rd/4th gear shift lever to engage with the 3rd gear.

4 Remove the 3rd/4th speed shift fork securing screw, tap the inner end of the shift rail to unseal the expansion plug from the front of the case; then withdraw the 3rd/4th shift rail from the front of the case. Collect the interlock pin from the shift rail.

5 Remove the 1st/2nd speed shift fork securing screw and slide the 1st/2nd speed shift rail out of the rear of the case.

6 Remove the interlock plug and detent plug from the top of the case.

7 Remove the snap-ring retaining the speedometer drivegear on the output shaft, then slide the gear off the shaft and collect the speedometer gear drive ball.

8 Remove the output shaft bearing retaining snap-ring and, using two screwdrivers, placed between the outer snap-ring and case, carefully lever the bearing out of the case and slide it off the end of the output shaft. If the bearing cannot be removed in this manner a special tool (No T 64P-7025-B) will be required.

9 Remove the input shaft and bearing assembly, and the blocking ring from the front of the case.

10 Move the output shaft to the right-hand side of the case, to provide clearance for the shift forks, then lift out the 3rd/4th and 1st/reverse shift forks.

11 Hold the thrust washer and 1st speed gear to prevent them from sliding off the shaft and remove the output shaft through the top of the case as shown in Fig. 6.25.

12 Remove the reverse gear shift fork set-screw, rotate the reverse shift rail 90°, and then slide the shift rail out of the rear of the case. Lift out the reverse shift fork.

13 Remove the reverse detent plug and spring.

14 Using a dummy shaft (a suitable piece of tubing will do) remove the reverse idler gear shaft as shown in Fig. 6.27.

15 Lift the reverse idler gear and thrust washers from the case, taking care to keep the dummy shaft in position to prevent the needle rollers dropping out.

16 Lift the countershaft gear, thrust washers and dummy shaft assembly from the case.

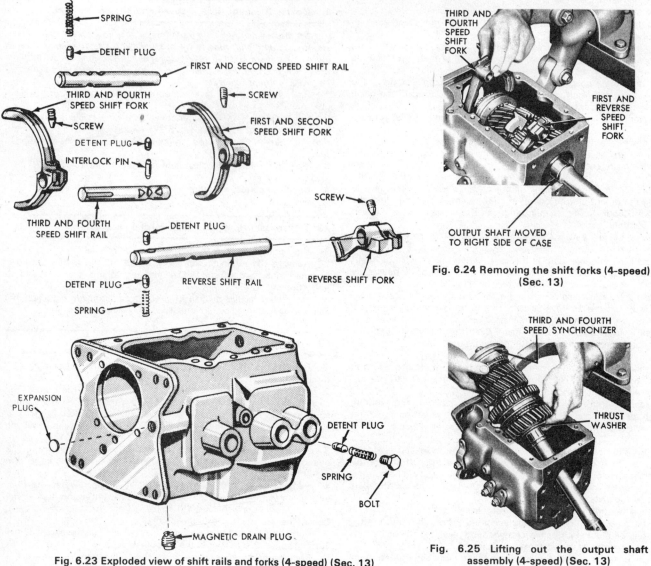

Fig. 6.23 Exploded view of shift rails and forks (4-speed) (Sec. 13)

Fig. 6.24 Removing the shift forks (4-speed) (Sec. 13)

Fig. 6.25 Lifting out the output shaft assembly (4-speed) (Sec. 13)

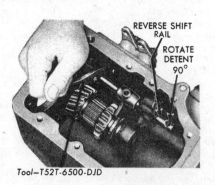

Tool—T52T-6500-DJD

Fig. 6.26 Rotating the reverse shift rail (4-speed) (Sec. 13)

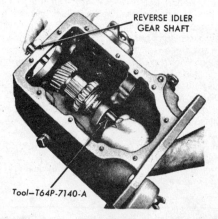

Tool—T64P-7140-A

Fig. 6.27 Removing the reverse idler gear shaft (4-speed) (Sec. 13)

17 Undo the retaining nuts and remove the three shift levers.
18 Remove the three cams and shafts from inside the case. Discard the O-ring from each shaft. The dismantling of the input and output shafts is described in the following Sections.

14 Input shaft (4-speed) – dismantling

This procedure is as described in Section 4.

15 Output shaft (4-speed) – dismantling

1   Refer to Section 5 and proceed as in paragraph 1.
2   Refer to Fig. 6.28. Remove the snap-ring from the front of the shaft and then slide the 3rd/4th gear synchro hub, blocking ring and 3rd gear off the shaft.
3   Remove the next snap-ring and the 2nd gear thrust washer, then slide the 2nd gear and the blocking ring off the shaft.
4   Remove the next snap-ring.
5   Remove the thrust washer, 1st gear and blocking ring from the rear of the shaft. Press the shaft out of the 1st/2nd synchro hub. Do not attempt to remove it by trying to hammer or pry it off with levers as this will probably damage the synchronizer assembly.
6   When dismantling the synchro hubs and sleeves, first refer to Fig. 6.29 and etch or lightly punch alignment marks on each part.
7   Push the sleeves off the hubs and separate the inserts and insert springs, making a note which way round they are installed. Do not mix the 1st/2nd synchro hub parts with those from the 3rd/4th synchro hub.

16 Transmission (4-speed) – examination and renovation

This procedure is as described in Section 6.

17 Input shaft (4-speed) – reassembly

This procedure is as described in Section 7.

18 Output shaft (4-speed) – reassembly

1   Assemble the synchronizers. Install the hub in the sleeve, making sure that the index marks, made at disassembly are in alignment. Position the three inserts into place on the hub then the insert springs, making sure that the irregular surface (hump) is seated in one of the inserts. Do not stagger the springs.
2   Before assembling the gears and synchro hub onto the output shaft, lubricate the splines and machined surfaces of the shaft with fresh transmission oil.
3   Install the 1st/2nd gear synchro hub onto the front of the output shaft with the shift fork groove toward the rear of the shaft. The synchro hub is a press-fit on the shaft and to avoid damaging the synchronizer assembly, install the synchro hub with the teeth end facing toward the rear of the shaft. Fit the snap-ring.
4   Place the blocking ring on the 2nd gear.
5   Slide the 2nd gear onto the shaft, making sure that the inserts in the synchronizer engage the notches in the blocking ring.
6   Install the 2nd gear thrust washer and snap-ring.

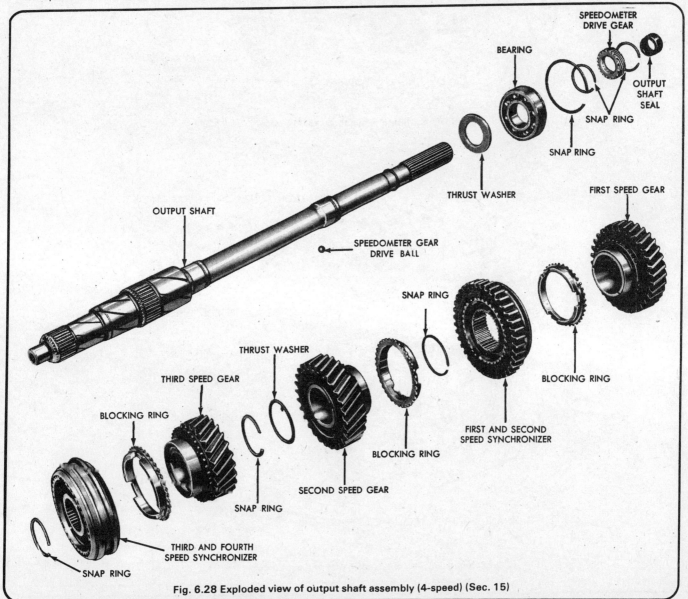

Fig. 6.28 Exploded view of output shaft assembly (4-speed) (Sec. 15)

6

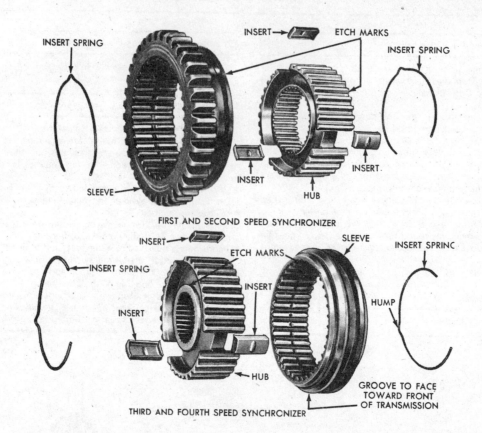

INSERT SPRING

INSERT → ETCH MARKS

INSERT SPRING

SLEEVE

INSERT

INSERT

HUB

FIRST AND SECOND SPEED SYNCHRONIZER

INSERT →

ETCH MARKS

SLEEVE

INSERT SPRINC

INSERT SPRING

INSERT

INSERT

HUMP

INSERT

HUB

GROOVE TO FACE TOWARD FRONT OF TRANSMISSION

THIRD AND FOURTH SPEED SYNCHRONIZER

Fig. 6.29 Dismantling the synchronizers (4-speed) (Sec. 15)

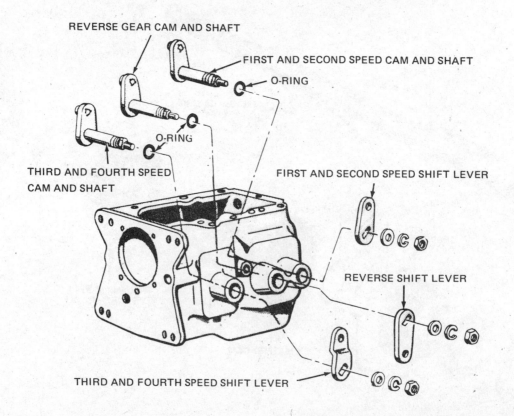

REVERSE GEAR CAM AND SHAFT

FIRST AND SECOND SPEED CAM AND SHAFT

O-RING

O-RING

THIRD AND FOURTH SPEED CAM AND SHAFT

FIRST AND SECOND SPEED SHIFT LEVER

REVERSE SHIFT LEVER

THIRD AND FOURTH SPEED SHIFT LEVER

Fig. 6.30 Exploded view of cams and shafts, and shift levers (4-speed) (Sec. 19)

7   Slide the 3rd gear onto the shaft with the tapered surface toward the front and then place a blocking ring on the 3rd gear.

8   Slide the 3rd/4th gear synchronizer onto the shaft and make sure that the inserts engage the notches in the blocking ring. Install the retaining snap-ring.

9   Install the blocking ring on the 1st gear and then slide the gear onto the rear of the output shaft.

10 Install the thrust washer on the rear of the shaft.

19   Transmission (4-speed) – reassembly

1   Lubricate the O-ring seals and install them on the shift lever shafts. Slide each cam and shaft into position in the transmission case, install the shift levers on the shafts and secure them with a flat washer, lockwasher and nut.

2   Smear some grease into each end of the countershaft gear and insert the 21 roller bearings and retaining washer in each end of the gear. Install the dummy shaft, used at dismantling, inside the countershaft gear to keep the bearings in place.

3   Refer to Section 9, and carry out the procedures described in paragraph 5 through 7.

4   Smear some grease in the bore at each end of the reverse idler gear, hold the dummy shaft in the gear and install the 22 roller bearings and the retainer washer in each end of the gear.

5   Install the reverse idler sliding gear on the reverse idler gear with the shift fork groove toward the front.

6   Apply a thin film of grease to the thrust surfaces in the case and locate the thrust washers in position, then install the reverse idler gear, sliding gear and dummy shaft in position and install the reverse idler shaft. Make sure the shift fork groove is toward the front of the case.

7   Check the reverse idler gear endplay with a feeler gauge. If the endplay is not within the limits given in Specifications at the beginning of this Chapter, replace the thrust washers, as necessary to obtain the specified endplay.

8   Install the reverse gear shift rail detent spring and plug, hold the

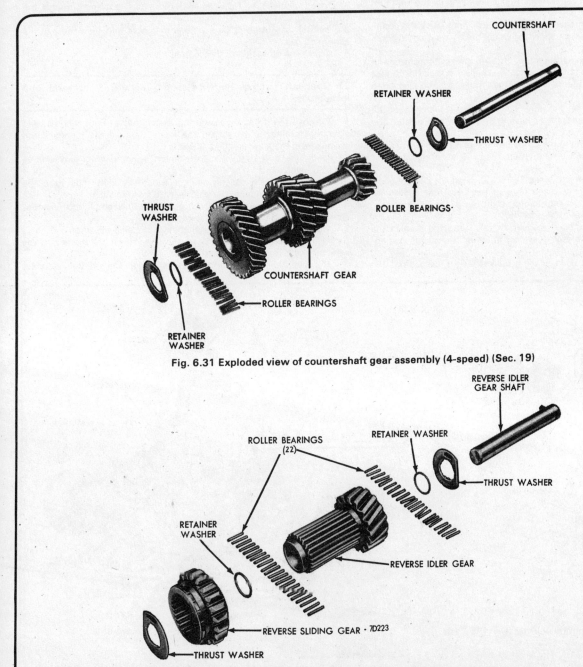

Fig. 6.31 Exploded view of countershaft gear assembly (4-speed) (Sec. 19)

Fig. 6.32 Exploded view of reverse idler gear assembly (4-speed) (Sec. 19)

reverse shift fork in place on the reverse idler sliding gear and push the shift rail in from the rear of the case. Install the shift fork securing screw.

9   Install the output shaft assembly through the top of the case, as shown in Fig. 6.25, taking care that the thrust washer does not slide off.

10 Install the 1st/2nd and 3rd/4th shift forks on their respective gears.

11 Install a detent plug in the detent hole and position the reverse shift rail in neutral, then smear the 3rd/4th gear shift rail interlock pin with grease and install it in the shift rail.

12 Push the 3rd/4th gear shift rail into place with the three detents towards the outside of the case.

13 Move the front synchronizer into 3rd gear and install the 3rd/4th gear shift fork securing screw, then move it to the neutral position and install the 3rd/4th gear shift rail detent plug, spring and bolt in the left-hand side of the case. Install the interlock pin (tapered ends) in the case.

14 Slide the 1st/2nd gear shift fork into place and install the shift fork securing screw.

15 Smear a thin film of grease in the bore of the input shaft and install the 15 roller bearings. Do not apply too much grease as it could block the oil holes.

16 Install the front blocking ring on the 3rd/4th gear synchronizer and install the input shaft gear in the case, making sure that the output shaft spigot enters the roller bearings in the input shaft and that none of the bearings drop out.

17 Place a new gasket on the input shaft bearing retainer, coat the securing bolts with sealant, then install the retainer and tighten the bolts to the specified torque.

18 Install a new snap-ring in the groove on the rear bearing and drive the bearing along the shaft until it enters the case, then install a new retaining snap-ring on the output shaft.

19 Position the case vertically (see Fig. 6.33), align the countershaft gear and thrust washers with the bore in the case then insert the countershaft gear and push the dummy shaft out of the countergear. Check that the countergear rotates freely.

20 Install the speedometer drive gear lock-ball into the hole in the output shaft and slide the drivegear over it. Install the retaining snap-ring.

21 Position a new extension housing gasket on the case. Coat the

attaching screws with sealant, install the extension housing and tighten the screws to the specified torque.

22 Install the drain and filler plugs.

23 Rotate the input shaft and check that all the gears can be selected in turn, and that both shafts rotate smoothly.

24 Install the remaining detent plug and spring in the case. On early models install the retaining screw; on later models the spring is retained by the cover.

25 Coat the cover securing screws with sealant and using a new gasket install the cover on the case. Tighten the securing capscrews to the specified torque.

26 Coat the 3rd/4th gear shift rail plug bore with sealant and install a new expansion plug.

20 Shift linkage (early 4-speed models) – adjustment

1   Loosen the three shift linkage adjustment nuts.

2   Insert a piece of 0.25 in (6.3 mm) diameter rod through the control bracket and levers as shown in Fig. 6.34.

3   Tighten the three linkage adjustment nuts and then remove the alignment rod.

4   Check the operation of the gearshift lever.

21 Gearshift control (early 4-speed models) – removal and installation

1   Remove the six screws securing the shift lever boot retainer, and slide the retainer and boot up the lever. Remove the plungers and springs from the lever (see Fig. 6.35).

2   Undo the two shift lever-to-trunnion securing bolts and remove the shift lever.

3   From under the car disconnect the three shift rods from the transmission by removing the hairpin-type retaining clips.

4   Remove the three bolts attaching the shift assembly to the extension housing and withdraw the shift assembly.

5   Remove the back-up light switch from the shift assembly.

6   Using snap-ring pliers, remove the snap-ring from the end of the selector shaft, then the flat washer and spring.

7   Remove the two securing bolts and pull the retainer, selector

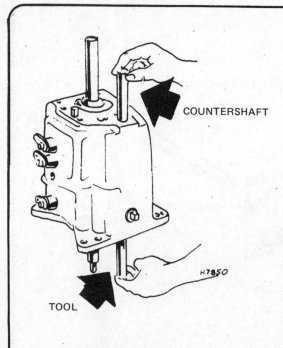

Fig. 6.33 Installing the countershaft (Sec. 19)

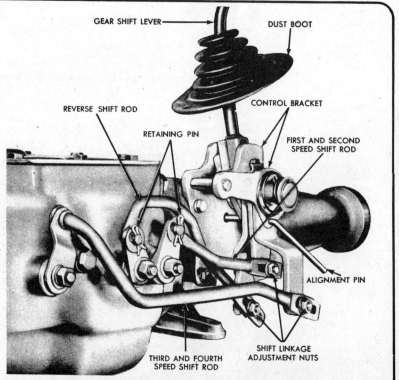

Fig. 6.34 Adjusting shift linkage (early 4-speed models) (Sec. 20)

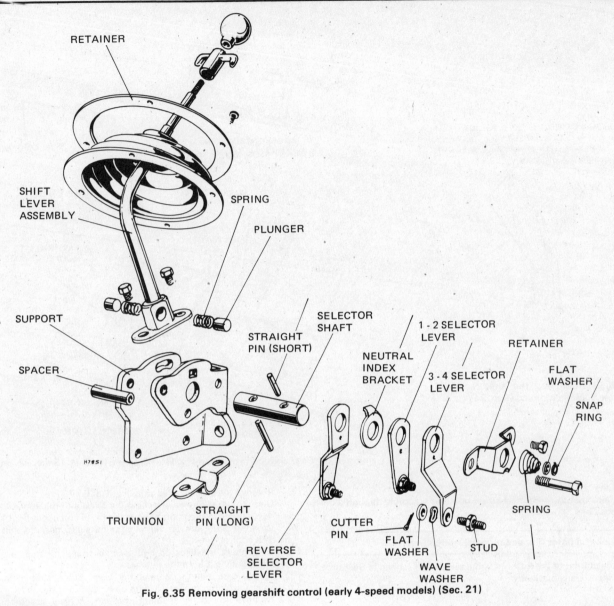

Fig. 6.35 Removing gearshift control (early 4-speed models) (Sec. 21)

levers and bracket from the shaft.

8   Using a pin punch drive the short selector lever pin from the shaft, then drive the long trunnion pin from the shaft, and remove the trunnion and shaft.

9   Clean and examine all the parts for wear and damage. Lubricate all friction surfaces.

10 Installation is the reverse of removal procedure. Adjust the shift linkage as described in Section 20.

22 Shift linkage (later 4-speed models) – adjustment

1   Disconnect the battery ground lead from the negative terminal.

2   With the shift lever in neutral, pull the lower boot up far enough to insert the alignment tool, (see Fig. 6.38) into the shift control assembly. Make sure the tool is completely through and located in the notches on both sides of the shift control housing.

3   If the alignment tool enters freely the adjustment is correct. For any lever that is out of alignment, loosen the nuts attaching the shift control rods to the shaft levers and disconnect the reverse shift rod at the shift control assembly. Rotate the reverse lever (the one in the center) clockwise to shift into reverse gear.

4   Tighten the two forward-speed shift rods at the control assembly.

5   Rotate the reverse lever counterclockwise until it stops, then attach the reverse shift rod to the control assembly.

6   Remove the alignment tool. Connect the battery ground lead and

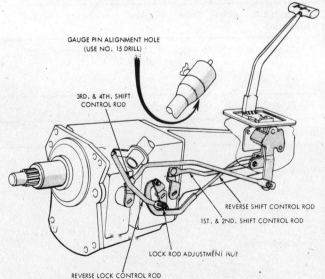

Fig. 6.36 Shift linkage (later 4-speed models)

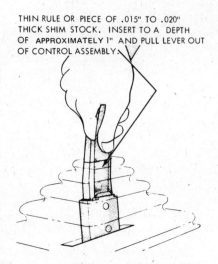

THIN RULE OR PIECE OF .015" TO .020" THICK SHIM STOCK. INSERT TO A DEPTH OF APPROXIMATELY 1" AND PULL LEVER OUT OF CONTROL ASSEMBLY.

Fig. 6.37 Removing the shift lever (later 4-speed models) (Sec. 24)

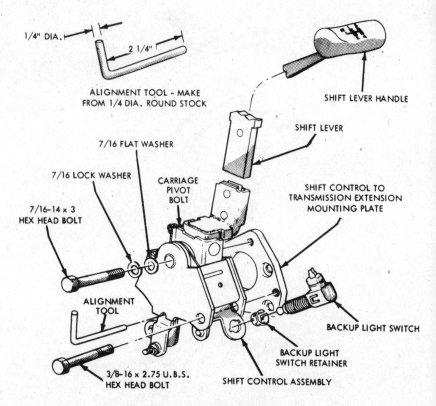

1/4" DIA.

2 1/4"

ALIGNMENT TOOL - MAKE FROM 1/4 DIA. ROUND STOCK

SHIFT LEVER HANDLE

SHIFT LEVER

7/16 FLAT WASHER

7/16 LOCK WASHER

CARRIAGE PIVOT BOLT

SHIFT CONTROL TO TRANSMISSION EXTENSION MOUNTING PLATE

7/16-14 x 3 HEX HEAD BOLT

ALIGNMENT TOOL

BACKUP LIGHT SWITCH

BACKUP LIGHT SWITCH RETAINER

3/8-16 x 2.75 U.B.S. HEX HEAD BOLT

SHIFT CONTROL ASSEMBLY

Fig. 6.38 Gear shift control assembly (later 4-speed models) (Secs. 22 and 24)

install the boot.

7   Check that the shift mechanism operates smoothly through all the shift positions.

23 Lock-rod (later 4-speed models) – adjustment

Adjustment of the lock-rod is the same as described in Section 11 for 3-speed transmissions.

24 Gearshift control (later 4-speed models) – removal and installation

1   Disconnect the battery ground lead from the negative terminal.

2   Remove the shift lever as shown in Fig. 6.37.

3   Undo the four screws attaching the bezel and the upper and lower shift lever boots to the floor; remove the bezel and upper boot.

4   Working under the car, remove the nuts securing the shift rods to the shift control levers.

5   Disconnect the back-up light switch connector and remove the switch by pulling it from the retainer.

6   Taking care not to damage the boot, pull the opening for the transmission shifter mounting plate down and over the shift assembly.

7   Remove the bolts securing the shift control assembly to the mounting plate on the extension housing and withdraw the control assembly.

8   Installation is the reverse of the removal procedure. Adjust the shift linkage as described in Sections 23 and 24. Check that the shift mechanism operates smoothly through all shift positions.

25 Fault diagnosis – manual transmission

Symptom	Reason/s
Weak or ineffective synchromesh	Synchronizing cones worn, split or damaged Worn blocking rings
Jumps out of gear	Detent springs broken Detent notches worn
Excessive noise	Oil level too low Incorrect grade of oil in transmission Bearings worn or damaged Gear teeth worn or damaged
Excessive difficulty in engaging gear	Clutch adjustment incorrect

PART B – Automatic transmission

26 General description

The three types of automatic transmission, C4, C6 and FMX, used on Mustang models are 3-speed units capable of providing automatic upshifts and downshifts through the three forward gear ratios, and also manual selection of first and second gears.

The transmissions are very similar consisting basically of a torque converter, planetary gear train, two multiple disc clutches and a hydraulic control system.

Due to the complexity of the automatic transmission unit, if performance is not up to standard, or overhaul is necessary, it is imperative that this be left to the local Ford repair station who will have the special equipment required for fault diagnosis and rectification. It is important that the fault is diagnosed before the transmission unit is removed from the car, if at all possible.

The content of the following Sections is therefore confined to supplying general information and any service information that can be used by the owner.

27 Special towing or recovery information

1 Should it be necessary to have the car towed to a repair station it must not be towed for more than 20 miles (32 km) and the speed must not exceed 30 mph (48 kph). Towing is permitted provided that the transmission is not damaged, that the oil level is correct and the selector lever is in the **N** position.
2 If there is a fault in the transmission or the towing distance is more than 20 miles (32 km), the driveshaft should be removed, as described in Chapter 7, and the rear of the transmission sealed to prevent the ingress of dirt. As an alternative, the car can be suspended and towed with the rear wheels off the ground.
3 On cars with automatic transmission it is not possible to tow-start the car.

28 Transmission fluid level – checking

1 When checking the fluid level, the fluid must be at its normal operating temperature – approximately 150°F (65°C). This is best achieved by driving the car for about 5 miles (8 km) under normal running conditions.
2 Park the car on level ground, apply the parking brake and depress the foot brake pedal.
3 Allow the engine to idle and shift the selector lever through all the positions three times, then position the lever at **P**. Do not switch off the engine during the fluid level check.
4 Pull the dipstick out of the tube, wipe it clean and push it all the way back into the tube, then pull it out and check the fluid level.
5 The fluid level should be above the *ADD* mark; if necessary, top-up with fluid, through the dipstick tube, to maintain the level between the *ADD* and *FULL* marks on the dipstick. Use only the specified fluid in the transmission.

29 Transmission – removal and installation

1 Jack-up the car, and support it securely with jack stands, to obtain the maximum possible working height under the car. Disconnect the battery.
2 Place a large drain pan beneath the transmission oil pan, then working from the rear, loosen the attaching bolts and allow the fluid to drain. Remove all the bolts except the two front ones, to drain as much fluid as possible, then temporarily refit two bolts at the rear to hold it in place. On PEA and PEF models of C4 transmission the fluid is drained by removing the dipstick/filler tube.
3 Remove the torque converter drain plug access cover from the lower front side of the converter housing.
4 Rotate the engine, by means of a wrench on the crankshaft pulley attaching bolt, until the converter drain plug is accessible, then remove the plug and collect the fluid in the drain pan. After the fluid has been drained, install and tighten the drain plug.
5 Remove the four flywheel-to-converter attaching nuts, cranking

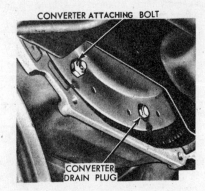

Fig. 6.39 Converter drain plug location (Sec. 29)

the engine as necessary to gain access to the nuts.
6 Remove the driveshaft, as described in Chapter 7, and cover the end of the transmission with a polythene bag to prevent the ingress of dirt.
7 Remove the starter motor retaining bolts and position the starter out of the way.
8 Remove the nuts that attach each muffler inlet pipe to the exhaust manifolds. Separate the pipes from the manifolds and allow the exhaust system to hang on the rear axle.
9 Disconnect the speedometer cable from the extension housing.
10 Disconnect the kickdown rod from the transmission downshift lever, and the shift rod from the manual lever. On models with a column lock-rod, disconnect the rod at the transmission.
11 Disconnect the vacuum hose from the vacuum unit and remove it from the attaching clip on the transmission.
12 Remove the filler tube and dipstick. On some models the filler tube is secured to the cylinder head with a bolt.
13 Disconnect the starter inhibitor (neutral start) switch leads from the retaining clips and connectors.
14 Position a trolley jack beneath the transmission and raise it so that it takes the weight of the transmission.
15 Remove the two nuts securing the engine rear support to the crossmember.
16 Raise the transmission just enough to remove the weight from the crossmember, remove the crossmember-to-frame side support securing nuts and lift out the crossmember.
17 Remove the bolts attaching the engine rear support to the extension housing and remove the support.
18 Disconnect the fluid cooler lines at the transmission and plug them to prevent the ingress of dirt.
19 Support the rear of the engine with a jack or other suitable support.
20 Ensure that the transmission is securely mounted on the trolley jack, then remove the converter-to-engine bolts (C4 – five bolts; C6 and FMX – six bolts).
21 Carefully move the transmission rearward and downward, and remove it from under the car.
22 Installation of the transmission is the reverse of the removal procedure, but the following points should be noted:
  (a) *Rotate the converter to align the drain plug with its hole in the flywheel*
  (b) *Do not allow the transmission to take a 'nose-down' attitude as the converter will move forward and disengage from the pump gear*
  (c) *Adjust the kickdown rod and selector linkage as described in Sections 30, 31 and 32*
  (d) *After lowering the car to the ground, fill the transmission with fluid to bring the level up to the FULL mark on the dipstick; then check and top-up the fluid level as described in Section 28.*

30 Manual shift linkage – adjustment

1 Place the transmission selector lever in the **D** position.
2 Jack-up and support the car. Working underneath the car, loosen

6

the manual lever shift rod retaining nut (see Fig. 6.40) and position the transmission manual lever in the **D** detent.

3   With the transmission selector lever and manual lever in the **D** positions, tighten the retaining nut to a torque of 10 to 20 lbf ft (1.3 to 2.7 kgf m).

4   Check the operation of the transmission in each selector lever position.

31 Transmission lock-rod – adjustment

On models from 1970 a transmission lock-rod connects the lower steering column shift tube to the manual reverse lever. It locks the transmission in reverse when the ignition switch is in the LOCK position. Before attempting to adjust the lock-rod ensure that the manual linkage is correctly adjusted as described in Section 30.

1   Loosen the lock-rod retaining nut (see Fig. 6.40) on the transmission manual lever.

2   Place the selector lever in the **D** position.

3   Align the hole in the steering column socket casting with the column alignment mark and insert a 0.18 in (4.5 mm) diameter pin. The column casting must not rotate with the pin in position.

4   Tighten the lock-rod retaining nut to a torque of 10 to 20 lbf ft (1.3 to 2.7 kgf m).

5   Remove the alignment pin and check the operation of the linkage.

32 Kickdown rod – adjustment

1   Disconnect the throttle and kickdown rod return springs.

2   Hold the carburetor throttle lever in wide open position against the stop.

3   Hold the kickdown rod against the 'through detent' stop.

4   Turn the adjustment screw on the carburetor kickdown lever to obtain a clearance of 0.04 to 0.08 in (1 to 2 mm) between the screw and the throttle lever.

5   Release the carburetor and transmission levers to the normal free position.

6   Install the throttle and kickdown rod return springs.

33 Neutral start switch (C4 and C6 transmissions) – adjustment

1   Loosen the two switch attaching bolts.

2   With the transmission selector lever in **N** (neutral) position, rotate the switch and install a No 43 drill into the gauge pin holes. It must be inserted a full 0.48 in (12.30 mm) into the three holes of the switch (see Fig. 6.41).

3   Tighten the switch attaching bolts and remove the drill.

4   Check the operation of the switch. The engine should start only when the transmission selector lever is in the **N** or **P** positions.

34 Neutral start switch (FMX transmission and C6 transmission with 429 CID engine) – adjustment

1   Shift the selector lever to **N** (neutral) position.

2   Undo the selector lever handle securing screws and remove the handle (see Fig. 6.40).

3   Remove the dial housing securing screws and remove the housing.

4   Remove the two pointer back-up shield securing screws and remove the shield.

5   Loosen the two screws securing the neutral start switch to the selector lever housing.

6   Adjust the switch in accordance with the information on the switch adjustment plate (see Fig. 6.42).

35 Intermediate band (C4 and C6) – adjustment

1   The intermediate band is used to hold the sun gear stationary to provide the second gear ratio. If it is not correctly adjusted there will be noticeable slip during first to second gear change instead of the usual crisp action.

2   To adjust the intermediate band, undo and remove the adjustment screw locknut located on the left-hand side of the transmission.

3   Tighten the adjusting screw, using a torque wrench set to 10 lbf ft (1.4 kgf m), and then back-off the adjustment screw $1\frac{3}{4}$ turns on C4 transmissions of $1\frac{1}{2}$ turns on C6 transmissions.

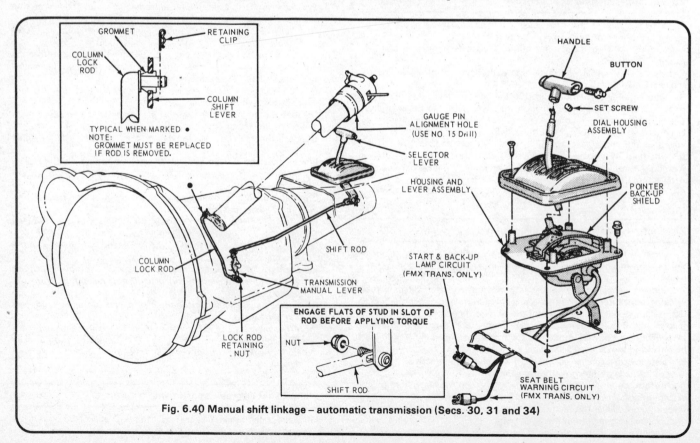

Fig. 6.40 Manual shift linkage – automatic transmission (Secs. 30, 31 and 34)

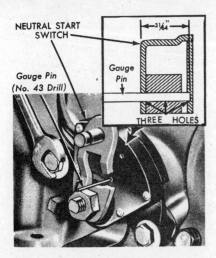

Fig. 6.41 Neutral start switch adjustment
(C4 and C6 transmission) (Sec. 33)

Fig. 6.43 Adjusting intermediate band
(Sec. 35)

Fig. 6.44 Adjusting low (reverse band
(Sec. 36)

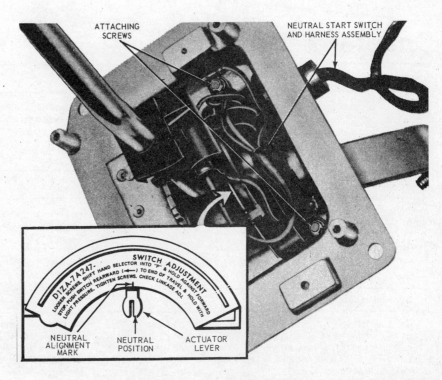

Fig. 6.42 Neutral start switch adjustment (FMX transmission and C6 transmission
with 429CID engine) (Sec. 34)

4   Install a new locknut and tighten it to the specified torque, while holding the adjusting screw to prevent it turning.

36 Low and reverse band (C4 only) – adjustment

1   The low and reverse band is in operation when the selector lever is in the 1 or R position. It holds the low and reverse pinion carrier stationary. If it is not correctly adjusted there will be a noticeable malfunction of the transmission, indicated by there being no drive in the R position and also no engine braking when the selector lever is in the first gear position.
2   To adjust the low/reverse band, undo and remove the adjusting screw locknut.
3   Tighten the adjusting screw, using a torque wrench set to 10 lbf ft (1.4 kgf m) and then back-off the adjusting screw a full three turns.
4   Install a new locknut and tighten it to the specified torque, while holding the adjusting screw to prevent it turning.

37 FMX transmission – band adjustment

Adjustment of the front and rear bands on FMX transmissions necessitates the removal of the transmission oil pan and special adjusting wrenches should be used. It is, therefore, recommended that this adjustment should be done by the local repair station.

38 Fault diagnosis – automatic transmission

As has been mentioned elsewhere in this Chapter, no service repair work should be considered by anyone without the specialist knowledge and equipment required to undertake this work. This is also relevant to fault diagnosis. If a fault is evident carry out the various adjustments previously described and if the fault still exists consult the local repair station or specialist.

6

Chapter 7 Driveshaft

Contents

Specifications

Type . . . .
One-piece tubular with single Cardan type universal joint at each end

Torque wrench settings

	lbf ft	kgf m
U-bolt nuts	8 to 15	2 to 2.07

1 General description

Drive is transmitted from the transmission to the rear axle by means of a finely balanced tubular driveshaft. Fitted at each end is a universal joint which allows for vertical movement of the rear axle. Each universal joint comprises a four legged center spider, four needle roller bearings and two yokes.

Fore-and-aft movement of the rear axle is absorbed by a sliding spline in the front of the driveshaft which slides over a mating spline on the rear of the transmission mainshaft.

All models are equipped with the sealed type of universal joint which requires no maintenance.

The driveshaft is a relatively simple component and is fairly easy to overhaul and repair, provided that spare parts are readily to hand.

2 Driveshaft – removal and installation

1   Chock the front wheels, jack-up the rear of the car or position the rear of the car over or on a ramp.
2   If the rear of the car is jacked-up, supplement the jack with support blocks so that danger is minimized should the jack fail.
3   If the rear wheels are off the ground, place the car in gear and apply the parking brake to ensure that the driveshaft does not turn when an attempt is made to loosen the four nuts securing the propeller shaft U-bolts to the rear axle pinion flange.
4   Mark the pinion flange, U-bolts and driveshaft so that they may be re-installed in their original position.
5   Undo and remove the four nuts securing the two U-bolts to the pinion flange, and remove the U-bolts.

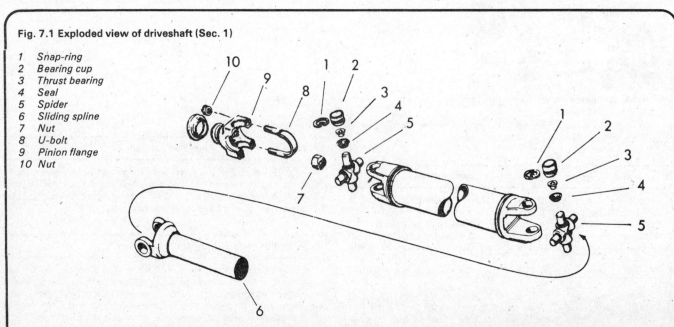

Fig. 7.1 Exploded view of driveshaft (Sec. 1)

1   Snap-ring
2   Bearing cup
3   Thrust bearing
4   Seal
5   Spider
6   Sliding spline
7   Nut
8   U-bolt
9   Pinion flange
10 Nut

6 Slightly push the driveshaft forward to separate the spider assembly from the pinion flange, then lower the end of the shaft and pull it rearward to disengage the transmission mainshaft splines.
7 Place a large can or tray under the rear of the transmission extension to catch any oil which is likely to leak from the end when the driveshaft is removed.
8 Installation of the driveshaft is a reversal of the above procedure. Ensure that the previously made mating marks are aligned.

3 Universal joints – inspection and repair

1 Wear in the needle roller bearings is characterised by vibration in the drive-line, 'clonks' on taking up the drive, and in extreme cases of lack of lubrication, metallic squeaking, and ultimately grating and shrieking.
2 It is easy to check if the needle roller bearings are worn with the driveshaft in position, by trying to turn the shaft with one hand, the other hand holding the rear axle pinion flange when the rear universal joint is being checked, and the front half coupling when the front universal is being checked. Any movement between the driveshaft and the front and the rear half couplings is indicative of considerable wear. If worn, the old bearings and spiders will have to be discarded and a repair kit, comprising new universal joint spiders, bearings, oil seals, and retainers purchased. Check also by trying to lift the shaft and noticing any movement in the joints.
3 Examine the driveshaft splines for wear. If worn it will be necessary to purchase a new front coupling, or if the yokes are badly worn, an exchange driveshaft. It is not possible to install oversize bearings and journals to the trunnion bearing holes.

4 Front universal joint – dismantling, overhaul and reassembly

1 Clean away all traces of dirt and grease from the snap-rings located on the ends of the bearing cups; remove the snap-rings by pressing their open ends together with a pair of snap-ring pliers, and lever them out with a screwdriver (photo). Note: If they are difficult to remove tap the bearing cup face resting on the top of the spider with a soft-faced hammer which will ease the pressure on the snap-ring.
2 Take off the bearing cups on the driveshaft yoke. To do this select two sockets from a socket set, one large enough to fit completely over the bearing cup and the other smaller than the bearing cup.
3 Open the jaws of the vise and with the sockets opposite each other and the universal joint in between, tighten the vise and force the narrower socket to move the opposite cup partially out of the yoke into the larger socket.
4 Remove the cup with a pair of pliers. Remove the opposite cup, and then free the yoke from the driveshaft.
5 To remove the remaining two cups now repeat the instructions in paragraph 3 or use a socket and hammer.
6 Recover the thrust bearing from inside each cup and remove the seal from the base of each spider journal.
7 Before reassembling, using new parts as necessary, thoroughly clean out the yokes and journals.
8 Install new oil seals to the spider journals and then assemble the needle rollers in the bearing cups with the assistance of some grease.
9 Fill each bearing cup about one third full with a universal grease, not forgetting to install the thrust bearings first.
10 Install the bearing cups on the spider and press them home so that they lie squarely in position. Install the snap-rings and settle the cups by tapping the whole assembly with a soft-faced hammer (photos).
11 Check that angular movement of the universal joint is free throughout its full range without signs of stiffness.

5 Rear universal joint – dismantling, overhaul and reassembly

This is easier than for the front universal joint as only two spider cups have to be removed as described in the previous Section. The remaining cups simply slide off the spider journals, these being held in position by two U-bolts and small lips on the pinion flange cup locations.

4.1 Removing a snap-ring

4.10A Installing the caps

4.10B Pressing in the caps

6 Driveshaft – balance

1   If the vibration from the drive-line has been traced to the driveshaft and yet there are no traces of wear, then the driveshaft is probably out-of-balance. This can also occur after overhaul.

2   First detach the driveshaft from the drive pinion flange and re-install, having rotated the shaft through 180°; if this does not cure the trouble then the following sequence should be followed:

3   Suitably support the rear of the car so that the wheels are clear of the ground. Chock the front wheels so that there is no chance of the car moving off the supports.

4   Start the engine and with top gear selected run at a speed of 40 to 50 mph (reading on speedometer).

5   An assistant should now place a crayon or piece of chalk so that it *just* contacts the rear end of the driveshaft. Obviously great care must be taken to avoid injury (Fig. 7.2).

6   Install two worm-drive type hose clips on the driveshaft so that the heads are 180° from the chalk mark. Tighten the clips (Fig. 7.3).

7   Start the engine again and run at a speed of 65 to 70 mph (reading on speedometer). If no vibration is felt, lower the car and road test.

8   Should, however, a vibration still exist, rotate the clips approximately 45° away from each other and retest (Fig. 7.4).

9   Continue to rotate the clips apart in smaller amounts until the vibration has been eliminated.

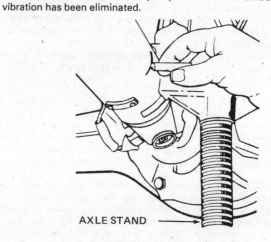

Fig. 7.2 Marking the driveshaft (Sec. 6)

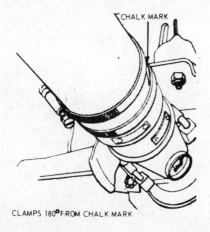

Fig. 7.3 Installing the worm-drive type clips (Sec. 6)

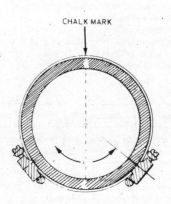

Fig. 7.4 Movement limit of clamps (Sec. 6)

7 Fault diagnosis – driveshaft

Symptom	Reason/s
Vibration	Wear in sliding sleeve splines Worn universal joint bearings Driveshaft out-of-balance Distorted driveshaft
Knock or 'clonk' when taking up drive	Worn universal joint bearings Worn rear axle drive pinion splines Loose rear drive flange bolts Excessive backlash in rear axle gears

Chapter 8 Rear axle

Contents

Specifications

Type .... Semi-floating hypoid with removable differential carrier

Ratios .... 3.00 : 1; 3.25 : 1, or 3.50 : 1 depending on engine type

Axle oil capacity .... 4.0 US pints (2 liters)

Oil type:
Conventional axle ESW-M2C-105-A
Limited slip axle ESW-M2C-119-A

Torque wrench settings

	lbf ft	kgf m
Bearing cap bolts	70 to 85	9.5 to 11.6
Adjusting nut lock bolts	12 to 25	1.66 to 3.46
Carrier to housing nuts	25 to 40	3.46 to 5.4
Pinion retainer to carrier bolts	30 to 45	4.15 to 6.1
Crownwheel attaching bolts	70 to 85	9.5 to 11.6
Axle shaft bearing retainer nuts	20 to 40	2.7 to 5.4
Pinion bearing preload (new bearing)	17 to 27	2.35 to 3.86

1 General description

The rear axle fitted to the Mustang models is a semi-floating hypoid gear type and is attached to the chassis by longitudinal leaf springs and telescopic shock absorbers.

The differential assembly has a removable carrier and the complete assembly can be withdrawn from the axle casing without having to remove the axle from the car.

The Traction-Lok limited slip differential is offered as equipment optional on some Mustang cars and provides improved traction in ice or snow conditions and also during hard acceleration. The procedure for removing and installing the limited slip differential is exactly the same as that used for the conventional type.

Unless the necessary tools and gauges are available, it is not recommended that the rear axle is overhauled, although the procedure is described later in this Chapter for those who have the necessary equipment.

With the removable carrier type axle, it is recommended that the differential unit is either renewed on an exchange basis, or the original unit taken to your Ford dealer for reconditioning.

2 Axleshaft – removal and installation

1 Place the car on level ground, chock the front wheels, loosen the rear wheel nuts on the side to be worked on, or both sides if both axleshafts are to be removed, then jack-up the rear of the car and remove the wheels. Position jack stands underneath the car.

2 Release the parking brake, then remove the brake drum securing screw and take off the brake drum.

3 Undo and remove the four bolts retaining the axleshaft bearing housing to the axle casing. These bolts are accessible with a socket on an extension through the holes in the axleshaft flange (Fig. 8.3).

4 It should be possible at this stage to remove the axleshaft by simply pulling on the flange, especially if taper bearings are installed, but if this fails, install the roadwheel on the studs and tighten down two opposite nuts just enough to prevent movement of the wheel on the studs.

5 Sitting on the ground, with one leg either side of the wheel and braced on the spring, get a firm hold on the outer edge of the tire and pull straight outward as hard as possible.

6 The axleshaft seals are made out of a synthetic material and are easily damaged. When withdrawing the shaft take care that the splined end does not cut the inner lip of the seal.

7 Installation is the reverse of the removal procedure but again, care must be taken to avoid damaging the seal. If a taper roller bearing is installed, the outer bearing should be removed from the axle housing using a slide hammer, and installed onto the taper bearing before installing the shaft.

3 Axleshaft oil seal – renewal (ball bearing type)

1 Remove the axleshaft as described in the previous Section.

2 The seal seats just inside the outer end of the axleshaft housing and ideally a slide hammer should be used to extract it. However, it can be removed using a hammer and chisel, but great care should be

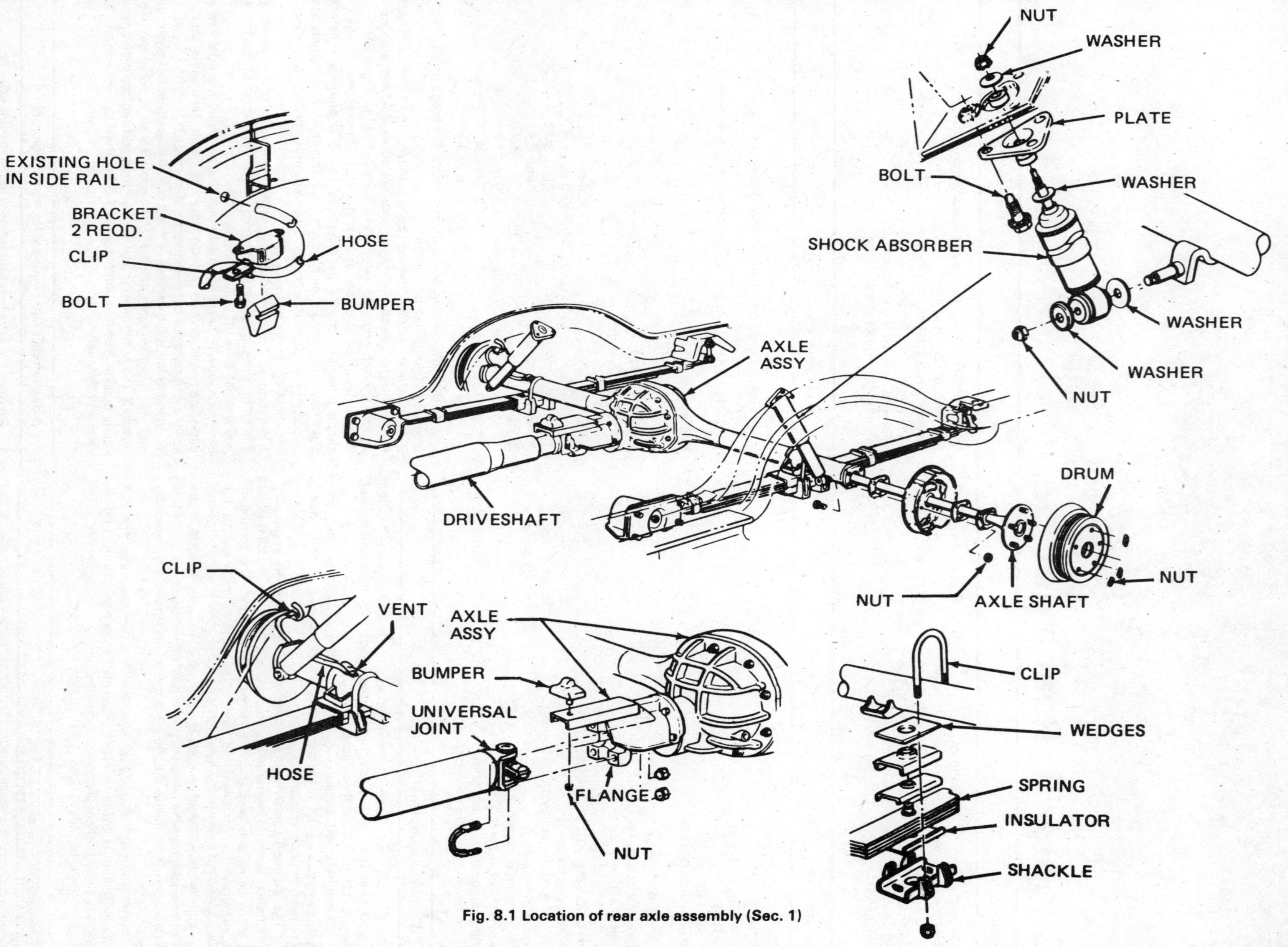

NUT
WASHER
PLATE
WASHER
WASHER
WASHER
NUT
WASHER
NUT
BOLT
SHOCK ABSORBER
DRUM
AXLE SHAFT
NUT
AXLE ASSY
DRIVESHAFT

CLIP
WEDGES
SPRING
INSULATOR
SHACKLE

VENT
AXLE ASSY
BUMPER
UNIVERSAL JOINT
FLANGE
NUT
HOSE
CLIP

EXISTING HOLE IN SIDE RAIL
HOSE
BUMPER
BRACKET 2 REQD.
CLIP
BOLT

Fig. 8.1 Location of rear axle assembly (Sec. 1)

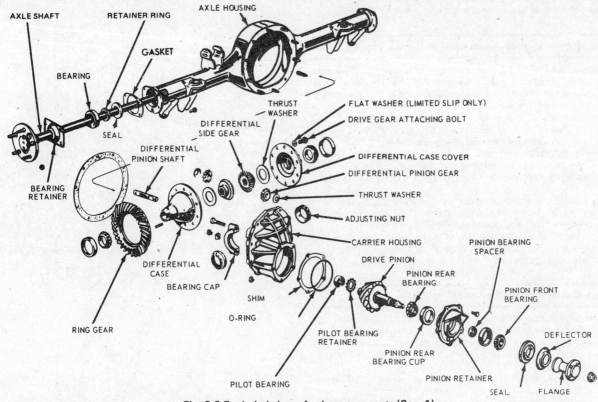

Fig. 8.2 Exploded view of axle components (Sec. 1)

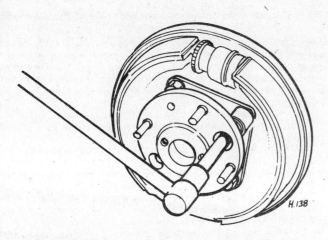

Fig. 8.3 Removing the axleshaft retaining nuts (Sec. 2)

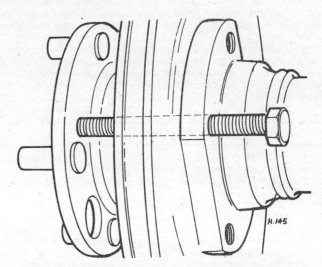

Fig. 8.4 Alternative method of extracting axleshaft (Sec. 2)

taken not to damage the axle housing, otherwise oil will seep past the outside of the new seal.

3 Make a note of which way round the seal is located in the housing before removing it; usually the metal clad side of the seal faces toward the roadwheel.

4 Smear some gasket sealer around the outside casing of the new seal and drive it evenly into place using a wood-block or a tubular drift having the same outside diameter as the seal.

5 Install the axleshaft as described in Section 2

4 Axleshaft bearing – renewal (ball bearing type)

1 Refer to Section 2 and remove the axleshaft assembly.

2 Using a hammer and sharp chisel make several deep nicks in the bearing retainer ring. This will release its grip on the axleshaft and

allow it to be slid off the shaft. If it is tight however, split it with a sharp chisel.

3 Place the axleshaft upside-down in a vise so that the bearing retainer is on the top of the jaws and the axleshaft flange is under them and, using a soft-faced hammer, drive the axleshaft through the bearing. If this proves difficult it will be necessary to use a garage press. Note which way round the bearing is installed.

4 Place the retainer plate and new bearing (correct way round) on the axleshaft.

5 Place the axleshaft vertically between the jaws of a bench vise, flange uppermost, so that the inner track is resting on the top of the vise jaws. Using a soft-faced hammer drive the axleshaft through the bearing until it is seating fully against the shaft shoulder.

6 The bearing retainer should next be installed, the sequence for this being the same as for the bearing. Do not attempt to install the bearing and retainer at one go.

7   Pack the bearing with a little multi-purpose grease.
8   Install the axleshaft assembly as described in Section 2.

5   Axleshaft bearing/oil seal – renewal (taper roller bearing type)

Note: *Because a special press has to be used to remove and re-install this type of bearing, it is recommended that the complete shaft assembly is taken to a Ford dealer who will have the proper equipment to carry out the job. However, the procedure is described for those who have the necessary equipment.*
1   Withdraw the axleshaft, as described in Section 2.
2   Secure the assembly in a vise, the jaws of which have been equipped with soft metal protectors.
3   Drill a hole in the bearing retainer and then remove by splitting it with a cold chisel. Take care not to damage the shaft during these operations.
4   Using a suitable press, draw off the combined bearing/oil seal.
5   To the axleshaft install the bearing retainer plate, the new bearing (seal side towards differential) and a new bearing retainer.
6   Apply pressure to the retainer only, using a press or bearing puller, and seat the components against the shoulder of the axleshaft flange.
7   Install the axleshaft, as described in Section 2.

6   Differential carrier – removal and installation

1   To remove the differential carrier assembly, drain the oil from the axle by removing the drain plug (if so equipped) in the base of the banjo casing, jack-up the rear of the vehicle, remove both roadwheels and brake drums and then partially withdraw both axleshafts as described in Section 2.
2   Disconnect the driveshaft at the rear end, as described in Chapter 7, Section 20.
3   Undo the self-locking nuts holding the differential carrier assembly to the axle casing. If an oil drain plug has not been fitted pull the assembly slightly forward and allow the oil to drain into a drain pan. The carrier complete with the differential unit can now be lifted clear with the gasket.
4   Before installing, carefully clean the mating surfaces of the carrier and the axle casing and obtain a new gasket. Installation is then a direct reversal of the above instructions. The nuts retaining the differential carrier assembly to the axle casing should be tightened to the specified torque.

7   Rear axle – removal and installation

1   Chock the front wheels, jack-up the rear of the car and support it on jack stands placed under the rear frame member.
2   Remove the wheels, brake drums and axleshafts as described in Section 2.
3   Remove the driveshaft as described in Chapter 7.
4   Disconnect the lower end of the shock absorbers from the axle housing.
5   Remove the brake vent tube (if so equipped) from the brake pipe junction and retaining clamp (see Chapter 9).
6   Remove the brake pipes from the clips that retain them to the axle, but do not disconnect any of the pipe unions.
7   Remove the brake linings and brake backplates, and support them with wire to avoid straining the hydraulic brake lines which are still attached (see Chapter 9).
8   Support the weight of the axle on a trolley jack and remove the nuts from the spring retaining U-bolts. Remove the bottom clamping plates.
9   Lower the axle assembly on the jack and withdraw it from the rear of the car.
10   The axle assembly is installed using the reverse procedure to that of removal. Tighten the U-bolt and shock absorber nuts to the torque figures given in Chapter 9 Specifications.

8   Differential – overhaul (conventional type)

Most professional garages will prefer to renew the complete differential carrier assembly as a unit if it is worn, rather than to

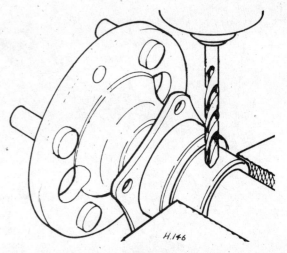

Fig. 8.5 Drilling the bearing retainer (taper bearing type) (Sec. 5)

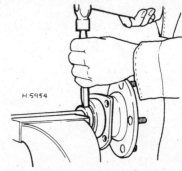

Fig. 8.6 Splitting the bearing retainer with a chisel (Secs. 4 and 5)

dismantle the unit to renew any damaged or worn parts. To do the job correctly requires the use of special and expensive tools which the majority of garages do not have. The primary object of these special tools is to enable the mesh of the crownwheel to the pinion to be very accurately set and thus ensure that noise is kept to a minimum and a long service life is achieved.
 The differential assembly should be stripped as follows:
1   Remove the differential assembly from the rear axle, as described in Section 6.
2   With the differential assembly on the bench begin dismantling the unit.
3   Undo and remove the bolts, spring washers and lockplates securing the adjustment cups to the bearing caps.
4   Release the tension on the bearing cap bolts and unscrew the differential bearing adjustment cups. Note from which side each cup originated, and mark with a punch or scriber.
5   Unscrew the bearing cap bolts and spring washers. Ensure that the caps are marked so that they may be installed in their original positions on reassembly.
6   Pull off the caps and then lever-out the differential unit complete with crownwheel and differential gears.
7   Recover the differential bearing outer tracks and inspect the bearings for wear or damage. If evident, the bearings will have to be renewed.
8   Using a universal puller and suitable thrust block draw off the old bearings.
9   Remove the bolts and washers that secure the crownwheel to the differential cage. Mark the relative positions of the cage and crownwheel, if new parts are not to be installed, and lift off the crownwheel.
10   Clamp the pinion flange in a vise and then undo the nut. Any damage caused to the edge of the flange by the vise should be carefully filed smooth.
11   With the nut removed, pull off the splined pinion flange. Tap the end of the pinion shaft, if the flange appears to be stuck.
12   The pinion, complete with spacer and rear bearing cone, may now be extracted from the rear of the housing.
13   Using a drift carefully tap out the pinion front bearing and oil seal.

14 Check the bearings for signs of wear and if evident the outer tracks must be removed using a suitable soft metal drift.

15 To dismantle the pinion assembly detach the bearing spacer and remove the rear bearing cone using a universal puller. Recover any shims found between the rear bearing and pinion head.

16 Tap out the differential pinion shaft locking pin which is tapered at one end and must be pushed out from the crownwheel side of the case.

17 Push the differential pinion shaft out of the case and rotate the pinions around the differential gears, so that they may be extracted through the apertures in the case. Cupped thrust washers are installed between the pinions and the case, and may be extracted after the pinions have been removed.

18 Remove the differential gears and thrust washers from the differential case.

19 Wash all parts and wipe dry with a clean lint-free cloth.

20 Again check all bearings for signs of wear or pitting; if evident a new set of bearings should be obtained.

21 Examine the teeth of the crownwheel and pinion for pitting, score-marks, chipping and general wear. If a crownwheel and pinion are required a matched assembly must be installed; under no circumstances may only one part of the two be renewed.

22 Inspect the differential pinions and side gears for signs of pitting, score-marks, chipping and general wear. Obtain new gears as necessary.

23 Inspect the thrust washers for signs of wear or deep scoring. Obtain new thrust washers as necessary.

24 Once the pinion oil seal has been disturbed it must be discarded and a new one obtained.

25 Commence reassembly by lubricating the differential gear thrust washers and then positioning a flat washer on each differential side gear. Position the two gears in the case.

26 Position the cupped thrust washers on the machined faces in the case, and retain in position with a smear of grease.

27 Locate the pinion gears in the case diametrically opposite each other, and rotate the gears to move the pinion gears in line with the holes in the shaft.

28 Check that the thrust washers are still in place and push the spider shaft through the case, thrust washers and pinions. If the pinions do not line-up they are not diametrically opposite each other, and should be extracted and repositioned. Measure the play of the gears and, if necessary select new thrust washers to obtain 0·005 to 0·007 in (0·13 to 0·18 mm) play.

29 Insert the locking pin (tapered end first) and lightly peen the case to prevent the pin working out.

30 Examine the bearing journals on the differential case for burrs, and

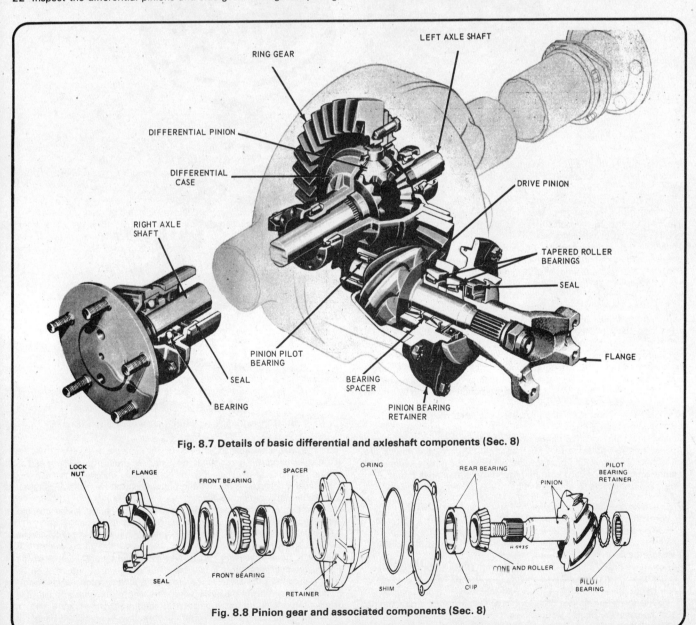

Fig. 8.7 Details of basic differential and axleshaft components (Sec. 8)

Fig. 8.8 Pinion gear and associated components (Sec. 8)

Fig. 8.9 Assembling the differential casing (Sec. 8)

install the differential bearing cones onto the differential case using a suitable diameter tubular drift. Make sure they are installed the correct way round.

31 Examine the crownwheel and differential case for burrs, score-marks and dirt. Clean as necessary and then install the crownwheel. Take care to line-up the bolt holes and any previously-made marks if the original parts are being re-used.

32 Install the crownwheel-to-differential case securing bolts and tighten in a diagonal manner to the specified torque wrench setting.

33 Using a suitable diameter drift carefully drive the pinion bearing cups into position in the final drive housing. Make sure that they are the correct way round.

34 Slide the shim onto the pinion shaft and locate behind the pinion head, then install the inner cone and race of the rear bearing. It is quite satisfactory to drive the rear bearing on with a piece of tubing 12 to 14 in (30 to 35 cm) long with sufficient internal diameter to just fit over the pinion shaft. With one end of the tube bearing against the race, tap the top end of the tube with a hammer, so driving the bearing squarely down the shaft and hard up against the underside of the thrust washer.

35 Slide a new collapsible spacer over the pinion shaft and insert the assembly into the differential carrier.

36 Install the pinion front bearing outer track and race followed by a new pinion oil seal.

37 Install the pinion drive flange and screw on the pinion self-locking nut and torque-tighten it to 175 lbf ft (24.1 kgf m) and check the pinion turning torque using either a suitable torque gauge or a spring balance and length of cord wrapped round the pinion drive flange. The correct pinion turning torque should be:

Original bearings

Torque wrench	12 to 18 lbf in	(0.14 to 0.216 kgf m)
Pull on spring balance	12 to 18 lbf	(5 to 8 kgf)

New bearings

Torque wrench	20 to 26 lbf in	(0.24 to 0.31 kgf m)
Pull on spring balance	20 to 26 lbf	(9 to 11 kgf)

38 To the foregoing figures add 3 lbf in (0.035 kgf m) if a new pinion oil seal has been installed.

39 Throughout the nut tightening process, hold the pinion flange

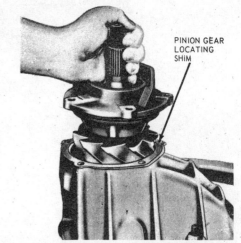

Fig. 8.10 Installing the pinion gear and retainer (Sec. 8)

quite still with a suitable tool.

40 If the pinion nut is overtightened, the nut cannot be unscrewed to correct the adjustment as the pinion spacer will have been over-compressed; the assembly will then have to be dismantled and a new collapsible type spacer installed.

41 Install the differential cage to the differential carrier and install the two bearing caps, locating them in their original positions.

42 Tighten the bearing cap bolts finger-tight and then screw in the two adjustment cups.

43 If it is now necessary to position the crownwheel relative to the pinion. If possible mount a dial indicator gauge and with the probe resting on one of the teeth of the crownwheel determine the backlash. Backlash may be varied by moving the whole differential assembly using the two adjustment cups until the required setting is obtained.

44 Tighten the bearing cap securing bolts and recheck the backlash setting.

Fig. 8.11 Crownwheel and pinion indexing marks (Sec. 8)

PAINT MARKING INDICATES POSITION IN WHICH GEARS WERE LAPPED

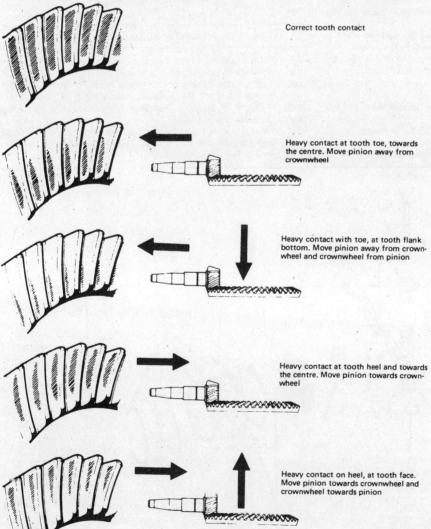

Correct tooth contact

Heavy contact at tooth toe, towards the centre. Move pinion away from crownwheel

Heavy contact with toe, at tooth flank bottom. Move pinion away from crownwheel and crownwheel from pinion

Heavy contact at tooth heel and towards the centre. Move pinion towards crownwheel

Heavy contact on heel, at tooth face. Move pinion towards crownwheel and crownwheel towards pinion

Fig. 8.12 Correct meshing of crownwheel and pinion, and repositioning guide for incorrect tooth meshing (Sec. 8)

H 1208

8

45 The best check the DIY motorist can make to ascertain the correct meshing of the crownwheel and pinion is to smear a little engineer's blue onto the crownwheel and then rotate the pinion. The contact mark should appear right in the middle of the crownwheel teeth. If the mark appears on the toe or the heel of the crownwheel then the crownwheel must be moved either nearer or further away from the pinion. The various tooth patterns that may be obtained are illustrated (Fig. 8.12).

46 When the correct meshing between the crownwheel and pinion has been obtained install the adjustment cup lock plates, bolts and spring washers.

47 The differential unit can now be installed to the axle casing.

9 Differential – overhaul (limited slip type)

The Traction-Lok limited slip differential is installed on some cars as an option to the conventional type. This type of differential is considerably more complicated than the conventional type, having a clutch mechanism attached to the crownwheel, the springs of which are preloaded to 1500 lbf (680 kgf). It is not therefore advisable for the home mechanic to attempt stripping and repairing this type of unit.

To check the operation of the limited slip facility the following tests can be carried out:

1 If the proper tool cannot be obtained, make up a torque wrench adaptor as shown in Fig. 8.14.

2 Jack-up one wheel and support that side of the car on a jack stand.

3 Remove the hub cap and attach the adaptor plate as shown in Fig. 8.14.

4 Make sure the transmission is in neutral and the parking brake is released and, using the torque wrench, attempt to turn the wheel.

5 The wheel should not start to turn until at least 40 lbf ft (5·5 kgf m) is showing on the torque wrench. Once the wheel is turning the torque required to keep it rotating may be lower than the initial breakaway torque figure but this is acceptable.

6 The wheel should turn with an even pressure throughout the check without slipping or binding.

7 If the initial rotation figure is below 40 lbf ft (5·5 kgf m) the limited slip facility is not operating to its full capability and, although it will not effect the normal running of the car, if maximum rear wheel traction is

a necessity it should be renewed. **WARNING**: *Never start the car and put it in gear with one wheel jacked up as, unlike the conventional differential, the limited slip type will cause the wheel still on the ground to turn with possibly disastrous results.*

10 Pinion oil seal – renewal

1 Jack-up the rear of the car and secure on stands under the bodyframe and axle casing.

2 Remove the roadwheels and brake drums.

3 Disconnect the driveshaft from the pinion drive flange as described in Chapter 7.

4 Using either a spring balance and a length of cord wrapped round the drive pinion, or a torque wrench (lbf in) check and record the turning torque of the pinion.

5 Hold the drive pinion quite still with a suitable tool and remove the pinion self-locking nut.

6 Remove the washer, drive flange and dust deflector, and then pry out the oil seal. Do not damage or lever against the pinion shaft splines during this operation.

7 Tap in the new oil seal using a piece of tubing as a drift. Do not inadvertently knock the end of the pinion shaft.

8 Repeat the operations described in paragraph 37 through 40 Section 8, but ensuring that the final pinion turning torque figure agrees with that recorded before dismantling.

9 Install the brake drums, driveshaft and roadwheels, and lower the car.

11 Wheel stud – removal and installation

1 The usual reasons for renewal of a wheel stud are that either the threads have been damaged or the stud has broken, this usually being caused by overtightening of the wheel nuts. To renew a wheel stud, remove the axleshaft assembly as described in Section 2. Using a parallel punch of suitable diameter drive the old stud through the flange towards the bearing.

2 To install a new stud place it in its hole from the rear of the flange and using a bench vise with a socket placed in front of the stud press it fully home in the flange (Fig. 8.15).

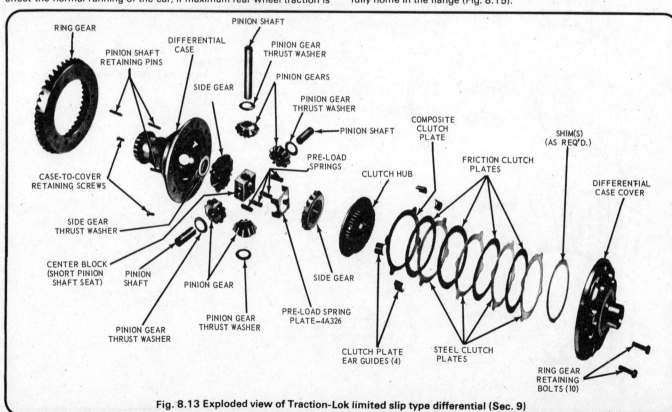

Fig. 8.13 Exploded view of Traction-Lok limited slip type differential (Sec. 9)

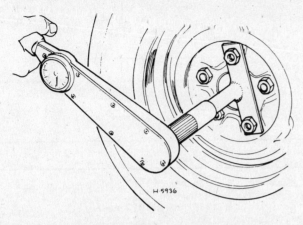

Fig. 8.14 Checking the operation of the limited slip facility on Traction-Lok differential (Sec. 9)

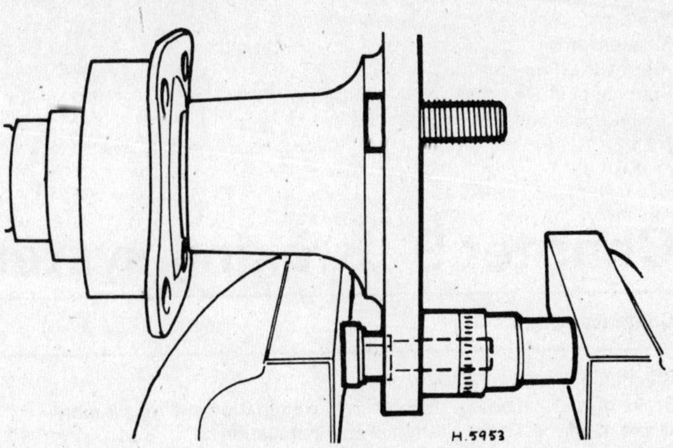

Fig. 8.15 Inserting a new stud into the axleshaft flange (Sec. 11)

12 Fault diagnosis – rear axle

Symptom	Reason/s
Vibration	Worn axleshaft bearings Loose drive flange bolts Out-of-balance driveshaft Wheels require balancing
Noise	Insufficient lubricant Worn gears and differential components generally
'Clunk' on acceleration or deceleration	Incorrect crownwheel and pinion mesh Excessive backlash due to wear in crownwheel and pinion teeth Worn axleshaft or differential side gear splines Loose drive flange bolts Worn drive pinion flange splines
Oil leakage	Faulty pinion or axleshaft oil seals Blocked axle housing breather

8

Chapter 9 Braking system

Contents

Specifications

System type . . . .   Drum brakes all round as standard, with option of servo-assisted front disc brakes

Service brake . . . .   Hydraulic

Parking brake . . . .   Mechanical, to rear wheels only

Drum brakes
Diameter . . . .   10 in (254 mm)
Wheel cylinder diameter . . . .   1.0 in (25.4 mm)
Drum regrinding limit . . . .   10.060 in (255.6 mm)
Brake lining wear limit:
    Riveted . . . . $\frac{1}{32}$ in (0.8 mm) from top of rivets
    Bonded . . . .   0.030 in (0.8 mm) total lining thickness

Disc brakes
Type:
    Models through 1967 . . . .   Four-piston, fixed caliper
    1968 through 1973 models . . . .   Single-piston, floating caliper
Brake dimensions (fixed caliper type):
    Lining thickness (new) . . . .   0.436 in (11.1 mm)
    Lining wear limit . . . .   0.066 in (1.8 mm)
    Rotor diameter . . . .   11.960 in (303.8 mm)
    Rotor thickness . . . .   1.240 in (31.5 mm)
Brake dimensions (floating caliper type):
    Lining thickness (outer) . . . .   0.333 in (8.5 mm)
    Lining thickness (inner) . . . .   0.362 in (9.2 mm)
    Lining wear limit . . . .   0.030 in (0.76 mm)
    Rotor diameter . . . .   11.29 in (286.8 mm)
    Rotor thickness . . . .   0.935 in (23.7 mm)

Note: *Regrinding the disc brake rotor to the correct limits requires the use of a special Rotunda finishing tool and this task should be entrusted to a Ford dealer*

Master cylinder
Type . . . .   Single cylinder (models through 1966) or tandem cylinder (1967 models onwards)
Bore . . . .   1.0 in (25.4 mm)

Brake pedal

	Max	Min
Free height (power brakes)	6.25 in (158 mm)	5.56 in (141 mm)
Free height (standard brakes)	7.49 in (190 mm)	6.43 in (163 mm)
Pedal travel (power brakes)	1.75 in (44 mm)	—
Pedal travel (standard brakes)	2.58 in (65 mm)	—

Torque wrench settings

	lbf ft	kgf m
Bleed valves (screws)	2.5 to 5.5	0.35 to 0.78
Hydraulic pipes:		
Brake hoses	12 to 20	1.6 to 2.77
Brake pipe	10 to 15	1.38 to 2.07
Upper anchor plate bolt (disc)	90 to 120	12.4 to 16.60
Lower anchor plate bolt (disc)	55 to 75	7.6 to 10.2
Parking brake assembly bolts	13 to 25	1.8 to 3.4
Master cylinder bolts	13 to 25	1.8 to 3.4
Wheel cylinder bolts	5 to 7	0.7 to 1.0
Pressure differential valve mounting nuts and bolts	7 to 11	1.0 to 1.53
Front backplate nuts and bolts	9 to 14	1.1 to 2.5
Rear backplate nuts and bolts	20 to 40	2.77 to 5.5
Servo unit to dashpanel	13 to 25	1.6 to 3.4
Parking brake securing bolts	20 to 25	2.77 to 3.4

1 General description

The standard braking system installed on the Mustang comprises hydraulically-operated drum brakes on the front and rear wheels, with a cable-operated parking brake actuating the rear brakes only. Front disc brakes and a vacuum brake booster are optional equipment on all models.

The front and rear drum brakes are virtually identical in design, being self-adjusting with a dual-piston wheel cylinder expanding both shoes. The self-adjuster mechanism comprises a cable, cable guide, adjusting lever, adjusting screw assembly and an adjuster spring. The cable is hooked over the anchor pin at the top and is connected to the lever at the bottom, and is passed along the web of the secondary brake shoe by means of the cable guide. The adjuster spring is hooked onto the primary brake shoe and also to the lever. The adjuster operates only when the brakes are applied and the car is backing-up. Also only when the secondary brake shoe is able to move towards the drum beyond a certain limit.

A dual master cylinder braking system is used on 1967 and later models, and comprises a dual master cylinder, pressure differential valve assembly and a switch. The switch is located on the differential valve and operates a dual brake warning light which is located on the instrument panel.

The self-centering pressure differential valve assembly body has a stepped bore to accommodate a sleeve and seal which is installed over the piston and into the large valve body bore in the front brake system area.

The brake warning light switch is located at the center of the valve body and the spring-loaded switch plunger locates in a tapered shoulder groove in the center of the piston. When in this condition the electrical circuit through the switch is broken and the warning light on the instrument panel is extinguished.

The front disc brake assembly comprises a ventilated disc which, on application of the brake pedal, is gripped between friction pads housed in a caliper unit. Models prior to 1968 are equipped with four-piston fixed caliper disc brakes while later models have the single piston floating caliper type.

All models equipped with disc brakes have a proportioning valve in the hydraulic pipeline to the rear brakes. This maintains a pre-determined pressure ratio between the front and rear brakes and reduces the possibility of the rear wheels locking-up under heavy braking conditions. 1972 and later Mustangs have a metering valve in the front brake line which prevents the front discs from carrying the majority of the braking loads at low operating pressures (light brake application), thus extending brake pad life.

2 Bleeding the hydraulic system

1 Removal of all the air from the hydraulic fluid in the braking system is essential to the correct working of the braking system. Before undertaking this task, examine the fluid reservoir cap to ensure that the vent hole is clear; also check the level of fluid in the reservoir and top-up if necessary.

2 Check all brake line unions and connections for possible leakage, and at the same time check the condition of the flexible hoses which may have perished.

3 If the condition of a caliper or wheel cylinder is in doubt, check for signs of fluid leakage.

4 If there is any possibility that incorrect fluid has been used in the system, drain all the fluid out and flush through with alcohol. Renew all piston seals and cups as they will be affected and could possibly fail under pressure.

5 Gather together a clean jar, a 12 inch (300 mm) length of rubber or plastic tubing which fits tightly over the bleed valves and a tin of the correct grade of brake fluid.

6 On models with the dual master cylinder the primary (front) and secondary (rear) hydraulic brake systems are individual systems and are therefore bled separately. Always bleed the longest line first.

7 To bleed the secondary system (rear) clean the area around the bleed valves and start at the rear right-hand wheel cylinder by first removing the cap over the end of the bleed valve.

8 Place the end of the tube in the clean jar which should contain sufficient fluid to keep the end of the tube submerged during the operation.

9 Open the bleed valve approx $\frac{3}{4}$ turn with a wrench and depress the brake pedal slowly through its full travel.

10 Close the bleed valve and allow the pedal to return to the released position.

11 Continue this sequence until no more air bubbles issue from the bleed tube. Give the brake pedal two more strokes to ensure that the line is completely free of air, and then tighten the bleed valve, ensuring that the bleed tube remains submerged until the valve is closed.

12 At regular intervals during the bleeding sequence, make sure that the reservoir is kept topped-up, otherwise air will enter again at this point. **Note**: *Do not re-use fluid bled from the system.*

13 Repeat the whole procedure on the rear left-hand brake line.

14 To bleed the primary system (front), start with the front right-hand side and finish with the front left-hand side cylinder. The procedure is identical to that previously described.

15 Some models have a bleed valve incorporated in the master cylinder. Where this is the case, the master cylinder should be bled before the brake lines. The bleeding procedure is identical to that already described.

16 Top-up the master cylinder to within 0.25 inch (6 mm) of the top of the reservoirs; check that the diaphragm type gasket is correctly located in the cover before the cover is installed.

3 Pressure differential valve – centralization

Models with the dual master cylinder are also equipped with a pressure differential valve. After any repair or bleed operations it is possible that the dual brake warning light will illuminate due to the pressure differential valve remaining in an off-center position.

1 To centralize the valve, first turn the ignition switch to the ON or ACC position.

9

2   Depress the brake pedal several times and the piston should center itself again causing the warning light to go out.
3   Turn the ignition switch off.
Note: *If difficulty is experienced in getting the valve to center, slacken the bleed valve on the brake opposite the one repaired and press the brake pedal very slowly until the warning light goes out. Tighten the bleed valve and top-up the brake fluid level.*

4   Flexible hoses – inspection, removal and installation

1   Inspect the condition of the flexible hydraulic hoses leading to each of the front brakes and the one at the front of the rear axle. If they are swollen, damaged or chafed, they must be renewed.
2   Wipe the top of the brake master cylinder reservoir and unscrew the cap. Place a piece of polythene sheet over the top of the reservoir and install the cap. This is to stop hydraulic fluid syphoning out during subsequent operations.
3   To remove a flexible hose wipe the union and any supports free from dust, and undo the union nuts from the metal pipe ends.
4   Remove the locknuts and washers securing each flexible hose end to the support and lift away the flexible hose.
5   Installation is the reverse sequence to removal. It will be necessary to bleed the brake hydraulic system as described in Section 2. On models with the dual master cylinder it is only necessary to bleed either the front or rear hydraulic system if one hose has been renewed.

5   Front disc brake pads (1964 through 1967 models) – removal, inspection and installation

1   The optional disc brakes on pre-1968 Mustangs are the four-piston fixed caliper type (see Fig. 9.1).
2   Jack-up the front of the car and support it on suitable jack stands. Remove the roadwheel.
3   Remove the two securing screws and withdraw the pad retaining clips and/or splash shield (see Fig. 9.1).
4   Using a large screwdriver or tire lever inserted between the pad shoe and lining, apply a steady pressure against the pad shoe and force the pistons to retract into the caliper bores.
5   Grip the metal flange on the outer end of each shoe using two pairs of pliers and pull the shoes straight out of the caliper assembly (Fig. 9.2).
6   To install the new pads, ensure that the pistons are fully retracted into the caliper bores and insert the pads into the caliper with the lining surfaces facing the rotor (disc). Ensure that the shoe flanges seat fully against the caliper bridges.
7   Install the pad retaining clips and/or splash shield and tighten the two securing screws.
8   Pump the brake pedal several times to seat the brake pads and check the brake master cylinder fluid level.
9   Install the roadwheel, lower the car and take it for a short road test to check the operation of the brakes.

6   Front disc brake calipers (1964 through 1967 models) – removal, overhaul and installation

1   Apply the parking brake, remove the front wheel trim, slacken the wheel nuts, jack up the front of the car and place on firmly based jack stands. Remove the front wheel.
2   Wipe the top of the master cylinder reservoir and unscrew the cap. Place a piece of polythene sheet over the top of the reservoir and re-install the cap.
3   Remove the friction pads as described in Section 5.
4   If it is intended to install new caliper pistons and/or the seals, depress the brake pedal to bring the pistons into contact with the disc and so assist subsequent removal of the pistons.
5   Wipe the area clean around the flexible hose bracket and detach the pipe as described in Section 4. Tape up the end of the pipe to stop the possibility of dirt ingress.
6   Using a screwdriver or chisel, bend back the tabs on the locking plate and undo the two caliper body mounting bolts.
7   Slide the caliper assembly off the disc and clamp the caliper mounting lugs in a soft-jawed vise.
8   Remove the hydraulic transfer pipe and bleed valve.

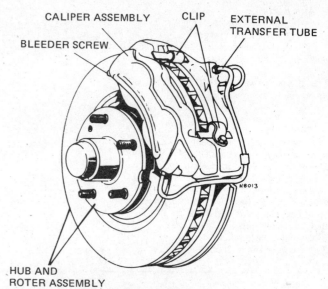

Fig. 9.1 Four-piston, fixed caliper type disc brake (Sec. 5)

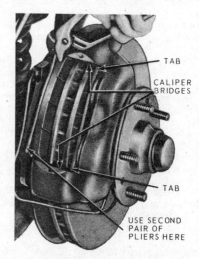

Fig. 9.2 Removing the brake pads – fixed caliper type (Sec. 5)

9   Remove the bridge bolts holding the caliper assembly together and separate the two halves (see Fig. 9.3).
10   Carefully pry the four dust boots from the grooves in the pistons and calipers, and remove the boots.
11   Tap the pistons out of the caliper bores and remove the piston seals using a small blunt screwdriver. Take great care not to scratch the surface of the caliper bores.
12   Thoroughly wash all parts in alcohol or clean hydraulic fluid. During reassembly new seals must be fitted; these should be well lubricated with clean hydraulic fluid.
13   Inspect the pistons and bores for signs of wear, score marks or damage; if evident new parts should be obtained or a new caliper obtained.
14   To reassemble, install one of the piston seals into the annulus groove in the cylinder bore.
15   Install the rubber boot in the cylinder bore groove so that the lip is turned outward.
16   Lubricate the seal and rubber boot with correct hydraulic fluid. Push the piston, crown first, through the rubber sealing boot and then into the cylinder bore. Take care as it is easy for the piston to damage the rubber boot.
17   With the piston half inserted into the cylinder bore, install the inner edge of the boot into the annular groove in the piston skirt.
18   Push the piston down the bore as far as it will go. Secure the rubber boot to the caliper with the circlip.
19   Install the remaining three pistons and boots using the same procedure, then make a final check to ensure that all the boots are

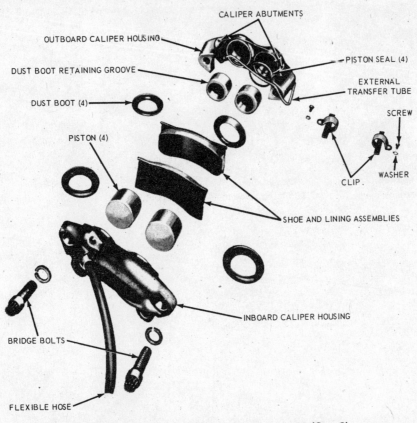

Fig. 9.3 Exploded view of fixed caliper type brake (Sec. 6)

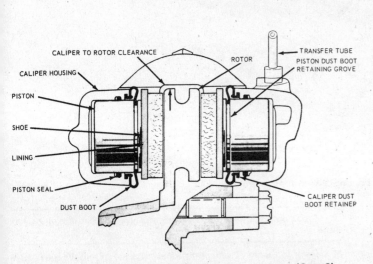

Fig. 9.4 Cross-sectional view of fixed caliper type brake (Sec. 6)

Fig. 9.5 Single-piston, floating caliper type disc brake (Sec. 7)

9

correctly located in the piston and caliper grooves.

20 Assemble the two caliper halves together and secure them with the two bridge bolts. Tighten the bolts to a torque wrench setting of 75 to 105 lbf ft (10.2 to 14.7 kgf m).

21 Connect the hydraulic transfer pipe and bleed valve to the caliper, and slide the caliper into position on the brake disc. Install the two caliper retaining bolts and tighten them to a torque wrench setting of 45 to 60 lbf ft (6.2 to 8.4 kgf m).

22 Reconnect the brake hose and install the brake pads as described in Section 5.

23 Bleed the braking system as described in Section 2, install the roadwheel and check the brakes for correct operation.

7 Front disc brake pads (1968 through 1973 models) – removal, inspection and installation

1 The optional disc brakes installed on 1968 through 1973 Mustangs are the single-piston floating caliper type (see Fig. 9.5).

2 To remove the brake pads, jack-up the front of the car, support it on suitable jack stands and remove the roadwheel.

3 Remove the two bolts securing the caliper assembly to the anchor plate and lift away the caliper. Support the caliper to avoid straining the flexible brake hose (photos).

4 Remove the two spring retaining clips using a screwdriver, and

7.3A Removing the caliper securing bolts

7.3B Lifting away the caliper and outer brake pad

7.5 Removing the inner brake pad

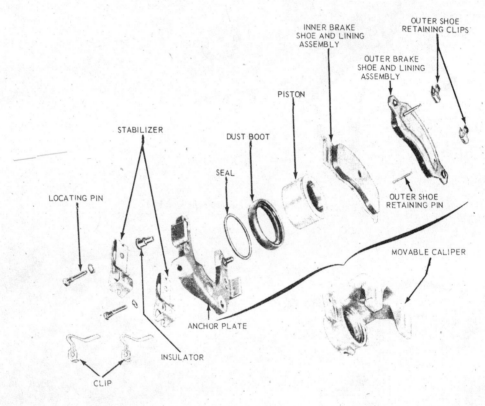

Fig. 9.6 Exploded view of floating caliper type brake (Sec. 8)

remove the outer brake pad and retaining pins from the caliper.

5　Remove the two retaining clips and lift out the inner brake pad (photo).

6　Examine the brake pad lining; if it has worn down close to the rivet head a replacement brake pad kit should be obtained from your Ford dealer. **Important**: The brake pad kit will also contain new retaining clips, insulator pins, and a stabilizer; these items must be used when installing new pads.

7　Push the retaining pins through the outer pad and caliper, and secure in place with new spring clips.

8　Slide the inner pad into position on the anchor plate and install the two spring retaining clips.

9　Slide the caliper into position over the disc and inner pad; and align the two mounting bolt holes.

10　Install and tighten both bolts finger-tight, then fully tighten the upper bolt to the specified torque wrench setting followed by the lower bolt. Secure both bolts with locking wire.

11　Check the brake fluid level in the master cylinder and pump the brake pedal several times to seat the brake pads.

12　Install the roadwheels, lower the car and take it for a short road test to check the operation of the brakes.

8　Front disc brake calipers (1968 through 1973 models) – overhaul

1　Refer to Section 7 and remove the caliper, and remove the flexible hose as described in Section 4.

2　Wrap a cloth around the caliper and using compressed air at the hydraulic fluid port carefully eject the pistons.

3　If the piston has seized in the bore carefully tap around the piston whilst applying air pressure. Remember the piston may come out with some force.

4　Remove the rubber dust boot from the caliper assembly.

5　Carefully remove the rubber piston seal from the cylinder bore with an old plastic knitting needle or something similar.

6　Thoroughly wash all parts in alcohol or clean hydraulic fluid. During reassembly new rubber seals must be installed and these should be well lubricated with clean hydraulic fluid before installation.

7　Inspect the piston and bore for signs of wear, score marks or other damage; if evident a new caliper assembly will be necessary.

8　To reassemble, first place the new caliper piston seal into its groove in the cylinder bore. The seal must not become twisted.

CALIPER HOUSING

PISTON

SHOE

LINING

ROTOR

DUST BOOT

PISTON SEAL

ANCHOR PLATE

Fig. 9.7 Cross-sectional view of floating caliper type brake (Sec. 8)

9   Install a new dust boot and ensure that the flange seats correctly in the outer groove of the caliper bore.

10 Carefully insert the piston into the bore. When it is about three-quarters of the way in, spread the dust boot over the piston. Seat the dust boot in the piston groove and push the piston fully into the bore.

11 Reassembly is now complete and the unit is ready for installing to the car.

9   Caliper anchor plate – removal and installation

1   Place chocks behind the rear wheels, apply the parking brake, loosen the front wheel nuts, jack-up the front of the car and support it on jack stands. Remove the roadwheel.

2   Remove the disc caliper and pads as described in Section 7.

3   Remove the upper and lower anchor plate bolts, and remove the anchor plate.

4   Before installing the anchor plate ensure that the mating surfaces of the plate and suspension spindle are clean and free from grit.

5   Because of the sheer force they are subject to, the old anchor plate retaining bolts should be discarded and new ones installed.

6   To avoid distorting the anchor plate, the upper bolts should be tightened to the specified torque figure followed by the lower bolts. Note that different torque figures are used for the upper and lower bolts (see Specifications).

10 Front brake disc and hub – removal and installation

1   Refer to the appropriate Sections, and remove the caliper and anchor plate assembly. To save extra work and time, if the caliper and anchor plate are not requiring attention, it is not necessary to disconnect the flexible brake hose from the caliper. Suspend the assembly with string or wire from the upper suspension arm.

2   Carefully remove the grease cap from the wheel spindle.

3   Withdraw the cotter pin and nut lock from the wheel bearing adjusting nut.

4   Undo and remove the wheel bearing adjusting nut from the spindle.

5   Grip the hub and disc assembly and pull it outwards far enough to loosen the washer and outer wheel bearing.

6   Push the hub and disc onto the spindle, and remove the washer and outer wheel bearing.

7   Grip the hub and disc assembly and pull it from the wheel spindle.

8   Carefully pry out the grease seal and lift away the inner tapered bearing from the back of the hub assembly.

9   Clean out the hub and wash the bearings with gasoline making sure that no grease or oil is allowed to get onto the brake disc.

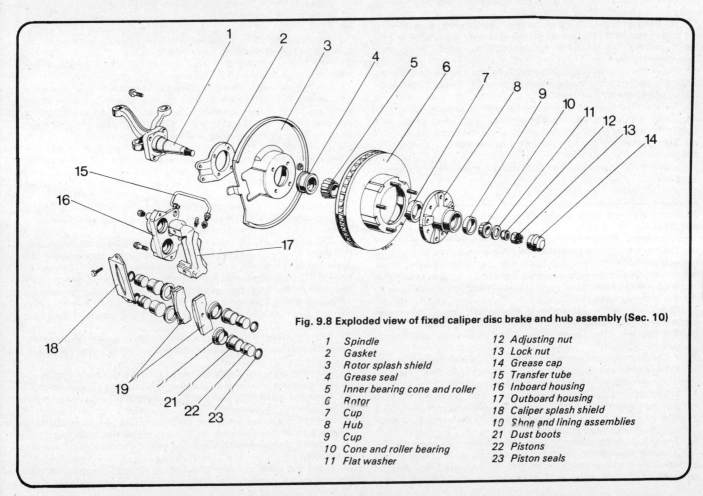

Fig. 9.8 Exploded view of fixed caliper disc brake and hub assembly (Sec. 10)

1	Spindle	12	Adjusting nut
2	Gasket	13	Lock nut
3	Rotor splash shield	14	Grease cap
4	Grease seal	15	Transfer tube
5	Inner bearing cone and roller	16	Inboard housing
6	Rotor	17	Outboard housing
7	Cup	18	Caliper splash shield
8	Hub	19	Shoe and lining assemblies
9	Cup	21	Dust boots
10	Cone and roller bearing	22	Pistons
11	Flat washer	23	Piston seals

9

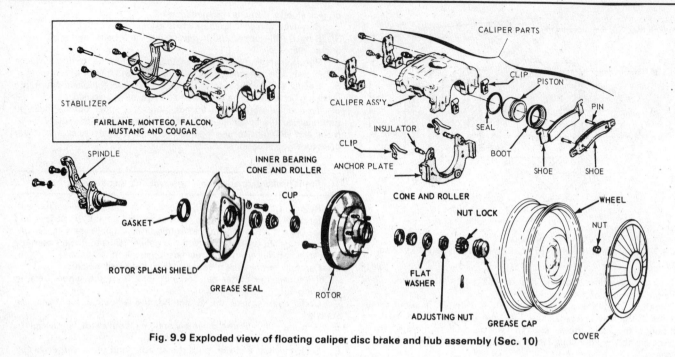

Fig. 9.9 Exploded view of floating caliper disc brake and hub assembly (Sec. 10)

10 Thoroughly clean the disc and inspect for signs of deep scoring or excessive corrosion. If these are evident the disc may be reground but the minimum thickness of the disc must not be less than the figure given in the Specifications. It is desirable however, to install a new disc if at all possible.

11 To reassemble, first work a suitable grease well into the bearings; fully pack the bearing cages and rollers.

12 To reassemble the hub install the inner bearing and then gently tap the grease seal back into the hub. A new seal must always be used as, during removal, the other one was probably damaged. The lip must face inward to the hub.

13 Install the hub and disc assembly onto the spindle keeping the assembly centered on the spindle to prevent damage to the inner grease seal or the spindle threads.

14 Place the outer wheel bearing and flat washer on the spindle.

15 Screw the wheel bearing adjusting nut onto the spindle and tighten finger-tight so that the hub and disc will still rotate freely.

16 Now tighten the nut using the method described in Chapter 11, and secure it with a new cotter pin and locknut.

17 Install the brake caliper and pads using the reverse procedure to removal.

11 Front and rear drum brake shoes – inspection, removal and installation

The front and rear drum brakes are basically the same design with the exception that the rear brakes are equipped with a parking brake mechanism. The following procedures apply to both the front and rear brakes, but references to the parking brake linkage obviously apply to the rear brakes only.

1 Chock the front or rear wheels as appropriate, jack-up the car and support on firmly based jack stands. Remove the roadwheel.

2 Remove the three Tinnerman nuts and remove the brake drum (photos).

3 If the drum will not come off, remove the rubber cover from the brake backplate and insert a narrow screwdriver through the slot. Disengage the adjusting lever from the adjusting screw.

4 Whilst holding the adjusting lever away from the screw, back off the adjusting screw with either a second screwdriver or shaped piece of metal as shown in Fig. 9.11. Take care not to burr, chip or damage the notches in the adjusting screw.

5 The brake linings should be renewed if they are so worn that the lining is only proud of the rivets by about 0.03 in (0.8 mm) or will be before the next routine check. If bonded linings are used they must be renewed when the lining material has worn down to 0.06 in (1.6 mm)

at its thinnest part.

6 To remove the brake shoes detach and remove the secondary shoe-to-anchor spring and lift away the spring.

7 Detach the primary shoe-to-anchor spring and lift away the spring.

8 Unhook the adjusting cable eye from the anchor pin.

9 Remove the shoe hold-down springs (photo) followed by the shoes, adjusting screw, pivot nut, socket and automatic adjustment parts.

10 Remove the parking brake link and spring. Disconnect the parking brake cable from the parking brake lever.

11 After the secondary shoe has been removed, the parking brake lever should be detached from the shoe.

12 It is recommended that only one brake assembly is overhauled at a time unless the parts are kept well apart. This is because the brake shoe adjusting screw assemblies are not interchangeable and, if interchanged, would in fact operate n reverse, thereby increasing the drum-to-lining clearance every time the car is backed up.

13 To prevent any mix up the socket end of the adjusting screw is stamped with an 'R' or 'L'. The adjusting pivot nuts can be identified by the number of grooves machined around the body of the nut. Two grooves on the nut indicate a right-hand thread and one groove indicates a left-hand thread.

14 If the shoes are to be left off for a while, place a warning on the steering wheel as accidental depression of the brake pedal will eject the pistons from the wheel cylinder.

15 Thoroughly clean all traces of dust from the shoes, backplate and brake drums using a stiff brush. Excessive amounts of brake dust can cause judder or squeal and it is therefore important to remove all traces. It is recommended that compressed air is *not* used for this operation as this increases the possibility of the dust being inhaled.

16 Check that the pistons are free in the cylinder, that the rubber dust covers are undamaged and in position, and that there are no hydraulic fluid leaks.

17 Prior to reassembly smear a trace of brake grease on the shoe support pads, brake shoe pivots and on the ratchet wheel face and threads.

18 To reassemble just install the parking brake lever to the secondary shoe, and secure with the spring washer and retaining clip.

19 Place the brake shoes on the backplate and retain with the hold-down springs.

20 Install the parking brake link and spring. Slacken off the parking brake adjustment and connect the cable to the parking brake lever.

21 Install the shoe guide (anchor pin) plate on the anchor pin (where applicable).

22 Place the cable eye over the anchor pin with the crimped side towards the backplate.

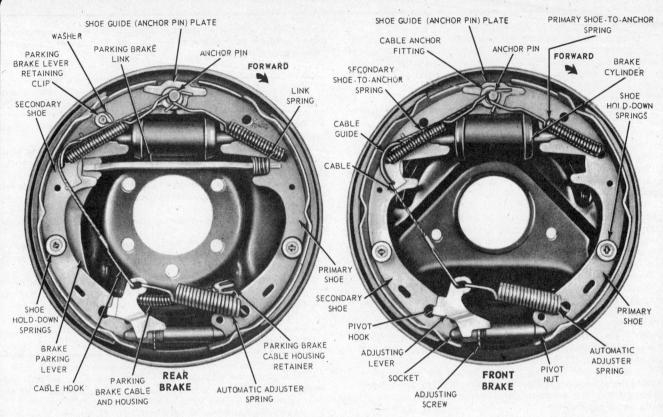

Fig. 9.10 Front and rear drum brakes (Sec. 11)

11.2A One of the Tinnerman type nuts securing the brake drum

11.2B Front brake drum removed; note that the hub assembly has also been removed to provide easier access to the shoes

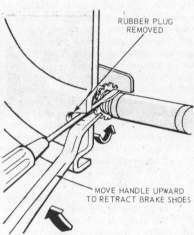

Fig. 9.11 Method of slackening the front and rear brake shoes (Sec. 11)

11.9 Removing a shoe retainer

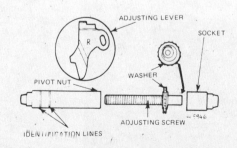

Fig. 9.12 Component parts of brake shoe adjuster (Sec. 11)

9

23 Install the primary shoe to anchor spring.
24 Install the cable guide into the secondary shoe web with the flanged hole fitted into the hole in the secondary shoe web. Thread the cable around the cable guide groove. It is very important that the cable is positioned in this groove and not between the guide and the shoe web.
25 Install the secondary shoe to anchor spring.
26 Check that the cable eye is not twisted or binding on the anchor pin when installed. All parts must be flat on the anchor pin.
27 Apply some brake grease to the threads and socket end of the adjusting screw. Turn the adjusting screw into the adjusting pivot nut fully and then back off $\frac{1}{2}$ turn.
28 Place the adjusting socket on the screw and install this assembly between the shoe ends with the adjusting screw toothed wheel nearest to the secondary shoe.
29 Hook the cable hook into the hole in the adjusting lever. The adjusting levers are stamped with an 'R' or 'L' to show their correct position on the left or right brake assembly (photo).
30 Position the hooked end of the adjuster spring completely into the large hole in the primary shoe web. The last coil of the spring must be at the edge of the hole.
31 Connect the loop end of the spring to the adjuster lever holes.
32 Pull the adjuster lever, cable and automatic adjuster spring down and towards the rear to engage the pivot hook in the large hole in the secondary shoe web (photos).
33 After reassembly check the action of the adjuster by pulling the section of the cable between the cable guide and the anchor pin towards the secondary shoe web far enough to lift the lever past a tooth on the adjusting screw wheel.
34 The lever should snap into position behind the next tooth, and releasing the cable should cause the adjuster spring to return the lever to its original position. This return motion of the lever will turn the adjusting screw one tooth.
35 If pulling the cable does not produce the desired action, or if the lever action is sluggish instead of positive and sharp, check the position of the lever on the adjusting screw toothed wheel. With the brake unit in a vertical position (the anchor pin at the top), the lever should contact the adjusting wheel 0.1875 in (4.763 mm) $\pm$ 0.0313 in (0.794 mm) above the center line of the screw.
36 Should the contact point be below this centerline lever will not lock on the teeth in the adjusting screw wheel, and the screw will not be turned as the lever is actuated by the cable.
37 Incorrect action should be checked as follows:
   (a) Inspect the cable and fittings. They should completely fill or extend slightly beyond the crimped section of the fittings. If this is not so, the cable assembly should be renewed.
   (b) Check the cable length. The cable should measure 8.41 in (213.5 mm) from the end of the cable anchor to the end of the cable hook
   (c) Inspect the cable guide for damage. The cable groove should be parallel to the shoe web, and the body of the guide should lie flat against the web. Renew the guide if it is damaged
   (d) Inspect the pivot hook on the lever. The hook surfaces should be square to the body of the lever for correct pivoting action. Renew the lever if the hook shows signs of damage
   (e) Check that the adjustment screw socket is correctly seated in the notch in the shoe web

38 Install the brake drum and roadwheel, lower the car to the ground and take it for a short road test to check the operation of the parking brake and/or footbrake.

12 Front and rear drum brake wheel cylinders – removal and installation

1 Refer to the previous Section and remove the brake shoes as described in paragraph 1 through 11.
2 If working on the rear brakes, slacken the brake pipe union from the rear of the wheel cylinder. Do not pull the pipe away from the cylinder as it will bend, making installation difficult.
3 On the front brakes, disconnect the inner end of the flexible brake hose as described in Section 4, then unscrew the other end of the hose from the wheel cylinder.
4 Undo and remove the two bolts securing the wheel cylinder to the brake backplate assembly.
5 Lift away the rear wheel cylinder assembly.
6 Plug the end of the hydraulic pipe to stop loss of too much hydraulic fluid.
7 Installation of the wheel cylinder is the reverse sequence to removal. It will be necessary to bleed the brake hydraulic system as described in Section 2.

13 Wheel cylinders – inspection and overhaul

1 Remove the wheel cylinder as described in the previous Section.
2 To dismantle the wheel cylinder, first remove the rubber boot from each end of the cylinder and push out the two pistons, cup seals and return spring (see Fig. 9.13).
3 Inspect the pistons for signs of scoring or scuff marks; if these are present the pistons should be renewed.
4 Examine the inside of the cylinder bore for score marks or corrosion. If these conditions are present the cylinder should be renewed.
5 If the cylinder is sound, thoroughly clean it out with alcohol or fresh hydraulic fluid.
6 Remove the bleed screw and check that the hole is clean.
7 The old rubber cups will probably be swollen and visibly worn. Smear the new rubber cups with clean brake fluid and insert one into the bore followed by one piston.
8 Place the return spring in the bore and push it until it contacts the rear of the first seal.
9 Install the second seal and piston into the cylinder bore.
10 Install the two rubber boots.
11 The wheel cylinder is now ready for installation to the brake backplate.

14 Rear drum brake backplate – removal and installation

1 Refer to Section 11, and remove the brake shoes and wheel cylinder from the backplate.
2 Disconnect the parking brake lever from the cable.
3 Refer to Chapter 8 and remove the axleshaft.
4 Disconnect the parking brake cable retainer from the backplate.

11.29 Cable correctly hooked onto the adjusting lever

11.32A Correct installation of adjusting lever, spring and cable

11.32B Location of lever on adjusting screw

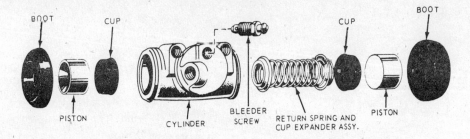

Fig. 9.13 Drum brake wheel cylinder components (Sec. 13)

5   The backplate and gasket may now be lifted away from the end of the axle housing.
6   Installation of the brake backplate is the reverse sequence to removal. It will be necessary to bleed the brake hydraulic system as described in Section 2. Do not forget to top-up the rear axle oil level if necessary.

15 Front drum brake backplate – removal and installation

1   Remove the brake shoes as described in Section 11 and the wheel cylinder as described in Section 12.
2   Remove the bolts securing the backplate to the wheel spindle assembly, and lift off the backplate and gasket.
3   Installation of the brake backplate is the reverse sequence to removal. It will be necessary to bleed the brake hydraulic system as described in Section 2.

16 Front and rear drum brake shoes – adjustment

Automatic adjusters are used on drum brakes and these operate when the car is backed-up and stopped. Should car use be such that it is not backed-up very often and the pedal movement has increased, then it will be necessary to adjust the brakes as follows:
1   Drive the car rearward and apply the brake pedal firmly. Now drive it forward, and again apply the brake pedal firmly.
2   Repeat the cycle until a desirable pedal movement is obtained. Should this not happen, however, it will be necessary to remove the drum and hub assemblies and inspect the adjuster mechanism as described in Section 11, paragraph 33 through 37.

17 Brake master cylinder – removal and installation

1   For safety reasons, disconnect the battery.
2   Withdraw the hairpin retainer and slide the stoplight switch off the brake pedal pin just sufficently for the switch outer hole to clear the pin. Lower the switch away from the pin. Lift the switch straight up from the pin taking great care not to damage the switch.
3   Slide the master cylinder pushrod, and the nylon washers and bushes from the brake pedal pin. **Note:** *On earlier models with the single master cylinder it is not necessary to remove the pushrod from the brake pedal; simply remove the rubber boot from the rear of the master cylinder to enable the pushrod to slide free when the cylinder is removed. This procedure also applies to all models with a brake servo unit.*
4   Unscrew the brake pipe from the master cylinder outlet port (two on the dual master cylinder). Plug the end of the pipe(s) to prevent dirt ingress and take suitable precautions to catch the hydraulic fluid as the pipe(s) is (are) removed from the master cylinder.
5   Undo and remove the two screws securing the master cylinder to the dashpanel (or servo unit).
6   Pull the master cylinder forwards and lift it upward from the car. Do not allow brake fluid to contact any paintwork as it acts as a solvent.
7   Install the master cylinder using the reverse procedure to removal. It will be necessary to bleed the hydraulic system as described in Section 2.

18 Brake master cylinder – dismantling, examination and reassembly

The following overhaul procedures are applicable to both single and dual master cylinders; however on the single type master cylinder there is no stop screw and only one piston assembly.

If a replacement master cylinder is to be installed, it will be necessary to lubricate the seals before installing to the car as they have a protective coating when originally assembled. Remove the blanking plugs from the hydraulic pipe union seatings. Inject some clean hydraulic fluid into the master cylinder and operate the pushrod several times so that the fluid spreads over all the internal working surfaces.

If the master cylinder is to be dismantled after removal proceed as follows:
1   Clean the exterior of the master cylinder and wipe dry with a lint-free cloth.
2   Remove the filler cover and diaphragm (gasket) from the top of the reservoir and pour out any remaining hydraulic fluid.
3   Undo and remove the secondary piston stop bolt from the bottom of the master cylinder body.
4   Undo and remove the bleed screw.
5   Depress the primary piston and remove the snap-ring from the groove at the rear of the master cylinder bore (Fig. 9.14).
6   Remove the pushrod and the primary piston assembly. *Do not remove the screw that retains the primary return spring retainer, return spring, primary cup and protector on the primary piston. This is factory set and must not be disturbed.*
7   Remove the secondary piston assembly. *Do not remove the outlet pipe seats, outlet check valves and outlet check valve springs from the master cylinder body.*
8   Examine the bore of the cylinder carefully for any signs of scores or ridges. If this is found to be smooth all over new seals can be installed. If however, there is any doubt of the condition of the bore then a new master cylinder must be obtained.
9   If examination of the seals shows them to be apparently swollen or very loose on the pistons, suspect oil contamination in the system. Oil will swell these rubber seals and if one is found to be swollen it is reasonable to assume that all seals in the braking system will need attention.
10 Thoroughly clean all parts in clean hydraulic fluid or alcohol.

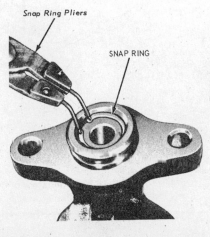

Fig. 9.14 Removing the master cylinder snap-ring (Sec. 18)

9

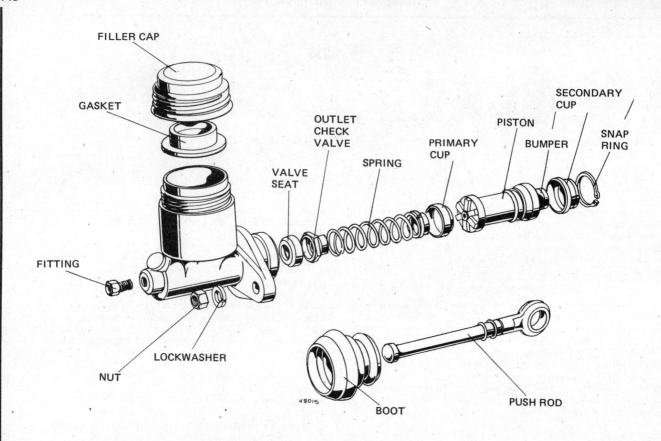

FILLER CAP

GASKET

OUTLET CHECK VALVE

VALVE SEAT

SPRING

PRIMARY CUP

PISTON

BUMPER

SECONDARY CUP

SNAP RING

FITTING

LOCKWASHER

NUT

BOOT

PUSH ROD

Fig. 9.15 Exploded view of single master cylinder (Sec. 18)

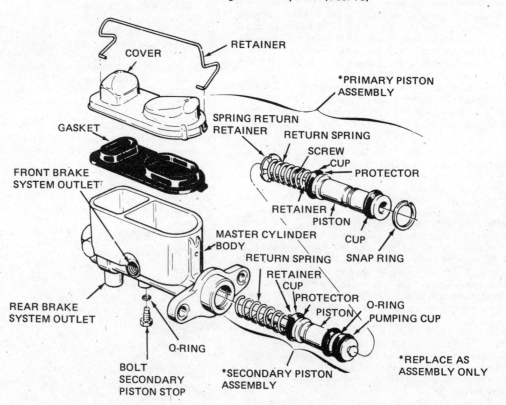

COVER

RETAINER

*PRIMARY PISTON ASSEMBLY

GASKET

SPRING RETURN RETAINER

RETURN SPRING

SCREW

CUP

PROTECTOR

FRONT BRAKE SYSTEM OUTLET

RETAINER

PISTON

CUP

SNAP RING

MASTER CYLINDER BODY

RETURN SPRING

RETAINER

CUP

PROTECTOR

PISTON

O-RING

PUMPING CUP

REAR BRAKE SYSTEM OUTLET

O-RING

BOLT SECONDARY PISTON STOP

*SECONDARY PISTON ASSEMBLY

*REPLACE AS ASSEMBLY ONLY

Fig. 9.16 Exploded view of dual master cylinder (Sec. 18)

Ensure that the ports are clear.

11 All components should be assembled wet after dipping in fresh brake fluid.

12 Carefully insert the complete secondary piston and return spring assembly into the master cylinder bore, easing the seals into the bore, taking care that they do not roll over. Push the assembly fully home.

13 Insert the primary piston assembly into the master cylinder bore.

14 Depress the primary piston and install the snap-ring into the cylinder bore groove.

15 Install the pushrod, boot and retainer onto the pushrod and push the assembly into the end of the primary piston. Check that the retainer is correctly seated and holding the pushrod securely.

16 Place the inner end of the pushrod boot in the master cylinder body retaining groove.

17 Install the secondary piston stop bolt and O-ring into the bottom of the master cylinder body.

18 Install the diaphragm into the filler cover making sure that it is correctly seated, and install the cover. Secure in position with the spring retainer.

19 Brake pedal – removal and installation

Manual transmission models

1 Remove the clutch cable retaining clip and remove the cable from the clutch pedal.

2 Disconnect the stoplight switch wires at the connector.

3 Remove the switch retainer and slide the stoplight switch from the brake pedal pin just sufficiently for the switch outer hole to clear the pin. Lower the switch away from the pin.

4 Slide the master cylinder pushrod, nylon washers and bush from the brake pedal pin.

5 Remove the self-locking nut and washer from the brake and clutch pedal shaft.

6 Remove the clutch pedal and shaft assembly. Follow this with the brake pedal assembly and bushes from the pedal support bracket.

7 Installation of the brake pedal is the reverse sequence to removal but the following additional points should be noted:

    (a) *Check and if necessary adjust the clutch pedal free-play as described in Chapter 5*

    (b) *Check and if necessary adjust the brake pedal free-play as described in Section 21*

    (c) *Lubricate all moving parts with a little grease*

Automatic transmission models

8 Disconnect the stoplight switch wires at the connector.

9 Withdraw the hairpin retainer and slide the stoplight switch off the brake pedal pin just sufficiently for the switch outer hole to clear the pin. Lower the switch away from the pin.

10 Slide the master cylinder pushrod, nylon washers and bush from the brake pedal pin.

11 Remove the self-locking nut and washer from the brake pedal shaft.

12 Remove the shaft, the brake pedal and the bushes from the pedal support bracket.

13 Installation of the brake pedal is the reverse sequence to removal, but the following points should be noted:

    (a) *Check and if necessary adjust the brake pedal free-play as described in Section 21*

    (b) *Lubricate all moving parts with a little grease*

20 Pressure differential valve – removal and installation

1 Disconnect the brake warning light connector from the warning light switch.

2 Disconnect the front inlet and rear outlet pipe unions from the valve assembly. Plug the ends of the pipes to prevent loss of hydraulic fluid or dirt ingress.

3 Undo and remove the two nuts and bolts securing the valve bracket to the underside of the wing apron.

4 Lift away the valve and bracket taking care not to allow any brake fluid to contact paintwork, as it acts as a solvent.

5 The valve cannot be overhauled or repaired, so if its performance is suspect a new unit will have to be obtained and installed.

6 Installation of the pressure differential valve and bracket is the reverse sequence to removal. It will be necessary to bleed the brake

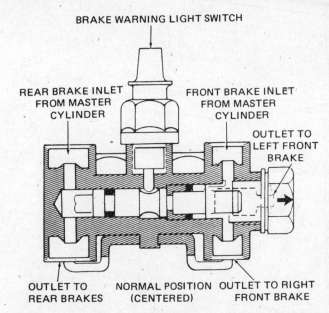

Fig. 9.17 Cross-sectional view of brake pressure differential valve (Sec. 20)

hydraulic system as described in Section 2, and possibly centralize the pressure differential valve as described in Section 3.

21 Brake pedal travel – measurement and adjustment

1 When the parking brake is fully released measure the brake pedal free height by first inserting a needle through the carpet and sound deadening felt until it contacts the metal dashpanel.

2 Measure the distance between the brake pedal to the metal dashpanel. This should be within the pedal height limits given in Specifications.

3 If the measurement obtained is not within the specified limit check the brake pedal linkage for missing, worn or damaged bushes, or loose securing bolts. Rectify as necessary.

4 If the measurement is still incorrect then the master cylinder should be checked to see if it has been correctly reassembled after overhaul.

5 To check the brake pedal travel measure and record the distance from the pedal free height position to the datum point which is the six o'clock position on the steering wheel rim.

6 Depress the brake pedal and take a second reading. The differences between the brake pedal free-height and the depressed

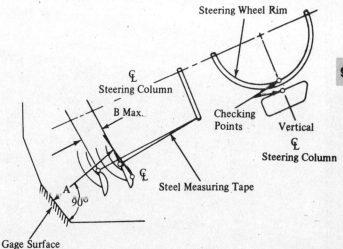

Fig. 9.18 Brake pedal free travel and height adjustment (Sec. 21)

9

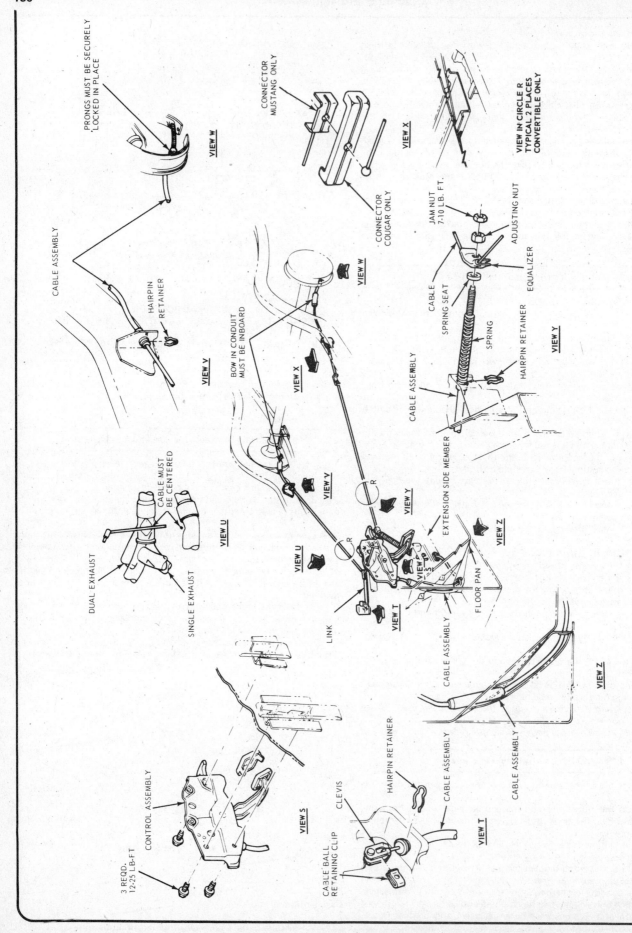

Fig. 9.19 Layout of parking brake and cable, pedal operated type (Sec. 23)

pedal measurement should be within the pedal travel figure given in Specifications.

7   If the pedal travel is more than that specified, adjust the brakes as described in Section 16.

8   Should this still not produce the desired results the drums will have to be removed to check that the linings are not badly worn and that the automatic adjusters are operating correctly. Rectify any faults found.

22 Parking brake – adjustment

1965 model Mustangs were equipped with a hand-operated parking brake while 1966 and later models were equipped with a pedal-operated parking brake.

1   To adjust the brake on all models, first block the front wheels, jack-up the rear of the car and support it on firmly-based jack stands.

2   On 1965 models, fully release the parking brake and then pull the handle up until the third 'click' is heard. Leave the handle in this position.

3   On later models equipped with a foot-operated parking brake, fully release the brake pedal and then depress it one 'click' from the released position. Note that on vacuum release brakes the first click occurs after approximately 2 in (50 mm) of travel.

4   On all models, slacken the locknut on the brake cable equalizer and turn the adjuster nut until the brake cables are just taut enough to cause the rear wheels to drag slightly when rotated by hand.

5   Tighten the equalizer locknut, release the parking brake and check that the rear wheels rotate freely.

6   Lower the car and check the operation of the parking brake.

23 Parking brake cable – removal and installation

1   Block the front wheels, jack-up the rear of the car and support on firmly-based jack stands. Remove the wheels.

2   Refer to Section 9 and remove the brake drums.

3   Release the parking brake and back-off the adjusting nut.

4   Remove the cable from the equalizer.

5   Remove the hairpin clips and pull the cable through the chassis brackets.

6   On models equipped with a foot-operated parking brake, release the front section of the cable from the pedal assembly by removing the spring clip (See Fig. 9.19)

7   Remove the self-adjuster springs and remove the cable retainers from the brake backplate.

8   Disconnect the ends of the cables from the parking brake levers on the secondary brake shoes.

9   Compress the cable retainer prongs and pull the cable ends from the backplates.

10   Installation of the parking brake cable is the reverse sequence to removal. It will be necessary to adjust the parking brake as described in Section 22.

24 Vacuum servo unit (brake booster) – description

1   A vacuum servo unit may be installed in the brake hydraulic circuit in series with the master cylinder, to provide assistance to the driver when the brake pedal is depressed. This reduces the effort required by the driver to operate the brakes under all braking conditions.

2   The unit operates by vacuum obtained from the intake manifold and comprises basically a booster diaphragm and check valve. The servo unit and hydraulic master cylinder are connected together so that the servo unit piston rod acts as the master cylinder pushrod. The driver's braking effort is transmitted through another pushrod to the servo unit piston and its built in control system. The servo unit piston does not fit tightly into the cylinder, but has a strong diaphragm to keep an air-tight seal between the two parts. The forward chamber is held under the vacuum conditions created in the intake manifold of the engine, and during periods when the brake pedal is not in use, the controls open a passage to the rear chamber, so placing it under vacuum conditions as well. When the brake pedal is depressed, the vacuum passage to the rear chamber is cut off and the chamber opened to atmospheric pressure. The consequent pressure differential pushes the servo piston forward in the vacuum chamber and operates the main pushrod to the master cylinder.

3   The controls are designed so that assistance is given under all conditions and, when the brakes are not required, vacuum in the rear chamber is established when the brake pedal is released. All air from the atmosphere entering the rear chamber is passed through a small air filter.

4   Under normal operating conditions the vacuum servo unit will give trouble-free service for a very long time. If however, it is suspected that the unit is faulty (ie increase in foot pressure is required to apply the brakes) it must be exchanged for a new unit. No attempt should be made to repair the old unit as it is not a repairable item.

25 Vacuum servo unit (brake booster) – removal and installation

1   Remove the stoplight switch and actuating rod from the brake pedal as described in Section 17.

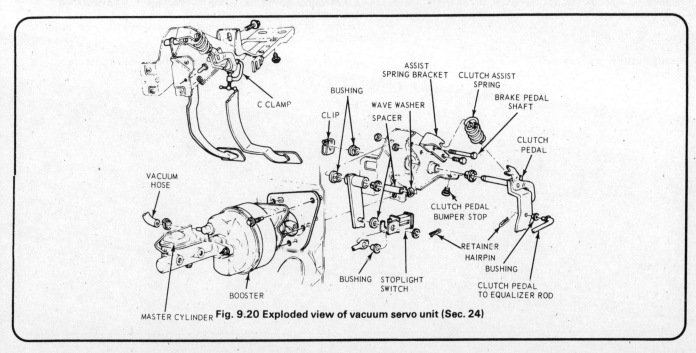

Fig. 9.20 Exploded view of vacuum servo unit (Sec. 24)

2   Working under the hood, remove the air cleaner from the car-buretor and the vacuum hose from the servo unit.
3   Refer to Section 17 and remove the master cylinder.
4   From inside the car, remove the nuts securing the servo unit to the dashpanel.
5   Working inside the engine compartment, move the servo unit

forward until the actuating rod is clear of the dashpanel, rotate it through 90° and lift the unit upward until clear of the engine compart-ment.
6   Installation of a new servo unit is the reverse sequence to removal. It will be necessary to bleed the brake hydraulic system as described in Section 2.

26 Fault diagnosis – braking system

Before diagnosing faults from the following chart, check that any braking irregularities are not caused by:

> *1 Uneven and incorrect tire pressures*
> *2 Incorrect 'mix' of radial and crossply tires*
> *3 Wear in the steering mechanism*
> *4 Defects in the suspension and dampers*
> *5 Misalignment of the bodyframe*

Symptom	Reason/s
Pedal travels a long way before the brakes operate	Brake shoes set too far from the drums (auto adjusters seized)
Stopping ability poor, even though pedal pressure is firm	Linings, discs or drums badly worn or scored One or more wheel hydraulic cylinders seized, resulting in some brake shoes not pressing against the drums (or pads against discs) Brake linings contaminated with oil Wrong type of linings fitted (too hard) Brake shoes wrongly assembled Servo unit not functioning
Car veers to one side when the brakes are applied	Brake pads or linings on one side are contaminated with oil Hydraulic wheel cylinder(s) on one side partially or fully seized A mixture of lining materials fitted between sides Brake discs not matched Unequal wear between sides caused by partially seized wheel cylinders
Pedal feels spongy when the brakes are applied	Air is present in the hydraulic system
Pedal feels springy when the brakes are applied	Brake linings not bedded into the drums (after fitting new ones) Master cylinder or brake backplate mounting bolts loose Severe wear in brake drums causing distortion when brakes are applied Discs out of true
Pedal travels right down with little or no resistance and brakes are virtually non-operative	Leak in hydraulic system resulting in lack of pressure for operating wheel cylinders If no signs of leakage are apparent the master cylinder internal seals are failing to sustain pressure
Binding, juddering, overheating	One or a combination of reasons given in the foregoing Sections

Chapter 10 Electrical system

Contents

Specifications

Battery

Type	Lead acid
Plates per cell/capacity:	
54	45 amp hr
66	55 amp hr
66	70 amp hr
78	80 amp hr

Alternator

Type	Autolite or Motorcraft
Color code	Purple, orange, red or green
Rating (at 15V):	
Purple	38 amps
Orange	42 amps
Red	55 amps
Green	61 amps
Output (at 15V):	
Purple	570 watts
Orange	630 watts
Red	825 watts
Green	915 watts
Field current (at 12V):	
Purple	2.4 amps
Orange, red, and green	2.9 amps
Cut-in speed	400 rpm
Rated output speed (engine rpm):	
Hot	2000 rpm
Cold	2900 rpm
Slip ring diameter (minimum)	1.22 in (30.988 mm)
Slip ring maximum run-out	0.0005 in (0.0127 mm)

10

Brush length:
    New length . . . .   0.5 in (12.7 mm)
    Minimum length . . . .   0.3125 in (7.9375 mm)

Alternator regulator
Type . . . .   Autolite, electro-mechanical
Setting . . . .   13.5 to 15.3V

Fusible link identification

Color	Wire gauge
Red	18
Orange	16
Green	14

Starter motor
Type . . . .   Autolite, positive engagement
Diameter . . . .   4.5 in (114.3 mm)
Current draw (normal load) . . . .   150 to 200 amps
Cranking speed . . . .   150 to 290 rpm
Minimum stall torque . . . .   15.5 lbf ft (2.13 kgf m)
Maximum load current . . . .   670 amps
No load current . . . .   70 amps
Brush length:
    New length . . . .   0.50 in (12.7 mm)
    Minimum length . . . .   0.25 in (6.35 mm)
Spring tension . . . .   40 oz
Maximum commutator run-out . . . .   0.005 in (0.127 mm)

Fuses and circuit breakers
Early models

Circuits	Location	Fuse or CB (Amps)
Ashtray light	Fuse panel	SFE 4
Back-up light	Fuse panel	AGC or SFE 15
Cigar lighter	Fuse panel	SFE 14
Clock feed	Fuse panel	SFE 14
Convertible top feed	Attached to starter motor relay	20CB
Convertible top motor	Integral part of motor	CB
Courtesy lights (C-Pillar)		
(Glove box)		
(Luggage compartment)		
(Map light)	Fuse panel	SFE 14
Emergency flashers	Fuse panel	AGC or SFE 20
Emission control and/or throttle solenoid	Fuse panel	SFE 14
Engine compartment light	Cartridge in feed line	SFE 7.5
Headlights	In switch	12CB
Heater and defroster	Fuse panel	SFE 14
Heater and defroster with air conditioning	Fuse panel	8AG or AGX 30
Horns	In headlight switch	15CB
Indicator lights (convenience control panel)	Fuse panel	AGC or SFE 20
Seat belt (instrument or convenience control panel) indicator	Fuse panel	AGC or SFE 15
Instrument panel lights (Clock light)		
(Heater and A/C controls)		
(Radio)	Fuse panel	SFE 4
License lights; Marker lights; Parking lights	In headlight switch	15CB
Power seats	On starter relay	20CB
Power seat motors	Integral part of motor	CB
Power window	Attached to starter motor relay	20CB
Power window motor	Integral with motor	CB
Power window relay feed; PRNDL (Auto/trans); Radio and/or stereo tape feed	Fuse panel	AGC or SFE 20
Speed control	Fuse panel	AGC or SFE 20
Stop lights	In headlight switch	15CB
Swing-tilt steering wheel	Fuse panel	AGC or SFE 20
Tail lights	In headlight switch	15CB
Transmission selector light	Fuse panel	AGC or SFE 20
Turn signals; Windshield washers	Fuse panel	AGC or SFE 20
Windshield wipers	Windshield wiper switch	6CB
Windshield wiper motor	Integral part of motor	CB

Later models
Fuses and circuit breakers not located in fuse panel (for fuse panel protected circuits refer to Chapter 10, Section 37).

1971 models

Circuit	Circuit protection and rating	Location
Headlamps	12 amp CB	Integral with lighting switch
Parking lamps; Marker lamps; License lamps; Tail lamps; (RPO PRNDL lamp)	15.amp CB	Integral with lighting switch
Engine compartment lamp	7.5 amp fuse (SFE 7.5)	Cartridge in feed line
Stop lamps	15 amp CB	On relay panel above glovebox
Power windows; power seat; power top and heated backlight	20 amp CB	On starter relay
Wiper (2-spd)	7 amp CB	In Wiper Switch
Intermittent wiper (RPO)	7 amp CB	
Front seat-back latch solenoid	CB	Integral with solenoid
Window motor; Seat motor; Top motor	CB	In motor

1972 models

Circuit	Circuit protection and rating	Location
Headlights	9 amp CB	Integral with lighting switch
Headlights with Grille Lights	13 amp CB	Integral with lighting switch
Parking lights; Marker lights; License lights; Tail lights; (RPO PRNDL Light); Headlight ON control	12 amp CB	Integral with lighting switch
Engine compartment light	7.5 amp fuse (SFE 7.5)	Cartridge in feed line
Stop lights; Hazard flasher	15 amp CB	On relay panel above glovebox
Power windows; Power seat; Power top; Heated backlight; Automatic seatback latch feed	20 amp CB	On starter relay
Wiper (2-spd)	7 amp CB	In wiper switch
Intermittent wiper (RPO)	7 amp CB	In wiper switch
Front seat back latch solenoid	CB	Integral with solenoid
Window motor; Seat motor; Top motor	CB	In motor

1973 models

Circuit	Circuit protection and rating	Location
Headlights	18 amp CB	Integral with lighting switch
Parking lights; Marker lights; License lights	15 amp CB	Integral with lighting switch
Tail lights; PRN21 light; Headlight ON control		
Stop lights; Hazard flasher	15 amp CB	On relay panel above glovebox
Power windows; Power seat; Power top; Engine compartment light; Automatic seatback latch feed	20 amp CB	On starter relay
Wiper (2-speed)	CB	In windshield wiper switch
Intermittent wiper (RPO)	CB	In windshield wiper switch
Heated back window	Fuse link	In harness
Window motor; Seat motor; Top motor	CB	In motor

Light bulb specification (typical)

Light description	Candle power or Wattage	Trade No.
Auto-trans quadrant	0.75 cp	1445
Back-up lamp	32 cp	1156
Cigar lighter bezel	2 cp	1895
Clock	2 cp	194
Cluster illumination	2 cp	194
Courtesy lamp – dome	12 cp	561
Courtesy lamps – under panel	6 cp	631
Electrical rear window defroster	—	(*)
Engine compartment	6 cp	631
Front park and turn signal	3-32 cp	1157 NA
Front side marker	2 cp	194
Gauges	2 cp	194
Glove compartment	2 cp	1895
Headlamps – high/low	50/60 watts	6014
Heater/Air Conditioner Control	0.75 cp	1445
High beam	2 cp	194
License plate lamp	4 cp	97
Lights bezel	2 cp	1895
Luggage compartment	6 cp	631
Map lamp	6 cp	212/212-1
Radio AM	2 cp	1893
Radio AM/FM	0.75 cp	1892
Radio AM/tape player	2 cp	1893
Rear side markers	2 cp	194

10

Light description

	Candle power or Wattage	Trade No.
Rear tail, stop and turn signal	3-32 cp	1157
Speedometer	2 cp	194
Spotlight	30 watts	4405
Turn signal indicators	2 cp	194
Warning lamps	2 cp	194
Wiper/washer bezel	2 cp	1895

(*) Bulb and wire assembly, Ford Part No. D1ZB-1 8 C6 22-AA

Torque wrench settings

	lbf ft	kgf m
Alternator pulley nut	60 to 100	8.3 to 13.8
Starter motor through-bolts	55 to 75	7.6 to 10.2
Starter motor mounting bolts	15 to 20	2.0 to 2.7

1 General description

The major components of the 12 volt negative ground system comprise a 12 volt battery, an alternator (driven from the crankshaft pulley), and a starter motor.

The battery supplies a steady amount of current for the ignition, lighting and other electrical circuits and provides a reserve of electricity when the current consumed by the electrical equipment exceeds that being produced by the alternator.

The alternator regulator ensures a high ouput if the battery is in a low state of charge and the demand from the electrical equipment is high, and a low output if the battery is fully charged and there is little demand for the electrical equipment.

When fitting electrical accessories to cars with a negative ground system, it is important, if they contain silicone diodes or transistors, that they are connected correctly, otherwise serious damage may result to the components concerned. Items such as radios, tape recorders, electronic ignition system, electric tachometer, automatic dipping etc, should all be checked for correct polarity.

It is important that the battery positive lead is always disconnected if the battery is to be boost-charged. Also, if body repairs are to be carried out using electric welding equipment, the alternator must be disconnected, otherwise serious damage can be caused. Whenever the battery has to be disconnected, it must always be reconnected with the negative terminal grounded.

2 Battery – removal and installation

1   The battery is on a carrier, installed on the right-hand side of the engine compartment. It should be removed once every three months for cleaning and testing. Disconnect the positive and then the ground cables from the battery terminals (photo).

2   Undo the securing nuts and remove the battery clamp. Carefully lift the battery from its carrier, holding it vertically to avoid spilling any

2.1 The battery is mounted at the front of the engine compartment on right-hand side

of the electrolyte.

3   Installation is the reverse of the removal procedure. **Note:** *Attach the ground cable first and smear the terminals with petroleum jelly to prevent corrosion. Never use ordinary grease.*

3 Battery – maintenance and inspection

1   Normal weekly battery maintenance consists of checking the electrolyte level of each cell to ensure that the separators are covered by $\frac{1}{4}$ inch of electrolyte. If the level has fallen, top-up the battery using distilled water only. Do not overfill. If a battery is overfilled or any electrolyte spilt, immediately wipe away and neutralize, as electrolyte attacks and corrodes any metal it comes into contact with very rapidly.

2   If the battery has the 'Auto-fil' device fitted, a special topping-up sequence is required. The white balls in the 'Auto-fil' battery are part of the automatic topping-up device which ensures correct electrolyte level. The vent chamber should remain in position at all times except when topping-up, or taking specific gravity readings. If the electrolyte level in any of the cells is below the bottom of the filling tube, top-up as follows:

(a) *Lift off the vent chamber cover*
(b) *With the battery level, pour distilled water into the trough until all the filling tubes and trough are full*
(c) *Immediately install the cover to allow the water in the trough and tubes to flow into the cells. Each cell will automatically receive the correct amount of water*

3   As well as keeping the terminals clean and covered with petroleum jelly, the top of the battery, and especially the top of the cells, should be kept clean and dry. This helps prevent corrosion and ensures that the battery does not become partially discharged by leakage through dampness and dirt.

4   Once every three months, remove the battery and inspect the battery securing bolts, the battery clamp plate, tray, and battery cables for corrosion (white fluffy deposits on the metal which are brittle to touch). If any corrosion is found, clean off the deposits with ammonia and paint over the clean metal with an anti-rust anti-acid paint.

5   At the same time inspect the battery case for cracks. If a crack is found, clean and plug it with one of the proprietary compounds marketed for this purpose. If leakage through the crack has been excessive, then it will be necessary to refill the appropriate cell with fresh electrolyte as detailed later. Cracks are frequently caused to the top of the battery case by pouring in distilled water in the middle of winter *after* instead of *before* a run. This gives the water no chance to mix with the electrolyte and so the former freezes and splits the battery case.

6   If topping-up the battery becomes excessive and the case has been inspected for cracks that could cause leakage, but none are found, the battery is being overcharged and the voltage regulator will have to be checked.

7   With the battery on the bench at the three monthly interval check, measure its specific gravity with a hydrometer to determine the state of charge and condition of the electrolyte. There should be very little variation between the different cells, and if a variation in excess of 0·025 is present it will be due to either:

(a) *Loss of electrolyte from the battery, at some time caused by spillage or a leak resulting in a drop in the specific gravity of the electrolyte, when the deficiency was replaced with distilled water instead of fresh electrolyte*
(b) *An internal short circuit caused by buckling of the plates or a similar malady pointing to the likelihood of total battery failure in the near future*

8 The specific gravity of the electrolyte for fully charged conditions at the electrolyte temperature indicated, is listed in Table A. The specific gravity of a fully discharged battery at different temperatures of the electrolyte is given in Table B.

Table A
Specific gravity – Battery fully charged
1.268 at 100°F or 38°C electrolyte temperature
1.272 at 90°F or 32°C electrolyte temperature
1.276 at 80°F or 27°C electrolyte temperature
1.280 at 70°F or 21°C electrolyte temperature
1.284 at 60°F or 16°C electrolyte temperature
1.288 at 50°F or 10°C electrolyte temperature
1.292 at 40°F or 4°C electrolyte temperature
1.296 at 30°F or –1.5°C electrolyte temperature

Table B
Specific gravity – Battery fully discharged
1.098 at 100°F or 38°C electrolyte temperature
1.102 at 90°F or 32°C electrolyte temperature
1.106 at 80°F or 27°C electrolyte temperature
1.110 at 70°F or 21°C electrolyte temperature
1.114 at 60°F or 16°C electrolyte temperature
1.118 at 50°F or 10°C electrolyte temperature
1.122 at 40°F or 4°C electrolyte temperature
1.126 at 30°F or –1.5°C electrolyte temperature

4 Battery – electrolyte replenishment

1 If the battery is in a fully charged state and one of the cells maintains a specific gravity reading which is 0·025 or more lower than the others, and a check of each cell has been made with a voltmeter to check for short circuits (a four to seven second test should give a steady reading of between 12 to 18 volts) then it is likely that electrolyte has been lost from the cell with the low reading.
2 Top-up the cell with a solution of 1 part sulphuric acid to 2·5 parts of water. If the cell is already fully topped up, draw some electrolyte out of it with a hydrometer. **Note**: *When mixing the sulphuric acid and water* **never add water to sulphuric acid,** *always pour the acid slowly onto the water in a glass container.* **If water is added to sulphuric acid it will explode.**
3 Continue to top-up the cell with the freshly made electrolyte and then recharge the battery and check the hydrometer readings.

5 Battery – charging

1 In winter time when heavy demand is placed upon the battery, such as when starting from cold, and much electrical equipment is continually in use, it is a good idea occasionally to have the battery fully charged from an external source at the rate of 3·5 to 4 amps.
2 Continue to charge the battery at this rate until no further rise in specific gravity is noted over a four hour period.
3 Alternatively, a trickle charger charging at the rate of about 1·5 amps can be safely used overnight.
4 Special rapid 'boost' chargers which are claimed to restore the power of the battery in 1 or 2 hours are to be avoided as they can cause serious damage to the battery plates through overheating.
5 While charging the battery, note that the temperature of the electrolyte should never exceed 100°F (37·8°C).

6 Alternator – general description

The main advantage of the alternator lies in its ability to provide a charge at low revolutions. Driving slowly in heavy traffic with a dynamo invariably means no charge is reaching the battery. In similar conditions even with the wiper, heating, lights and perhaps radio switched on the alternator will ensure a charge reaches the battery.
The alternator is of the rotating field, ventilated design. It comprises 3-phase output winding; a twelve pole rotor carrying the field windings – each end of the rotor shaft runs in ball race bearings which are lubricated for life; natural finish aluminium die-cast end brackets incorporating the mounting lugs; a rectifier pack for converting ac

output of the machine to dc for battery charging, and an output control regulator.
The rotor is belt driven from the engine through a pulley keyed to the rotor shaft. A pressed steel fan adjacent to the pulley draws cooling air through the unit. This fan forms an integral part of the alternator specification. It has been designed to provide adequate air flow with minimum noise, and to withstand the high stresses associated with the maximum speed. Rotation is clockwise viewed on the drive end. Maximum continuous rotor speed is 12 500 rpm.
Rectification of the alternator output is achieved by six silicone diodes housed in a rectifier pack and connected as a 3-phase full wave bridge. The rectifier pack is attached to the outer face of the slip ring end bracket and contains also three 'field' diodes. At normal operating speeds, rectified current from the stator output windings flows through these diodes to provide the self excitation of the rotor field, via brushes bearing on face type slip rings.
The slip rings are carried on a small diameter moulded drum attached to the rotor shaft, outboard of the slip ring end bearing. The inner ring is centered on the rotor shaft axle, while the outer ring has a mean diameter of ¾ inch approximately. By keeping the mean diameter of the slip rings to a minimum, relative speeds between brushes and rings, and hence wear, are also minimal. The slip rings are connected to the rotor field windings by wires carried in grooves in the rotor shaft.
The brush gear is housed in a moulding fitted to the inside of the rear casing. This moulding thus encloses the slip ring and brush gear assembly, and, together with the shielded bearing, protects the assembly against the entry of dust and moisture.
The regulator is located on the right-hand side of of the engine compartment. It is a factory-calibrated unit and is not to be adjusted. Should its operation be faulty it must be renewed as a complete unit.

7 Alternator – maintenance

1 The equipment has been designed for the minimum amount of maintenance in service, the only items subject to wear being the brushes and bearings.
2 Brushes should be examined after about 75 000 miles (120 000 km) and renewed if necessary. The bearings are pre-packed with grease for life, and should not require further attention.
3 Check the drive belt at the specified service intervals for correct adjustment which should be 0·5 inch (13 mm) total movement at the center of the run between the alternator and water pump pulleys.

8 Alternator – special procedures

Whenever the electrical system of the car is being attended to, and external means of starting the engine are used, there are certain precautions that must be taken otherwise serious and expensive damage to the alternator can result.
1 Always make sure that the negative terminal of the battery is grounded. If the terminal connections are accidentally reversed or if the battery has been reverse charged the alternator diodes will be damaged.
2 The output terminal on the alternator marked *BAT* or *B+* must never be grounded but should always be connected directly to the positive terminal of the battery.
3 Whenever the alternator is to be removed or when disconnecting the terminals of the alternator circuit, always disconnect the battery ground terminal first.
4 The alternator must never be operated without the battery to alternator cable connected.
5 If the battery is to be charged by external means always disconnect both the battery cables before the external charger is connected.
6 Should it be necessary to use a booster charger or booster battery to start the engine always double-check that the negative cable is connected to negative terminal and the positive cable to positive terminal.

9 Alternator – removal and installation

1 Disconnect the battery cables.
2 Loosen the alternator mounting bolts and remove the adjustment arm-to-alternator attaching bolt. Push the alternator in towards the engine and remove the drive belt.

10

9.2 Loosen the alternator adjustment arm bolt

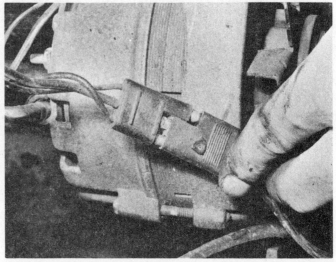

9.3 Disconnecting the alternator wiring at the multi-socket

3   Remove the electrical connectors from the alternator. The stator and field connectors are the push-on type, they should be pulled straight off the terminal studs. On some models a multi-socket can be disconnected and the wires left connected to the alternator (photo).
4   Remove the two mounting bolts and carefully lift away the alternator.
5   Take care not to knock or drop the alternator otherwise this can cause irreparable damage.
6   Installing the alternator is the reverse sequence to removal.
7   Adjust the drivebelt so that it has 0·5 inch (13 mm) total movement at the center of the run between the alternator and water pump pulleys. **Note**: *It may be necessary to remove other accessory drivebelts before the alternator drivebelt can be removed (see Chapter 2).*

10 Alternator – fault diagnosis and repair

Due to the specialist knowledge and equipment required to test or service an alternator it is recommended that if the performance is suspect the car be taken to an automobile electrician who will have the facilities for such work. Because of this recommendation, information is limited to the inspection and renewal of the brushes.

The ammeter *(ALT)* gauge on the instrument panels indicates the charge *(C)* or discharge *(D)* current passing into, or out of the battery. With the electrical equipment switched on and the engine idling the gauge needle may show a discharge condition. However, at fast idle or normal driving speeds the needle should stay on the *C* side of the gauge; just how far over will depend on the charged state of the battery.
   If the gauge does not show a charge under these conditions there is a fault in the system and the following points should be checked before inspecting the brushes or, if necessary, renewing the alternator:

(a) *Check the drivebelt tension, as described in Section 7*
(b) *Check the battery, as described in Section 3*
(c) *Check all electrical cable connections for cleanliness and security*

11 Alternator brushes – removal, inspection and installation

1   First remove the alternator as described in Section 9.
2   Scratch a line across the length of the alternator housing to ensure correct reassembly.
3   Remove the three housing through-bolts, and the nuts and insulators from the rear housing. Make a careful note of all insulator positions.

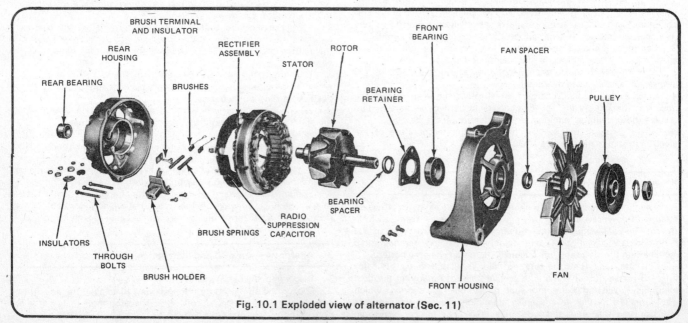

Fig. 10.1 Exploded view of alternator (Sec. 11)

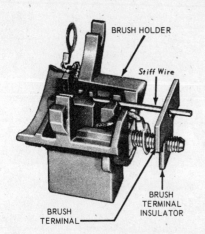

Fig. 10.2 Installing the springs and brushes into the holder assembly (Sec. 11)

4   Withdraw the rear housing section from the stator, rotor and front housing assembly.
5   Remove the brushes and springs from the brush holder assembly which is located inside the rear housing.
6   Check the length of the brushes against the wear dimension given in the Specifications at the beginning of this Chapter and renew if necessary.
7   Install the springs and brushes into the holder assembly and retain them in place by inserting a piece of wire through the rear housing and brush terminal insulator as shown in Fig. 10.2. Make sure enough wire protrudes through the rear of the housing so that it may be withdrawn at a later stage.
8   Refit to the stator the rear housing rotor and front housing assembly, making sure that the scribed marks line up.
9   Install the three housing through-bolts and rear end insulators and nuts, but do not tighten.
10 Carefully extract the piece of wire from the rear housing and ascertain as far as possible that the brushes are seated on the slip ring. Tighten the through-bolts and rear housing nuts.
11 Install the alternator as described in Section 9.

12 Starter motor – general description

The starter motor system comprises a motor with an integral positive engagement drive, the battery, a remote control starter switch, a neutral start switch, the starter relay and the necessary wiring.
When the ignition switch is turned to the start position the starter relay is energised through the starter control circuit. The relay then connects the battery to the starter motor.
Cars fitted with an automatic transmission have a neutral start switch in the starter control circuit which prevents operation of the starter if the selector lever is not in the N or P positions.
With the starter in its rest positionone a set of the field coils is connected directly to ground through a set of contacts. When the starter is first connected to the battery, a large current flows through the grounded field coil and operates a movable pole shoe. The pole shoe is attached to the starter drive plunger lever and so the drive is engaged with the ring gear on the flywheel.
When the movable pole shoe is fully seated, it opens the field coil grounding contacts and the starter is in a normal operational condition.

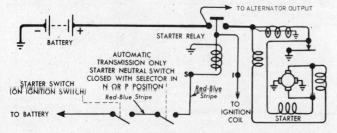

Fig. 10.3 Starting circuit (Sec. 12)

A special holding coil is used to maintain the movable pole shoe in the fully seated position whilst the starter is turning the engine.

13 Starter motor – testing on the car

1   If the starter motor fails to operate, then check the condition of the battery by turning on the headlights. If they glow brightly for several seconds and then gradually dim, the battery is in a discharged condition.
2   If the headlights continue to glow brightly and it is obvious that the battery is in good condition, check the tightness of the battery leads and all cables relative to the starting system. If possible, check the wiring with a voltmeter or test light for breaks or short circuits.
3   Check that there is current at the relay when the ignition switch is operated. If there is, then the relay should be suspect.
4   If there is no current at the relay, then suspect the ignition switch. On models with automatic transmission check the neutral start switch.
5   Should the above checks prove negative then the starter motor brushes probably need renewal or at the worst there is an internal fault in the motor.

14 Starter motor – removal and installation

1   Chock the rear wheels, apply the parking brake, jack-up the front of the car and support on firmly based stands.
2   Disconnect the starter cable at the starter.
3   Remove the starter motor securing bolts and lift the starter out towards the front of the engine.
4   Installation is the reverse of the removal procedure.

15 Starter motor – dismantling, overhaul and reassembly

1   Slacken the brush cover band retaining screw and remove the brush cover band and starter drive plunger lever cover.
2   Note the positions of the leads to ensure correct reassembly and then remove the commutator brushes from the brush holder.
3   Undo and remove the long through-bolts and lift off the drive end housing.
4   Remove the starter drive plunger lever return spring.
5   Remove the pivot pin that retains the starter gear plunger lever, using a suitable diameter pin punch.
6   Lift away the lever and withdraw the armature.
7   Remove the stop ring retainer followed by the stop ring that retains the starter drive gear onto the end of the armature shaft. The stop ring must be discarded and a new one obtained ready for reassembly.
8   Slide the starter drive assembly from the end of the armature.
9   Remove the brush endplate.
10 Unscrew the two screws that secure the ground brushes to the frame.
11 Dismantling should now be considered to be complete as removal of the field coils requires special equipment.
12 Clean the field coils, armature, commutator, armature shaft, brush endplate and drive end housing using a non-fluffy cloth and brush. Other parts may be washed in a suitable solvent.
13 Carefully inspect the armature windings for broken or burnt insulation and unsoldered connections.
14 Test the four field coils for an open circuit. Connect a 12 volt battery and 12 volt bulb to one of the leads between the field terminal post and the tapping point of the field coils to which the brushes are connected. An open circuit is proved by the bulb not lighting.
15 If the bulb lights, it does not necessarily mean that the field coils are in order, as there is a possibility that one of the coils could be grounded to the starter yoke or pole shoes. To check this, remove the lead from the brush connector and place it against a clean portion of the starter yoke. If the bulb lights, the field coils are grounding.
16 Renewal of the field coils calls for the use of a wheel operated screwdriver, a soldering iron, caulking and riveting operations, and is considered beyond the scope of the majority of owners. The starter yoke should be taken to a reputable electrical engineering works for new field coils to be installed. Alternatively purchase an exchange starter motor.
17 If the armature is damaged this will be evident on inspection. Look

10

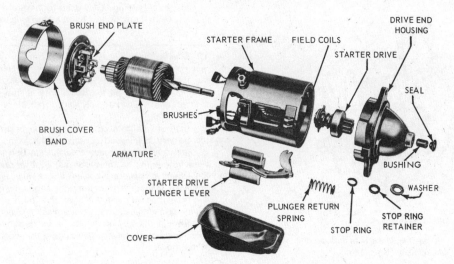

BRUSH END PLATE

STARTER FRAME   FIELD COILS

DRIVE END HOUSING

STARTER DRIVE

SEAL

BRUSHES

BRUSH COVER BAND

ARMATURE

BUSHING

STARTER DRIVE PLUNGER LEVER

PLUNGER RETURN SPRING

WASHER

STOP RING RETAINER

STOP RING

COVER

Fig. 10.4 Exploded view of starter motor (Sec. 15)

for signs of burning, discoloration and for conductors that have lifted away from the commutator. Reassembly is a straightforward reversal of the dismantling procedure.

18 If a bearing is worn, so allowing excessive side-play of the armature shaft, the bearing bush must be renewed. Drive out the old bush with a piece of suitable diameter rod, preferably with a shoulder on it to stop the bush collapsing.

19 Soak a new bush in engine oil for 24 hours or, if time does not permit, heat in an oil bath at 100°C (212°F) for two hours prior to installation.

20 As a new bush must not be reamed after installation, it must be pressed into position using a small mandrel of the same internal diameter as the bush and with a shoulder on it. Place the bush on the mandrel and press into position using a bench vise.

21 If the brushes are renewed, their flexible connectors must be unsoldered and the connectors of new brushes soldered in their place. Check that the new brushes move freely in their holders as detailed above. If cleaning the commutator with gasoline fails to remove all the burnt areas and spots, then wrap a piece of glass paper around the commutator and rotate the armature.

22 If the commutator is very badly worn, remove the drive gear. Then mount the armature in a lathe and, with the lathe turning at high speed, take a very fine cut off the commutator and finish the surface by polishing with glass paper. *Do not undercut the mica insulators between the commutator segments.*

23 Make sure that the drive moves freely on the armature shaft splines without binding or sticking.

24 To reassemble the starter motor is the reverse sequence to dismantling. The following additional points should be noted:

(a) *Fill the drive end housing approximately ¼ full with grease*
(b) *Always use a new stop ring*
(c) *Lightly lubricate the armature shaft splines with a Lubriplate 777 or thin oil*

16 Starter relay – removal and installation

1 For safety reasons, disconnect the battery.
2 Make a note of and then disconnect the battery cables, ignition switch and coil wire from the relay.
3 Undo and remove the two screws that secure the relay to the fender apron and lift away the relay.
4 Installing the starter relay is the reverse sequence to removal.

17 Fusible link – testing, removal and installation

1 A fusible link is used to protect the alternator from overload and is located in the wiring harness connecting the starter relay and *BAT* terminal on the alternator.
2 If it is suspected that the alternator is not charging, first check that

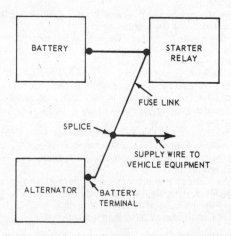

BATTERY

STARTER RELAY

FUSE LINK

SPLICE

SUPPLY WIRE TO VEHICLE EQUIPMENT

ALTERNATOR

BATTERY TERMINAL

Fig. 10.5 Installing the fusible link (Sec. 17)

the battery is fully charged and the terminals are clean.
3 Using a voltmeter, check that there is voltage at the *BAT* terminal at the rear of the alternator. No reading indicates that the fusible link has probably burned out. Check the fuse visually.
4 To install a new fusible link disconnect the battery ground terminal first.
5 Disconnect the fusible link eyelet terminal from the battery terminal of the starter relay.
6 Cut the fusible link and the splice(s) from the wire(s) to which it is attached.
7 Splice and solder the new fusible link to the wire from which the old link was cut. Protect the splice with insulation tape.
8 Securely connect the eyelet terminal to the battery stud on the starter relay.
9 Reconnect the battery ground terminal.

18 Headlight unit – removal and installation

1 Undo the headlight door retaining screws and remove the headlight door (photo).
2 Undo the three screws that hold the headlight retainer to the adjusting ring and remove the retainer (photo).
3 Pull the headlight sealed beam unit forward and disconnect the wiring assembly connector (photo).
4 Installation is the reverse of the removal sequence. Locate the sealed beam unit glass tabs in the positioning slots. It is recommended that whenever the sealed beam unit is changed, the headlight alignment is checked (see Section 19).

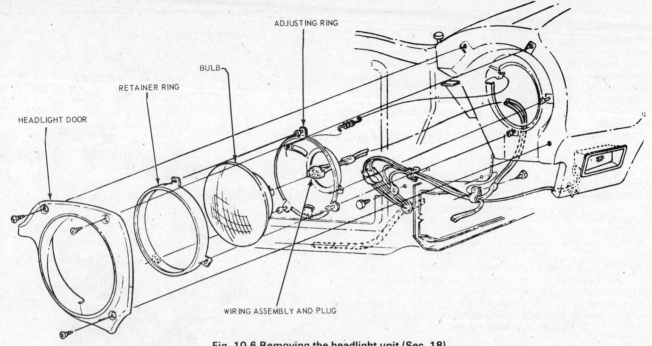

HEADLIGHT DOOR

RETAINER RING

BULB

ADJUSTING RING

WIRING ASSEMBLY AND PLUG

Fig. 10.6 Removing the headlight unit (Sec. 18)

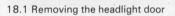

18.1 Removing the headlight door

18.2 Undo the screws and remove the headlight retainer

18.3A Pull the headlight unit forward ...

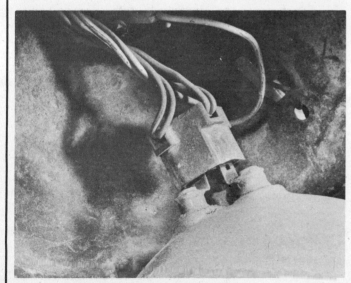

18.3B ... and disconnect the wiring connector

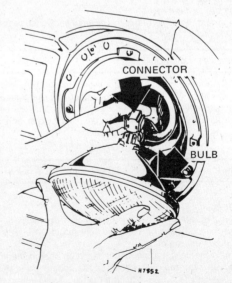

CONNECTOR

BULB

H7552

Fig. 10.7 Disconnecting the wiring connector (Sec. 18)

10

19 Headlights – alignment

It is always advisable to have the headlights aligned on proper optical beam-setting equipment but if this is not available the following procedure may be used:
1   Position the car on level ground 10 ft (3 metres) in front of a dark wall or board. The wall or board must be at right-angles to the center-line of the car.
2   Draw a vertical line on the board or wall in line with the center-line of the car.
3   Bounce the car on its suspension to ensure correct settlement and then measure the height between the ground and the center of the headlights.
4   Draw a horizontal line across the board or wall at this measured height. On this horizontal line mark a cross on either side of the vertical center-line, the distance between the center of the light unit and the center of the car.
5   Remove the headlight doors and switch the headlights onto full beam.
6   By careful adjusting of the horizontal and vertical adjusting screws on each light, align the centers of each beam onto the crosses which were previously marked on the horizontal line.
7   Bounce the car on its suspension again and check that the beams return to the correct positions. At the same time check the operation of the dimmer switch. Install the headlight doors.

20 Headlight switch – removal and installation

1   Disconnect the battery ground cable.
2   Working through the access hole in the underside of the instrument panel, press the release button using a small screwdriver (Fig. 10.18) and remove the switch knob and shaft.
3   Remove the bezel nut and lift out the switch body from behind the instrument panel. Disconnect the wiring harness connector.
4   Install the switch using the reverse procedure to removal.

21 Headlight dimmer switch – removal and installation

1   Disconnect the battery ground cable.
2   Carefully pull back the carpet from around the dimmer switch, removing the scuff plate and cowl trim screws if necessary.
3   Undo and remove the two screws securing the dimmer switch to the mounting bracket.
4   Draw the switch forwards and disconnect the multi-pin connector from the rear of the switch.
5   Lift away the dimmer switch.
6   Installing the dimmer switch is the reverse sequence to removal.

22 Headlight ON indicator

Later models have a headlight ON indicator and buzzer system to warn the driver that the lights have been left on. An indicator light, which contains a built-in flasher, and a buzzer are connected in parallel between the headlight switch and a relay. The buzzer and relay are mounted on a relay panel above the glovebox.

23 Front parking and turn signal lights – removal and installation

Early models
1   The front parking lights are located in two openings in the front bumper, and the bulb can be renewed by undoing the lens securing screws and removing the bulb.
2   The wire to the light unit connects to a plug behind the light body. The light body is mounted by a bracket to the upper side of the bumper opening.
3   The light body and lead wire are removed from underneath the car after disconnecting the wire at the plug and disengaging it from the retaining clips.
4   Installation is the reverse of the removal sequence.

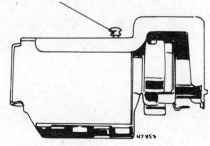

KNOB RELEASE BUTTON

Fig. 10.8 Headlight switch removal (Sec. 20)

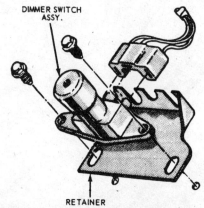

DIMMER SWITCH ASSY.

RETAINER
Fig. 10.9 Removing the dimmer switch (Sec. 21)

Later models
5   The parking lights are located in the radiator grille. To renew the bulb, twist the bulb socket then pull the socket and bulb from the light body.
6   To remove the light body undo the two screws attaching the parking light and door to the grille and lift away the light body.
7   Installation is the reverse of the removal procedure.

24 Rear light cluster – removal and installation

1   Renew the bulbs by disengaging the sockets from the light body inside the luggage compartment.
2   To remove the light body, move the spare tire to one side and then withdraw the three light sockets from the light body.
3   Remove the two nuts attaching the wire harness clips to the light body.
4   Undo the four nuts securing the light body to the rear panel and remove the light body assembly from the outside.
5   The light body can now be separated from the bezel and lens by removing the attaching screws.
6   Installation is the reverse of the removal procedure.

25 Front side marker lights – removal and installation

1   To renew the bulb, reach behind the fender and disengage the bulb socket from the light body by turning the socket counterclockwise. Remove the bulb from the socket.
2   Undo the light body securing nuts and the wire retaining clip, then remove the light body and the retainer.
3   Installation is the reverse of the removal procedure.

26 Rear side marker lights – removal and installation

1   Remove the lower rear corner of the trim panel in the luggage compartment.
2   Remove the bulb socket from the light body by turning it

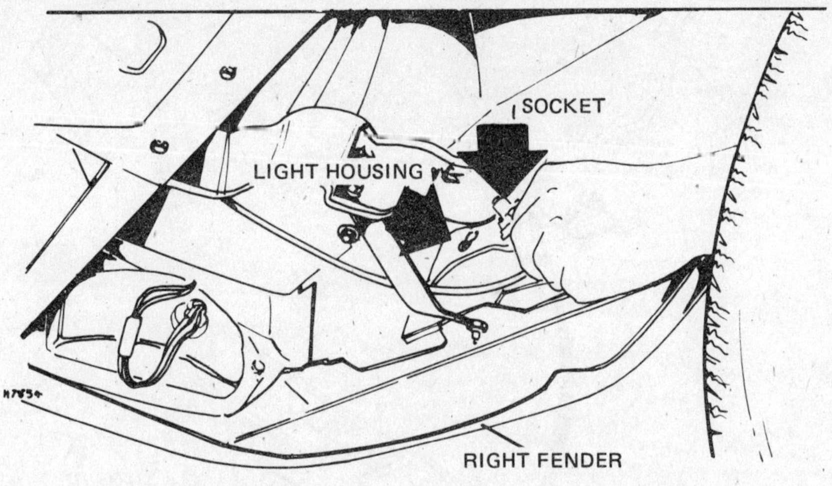

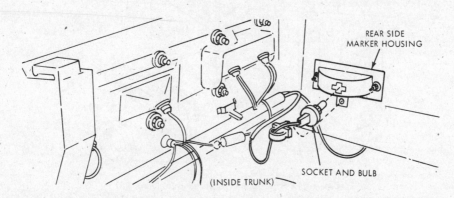

Fig. 10.10 Removing the front side marker lights (Sec. 25)

Fig. 10.11 Removing the rear side marker lights (Sec. 26)

counterclockwise and pulling it out, then remove the bulb.
3   Undo the nuts from the bezel studs (inside the luggage compartment) and remove the bezel, lens and light body from the outside.
4   Installation is the reverse of the removal procedure.

27 License plate light

The license plate light is removed by disconnecting the connector plug from inside the luggage compartment, undoing the two light body retaining screws and lifting out the light body assembly.

28 Stoplight switch – removal and installation

1   Disconnect the battery.
2   Disconnect the wires at the switch connector.
3   Withdraw the hairpin retainer, slide the stoplight switch, the pushrod, nylon washers and bushing away from the brake pedal and remove the switch (Fig. 10.12).
4   Installing the switch is the reverse of the removal procedure.

29 Turn signal/hazard flasher switch – removal and installation

1   Disconnect the battery ground terminal.
2   Remove the steering wheel as described in Chapter 11.
3   Remove the wiring cover from the steering column, if equipped with a fixed steering column. Disconnect the multi-connector at the base of the steering column.
4   Make a note of the color code and location of each wire, then disconnect the wires from the connector plug, using a very small

screwdriver or a piece of wire (Fig. 10.13).
5   Remove the wire cover plastic sleeve. If equipped with a tilt steering column, tape the wire ends together and attach a piece of strong cord to the wires to help pull the wires through the steering column when installing the switch.
6   Unscrew the turn signal switch lever.
7   On tilt steering columns remove the two steering column upper collar retaining screws and remove the collar. Push the steering column upper collar down and remove the wiring retaining clip from the column jacket.
8   Undo the two switch securing screws and remove the switch and wire assembly.
9   Installing the switch is the reverse of the removal procedure.

30 Turn signal circuit – fault diagnosis and rectification

Should the flasher unit fail to operate, or work very slowly or rapidly, check out the turn signal circuit before assuming that there is a fault in the unit.
1   Examine the turn signal light bulbs, both front and rear, for broken filaments.
2   If the external flashers are working, but either of the internal flasher warning lights have ceased to function, check the filaments in the warning light bulbs and renew if necessary.
3   If a flasher bulb is sound but does not work check all the flasher circuit connections with the aid of the relevant wiring diagram at the end of this Chapter.
4   With the ignition switched on check that the correct voltage is reaching the flasher unit by connecting a voltmeter between the plus terminal and ground. If it is found that voltage is correct at the unit, connect the two flasher unit terminals together and operate the turn signal switch. If one of the flasher warning lights comes on this proves

10

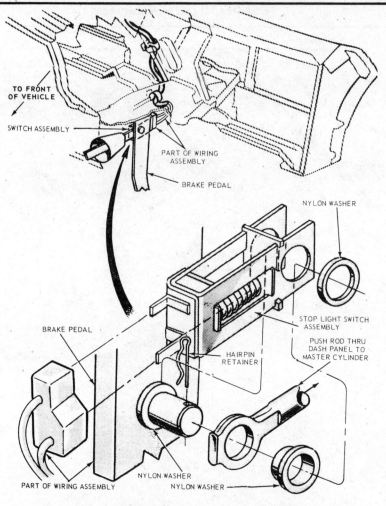

TO FRONT OF VEHICLE

SWITCH ASSEMBLY

PART OF WIRING ASSEMBLY

BRAKE PEDAL

NYLON WASHER

STOP LIGHT SWITCH ASSEMBLY

PUSH ROD THRU DASH PANEL TO MASTER CYLINDER

BRAKE PEDAL

HAIRPIN RETAINER

NYLON WASHER

PART OF WIRING ASSEMBLY

NYLON WASHER

Fig. 10.12 Stoplight switch removal (Sec. 28)

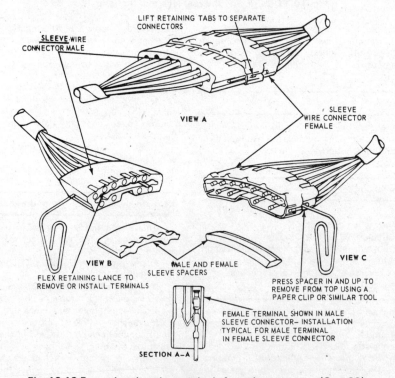

LIFT RETAINING TABS TO SEPARATE CONNECTORS

SLEEVE WIRE CONNECTOR MALE

SLEEVE WIRE CONNECTOR FEMALE

VIEW A

VIEW B

MALE AND FEMALE SLEEVE SPACERS

VIEW C

FLEX RETAINING LANCE TO REMOVE OR INSTALL TERMINALS

PRESS SPACER IN AND UP TO REMOVE FROM TOP USING A PAPER CLIP OR SIMILAR TOOL

FEMALE TERMINAL SHOWN IN MALE SLEEVE CONNECTOR– INSTALLATION TYPICAL FOR MALE TERMINAL IN FEMALE SLEEVE CONNECTOR

SECTION A–A

Fig. 10.13 Removing the wire terminals from the connector (Sec. 33)

that the flasher unit itself is at fault and must be renewed as it is not possible to dismantle and repair it.

31 Turn signal flasher unit – renewal

1 The turn signal flasher unit is located on the steering column bracket behind the instrument panel on early models. On later models it is attached to the bracket above the glovebox under the instrument panel.
2 To renew the flasher unit, disconnect the wiring connector from the unit and remove it from the mounting clip. Tab-and-slot mounted flashers are removed by rotating the unit 90 degrees counterclockwise to disengage it from the mounting slot.
3 Ensure that the new flasher unit has the same color code and part number as the old unit.

32 Hazard warning lights flasher unit – renewal

1 The hazard warning lights flasher unit is installed behind the instrument panel near the ashtray on early models. On later models it is taped to the wiring harness above the fuse panel.
2 Removal procedure is the same as that described in Section 31.

33 Speedometer cable – removal and installation

Inner cable

1 Working behind the instrument panel disconnect the speedometer cable from the rear of the speedometer head (see Fig. 10.14).
2 Carefully pull the speedometer inner cable out from the upper end of the speedometer cable outer casing.
3 If the inner cable is broken, raise the car and, working underneath, undo and remove the bolt that secures the speedometer cable mounting clip to the transmission (see Fig. 10.15).

4 Remove the speedometer cable shaft and driven gear from the transmission.
5 Remove the driven gear retainer and the driven gear and shaft from the cable.
6 Remove the lower part of the broken inner cable from the end of the outer casing.
7 Installing the new speedometer inner cable is the reverse sequence to removal.
8 Lightly lubricate the inner cable and insert into the outer casing. When the cable has nearly all been inserted turn the end to ensure that the squared end is engaged with the speedometer driven gear.

Outer cable

9 Working behind the instrument panel, disconnect the speedometer cable from the rear of the speedometer head.
10 Push the outer cable and grommet through the opening in the dashboard panel.
11 Raise the car and, working underneath, detach the cable from all its retaining clips.
12 Disconnect the cable from the transmission as described earlier in this Section and withdraw from under the car.
13 Install the speedometer cable using the reverse procedure to removal.

34 Instrument panel cluster – removal and installation

1 Disconnect the battery ground terminal.

1965/66 models

2 Disconnect the speedometer cable at the rear of the panel.
3 Remove the six attaching screws and tilt the cluster forward, just enough to disconnect the wiring and the bulb sockets, then remove the cluster assembly (photos).
4 The instruments and gauges can now be removed, if necessary, for servicing or renewal.
5 Installing the cluster is the reverse of the removal procedure.

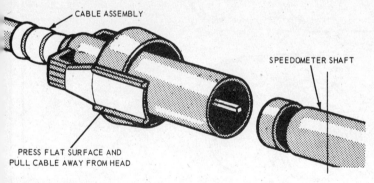

CABLE ASSEMBLY

SPEEDOMETER SHAFT

PRESS FLAT SURFACE AND PULL CABLE AWAY FROM HEAD

Fig. 10.14 Speedometer cable-to-speedometer head connection (Sec. 33)

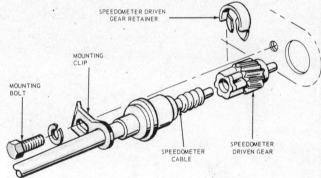

SPEEDOMETER DRIVEN GEAR RETAINER

MOUNTING CLIP

MOUNTING BOLT

SPEEDOMETER CABLE

SPEEDOMETER DRIVEN GEAR

Fig. 10.15 Speedometer cable-to-transmission connection (Sec. 33)

34.3A Removing the instrument panel bottom attaching screws

34.3B ... and the top attaching screws

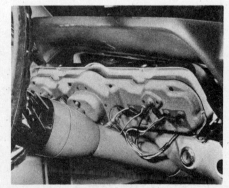

34.3C Rear view of the instrument panel

10

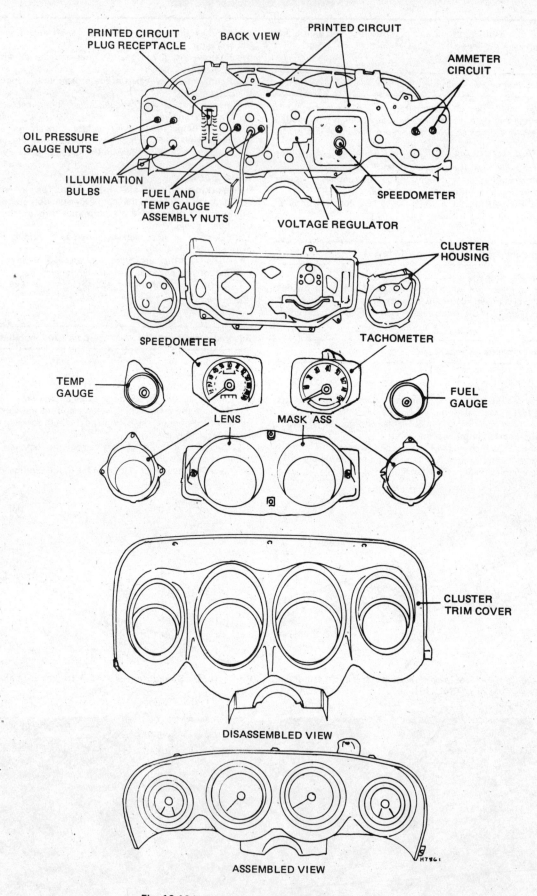

PRINTED CIRCUIT
PLUG RECEPTACLE

BACK VIEW

PRINTED CIRCUIT

AMMETER
CIRCUIT

OIL PRESSURE
GAUGE NUTS

ILLUMINATION
BULBS

FUEL AND
TEMP GAUGE
ASSEMBLY NUTS

SPEEDOMETER

VOLTAGE REGULATOR

CLUSTER
HOUSING

SPEEDOMETER

TACHOMETER

TEMP
GAUGE

FUEL
GAUGE

LENS

MASK ASS

CLUSTER
TRIM COVER

DISASSEMBLED VIEW

ASSEMBLED VIEW

Fig. 10.16 Instrument cluster – 1969/70 (Sec. 34)

1967/68 models

6 Remove the instrument panel pad assembly.

7 Remove the heater control attaching screws and withdraw the control assembly.

8 Disconnect the speedometer cable from the speedometer head.

9 Disconnect the cigar lighter wiring connector, undo the ashtray attaching screws and remove the ashtray.

10 Working through the ashtray opening, undo the nut attaching the instrument cluster to the panel.

11 Remove the seven attaching screws and withdraw the cluster forward; disconnect the two multi-connectors and remove the instrument cluster.

12 Installing the instrument cluster is the reverse of the removal procedure.

1969/70 models

13 Remove the instrument panel pad as described in Chapter 12, Section 29.

14 Remove the six attaching screws and withdraw the cluster, just enough to provide access, and disconnect the multiple plug to the printed circuit and, if so equipped, the tachometer plug. Remove the instrument cluster.

15 Installing the instrument cluster is the reverse of the removal procedure.

1971/73 models

16 Remove the instrument panel end-finish panel and the cluster opening finish panel.

17 Remove the four cluster attaching screws and pull the cluster

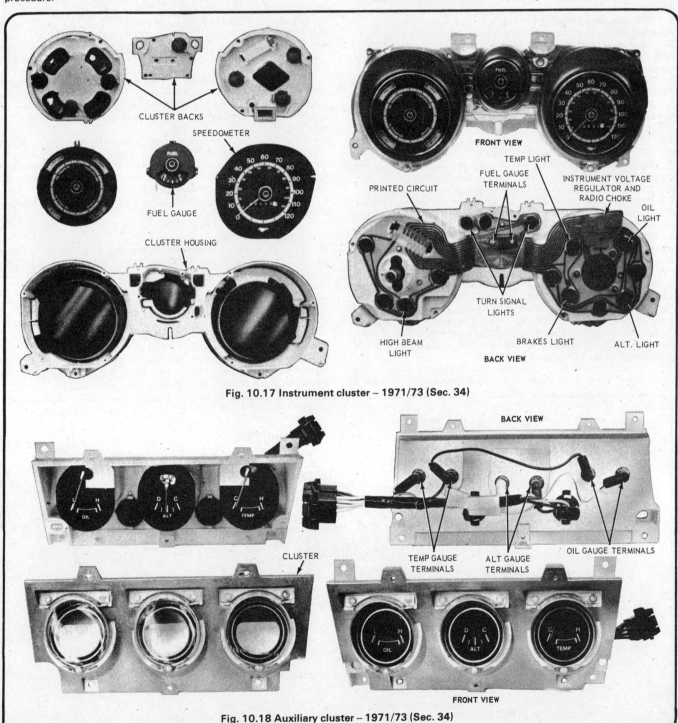

CLUSTER BACKS

SPEEDOMETER

FUEL GAUGE

CLUSTER HOUSING

FRONT VIEW

PRINTED CIRCUIT

TEMP LIGHT

FUEL GAUGE TERMINALS

INSTRUMENT VOLTAGE REGULATOR AND RADIO CHOKE

OIL LIGHT

TURN SIGNAL LIGHTS

HIGH BEAM LIGHT

BRAKES LIGHT

ALT. LIGHT

BACK VIEW

Fig. 10.17 Instrument cluster – 1971/73 (Sec. 34)

BACK VIEW

CLUSTER

TEMP GAUGE TERMINALS

ALT GAUGE TERMINALS

OIL GAUGE TERMINALS

FRONT VIEW

Fig. 10.18 Auxiliary cluster – 1971/73 (Sec. 34)

10

away from the instrument panel.

18 Disconnect the wiring connectors and the speedometer cable, then remove the cluster.

19 To remove the auxiliary cluster, undo the instrument panel center finish panel attaching screws (4) and disconnect the wiring. Remove the four screws attaching the cluster to the finish panel and lift away the auxiliary cluster.

20 Installing the instrument cluster and auxiliary cluster is the reverse of the removal procedure.

35 Ignition switch – removal and installation

1965/69 models

1   Disconnect the battery ground cable.

2   Insert the ignition key into the switch and turn to the ACC position.

3   Insert a piece of wire into the hole of the lock cylinder. Push the wire inward, to depress the lock pin, then turn the key counterclockwise and withdraw the lock cylinder.

4   Press the rear of the switch and rotate it counterclockwise. Remove the bezel, switch and spacer.

5   Disconnect the wiring and plug from the rear of the switch.

6   Installation is the reverse of the removal procedure.

1970/73 models

7   Disconnect the battery ground cable.

8   Remove the steering column shroud and detach the steering column from the brake support bracket (see Chapter 11).

9   Disconnect the switch wiring at the multiple plug.

10 Undo the two nuts securing the switch to the steering column, then remove the pin connecting the switch plunger directly to the actuator and remove the switch.

11 When installing the ignition switch, both the locking mechanism at the top of the column and the switch itself must be in the LOCK position for correct adjustment.

12 To hold the mechanical parts of the column in the LOCK position, move the shift lever to P (automatic transmission) or reverse gear (manual transmission), turn the key to the LOCK position and remove the key. New switches are supplied already pinned in the LOCK position by a plastic pin inserted in a locking hole on top of the switch. To pin an existing switch, pull the switch plunger out as far as it will go and then move it in one detent. Insert a 0·090 in (2·38 mm) diameter wire in the locking hole on top of the switch.

13 Connect the switch plunger to the switch actuator rod.

14 Install the switch on the column. Install the securing nuts but do

not tighten them.

15 Move the switch up and down on the column to locate the middle position of rod lash and then tighten the securing nuts.

16 Remove the plastic locking pin or wire.

17 Connect the battery ground cable and check the operation of the switch in all positions.

18 Attach the steering column to the brake support and install the shrouds.

36 Ignition switch lock cylinder (1970 through 1973 models) – removal and installation

Fixed steering column

1   Disconnect the battery ground cable.

2   Remove the steering wheel as described in Chapter 11.

3   Insert a wire pin, 0·09 in (2·38 mm) diameter in the hole located inside the column halfway down the lock cylinder housing (see Fig. 10.19).

4   Place the gearshift lever in the P position (automatic transmission) or reverse gear (manual transmission) position, and turn the lock cylinder with the ignition key to the RUN position.

5   Depress the wire pin and pull the lock cylinder out. Remove the wire pin.

6   When installing the lock cylinder, make sure the locking pin is depressed, then insert the cylinder into its housing and turn the key to the OFF position. The cylinder must be fully inserted before turning the key to OFF position as this action extends the cylinder retaining pin into the cylinder housing. Reconnect the battery.

7   Check for correct operation in all positions and install the steering wheel.

Tilt steering column

8   It is not necessary to remove the steering wheel. Insert the wire pin in the hole located on the outside of the column (see Fig. 10.19) and proceed as for the fixed steering column.

37 Horns – adjustment

1   If the horns are faulty or fail completely, check the wiring and the connections at the terminals and the switch.

2   Connect a voltmeter and ammeter to the horn and to a voltage supply as shown in Fig. 10.21 and check the current draw which should be 4 to 5 amperes at 12 volts.

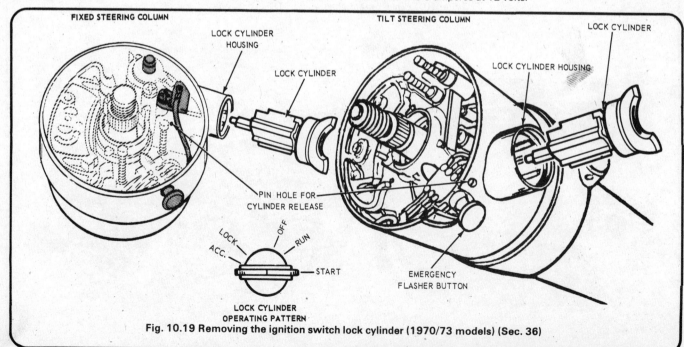

FIXED STEERING COLUMN   TILT STEERING COLUMN

LOCK CYLINDER HOUSING   LOCK CYLINDER

LOCK CYLINDER

LOCK CYLINDER HOUSING

PIN HOLE FOR CYLINDER RELEASE

LOCK
ACC.
OFF
RUN
START

LOCK CYLINDER OPERATING PATTERN

EMERGENCY FLASHER BUTTON

Fig. 10.19 Removing the ignition switch lock cylinder (1970/73 models) (Sec. 36)

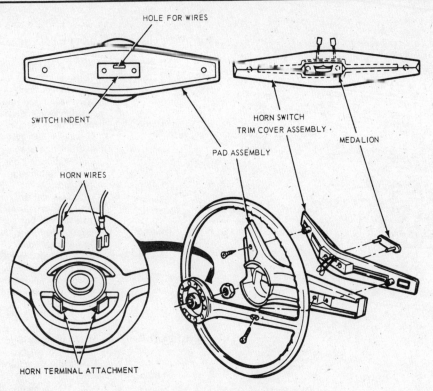

Fig. 10.20 Exploded view of horn switch (Sec. 37)

3   Adjust, if necessary, by turning the self-locking adjusting screw to change the contact tension. If the current cannot be adjusted to within the specified limits, the horn must be renewed.

38 Fuses and circuit breakers

1   The fuse panel is located on a bracket attached to the lower right flange of the brake pedal support on later models. On earlier models the fuse panel is located on the left side dash panel.
2   Most of the electrical circuits are protected by fuses and circuit breakers. Fuse identification is given in Figs. 10.22, 10.23 and 10.24, and in the Specifications at the beginning of this Chapter.
3   If a fuse blows always trace the cause and rectify before renewing the fuse. Always install a fuse of the correct amperage.

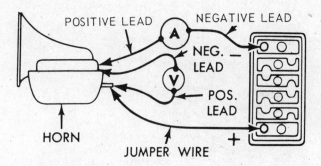

Fig. 10.21 Checking the horn current draw (Sec. 37)

Fig. 10.22 Fuse panel – 1971 models (Sec. 38)

1	20 amp	Horns
2	14 amp	Courtesy lamps: Instrument panel, door, C-pillar, glovebox, map lamp, luggage compartment lamp, dome lamp, cigar lighter feed, ignition key buzzer and automatic seat back latch and clock feed
2	4 amp	Instrument panel illumination: Heater switch, headlight switch, wiper/washer switch, ashtray, radio, clock and gauge illumination
4	14 amp	Indicator lamps. Seat belt and emission control, door ajar, parking brake, dual brake
5	14 amp	Heater defroster: **NOTE:** *30 amp required for air conditioner*
6	15 amp	Back-up lamps, radio, wipers, low fuel and turn signal indicator
7	20 amp	Accessory feed

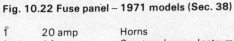

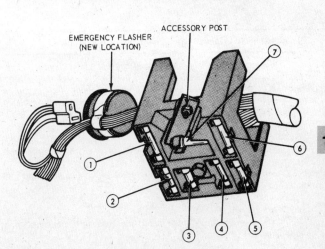

FUSE PANEL LOCATED ON PLATE ATTACHED
TO LOWER RIGHT HAND FLANGE OF BRAKE PEDAL SUPPORT

10

FUSE PANEL LOCATED AT RIGHT OF
STEERING COLUMN ATTACHED TO LOWER RIGHT
FLANGE OF BRAKE PEDAL SUPPORT

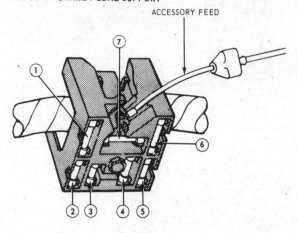

ACCESSORY FEED

Fig. 10.23 Fuse panel – 1972 models (Sec. 38)

1	20 amp	Horns and cigar lighter
2	14 amp	Courtesy: Dome or C-pillar, map, luggage and glove compartment lights, automatic seat back latch release coil feed, clock feed, ignition key and headlights *ON* buzzer
3	4 amp	Instrument panel illumination: Heater switch, headlight switch, wiper/washer switch, ashtray, radio and gauge illumination, clock illumination, cigar light and instrument cluster illumination
4	14 amp	Indicator lights: Oil pressure, seat belt, emission control or throttle solenoid positioner, door ajar and parking brake, seat belt time delay relay
5	14 amp	Heater defroster: **NOTE**: *30 amp required for air conditioner*
6	15 amp	Back-up lights, radio, windshield washer, and turn signal flasher
7	20 amp	Accessory feed: Parking brake indicator light, power window and back light safety relay coil feed

Fig. 10.24 Fuse panel – 1973 models (Sec. 38)

1	20 amp	Horns and cigar lighter
2	14 amp	Courtesy: Dome or C-pillar, map, luggage and glove compartment lights, automatic seat back latch relay coil feed, clock feed, ignition key warning and headlights *ON* buzzer
3	4 amp	Instrument panel and cluster illumination: Ashtray, clock, radio, wiper/washer switch, heater control, headlight switch, cigar lighter and gauge illumination
4	14 amp	Indicator lights: Oil pressure, engine water temperature, dual brake system, seat belt warning lamp and buzzer, emission control solenoids, throttle solenoid positioner, electronic spark control
5	14 amp	Heater defroster: **NOTE**: *30 amp required for air conditioner*
6	15 amp	Back-up lights, radio and stereo tape player, windshield washer and turn signal system
7	20 amp	Accessory feed: Parking brake warning lamp, power window and heated rear window relay coil feed

ACCESSORY FEED

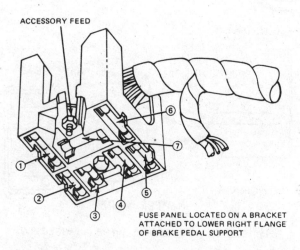

FUSE PANEL LOCATED ON A BRACKET
ATTACHED TO LOWER RIGHT FLANGE
OF BRAKE PEDAL SUPPORT

39 Windshield wiper blades – removal and installation

The windshield wiper blades can be one of two types. With the bayonet type the blade saddle slides over the end of the arm and is engaged by a locking stud. With the blade saddle pin type, a pin on the arm indexes into the side of the blade saddle and engages a spring loaded clip in the saddle.

Bayonet type – Trico
1 To remove a Trico blade press down on the arm to disengage the top stud.
2 Depress the tab on the saddle to release the top stud and pull the blade from the arm.

Bayonet type – Anco
To remove an Anco blade press inwards on the tab and pull the blade from the arm.

Saddle pin type – Trico
To remove a pin type Trico blade insert a screwdriver into the spring release opening of the blade saddle, depress the spring clip and pull the blade from the arm.

40 Windshield wiper arm – removal and installation

1 Swing the arm away from the windshield and insert a 0·09 in (2·38 mm) pin (drill or pop rivet) through the pin hole, as shown in Fig. 10.25, to release the arm which can now be pulled off. Do not pry it off with a screwdriver.
2 Leave the pin in position until the arm is installed. With the pivot shaft in the park position, push the arm on and remove the pin.

41 Windshield wiper mechanism – fault diagnosis and rectification

1 Should the windshield wiper fail, or work very slowly, then check the terminals on the motor for loose connections, and make sure that the insulation of all the wiring is not cracked or broken, thus causing a short circuit. If this is in order then check the current the motor is taking by connecting an ammeter in the circuit and turning on the wiper switch. Consumption should be between 2·3 to 3·1 amps.
2 If no current is passing through the motor, check that the switch is operating correctly.
3 If the wiper motor takes a very high current check the wiper blades

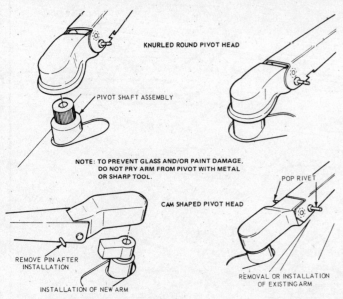

KNURLED ROUND PIVOT HEAD

PIVOT SHAFT ASSEMBLY

NOTE: TO PREVENT GLASS AND/OR PAINT DAMAGE,
DO NOT PRY ARM FROM PIVOT WITH METAL
OR SHARP TOOL.

CAM SHAPED PIVOT HEAD

POP RIVET

REMOVE PIN AFTER
INSTALLATION

INSTALLATION OF NEW ARM

REMOVAL OR INSTALLATION
OF EXISTING ARM

**Fig. 10.25 Installing windshield wiper arm to pivot shaft
(Sec. 40)**

for freedom of movement. If this is satisfactory, check the gearbox
cover and gear assembly for damage.
4   If the motor takes a very low current ensure that the battery is fully
charged. Check the brush gear and ensure the brushes are bearing on
the commutator. If not, check the brushes for freedom of movement
and, if necessary, renew the tension springs. If the brushes are very
worn they should be renewed. Check the armature by substitution if
this unit is suspect.

42 Windshield wiper motor – removal and installation

1965/66 models
1   Disconnect the battery ground cable.
2   Disconnect the wiring from the wiper motor.
3   Remove the three bolts securing the wiper motor bracket to the
dash panel, lower the wiper and bracket assembly, and disconnect the
wiper linkage from the motor.
4   Lift out the wiper motor and bracket assembly.
5   Installing the wiper motor is the reverse of the removal procedure.

1967/68 models
6   Disconnect the wiper motor wiring connector.
7   Undo the attaching nut and disconnect the pivot arm and wiper
arms from the motor.
8   Remove the bolts securing the motor to the mounting bracket and
withdraw the wiper motor.
9   Installing the motor is the reverse of the removal procedure.

1969/70 models
10   Remove the wiper arm and blade assemblies from the pivot shafts,
and disconnect the washer hose at the T-fitting on the cowl grille.
11   Remove the eight securing screws and lift off the cowl top grille.
12   The motor is located in the left side fresh air plenum chamber.
Disconnect the motor ground wire by removing the attaching screw at
the front edge of the plenum chamber.
13   Disconnect the motor wire harness at the plug and push it back
into the chamber.
14   Remove the retaining clip and disconnect the linkage drive arm
from the motor output arm crankpin.
15   Remove the three bolts securing the motor to the mounting
bracket, rotate the motor output arm 180 degrees and lift out the
motor.
16   Installing the motor is the reverse of the removal procedure but,
before installing, rotate the output arm 180 degrees. Before connecting the linkage drive arm to the motor, turn the ignition switch to ACC

so that the motor is in the park position.

1971/73 models
17   Disconnect the wiper motor wiring connector.
18   Remove the cowl top left vent screen.
19   Disconnect the wiper link from the wiper motor arm by removing
the retaining clip.
20   Undo the three wiper motor securing bolts and remove the wiper
motor and mounting bracket.
21   Installing the wiper motor is the reverse of the removal procedure.
Ensure that the connecting clip locking flange is forced into the locked
position (see Fig. 10.26). Check the motor operation.

43 Windshield wiper pivot shaft and link assembly – removal and installation

1   Remove the wiper arms and blades as described in Section 40.
2   Remove the four retaining drive pins and lift off the cowl top left
vent.
3   Remove the drive arm-to-pivot retaining clip.
4   Undo the three retaining screws from each pivot, and remove the
pivot shaft and link assembly.
5   Installing the wiper pivot shafts and linkage is the reverse of the
removal procedure. Ensure that the retaining clips are in the locked
position (see Fig. 10.26).

44 Windshield wiper motor – dismantling, inspection and reassembly

1   Undo the securing screws and remove the ground terminal and
cover (Fig. 10.27).
2   Carefully remove the idler gear and pinion retainer.
3   Lift away the idler gear and pinion.
4   Undo and remove the two long motor through-bolts, and separate
the housing, switch terminal insulator sleeve and armature.
5   Suitably mark the position of the output arm relative to the shaft,
to ensure correct reassembly.
6   Undo and remove the output arm retaining nut, output arm, spring
washer, spacer washer, O-ring, output gearshaft assembly, parking
switch lever and washer, in that order.
7   Remove the brushes and brush springs.
8   Remove the brushplate and switch assembly and finally remove
the switch contact to parking lever pin from the gear housing.
9   Thoroughly clean all parts and then inspect the gear housing for
signs of cracks, distortion, or damage.
10   Carefully check all shafts, bushes and gears for signs of scoring or
damage.
11   If the brushes are worn they should be renewed.
12   Any serious fault with the armature such as a breakdown in insulation necessitates a new motor assembly.
13   Reassembly of the windshield wiper motor is the reverse sequence
to dismantling and will present no problems provided that care is
taken.

45 Windshield washer nozzles – adjustment

To adjust the washer nozzles use a pair of thin-nosed pliers and
carefully bend the nozzle in the required direction. Do not squeeze the
nozzle too hard otherwise it will be crimped closed.

46 Windshield washer reservoir and pump – removal and installa-tion

Early models
1   The reservoir, pump and motor are supplied as a complete
assembly and cannot be repaired, except for the renewal of the screen
in the top of the reservoir.
2   To remove the assembly, disconnect the wiring connector and
hose, remove the retaining screws and lift the complete assembly from
the left fender apron.

10

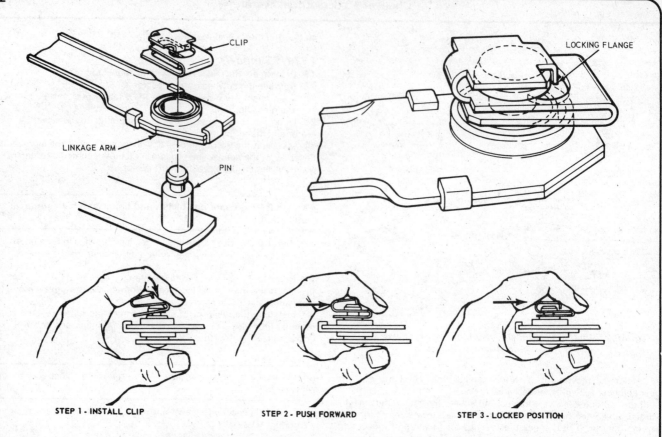

CLIP

LINKAGE ARM

PIN

LOCKING FLANGE

STEP 1 - INSTALL CLIP   STEP 2 - PUSH FORWARD   STEP 3 - LOCKED POSITION

Fig. 10.26 Installing the windshield wiper arm retaining clips (Secs. 42 and 43)

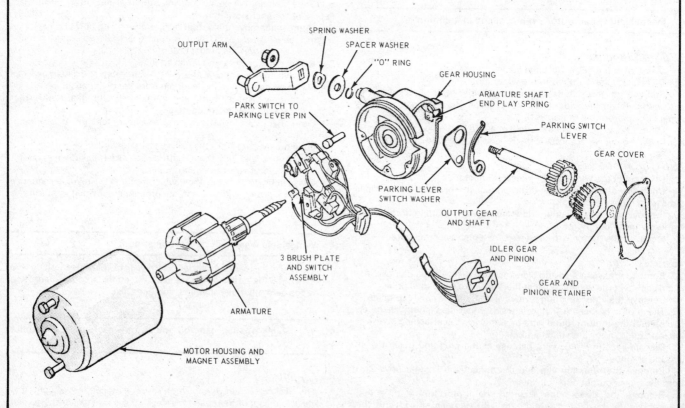

OUTPUT ARM

SPRING WASHER

SPACER WASHER

"O" RING

GEAR HOUSING

ARMATURE SHAFT END PLAY SPRING

PARKING SWITCH LEVER

GEAR COVER

PARK SWITCH TO PARKING LEVER PIN

PARKING LEVER SWITCH WASHER

OUTPUT GEAR AND SHAFT

IDLER GEAR AND PINION

GEAR AND PINION RETAINER

3 BRUSH PLATE AND SWITCH ASSEMBLY

ARMATURE

MOTOR HOUSING AND MAGNET ASSEMBLY

Fig. 10.27 Exploded view of windshield wiper motor (Sec. 44)

Later models
3   Remove the wiring connector plug and washer hose.
4   Undo and remove the retaining screws, and lift the washer and motor assembly away from the left-hand side fender apron.
5   To remove the pump motor from the reservoir, pry out the retaining ring and carefully pull the motor out of the reservoir recess (see Fig. 10.28).
6   The motor and pump assembly cannot be repaired, and if faulty must be renewed.
7   When installing the motor into the reservoir, make sure the projection on the motor body is lined up with the slot in the reservoir.
8   Press on the motor retaining ring and install the reservoir assembly to the car using the reverse procedure to removal.

47 Radio – removal and installation

1965/66 models
1   Disconnect the battery ground cable.

2   Remove the control knobs and the nuts attaching the radio to the instrument panel.
3   Disconnect the antenna and the speaker wire.
4   Disconnect the wire at the fuse panel and the pilot light wire.
5   Undo the radio-to-bracket attaching bolts and remove the radio from the instrument panel.
6   Installation is the reverse of the removal procedure.

1967/68 models
7   Disconnect the battery ground cable.
8   Remove the right and left supports from the support bracket, and remove the console assembly.
9   Disconnect the wiring connections and the antenna from the radio.
10 Remove the radio control knobs.
11 Remove the nuts from the radio control shafts and lift out the radio.
12 Installation is the reverse of the removal procedure.

1969/70 models
13 Disconnect the battery ground cable.

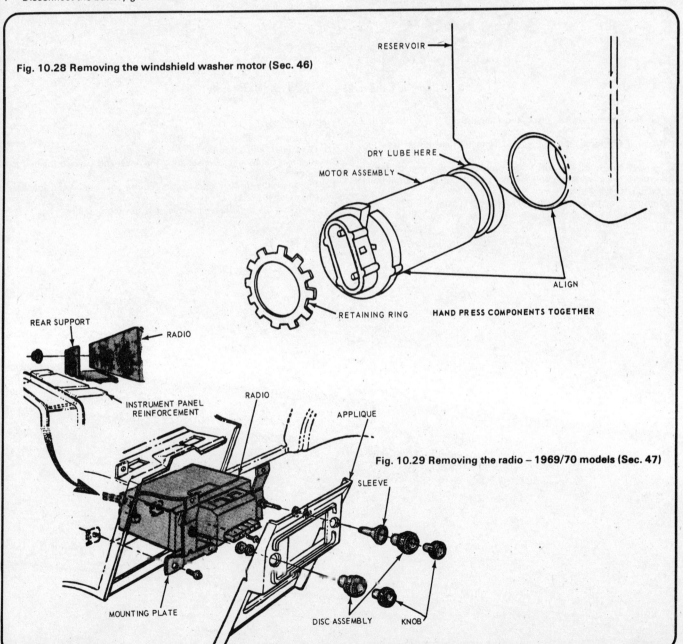

Fig. 10.28 Removing the windshield washer motor (Sec. 46)

RESERVOIR

DRY LUBE HERE

MOTOR ASSEMBLY

ALIGN

RETAINING RING

HAND PRESS COMPONENTS TOGETHER

REAR SUPPORT

RADIO

INSTRUMENT PANEL REINFORCEMENT

RADIO

APPLIQUE

Fig. 10.29 Removing the radio – 1969/70 models (Sec. 47)

SLEEVE

MOUNTING PLATE

DISC ASSEMBLY

KNOB

10

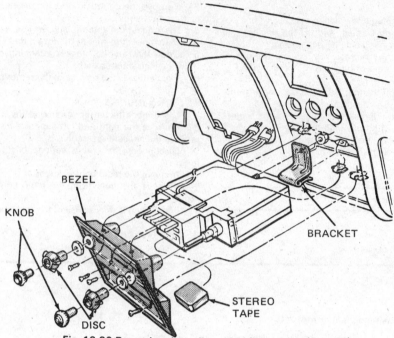

KNOB

BEZEL

BRACKET

STEREO
TAPE

DISC

Fig. 10.30 Removing the radio – 1971/73 models (Sec. 47)

14 Pull the control knobs, discs and sleeve from the radio control shafts.
15 Remove the radio applique from the instrument panel (see Fig. 10.29).
16 Remove the right and left finish panels and the two mounting plate attaching screws, then pull the radio out of the instrument panel and disconnect the wiring.
17 Remove the mounting plate and rear support from the radio.
18 Installing the radio is the reverse of the removal procedure.

1971/73 models

19 Disconnect the battery ground cable.
20 Disconnect the antenna.
21 Remove the four screws securing the bezel and radio to the instrument panel.
22 Pull the radio forward and disconnect the power lead and speaker; then lift away the radio.
23 Installing the radio is the reverse of removal procedure.

48 Fault diagnosis – electrical system

Symptom	Reason/s
No voltage at starter motor	Battery discharged Battery defective internally Battery terminal leads loose or ground lead not securely attached to body Loose or broken connections in starter motor circuit Starter motor switch or solenoid faulty
Voltage at starter motor: faulty motor	Starter motor pinion jammed in mesh with flywheel gear ring Starter brushes badly worn, sticking, or brush wires loose Commutator dirty, worn or burnt Starter motor armature faulty Field coils grounded
Electrical defects	Battery in discharged condition Starter brushes badly worn, sticking, or brush wires loose Loose wires in starter motor circuit
Dirt or oil on drive gear	Starter motor pinion sticking on screwed sleeve
Mechanical damage	Pinion or flywheel gear teeth broken or worn
Lack of attention, or mechanical damage	Pinion or flywheel gear teeth broken or worn Starter drive main spring broken Starter motor retaining bolts loose
Wear or damage	Battery defective internally Electrolyte level too low or electrolyte too weak due to leakage Plate separators no longer fully effective Battery plates severely sulphated
Insufficient current flow to keep battery charged	Drivebelt slipping Battery terminal connections loose or corroded Alternator not charging properly Short in lighting circuit causing continual battery drain Regulator unit not working correctly
Alternator not charging *	Drivebelt loose and slipping, or broken Brushes worn, sticking, broken or dirty Brush springs weak or broken

* If all appears to be well but the alternator is still not charging, take the car to an automobile electrician to check the alternator and regulator

10

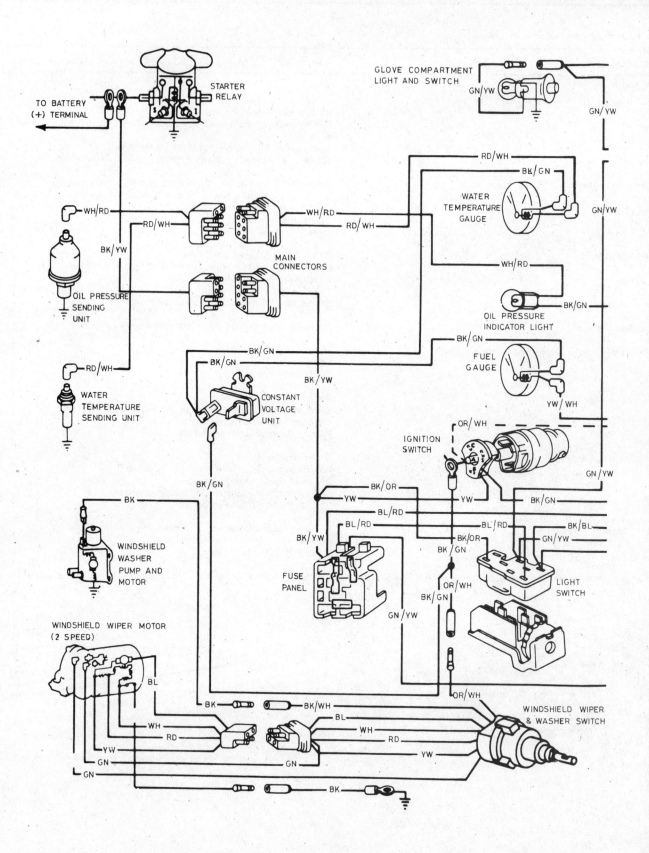

Fig. WD1A Interior light, wiper and gauge wiring diagram – 1965

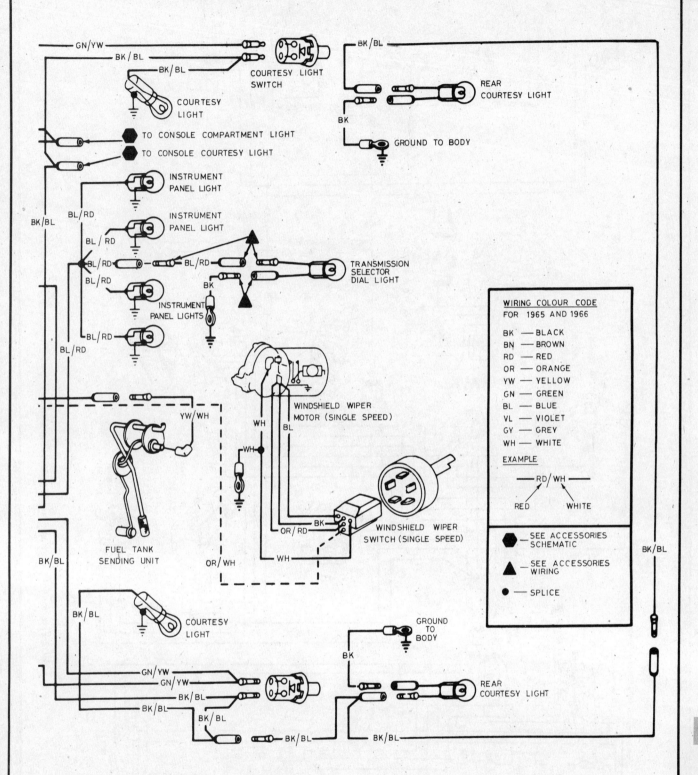

Fig. WD1B Interior light, wiper and gauge wiring diagram – 1965 (continued)

10

Fig. WD2 Exterior light, horn and turn signal wiring diagram – 1965 (see page 177 for Wiring Color Code)

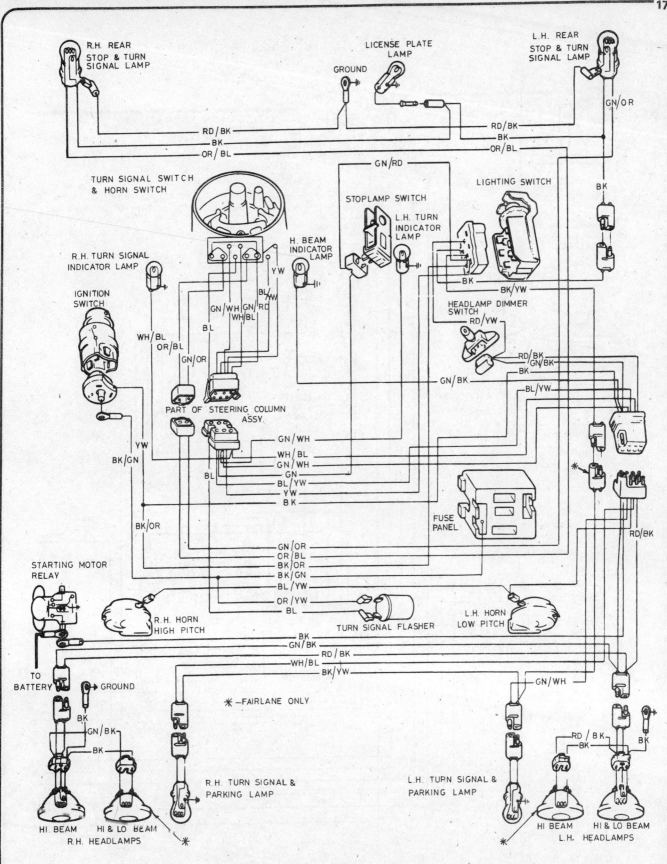

Fig. WD3 Exterior light, horn and turn signal wiring diagram – 1966 (see page 177 for Wiring Color Code)

10

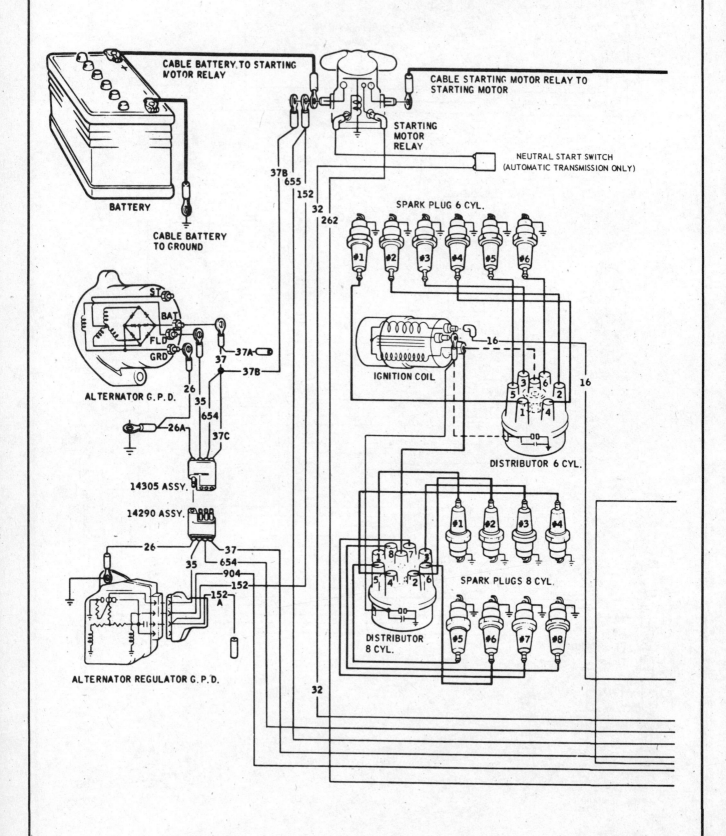

Fig. WD4A Ignition, starting, charging and gauges wiring diagram – 1966

WIRING COLOR CODE

16B	16	RED-GREEN STRIPE
	16A	PINK
654 152A 152	21	YELLOW
	26A 26	BLACK-RED STRIPE
	29	YELLOW-WHITE STRIPE
30C 30B 30A	30	BLACK-GREEN STRIPE
	31	WHITE-RED STRIPE
	32A 32	RED-BLUE STRIPE
	35	WHITE
37C 37B 37A	37	BLACK-YELLOW STRIPE
	39	RED-WHITE STRIPE
	57	BLACK
	262	BROWN
297A	297	BLACK-GREEN STRIPE
	655	RED
	904	GREEN-RED STRIPE
	640	RED-YELLOW STRIPE
●		SPLICE

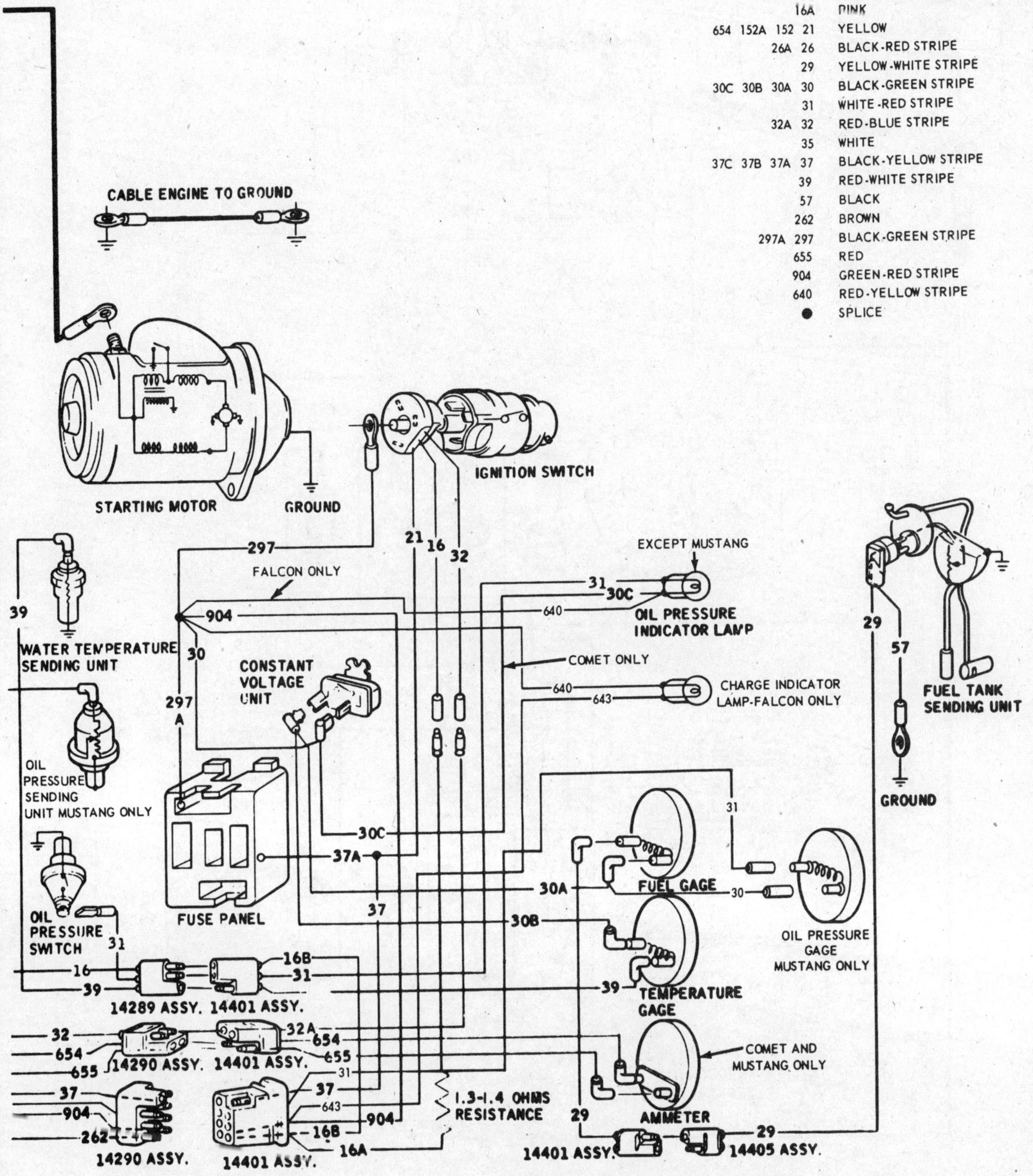

CABLE ENGINE TO GROUND

STARTING MOTOR GROUND

IGNITION SWITCH

EXCEPT MUSTANG

297

FALCON ONLY

21 16 32

31
30C

640

OIL PRESSURE
INDICATOR LAMP

39

WATER TEMPERATURE
SENDING UNIT

904

30

297
A

CONSTANT
VOLTAGE
UNIT

COMET ONLY

640
643

CHARGE INDICATOR
LAMP-FALCON ONLY

29

57

FUEL TANK
SENDING UNIT

GROUND

OIL PRESSURE
SENDING
UNIT MUSTANG ONLY

OIL PRESSURE
SWITCH

31

16
39

14289 ASSY. 14401 ASSY.

32
654
655 14290 ASSY.

37
904
262 14290 ASSY.

30C

37A

37

FUSE PANEL

16B
31

32A
654
655 14401 ASSY.

31

37
643
904
16B
16A 14401 ASSY.

1.3-1.4 OHMS
RESISTANCE

30A

30B

39

FUEL GAGE

31

30

TEMPERATURE
GAGE

OIL PRESSURE
GAGE
MUSTANG ONLY

COMET AND
MUSTANG ONLY

29 AMMETER

29
14401 ASSY. 29 14405 ASSY.

Fig. WD4B Ignition, starting, charging and gauges wiring diagram – 1966 (continued)

10

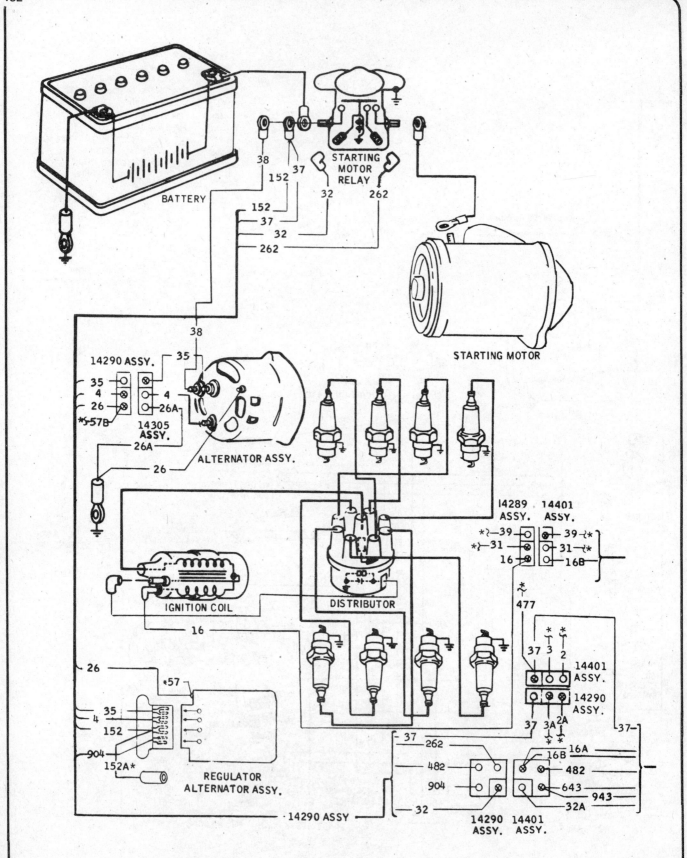

Fig. WD5A Ignition, starting and charging wiring diagram – 1967

WIRING COLOR CODE

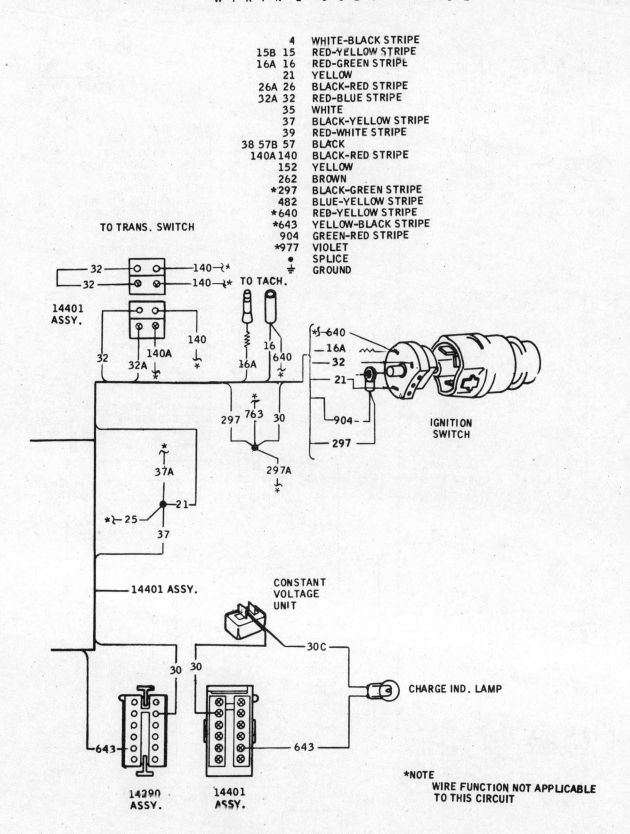

	4	WHITE-BLACK STRIPE
15B	15	RED-YELLOW STRIPE
16A	16	RED-GREEN STRIPE
	21	YELLOW
26A	26	BLACK-RED STRIPE
32A	32	RED-BLUE STRIPE
	35	WHITE
	37	BLACK-YELLOW STRIPE
	39	RED-WHITE STRIPE
38 57B	57	BLACK
140A	140	BLACK-RED STRIPE
	152	YELLOW
	262	BROWN
*297		BLACK-GREEN STRIPE
	482	BLUE-YELLOW STRIPE
*640		RED-YELLOW STRIPE
*643		YELLOW-BLACK STRIPE
	904	GREEN-RED STRIPE
*977		VIOLET
•		SPLICE
⏚		GROUND

*NOTE
WIRE FUNCTION NOT APPLICABLE
TO THIS CIRCUIT

Fig. WD5B Ignition, starting and charging wiring diagram – 1967 (continued)

10

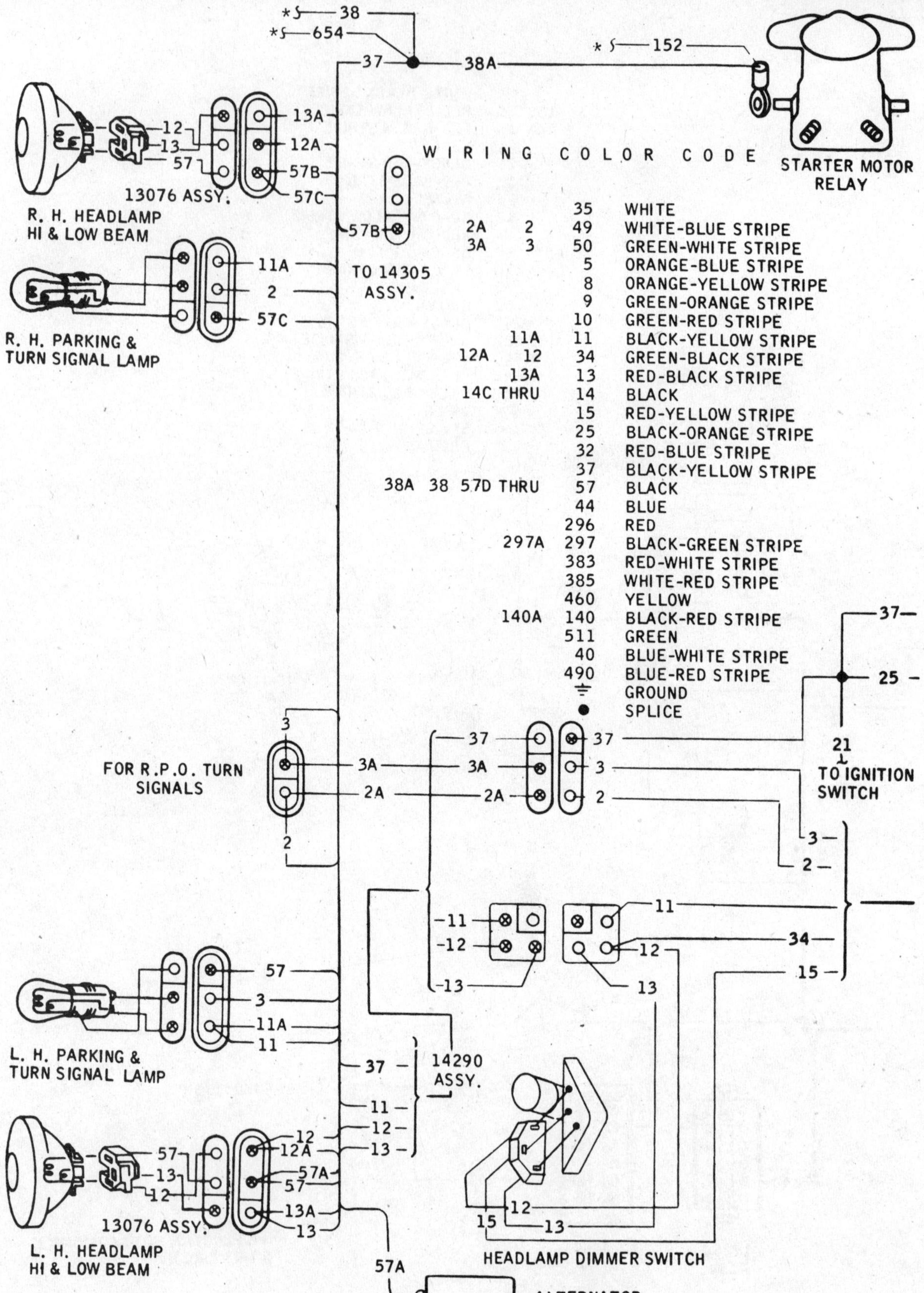

WIRING COLOR CODE

R. H. HEADLAMP
HI & LOW BEAM

13076 ASSY.

R. H. PARKING &
TURN SIGNAL LAMP

STARTER MOTOR
RELAY

TO 14305
ASSY.

		35	WHITE
2A	2	49	WHITE-BLUE STRIPE
3A	3	50	GREEN-WHITE STRIPE
		5	ORANGE-BLUE STRIPE
		8	ORANGE-YELLOW STRIPE
		9	GREEN-ORANGE STRIPE
		10	GREEN-RED STRIPE
11A		11	BLACK-YELLOW STRIPE
12A	12	34	GREEN-BLACK STRIPE
13A		13	RED-BLACK STRIPE
14C THRU		14	BLACK
		15	RED-YELLOW STRIPE
		25	BLACK-ORANGE STRIPE
		32	RED-BLUE STRIPE
		37	BLACK-YELLOW STRIPE
38A 38 57D THRU		57	BLACK
		44	BLUE
		296	RED
297A	297	BLACK-GREEN STRIPE
		383	RED-WHITE STRIPE
		385	WHITE-RED STRIPE
		460	YELLOW
140A	140	BLACK-RED STRIPE
		511	GREEN
		40	BLUE-WHITE STRIPE
		490	BLUE-RED STRIPE
			GROUND
			SPLICE

FOR R.P.O. TURN
SIGNALS

TO IGNITION
SWITCH

L. H. PARKING &
TURN SIGNAL LAMP

14290
ASSY.

L. H. HEADLAMP
HI & LOW BEAM

13076 ASSY.

HEADLAMP DIMMER SWITCH

ALTERNATOR
REGULATOR

Fig. WD6A Exterior lighting and turn signals wiring diagram – 1967

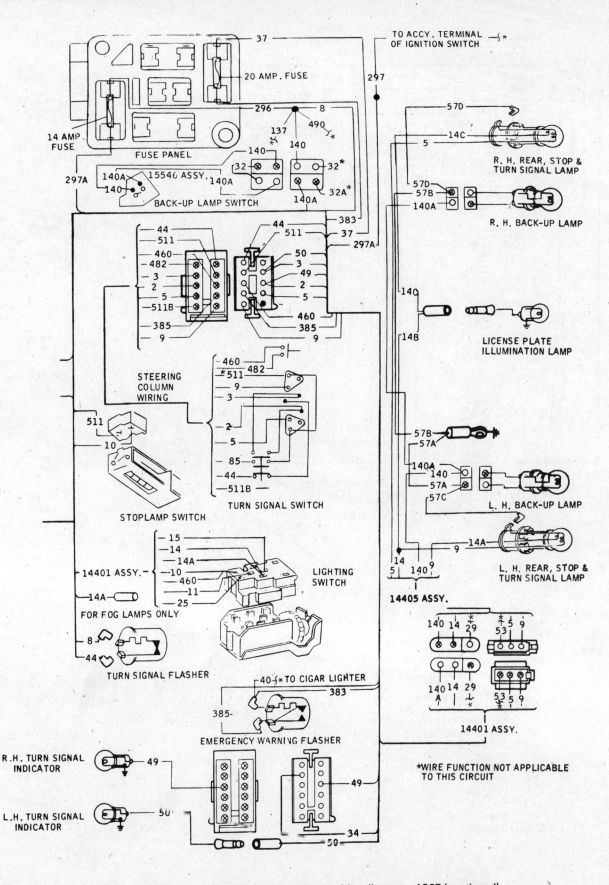

Fig. WD6B Exterior lighting and turn signals wiring diagram – 1967 (continued)

10

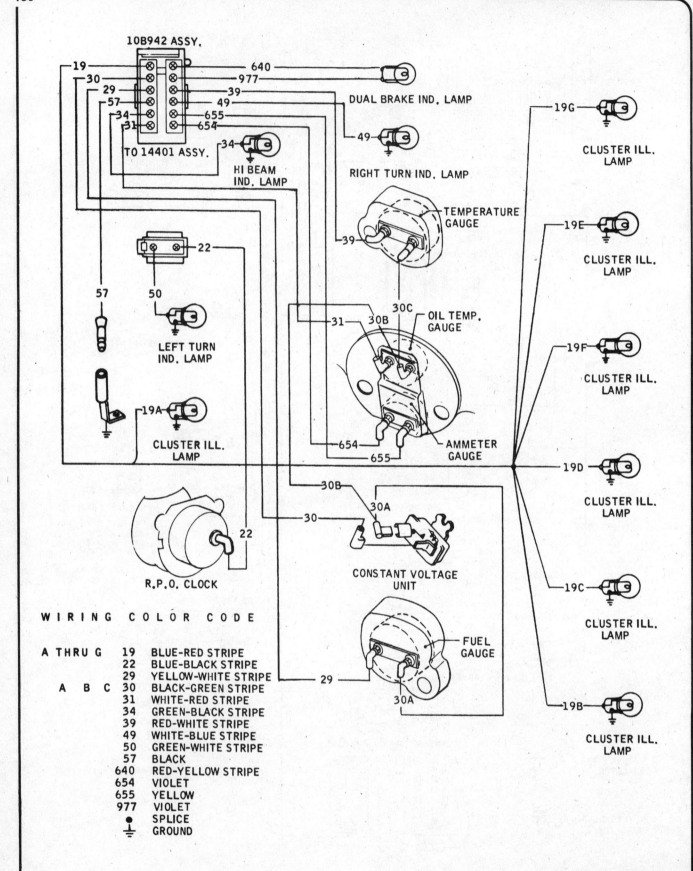

WIRING COLOR CODE

A THRU G	19	BLUE-RED STRIPE
	22	BLUE-BLACK STRIPE
	29	YELLOW-WHITE STRIPE
A B C	30	BLACK-GREEN STRIPE
	31	WHITE-RED STRIPE
	34	GREEN-BLACK STRIPE
	39	RED-WHITE STRIPE
	49	WHITE-BLUE STRIPE
	50	GREEN-WHITE STRIPE
	57	BLACK
	640	RED-YELLOW STRIPE
	654	VIOLET
	655	YELLOW
	977	VIOLET
●		SPLICE
⏚		GROUND

Fig. WD7 Pre-wired instrument cluster wiring diagram – 1967

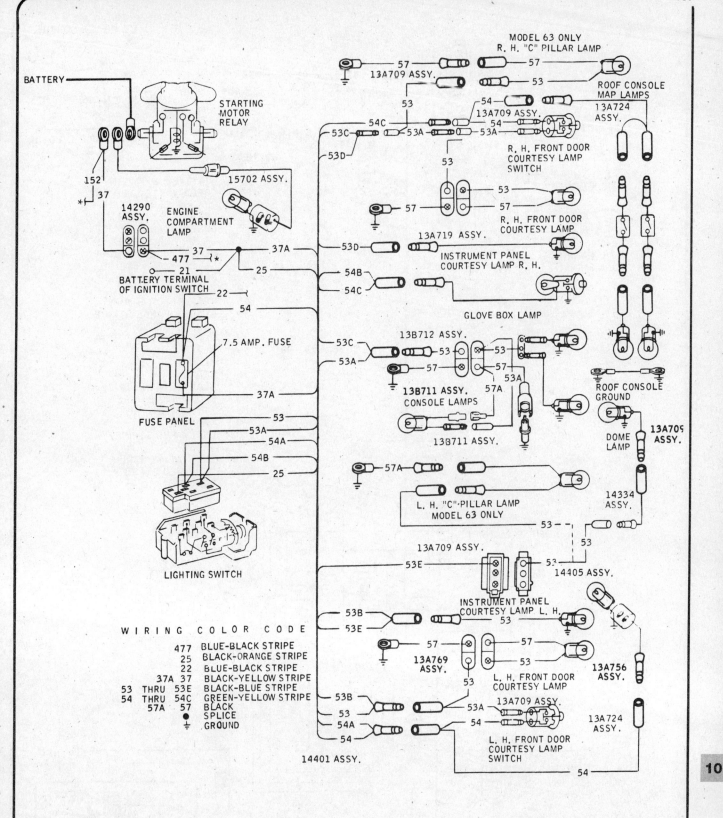

Fig. WD8 Interior lighting wiring diagram – 1967

WIRING COLOR CODE

477 BLUE-BLACK STRIPE
25 BLACK-ORANGE STRIPE
22 BLUE-BLACK STRIPE
37A 37 BLACK-YELLOW STRIPE
53 THRU 53E BLACK-BLUE STRIPE
54 THRU 54C GREEN-YELLOW STRIPE
57A 57 BLACK
● SPLICE
⏚ GROUND

*NOTE:
WIRE FUNCTION NOT APPLICABLE
TO THIS CIRCUIT

10

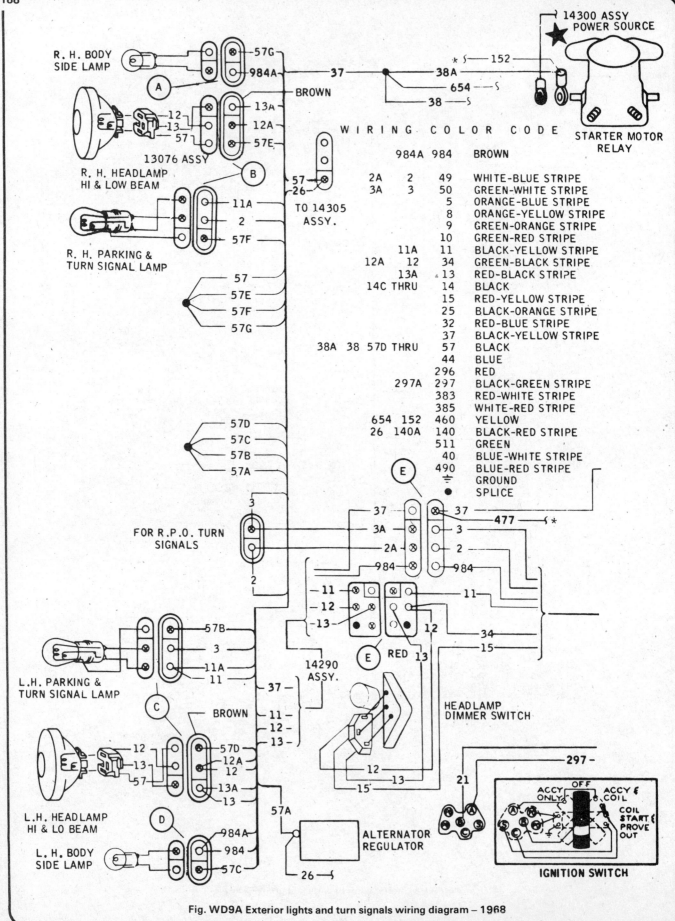

Fig. WD9A Exterior lights and turn signals wiring diagram – 1968

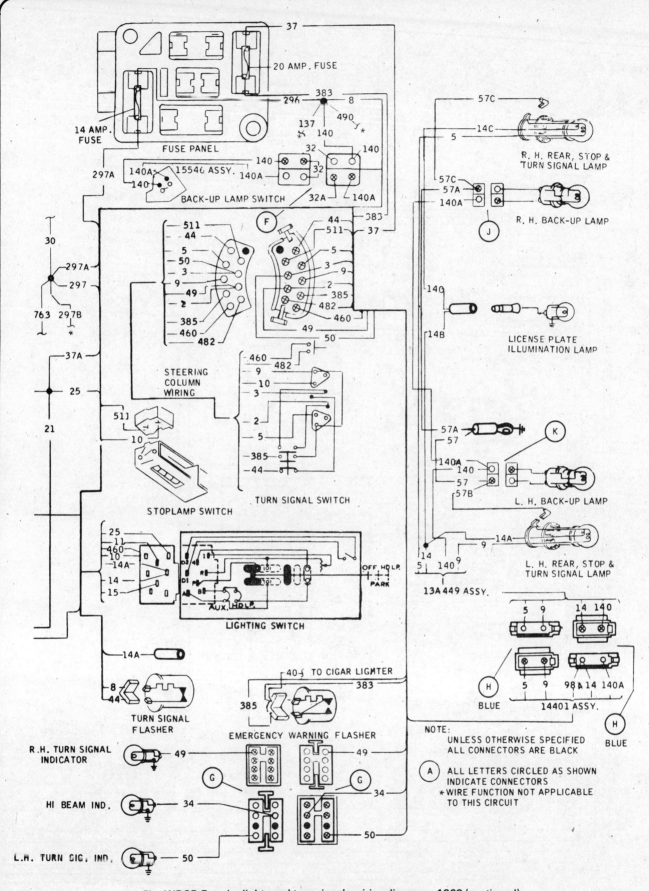

Fig. WD9B Exterior lights and turn signals wiring diagram – 1968 (continued)

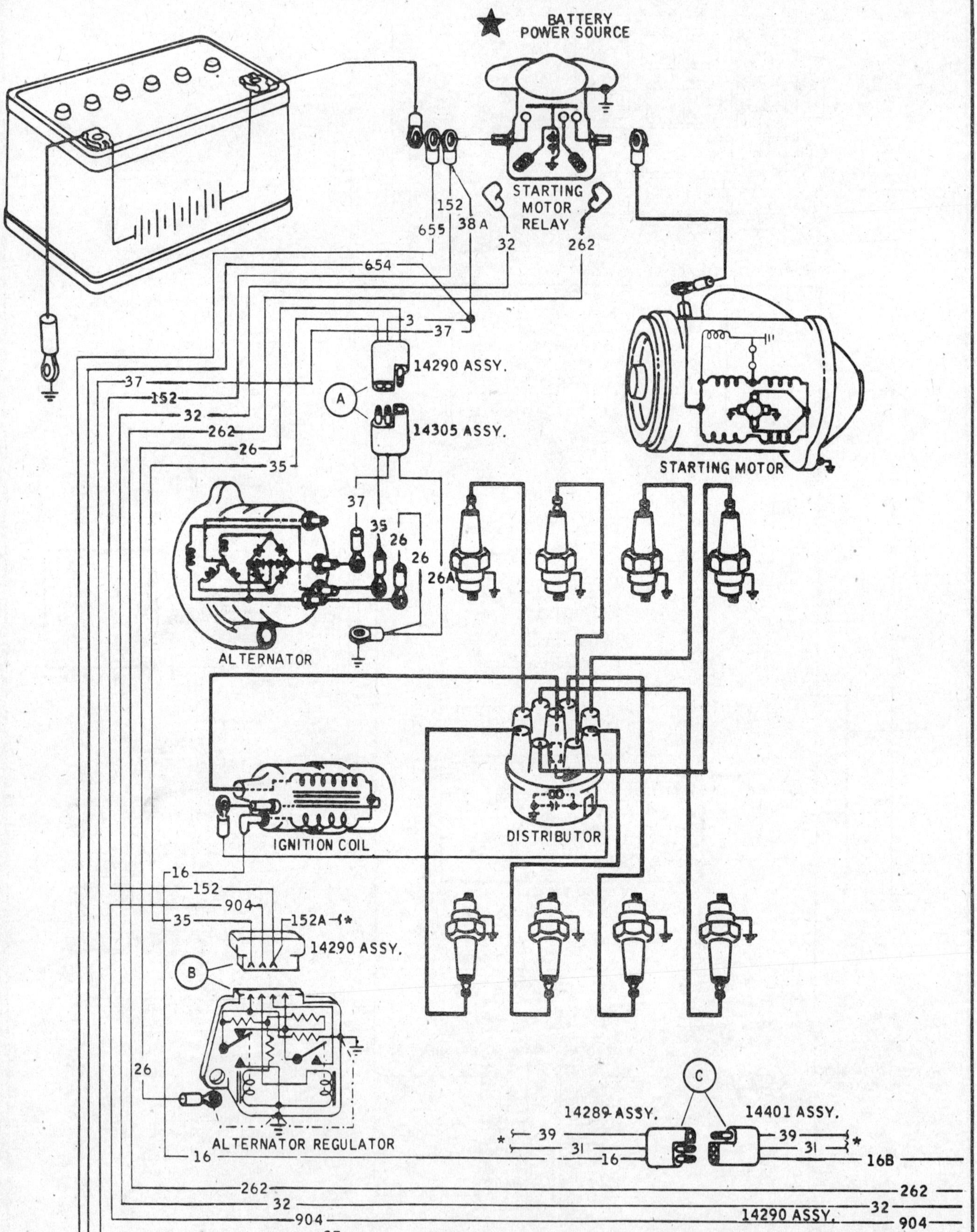

BATTERY
POWER SOURCE

STARTING
MOTOR RELAY

152
655
38 A
32
262

654

3
37

37
152
32
262
26
35

14290 ASSY.

A

14305 ASSY.

STARTING MOTOR

ALTERNATOR

37
35
26
26
26A

IGNITION COIL

DISTRIBUTOR

16
152
904
35
152A
14290 ASSY.

B

26

ALTERNATOR REGULATOR

16

C

14289 ASSY.   14401 ASSY.

*   39
31
16
39
31   *
16B

262   262
32   32
904   14290 ASSY.   904
37
654
655

Fig. WD10A Ignition, starting and charging wiring diagram – 1968

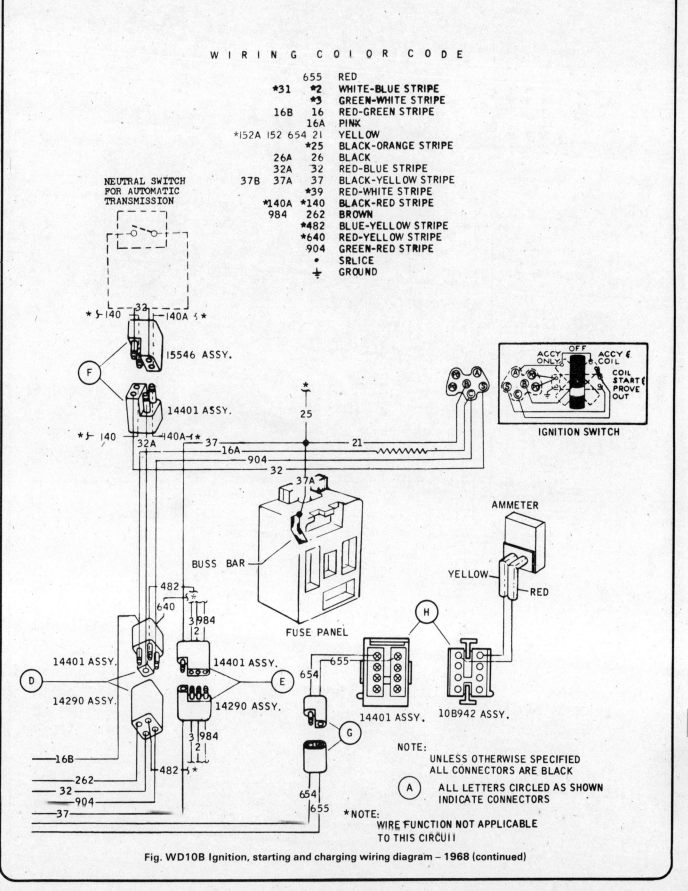

Fig. WD10B Ignition, starting and charging wiring diagram – 1968 (continued)

10

192

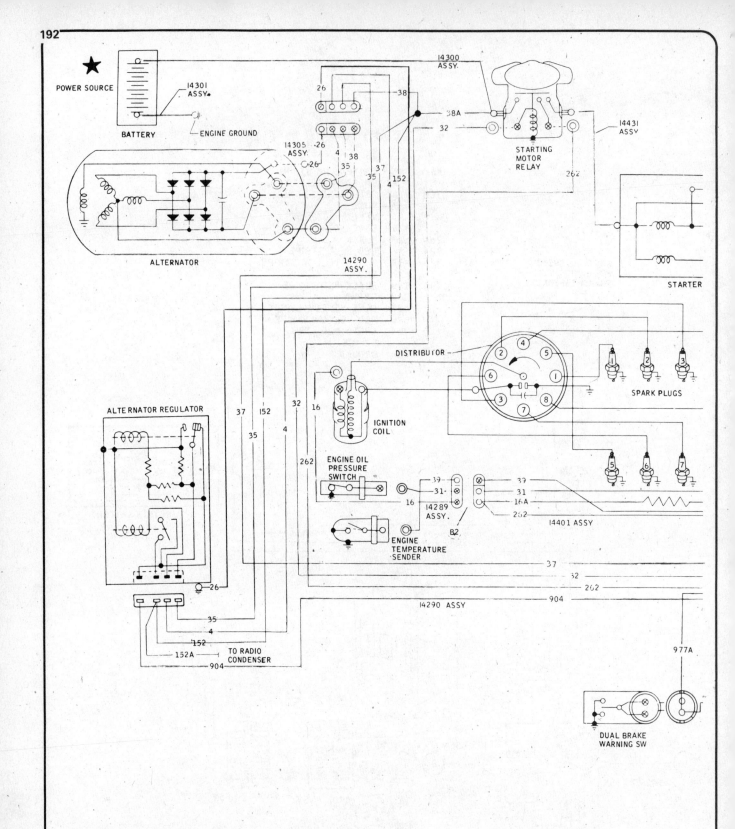

Fig. WD11A Ignition, starting and charging wiring diagram – 1969

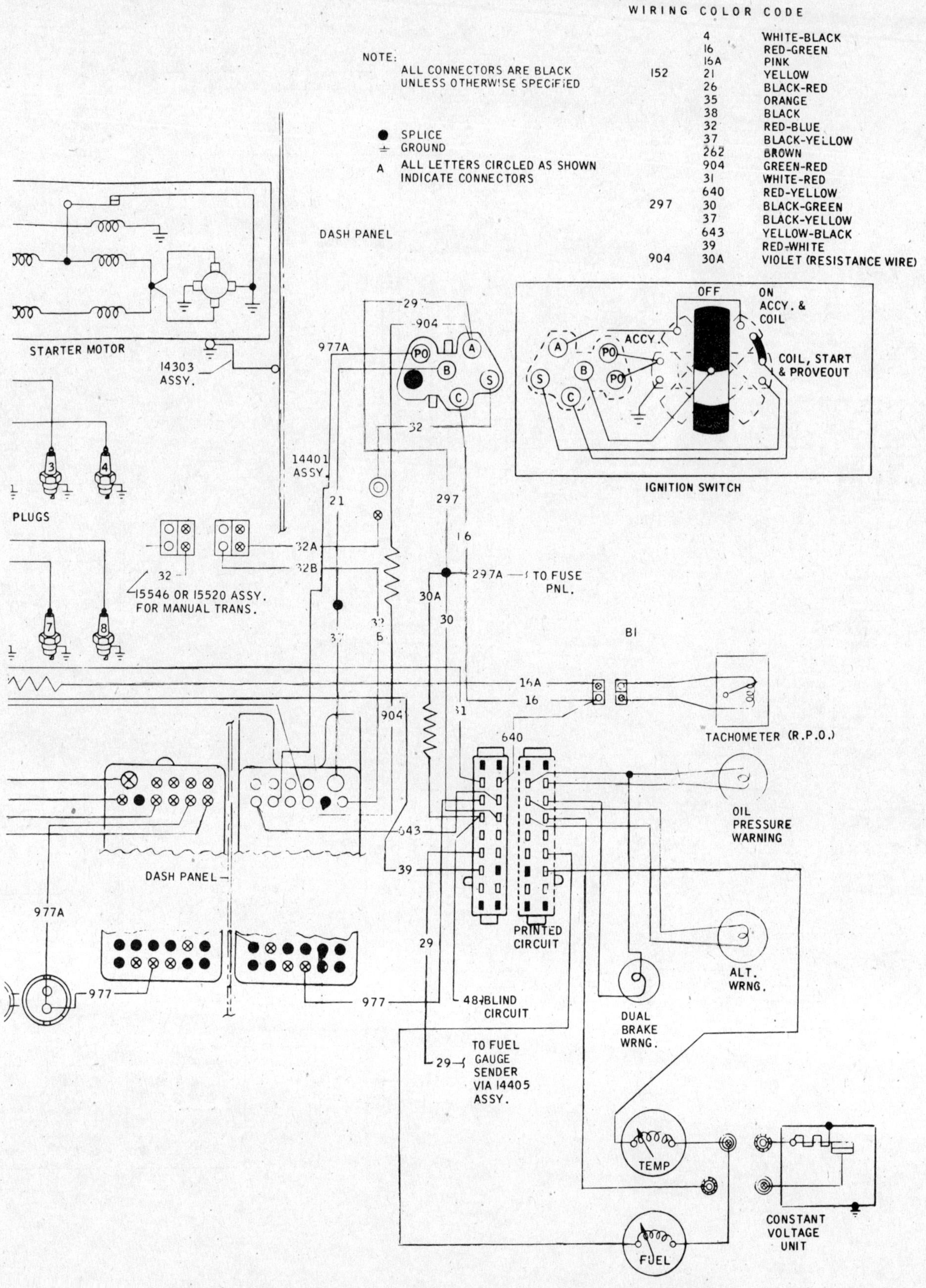

WIRING COLOR CODE

	4	WHITE-BLACK
	16	RED-GREEN
	16A	PINK
152	21	YELLOW
	26	BLACK-RED
	35	ORANGE
	38	BLACK
	32	RED-BLUE
	37	BLACK-YELLOW
	262	BROWN
	904	GREEN-RED
	31	WHITE-RED
	640	RED-YELLOW
297	30	BLACK-GREEN
	37	BLACK-YELLOW
	643	YELLOW-BLACK
	39	RED-WHITE
904	30A	VIOLET (RESISTANCE WIRE)

NOTE:
ALL CONNECTORS ARE BLACK
UNLESS OTHERWISE SPECIFIED

● SPLICE
⏚ GROUND
Ⓐ ALL LETTERS CIRCLED AS SHOWN
INDICATE CONNECTORS

DASH PANEL

STARTER MOTOR

14303 ASSY.

PLUGS

3   4

14401 ASSY.

977A

904

PO

A

B

S

C

32

OFF
ON
ACCY. &
COIL

ACCY

A
PO
S
B
PO
C

COIL, START
& PROVEOUT

IGNITION SWITCH

21   297

32A
32B

32
15546 OR 15520 ASSY.
FOR MANUAL TRANS.

7   8

16

297A   TO FUSE PNL.

30A
30

32
6
37

BI

16A
16

904
31

TACHOMETER (R.P.O.)

640

OIL
PRESSURE
WARNING

643

39

DASH PANEL

977A

977

977

29

29

PRINTED
CIRCUIT

48 BLIND
CIRCUIT

TO FUEL
GAUGE
SENDER
VIA 14405
ASSY.

DUAL
BRAKE
WRNG.

ALT.
WRNG.

TEMP

FUEL

CONSTANT
VOLTAGE
UNIT

Fig. WD11B Ignition, starting and charging wiring diagram – 1969 (continued)

Fig. WD12A Exterior lights, turn signals and brake lights wiring diagram – 1969

NOTE:
(A) ALL LETTERS CIRCLED AS SHOWN INDICATE CONNECTORS

DASH PANEL

TO 7200 ASSY.

385
2 (18)
19
9 (18)
3 (18)
5 (18)
50
44
511

297
297(2)
297A

21 (12)

TO IGNITION SWITCH

14303 ASSY.

DASH PANEL GROUND

INSTRUMENT PANEL GROUND

57 (20)
49 (20)
34
50 (20)

TO PRINTED CKT. BOARD

TURN SIGNAL FLASHER

8 (18)
44 (18)

140 (18)
140A (18)

385 (16)
383 (16)

EMERGENCY WARNING FLASHER

8
140
296

15 (16)
14 (18)
11 (18)
25 (12)
10

TO HEADLAMP SWITCH

STOPLAMP SWITCH

21
25
37A

383

296 (18)

14
984
140A

TO 14405

12 (16)
11
3
2
37 (12)
13 (16)

15   34 (16)
12

20A.   20A.
37A (14)   20A.   20A.

297A (12)

14A.   4A.   14A.

FUSE PANEL

984 (18)

HEADLAMP DIMMER SWITCH

5
9
(RED)
TO 14405

Fig. WD12B Exterior lights, turn signals and brake lights wiring diagram – 1969 (continued)

10

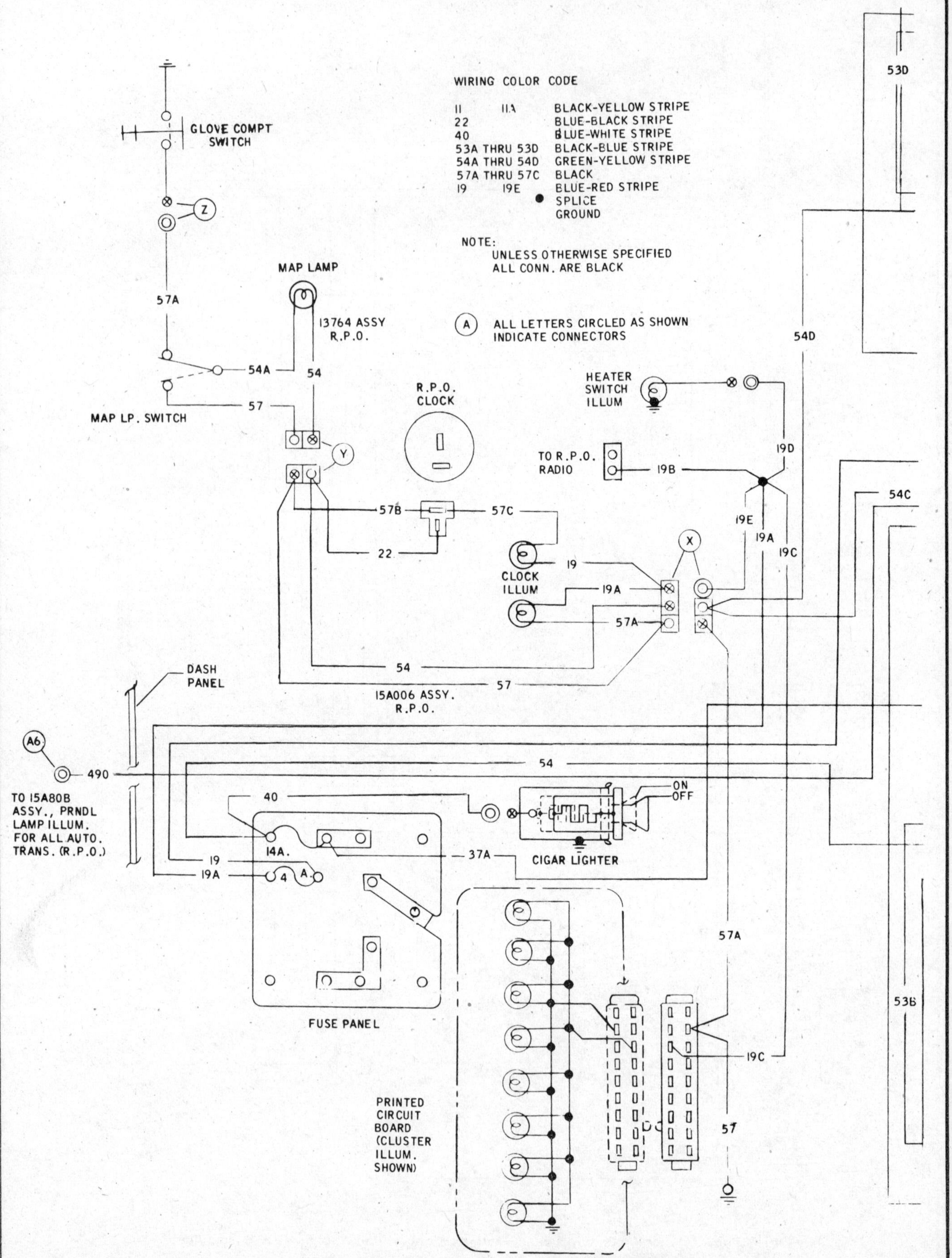

GLOVE COMPT SWITCH

Z

57A

MAP LAMP

13764 ASSY R.P.O.

54A

54

57

MAP LP. SWITCH

WIRING COLOR CODE

11	11A	BLACK-YELLOW STRIPE
22		BLUE-BLACK STRIPE
40		BLUE-WHITE STRIPE
53A THRU 53D		BLACK-BLUE STRIPE
54A THRU 54D		GREEN-YELLOW STRIPE
57A THRU 57C		BLACK
19	19E	BLUE-RED STRIPE
	●	SPLICE
		GROUND

NOTE:
UNLESS OTHERWISE SPECIFIED
ALL CONN. ARE BLACK

A   ALL LETTERS CIRCLED AS SHOWN
     INDICATE CONNECTORS

53D

54D

54C

R.P.O. CLOCK

HEATER SWITCH ILLUM

TO R.P.O. RADIO

19B

19D

19E

19A

19C

Y

57B   57C

22

CLOCK ILLUM

19

19A

57A

X

54

57

15A006 ASSY. R.P.O.

DASH PANEL

A6

490

TO 15A80B ASSY., PRNDL LAMP ILLUM. FOR ALL AUTO. TRANS. (R.P.O.)

40

19

14A.

19A

4   A

54

ON OFF

CIGAR LIGHTER

37A

57A

FUSE PANEL

53B

19C

57

PRINTED CIRCUIT BOARD (CLUSTER ILLUM. SHOWN)

Fig. WD13A Interior lights wiring diagram – 1969

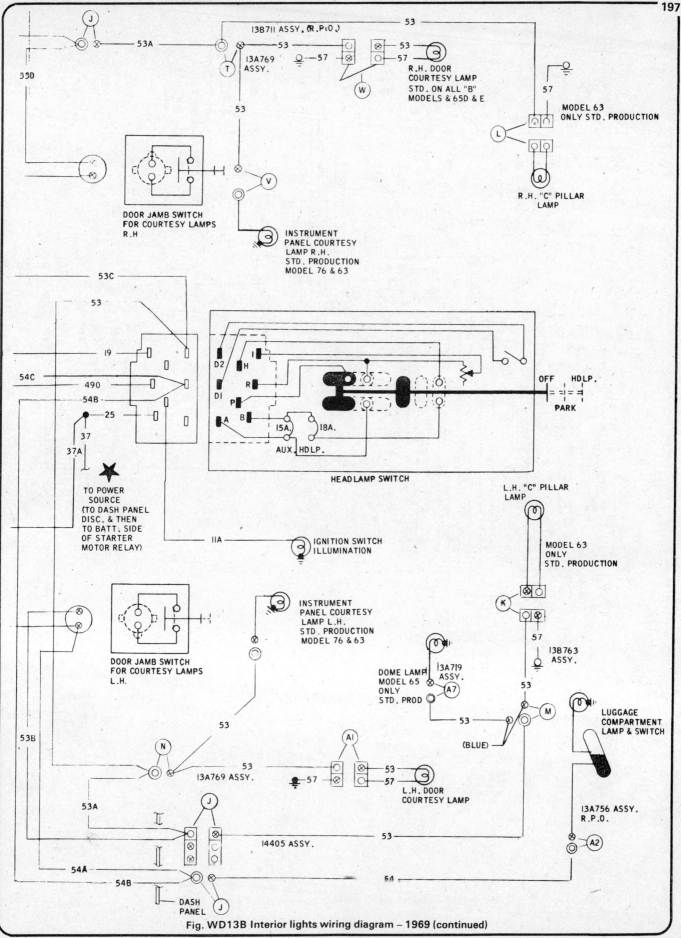

Fig. WD13B Interior lights wiring diagram – 1969 (continued)

10

Fig. WD14A Ignition, starting and charging wiring diagram – 1970

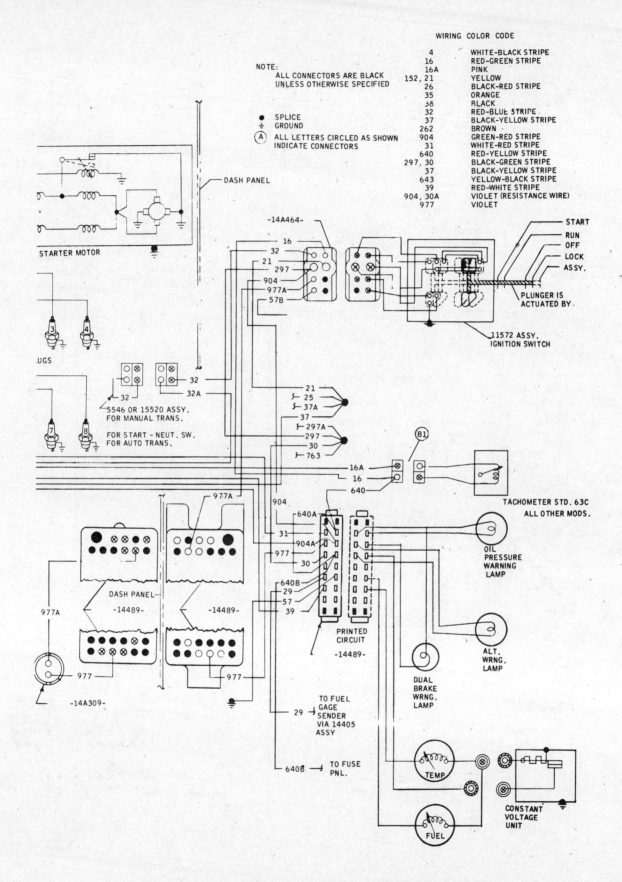

Fig. WD14B Ignition, starting and charging wiring diagram 1970 (continued)

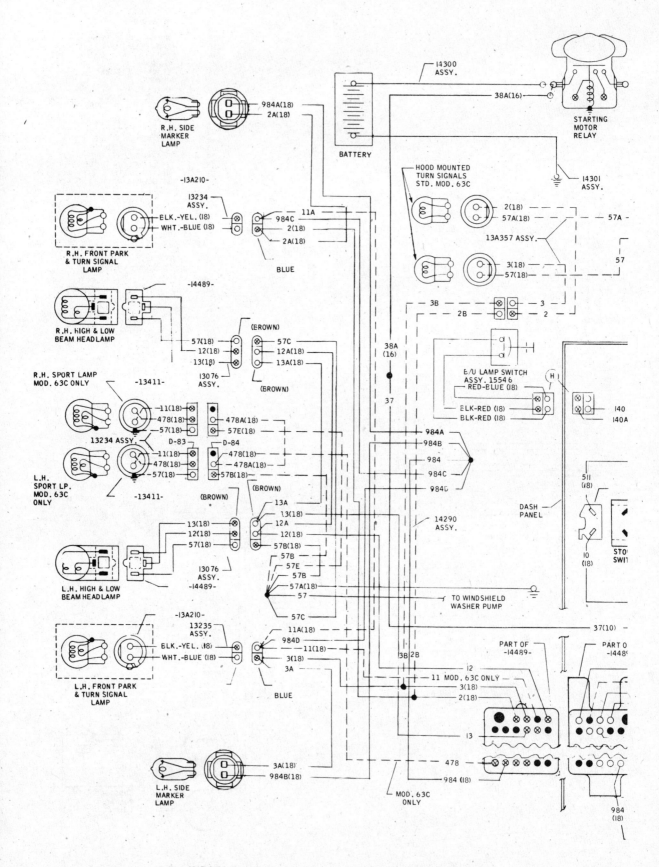

Fig. WD15A Exterior lights and turn signals wiring diagram – 1970

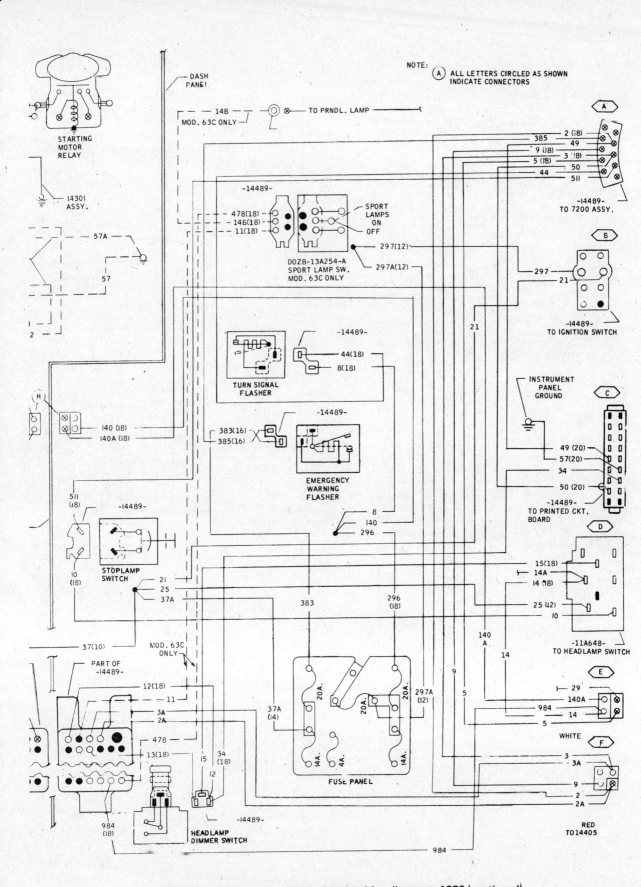

NOTE: (A) ALL LETTERS CIRCLED AS SHOWN
INDICATE CONNECTORS

Fig. WD15B Exterior lights and turn signals wiring diagram – 1970 (continued)

10

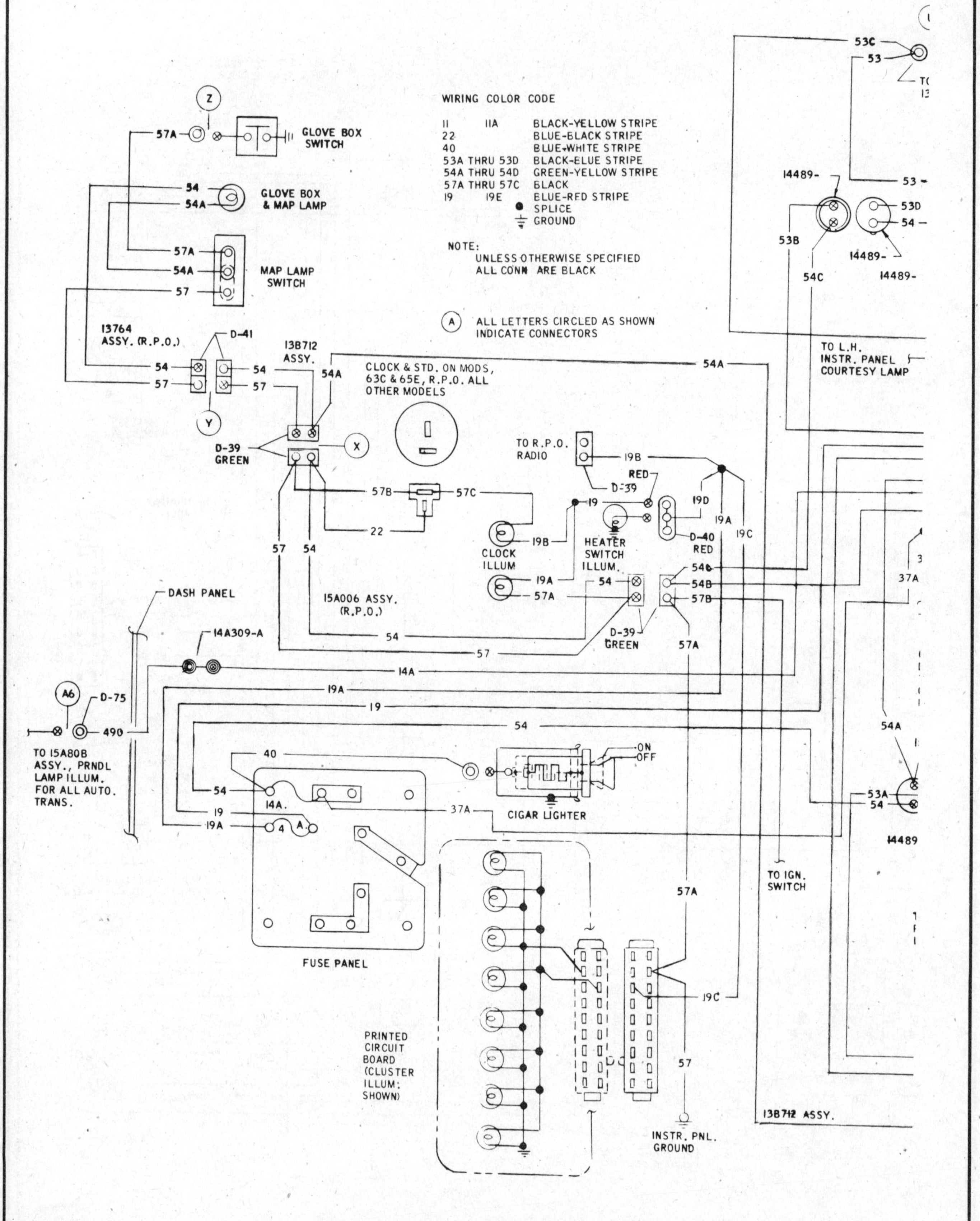

GLOVE BOX SWITCH

57A

Z

GLOVE BOX & MAP LAMP

54
54A

MAP LAMP SWITCH

57A
54A
57

13764 ASSY. (R.P.O.)

D-41

54
57

54
57

13B712 ASSY.

54A

Y

D-39 GREEN

X

57
54

57B — 57C

22

57
54

DASH PANEL

14A309-A

15A006 ASSY. (R.P.O.)

54
57

14A

19A

19

A6

D-75

490

TO I5A80B ASSY., PRNDL LAMP ILLUM. FOR ALL AUTO. TRANS.

54
14A.
19
19A

40

4

A

37A

FUSE PANEL

CIGAR LIGHTER

ON
OFF

PRINTED CIRCUIT BOARD (CLUSTER ILLUM. SHOWN)

INSTR. PNL. GROUND

57A

57

19C

WIRING COLOR CODE

11	11A	BLACK-YELLOW STRIPE
22		BLUE-BLACK STRIPE
40		BLUE-WHITE STRIPE
53A THRU 53D		BLACK-BLUE STRIPE
54A THRU 54D		GREEN-YELLOW STRIPE
57A THRU 57C		BLACK
19	19E	BLUE-RED STRIPE

● SPLICE
⏚ GROUND

NOTE:
UNLESS OTHERWISE SPECIFIED ALL CONN ARE BLACK

A ALL LETTERS CIRCLED AS SHOWN INDICATE CONNECTORS

CLOCK & STD. ON MODS, 63C & 65E, R.P.O. ALL OTHER MODELS

TO R.P.O. RADIO

19B

RED

D-39

19

19D

HEATER SWITCH ILLUM.

D-40 RED

19A

19C

CLOCK ILLUM.

19B

19A
57A

54
54

57B

D-39 GREEN

57A

54
54A
57B

53C
53

14489-

53
53D
54

54C

53B
14489-

14489-

TO L.H. INSTR. PANEL COURTESY LAMP

54A

37A

37A

54A

53A
54

14489

TO IGN. SWITCH

13B712 ASSY.

Fig. WD16A Interior lights wiring diagram – 1970

Fig. WD16B Interior lights wiring diagram – 1970 (continued)

Fig. WD17A Ignition, charging and starting wiring diagram – 1971

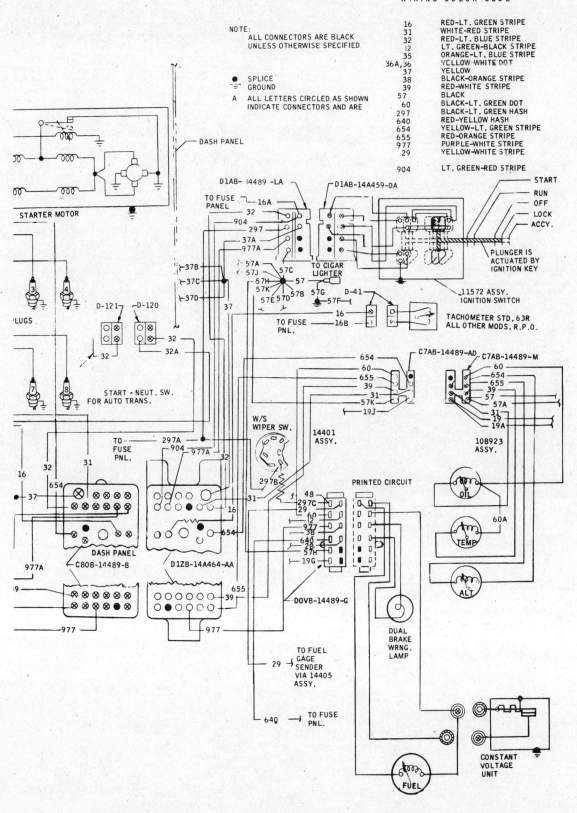

Fig. WD17B Ignition, charging and starting wiring diagram – 1971 (continued)

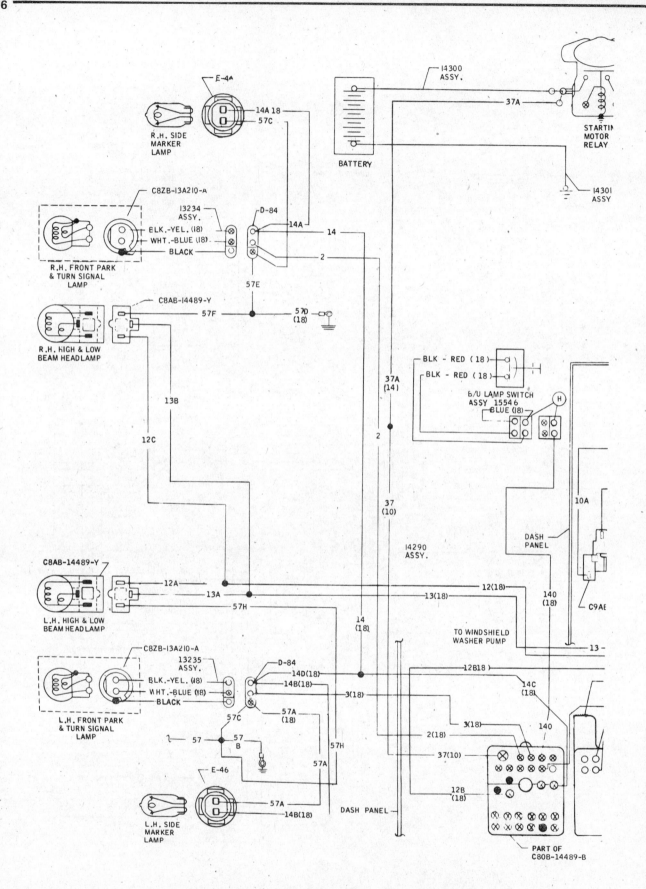

Fig. WD18A Exterior lights and turn signals wiring diagram – 1971

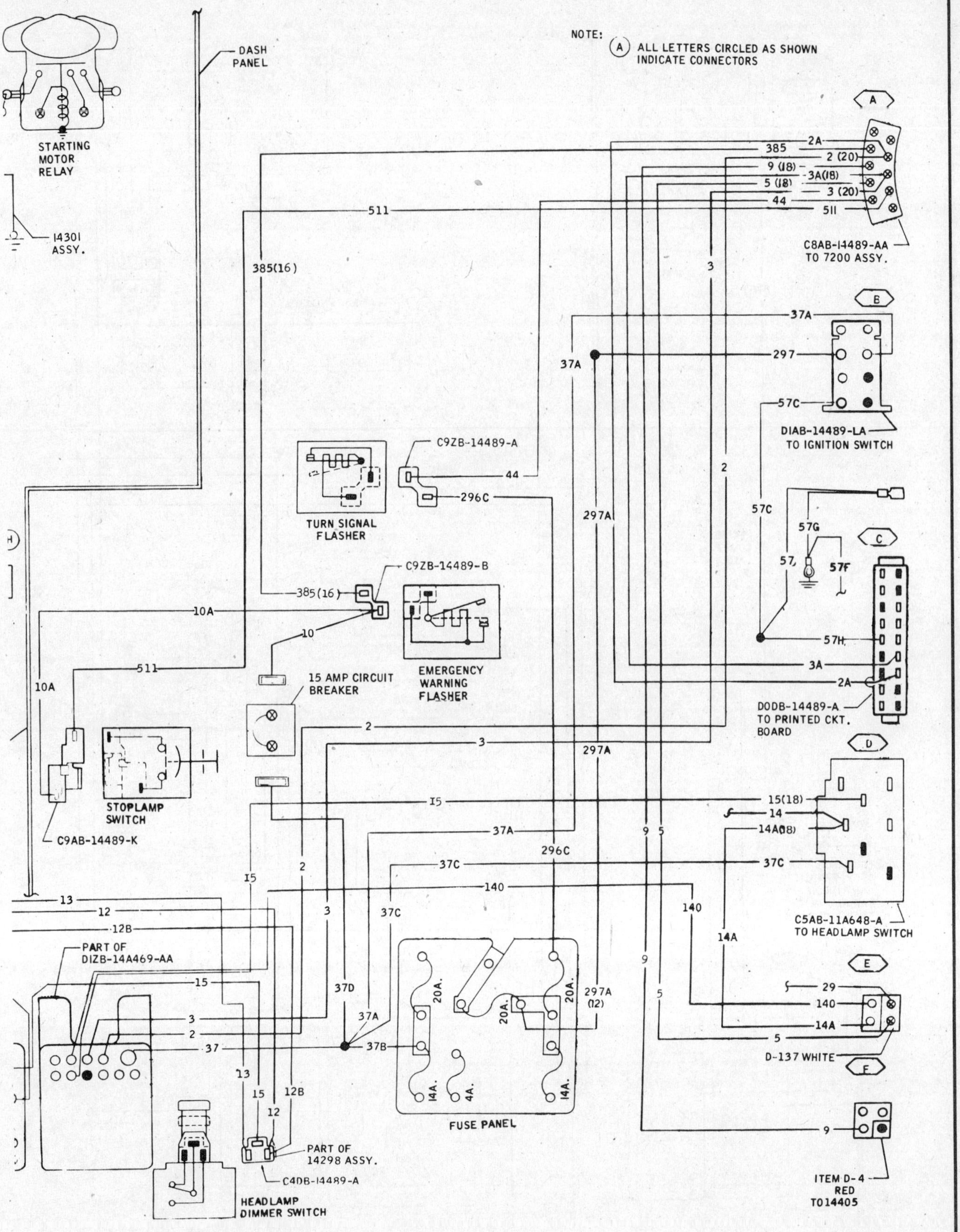

STARTING MOTOR RELAY

14301 ASSY.

DASH PANEL

NOTE:
(A) ALL LETTERS CIRCLED AS SHOWN INDICATE CONNECTORS

385 — 2A
2 (20)
9 (18)
5 (18) — 3A(18)
3 (20)
44 — 511

511
385(16)

3

C8AB-14489-AA TO 7200 ASSY.

37A
37A — 297
57C
DIAB-14489-LA TO IGNITION SWITCH

2

297A
57C
57G
57, 57F
57H
3A
2A
D0DB-14489-A TO PRINTED CKT. BOARD

C9ZB-14489-A
44
296C
TURN SIGNAL FLASHER

C9ZB-14489-B
385(16)
10A
10
EMERGENCY WARNING FLASHER

15 AMP CIRCUIT BREAKER

511
10A

STOPLAMP SWITCH
C9AB-14489-K

2
3
15
37A
296C
37C
140

15(18)
14
14A(18)
37C
C5AB-11A648-A TO HEADLAMP SWITCH

13
12
12B
PART OF DIZB-14A469-AA
15
3
2
37
37D
37A
37B
20A. 20A. 20A.
297A (12)
14A. 4A. 14A.
FUSE PANEL

29
140
14A
5
D-137 WHITE

9 5
140
14A
5
9

ITEM D-4 RED TO14405

13
15 12B
12
PART OF 14298 ASSY.
C4DB-14489-A
HEADLAMP DIMMER SWITCH

10

Fig. WD18B Exterior lights and turn signals wiring diagram – 1971 (continued)

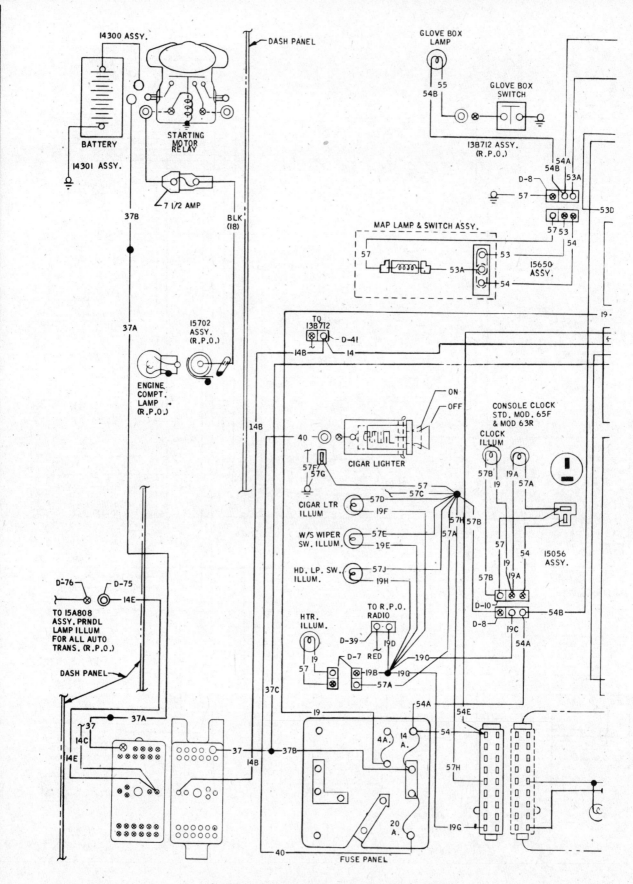

Fig. WD19A Interior lights wiring diagram – 1971

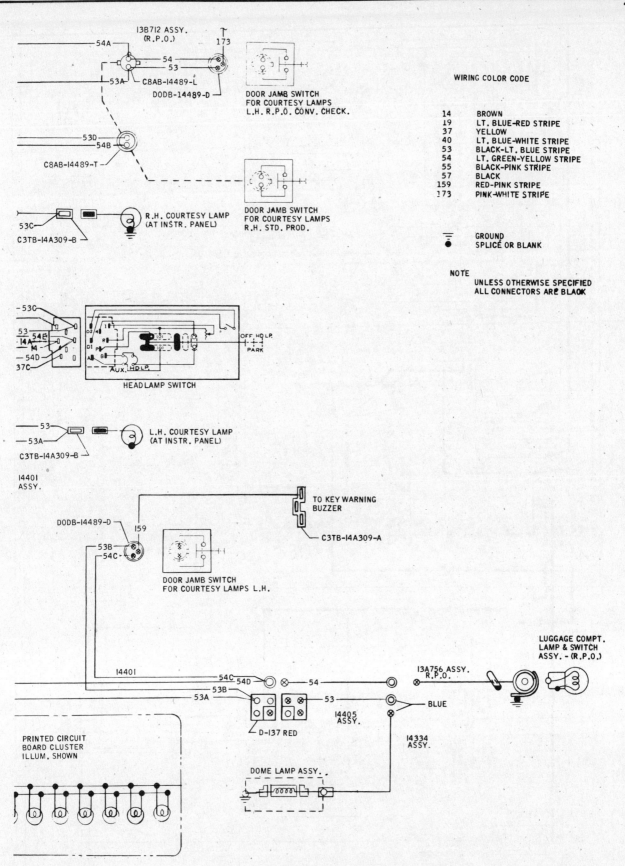

Fig. WD19B Interior lights wiring diagram – 1971 (continued)

Fig. WD20A Wiring diagram – 1972 (see pages 217 and 218 for 'Key')

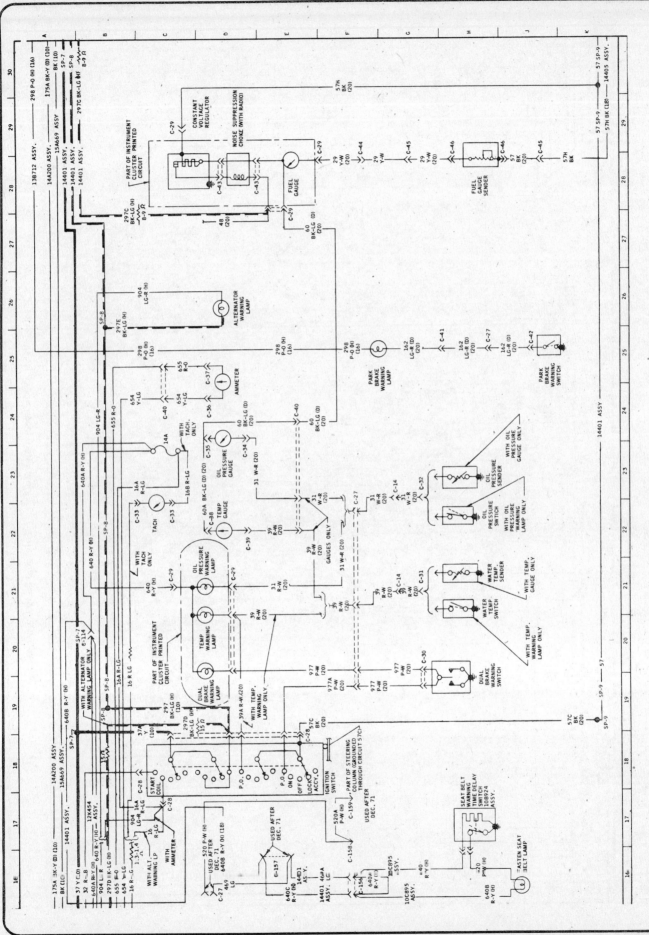

Fig. WD20B Wiring diagram – 1972 (continued) (see pages 217 and 218 for 'Key')

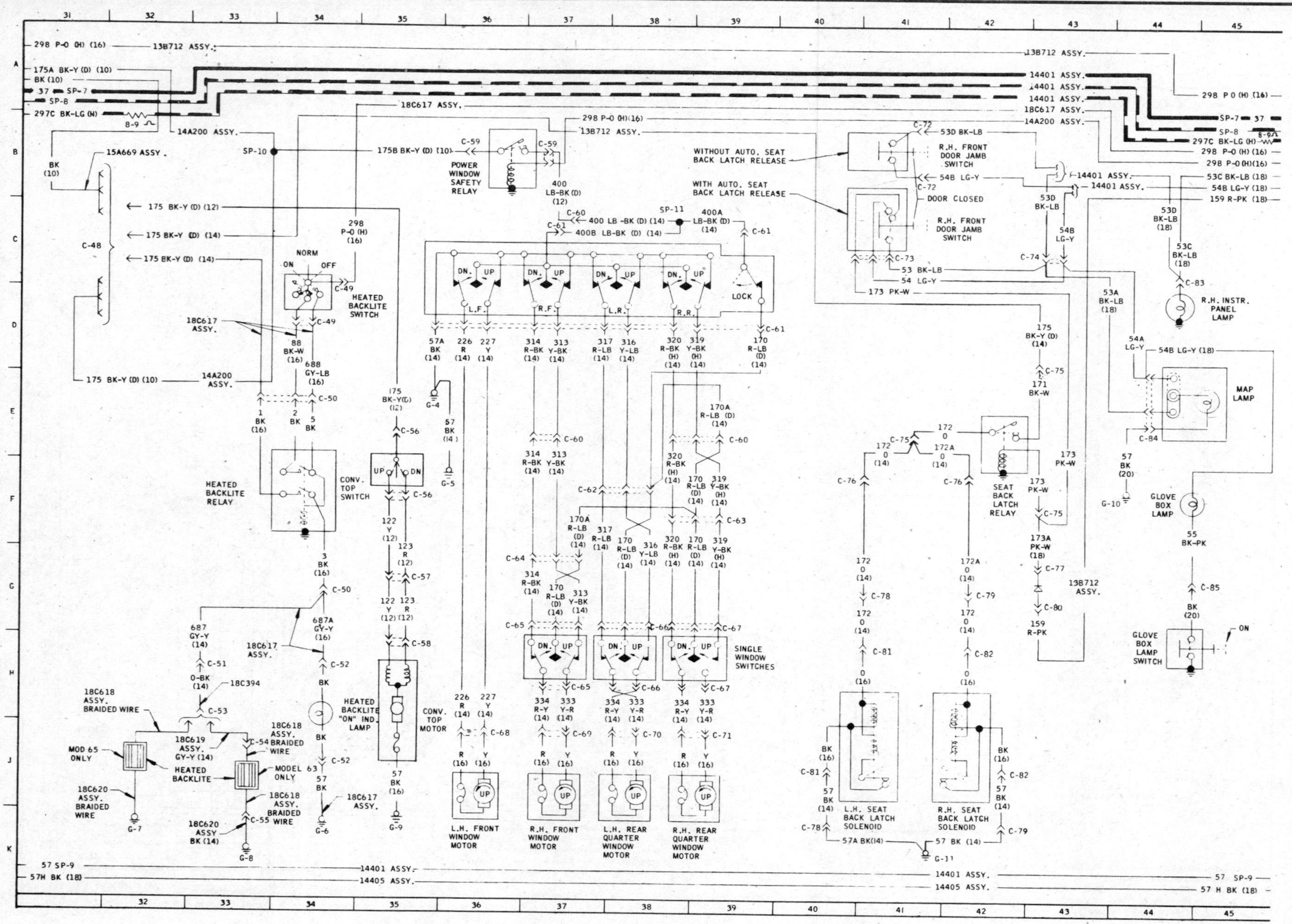

MAP LAMP

R.H. INSTR. PANEL LAMP

GLOVE BOX LAMP

GLOVE BOX LAMP SWITCH

ON

SEAT BACK LATCH RELAY

R.H. SEAT BACK LATCH SOLENOID

L.H. SEAT BACK LATCH SOLENOID

R.H. FRONT DOOR JAMB SWITCH

R.H. FRONT DOOR JAMB SWITCH

DOOR CLOSED

WITHOUT AUTO. SEAT BACK LATCH RELEASE

WITH AUTO. SEAT BACK LATCH RELEASE

LOCK

POWER WINDOW SAFETY RELAY

SINGLE WINDOW SWITCHES

R.H. REAR QUARTER WINDOW MOTOR

L.H. REAR QUARTER WINDOW MOTOR

R.H. FRONT WINDOW MOTOR

L.H. FRONT WINDOW MOTOR

R.R.

L.R.

R.F.

L.F.

UP / DN

CONV. TOP MOTOR

CONV. TOP SWITCH

UP / DN

HEATED BACKLITE SWITCH

NORM / OFF / ON

HEATED BACKLITE "ON" IND. LAMP

HEATED BACKLITE RELAY

HEATED BACKLITE

MODEL 63 ONLY

MOD 65 ONLY

18C618 ASSY. BRAIDED WIRE

18C620 ASSY. BRAIDED WIRE

Fig. WD20C Wiring diagram – 1972 (continued) (see pages 217 and 218 for 'Key')

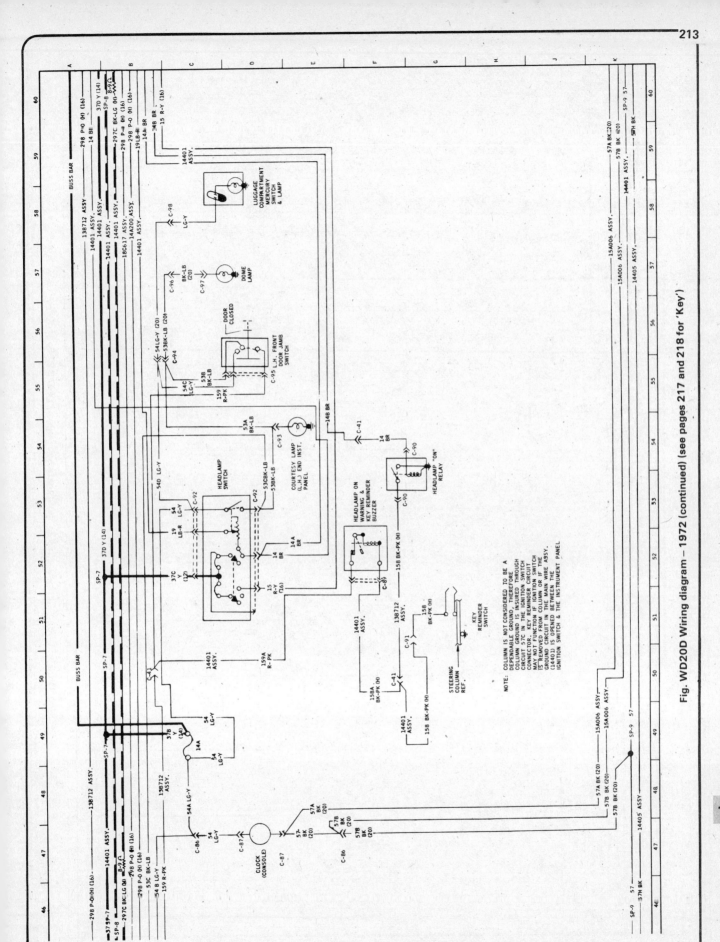

Fig. WD20D Wiring diagram — 1972 (continued) (see pages 217 and 218 for 'Key')

10

BUSS BAR

HORN SWITCH
ON OFF
460 Y-LB (D) 14
C-91
HI PITCH HORN
LO PITCH HORN
C-106
C-105
C-27
DB (14)
DB (14)
DB (14)
1A DB (14)

CIGAR LIGHTER
460 Y-LB (D) (14)
C-104
C-103
57 BK (1B)
57G BK (16)
57F BK
G-6
G-10

20A
40 LB-W (16)
BUSS BAR

CLUSTER ILLUMINATION
C-29
57H (20)
PART OF PRINTED CIRCUIT BOARD

20A
297 A BK-LG (H) (10)
ACCESSORY STUD (ON FUSE PANEL)
BUSS BAR
C-100
C-109
19G 28 - R (20)

GAGE PACK ILLUM
19A LB-R (20)
57A BK (20)
C-40
C-40
57A BK (20)

19J LB-R (20)
19 LB-R (20)
57 BK (20)
57A BK (20)

P-O (H) (14)
14A318 ASSY.
C-99

RADIO ILLUM
19D LB-R (20)
C-102

HEATER CONTROLS ILLUM.
19B LB-R (20)
19 LB-R (20)
C-101
57 BK (20)
C-101
57A BK (20)

W/S WIPER SWITCH ILLUM.
19E LB-R (20)
57E BK (20)
57E BK (20)

CIGAR LIGHTER ILLUM.
19F LB-R (20)
57D BK (20)
57D BK (20)

HEADLAMP SWITCH ILLUM.
19A LB-R (20)
SP-12
19H LB-R (20)
57J BK (20)

4A

CLOCK ILLUM (CONSOLE)
19 LB-R (20)
57B BK (20)
19C LB-R (20)
C-86
19A LB-R (20)
57A BK (20)
154006 ASSY.

BUSS BAR
14 BR (1B)
370 Y (14)
SP-8
297C BK-LG (H)
14B BR
15 R-Y (16)
14401 ASSY.
57H BK
SP-9

298 P-O (H) (16)
14 BR
370 Y (14)
SP-8
297C BK-LG (H) (16)
298 P-O (H) (16)
19 LB-P
14A BR
15 R-Y (16)
57 SP-9
57H BK

138712 ASSY.
298 P-O (H) (16)
18C617 ASSY
14A200 ASSY

14401 ASSY.
14405 ASSY.

Fig. WD20E Wiring diagram – 1972 (continued) (see pages 217 and 218 for 'Key')

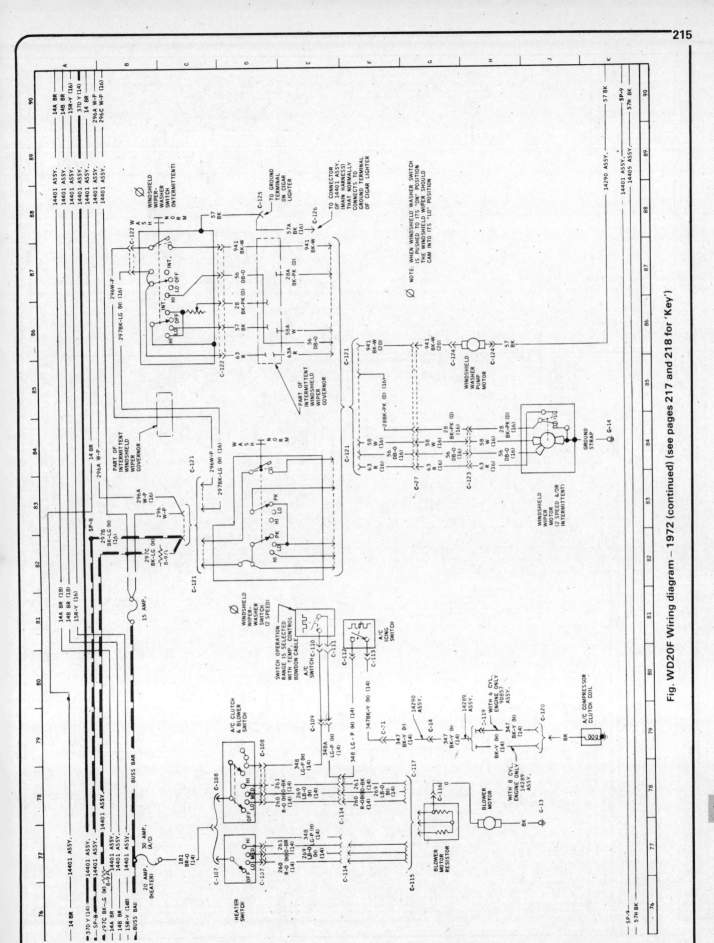

Fig. WD20F Wiring diagram — 1972 (continued) (see pages 217 and 218 for 'Key')

Fig. WD20G Wiring diagram – 1972 (continued) (see pages 217 and 218 for 'Key')

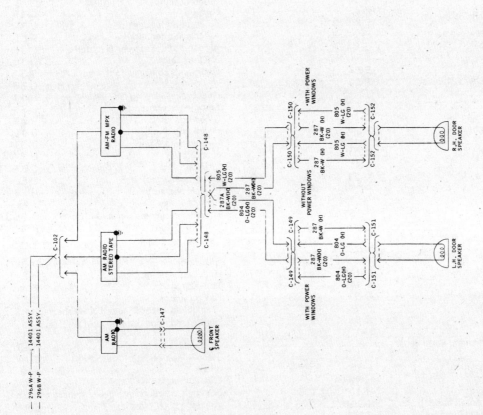

Wiring color key
Primary colors

Black	BK
Brown	BR
Tan	T
Red	R
Pink	PK
Orange	O
Yellow	Y
Dark Green	DG
Light Green	LG
Dark Blue	DB
Light Blue	LB
Purple	P
Gray	GY
White	W
Hash	(H)
Dot	(D)

Stripe is understood and has no
color key

Heavy solid line represents battery feed ——————
Heavy dashed line represents accessory feed --------

Fig. WD20H Wiring diagram – 1972 (continued) (see pages 217 and 218 for 'Key')

10

Key to Wiring Diagram – 1972

Component	Location
Air conditioner clutch	K-79
Alternator	F-3
Alternator regulator	J-4
Clock	D-47
Circuit breakers	
Power assist	B-8
Stop lamp	C-97
Capacitor (condenser) noise suppression	J-5
Choke-noise suppression	D-28
Battery	B-2
Buzzer (Headlamp 'ON') and key warning	F-53
Cigar lighter	D-73
Distributor	F-G-H-7
Engine governor	F-10
Flashers	
Emergency warning	D-96
Turn signal	B-91
Gauges	
Ammeter	D-25
Fuel	E-28
Instrument voltage regulator	C-28
Oil pressure	D-24
Tachometer	C-22
Temperature	D-22
Governor (intermittent wiper)	B-84,85 & D-86,87
Heated back-light (heater elements)	J-32,33
Heater, A/C blower resistor	G-78
Horns	G,H-74
Ignition coil	F-12
Illumination lamps	
Cigar lighter	E-65
Clock (console)	F-62
Gauge cluster	F-69,70
Headlamp switch	F-64
Heater controls	G-67
Main cluster	E,F,G,H,J-71
Radio	E-68
W/S wiper-washer switches	F-66
Indicator lamps	
Alternator	D-26
Dual brake warning	D-20
Heated back-light 'ON'	J-34
High beam	H-100
High-water temp	D-21
Left turn	F-91
Low oil pressure	D-21
Parking brake	F-25
Right turn	F-92
Seat belt	J-16
Lights	
Eng. compt. (light and switch)	E-7
Back-up LH	H-102
Back-up RH	H-104
Grille lamps (2 lamps)	J-97
Glove box	F-44
Dome	D-57
Headlights	H-98,99
PRND21	H-96
License plate	H-103
Luggage compartment (light & switch)	D-59
Map (light and switch)	E-45
Parking	H-92,94
Rear (tail, stop & turn) (4 lamps)	H-101,102,105
Side marker - front (2 lamps)	J-93,95
- rear (2 lamps)	J-103
Instr. panel ctsy. (2 lamps)	D-44 & E-54
Motors	
Air conditioner or heater blower	H-78
Convertible top	J-35

Component	Location
Power windows	
LH front door	J-36
RH front door	J-37
RH rear quarter	J-39
LH rear quarter	J-38
Starting	C-14
Windshield washer	H-86
Windshield wiper	J-84
Radios	
AM	C-115
AM and stereo tape unit	C-117
AM-FM multiplex	C-119
Senders	
Fuel gauge	H-28
Oil pressure gauge	H-23
Water temperature gauge	H-21
Solenoids	
Seat back latch	J-41,42
Throttle position	K-6
Emission vacuum	K-8
Relays	
Starting motor	B-9
Power window safety	B-36
Heated back-light	F-34
Seat back latch	E-42
Headlamp on	F-54
Speakers	
Front	E-115
LH door	J-116
RH door	J-119
Speed sensor (emission control)	J-15
Spark control unit (emission control)	K-13
Switches	
Ambient temp. sensor (emission control)	G-15
Air conditioner control	E-81
Air conditioner icing	F-81
Air conditioner blower & clutch	D-78
Back-up light	D-103,D-104
Door jamb courtesy light – front RH	B,C-41
LH	D-56
Dual brake warning	H-19
Emergency warning	C-95
Glove box lamp	H-45
Headlamp dimmer	D-100
Heated back-light	D-34
Heater blower	D-77
Ignition	C,D,E-18
Light (headlamp)	C-52
Low oil pressure	H-22
Parking brake	J-25
Power window master and LH front	D-36,37,38,39
RH front door	H-37
LH rear quarter	H-38
RH rear quarter	H-39
Stop light	D-98
High water temp	H-21
Turn signal	C-94
Key reminder	G-51
Windshield wiper 2-speed & washer	D-83
Windshield wiper intermittent & washer	C-87
Convertible top	F-35
'Park' – 'neutral' start (auto trans. only)	F-14
Eng. compt. lamp	E-7
Seat belt warning time delay switch	H-16
map (switch & lamp)	E-44
Luggage compt. switch & lamp	D-59
Eng. compt. (switch & lamp)	E-7
Horn	D-74
Transmission (emission control)	K-11

Key to Wiring Diagram – 1973

Component	Location
Air conditioner	
clutch solenoid	F-70
Alternator	A-1
Alternator regulator	F-1
Ammeter	A-3
Automatic seat back latch solenoid	E-47,E-48
Battery	C-5
Blower motor resistor	E-69,E-71
Cigar lighter	C-32
Clock	D-31
Cluster clock	B-37
Constant voltage unit	F-19
Distributors	
6 cylinder 250 CID	D-3
8 cylinder 302 CID	E-3
8 cylinder 351 CID	F-3
Electric choke	E-5
Emission systems	
Ambient temp sensor SW	C-84
EGR cutout solenoid	C-87
Spark vacuum, module sol	E-87
Spark delay valve bypass solenoid	E-88
EGR control module	A-85
Speed sensor	C-85
Transmission regulator spark control solenoid	E-85
TRS switch	F-86
Throttle positioner solenoid	C-88
Flashers	
Emergency warning	E-34
Turn signal	B-34
Gauges	
Engine temperature	F-10
Fuel	C-20
Oil pressure	F-12
Tachometer	B-11
Heated back-light	E-52
Horns	E-31,E-32
Ignition coil	F-6
Illumination lamps	
Cigar	F-26
Clock	D-30
Gauge	D-29
Headlamp switch	F-27
Heater switch	F-25
Instrument cluster	F-29
PRNDL	E-35
Windshield washer switch	F-26
Immersion heater	D-55
Indicators	
Alternator warning	E-9
Dual brake warning	F-14
Engine temp. warning	F-14
Heated back-light on	E-51
High beam	B-37
Oil pressure	F-13
Parking brake warning	C-46
Seat belt warning	D-21
Turn signal	
LH	B-36
RH	C-36
Key reminder buzzer	C-41
Junction block	C-3
Lamps	
Back-up	
LH	F-23
RH	F-24
Courtesy	E-42,E-43
Dome	D-40
Engine compartment	C-7
Glove box	E-11
Headlamps	
LH	E-37
RH	E-36
License	F-40

Component	Location
Map	B-45
Park and turn front	
LH	F-33
RH	F-35
Switches	
A/C blower	B-69
Back-up lamp (manual)	C-24
Convertible top	B-54
Deicing	E-70
Door jambs	B-40,C-43,C-44
Dual brake warning	F-15
Emergency warning	B-34
Glove box	F-44
Headlamp	C-38
Headlamp dimmer	C-36
Heated back-light	B-51
Heater blower	B-71
Horn	C-31
Ignition	D-15
Key reminder	E-41
Map lamp	B-45
Master control power	
Window	A-77
Mode (A/C)	C-70
Parking brake	F-46
Power window	E-77,E-78,E-80
Oil pressure	F-13
Seat belt retractors	
LH	F-22
RH	F-21
Seat belt warning (manual trans)	C-22
Seat sensor	F-21
Start interlock and backup lamp	B-21
Stoplamp	D-34
Turn signal	B-33
Water temperature	F-11
Windshield wiper and washer	C-60
Windshield wiper and washer 2-speed intermittent	A-63
W/S/W/Governor	C-63
Rear tail stop	
LH	F-39,F-40
RH	F-37,F-38
Side markers	
L Front	F-33
R Front	F-34
L Rear	F-39
R Rear	F-37
Trunk	E-45
Motors	
Blower	F-69
Convertible top	F-53
Heater blower	F-72
Power window	F-76,F-77, F-79,F-80
Starter	F-7
Windshield wiper	F-62
W/S washer pump	E-58
Noise suppression capacitor	E-2
Radio noise suppression (choke)	E-19
Radios	
AM	B-25
AM/FM/MPX	B-27
AM/tape	B-26
Radio speakers	E-25,E-26,E-27
Relays	
Headlamp on warning	F-43
Heated back-light	C-90
Power window	D-74
Seat back latch	C-48
Starting motor	B-6
Seat belt warning buzzer	C-21
Senders	
Fuel gauge	F-20
Oil pressure	F-12
Water temperature	E-10

10

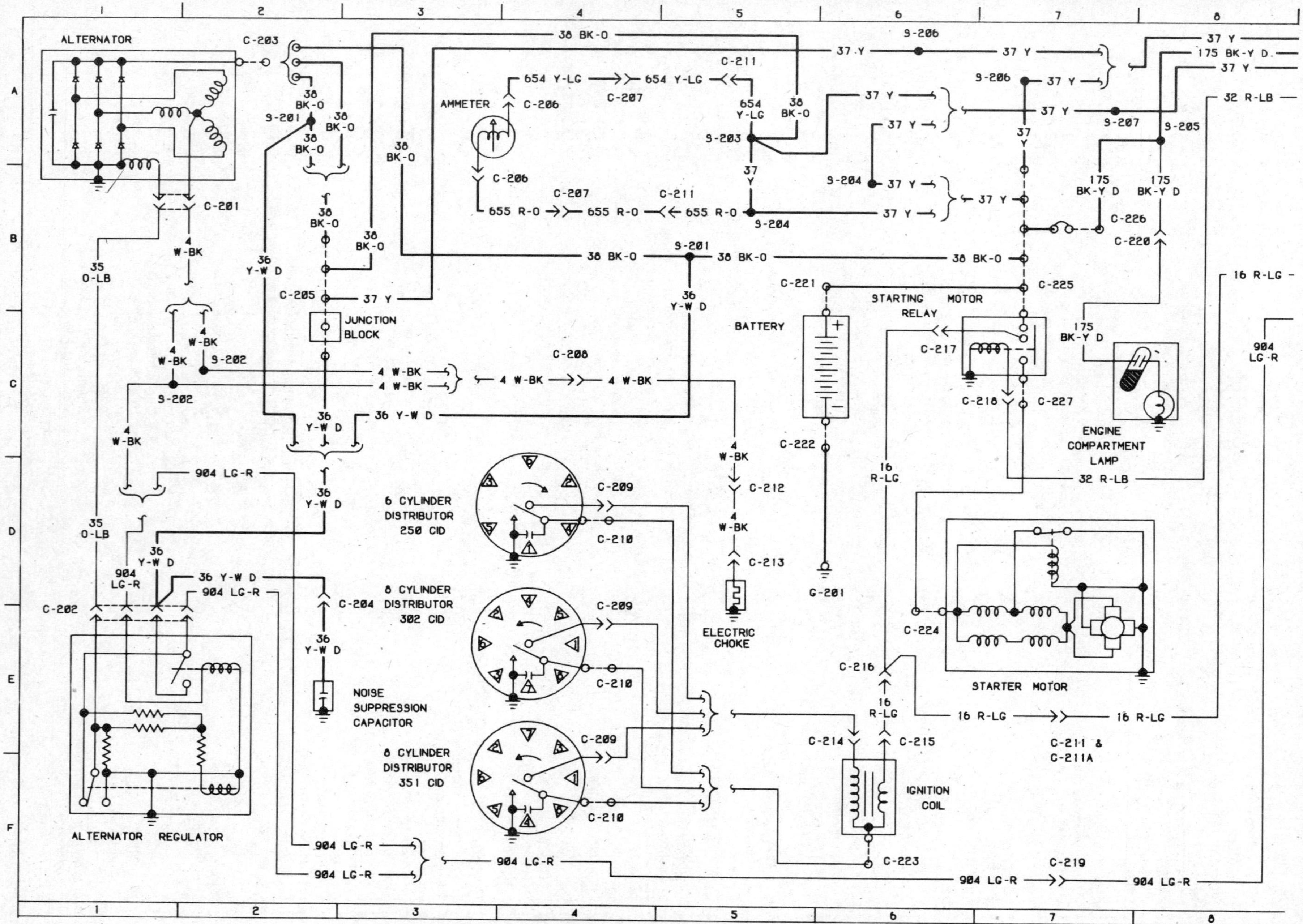

6 7 7 6 5 4 3 2 1

37 Y
175 BK-Y D
37 Y
32 R-LB
16 R-LG
904 LG-R

S-205
S-207
175 BK-Y D
C-226
C-220
175 BK-Y D
ENGINE COMPARTMENT LAMP
32 R-LB
STARTER MOTOR
16 R-LG
C-211 & C-211A

37 Y
S-206
37 Y
C-225
C-227
C-218
C-224
16 R-LG

STARTING MOTOR RELAY
C-217
C-216
16 R-LG
C-215
IGNITION COIL
C-214
C-223

37 Y
S-204
37 Y
S-203
654 Y-LG
654 Y-LG
C-211
C-207
36 BK-O
C-221
BATTERY
C-222
G-201
16 R-LG

S-204
S-204
655 R-O
C-211
36 BK-O
S-201
36 Y-W D

W-BK
C-212
W-BK
C-213
ELECTRIC CHOKE

AMMETER
C-206
654 Y-LG
C-207
655 R-O
C-207
36 BK-O
C-200
4 W-BK

6 CYLINDER DISTRIBUTOR 250 CID
8 CYLINDER DISTRIBUTOR 302 CID
8 CYLINDER DISTRIBUTOR 351 CID
C-209 C-210

904 LG-R
C-219
904 LG-R

C-206
C-211
36 BK-O
36 Y-W D
4 W-BK

30 BK-O
30 BK-O
37 Y
JUNCTION BLOCK
C-205
36 Y-W D
36 Y-W D
C-204
NOISE SUPPRESSION CAPACITOR
904 LG-R
904 LG-R

S-201
C-203
36 Y-W D
36 Y-W D
36 Y-W D
904 LG-R

ALTERNATOR
C-201
4 W-BK
S-202
W-BK
35 O-LB
C-202
ALTERNATOR REGULATOR
36 Y-W D
904 LG-R

Fig. WD21A Wiring diagram — 1973 (see pages 219 and 231 for 'Key')

A B C D E F

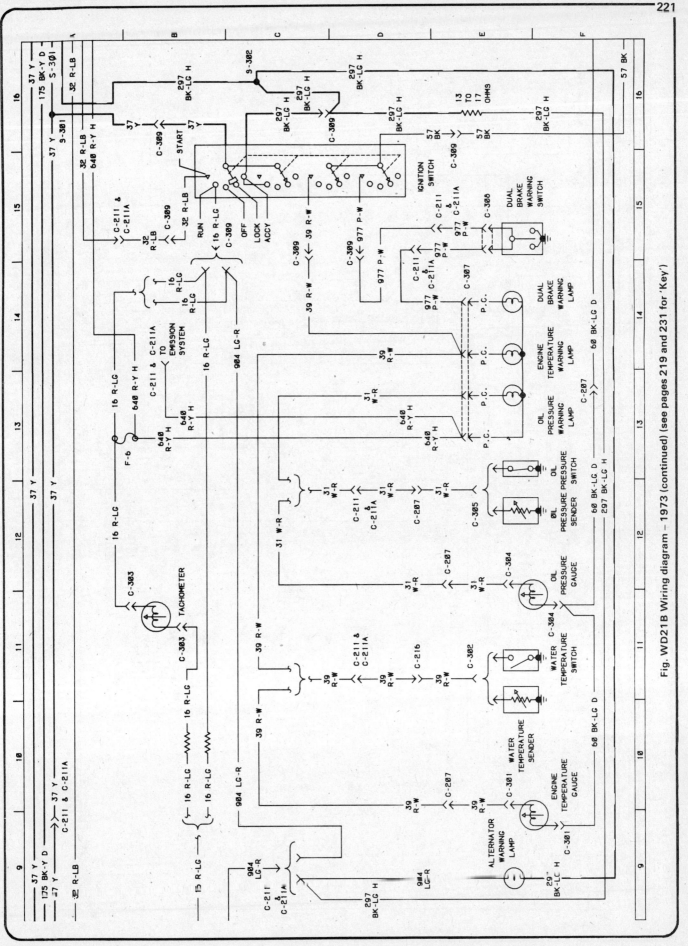

Fig. WD21B Wiring diagram – 1973 (continued) (see pages 219 and 231 for 'Key')

10

Fig. WD21C Wiring diagram – 1973 (continued) (see pages 219 and 231 for 'Key')

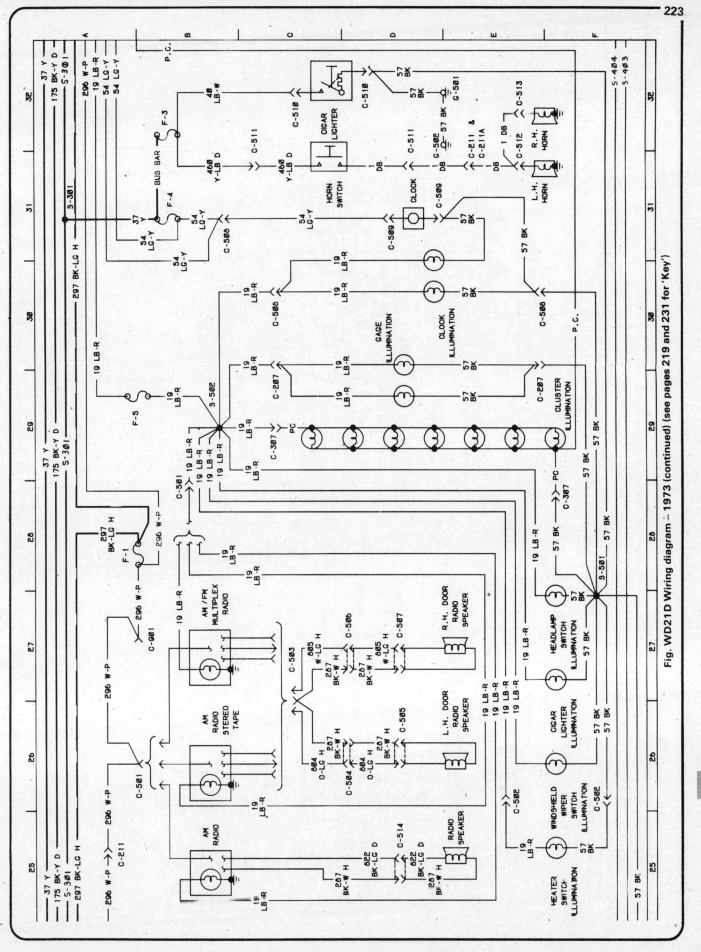

Fig. WD21D Wiring diagram — 1973 (continued) (see pages 219 and 231 for 'Key')

10

Fig. WD21E Wiring diagram – 1973 (continued) (see pages 219 and 231 for 'Key')

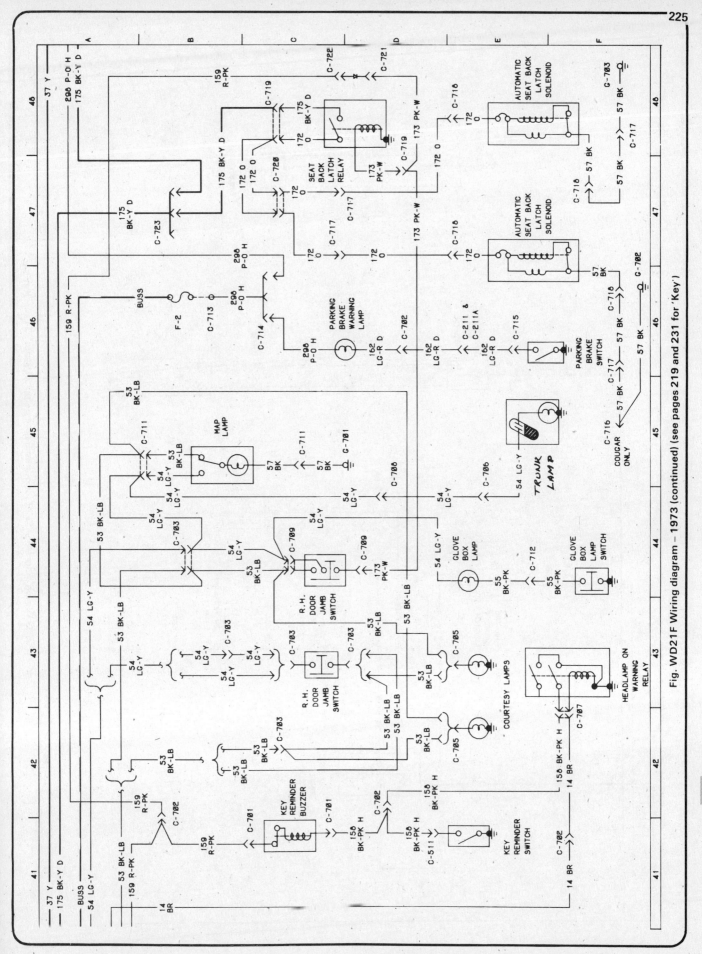

Fig. WD21F Wiring diagram – 1973 (continued) (see pages 219 and 231 for 'Key')

10

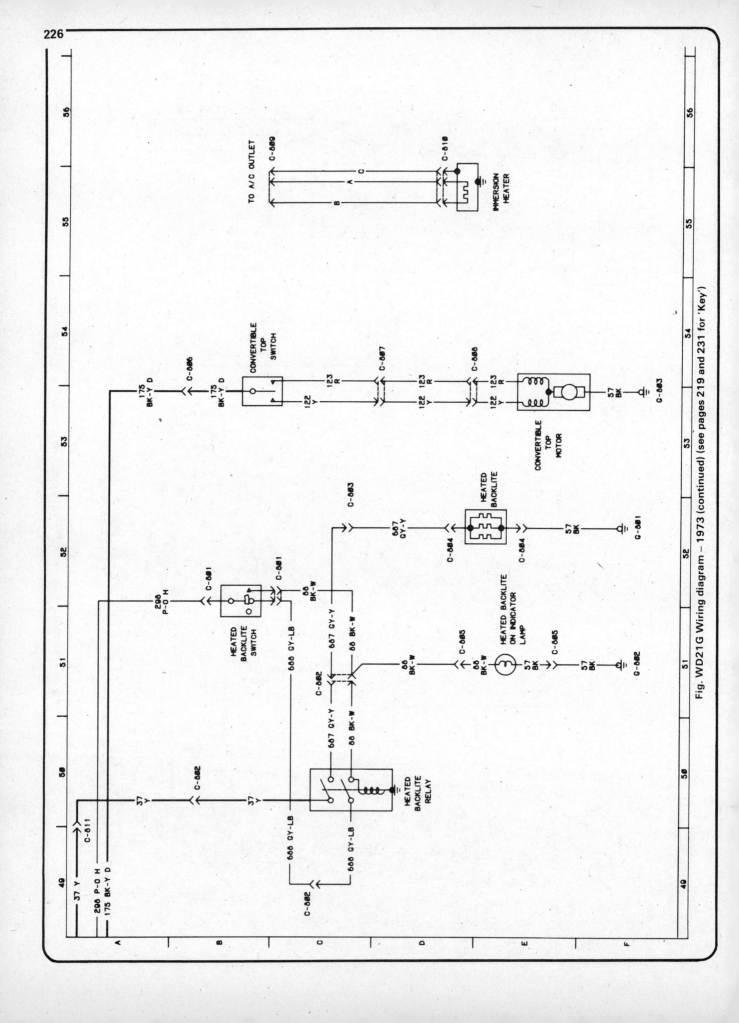

Fig. WD21G Wiring diagram – 1973 (continued) (see pages 219 and 231 for 'Key')

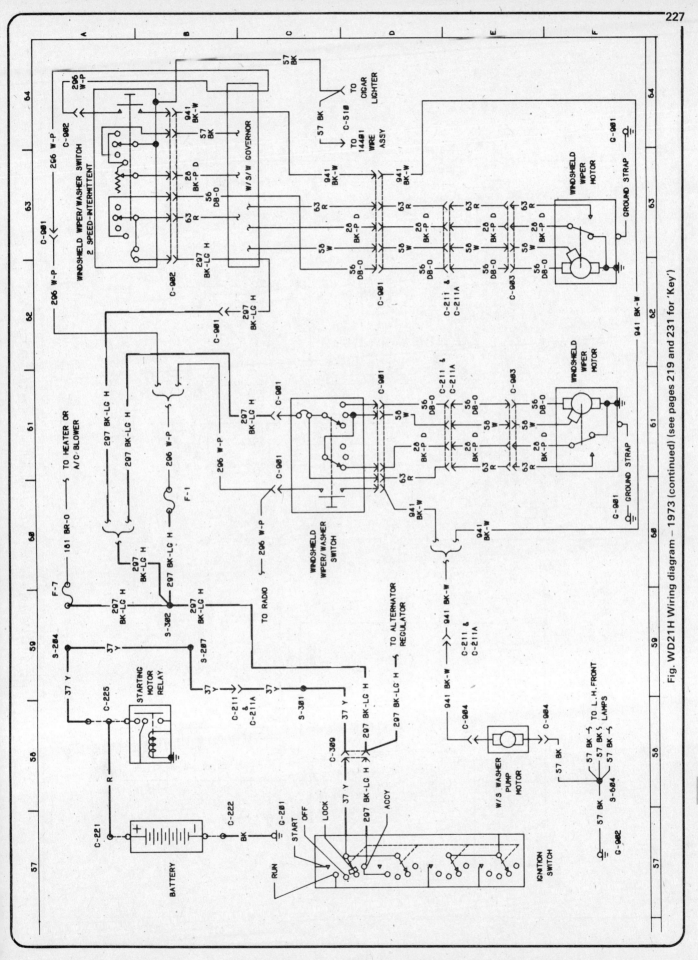

Fig. WD21H Wiring diagram – 1973 (continued) (see pages 219 and 231 for 'Key')

10

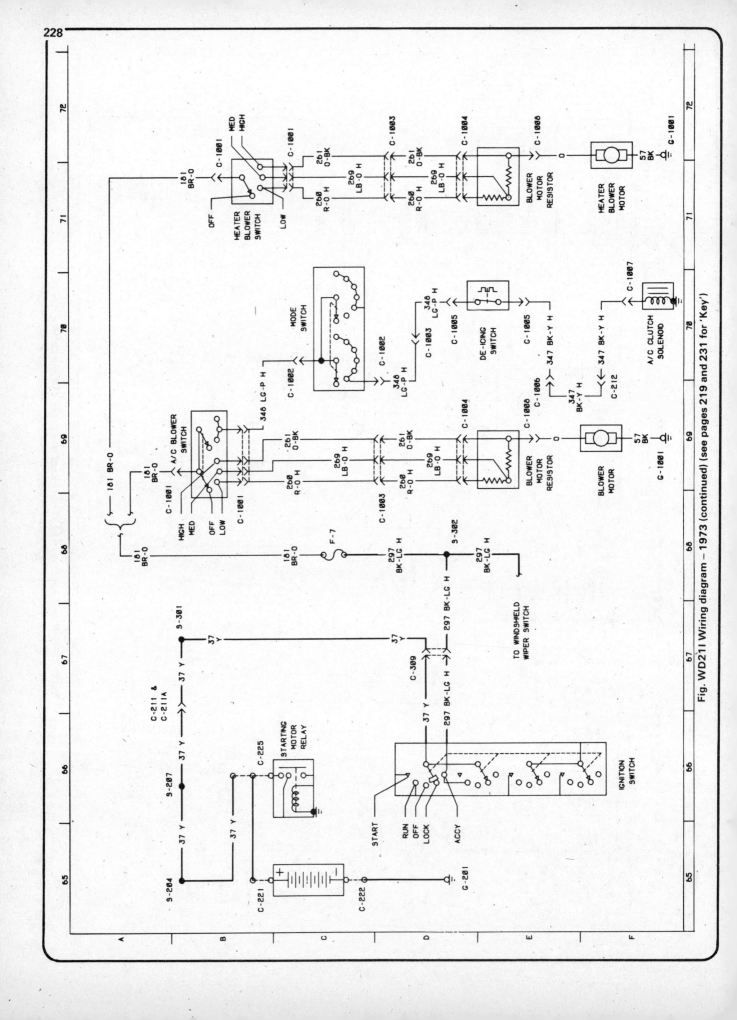

Fig. WD211 Wiring diagram – 1973 (continued) (see pages 219 and 231 for 'Key')

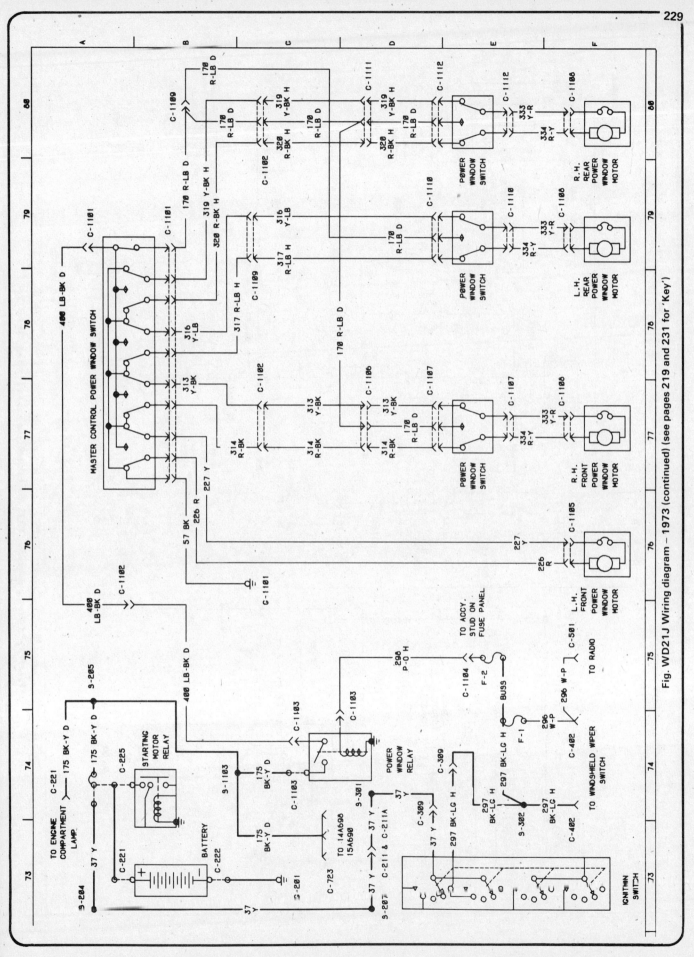

Fig. WD21J Wiring diagram – 1973 (continued) (see pages 219 and 231 for 'Key')

10

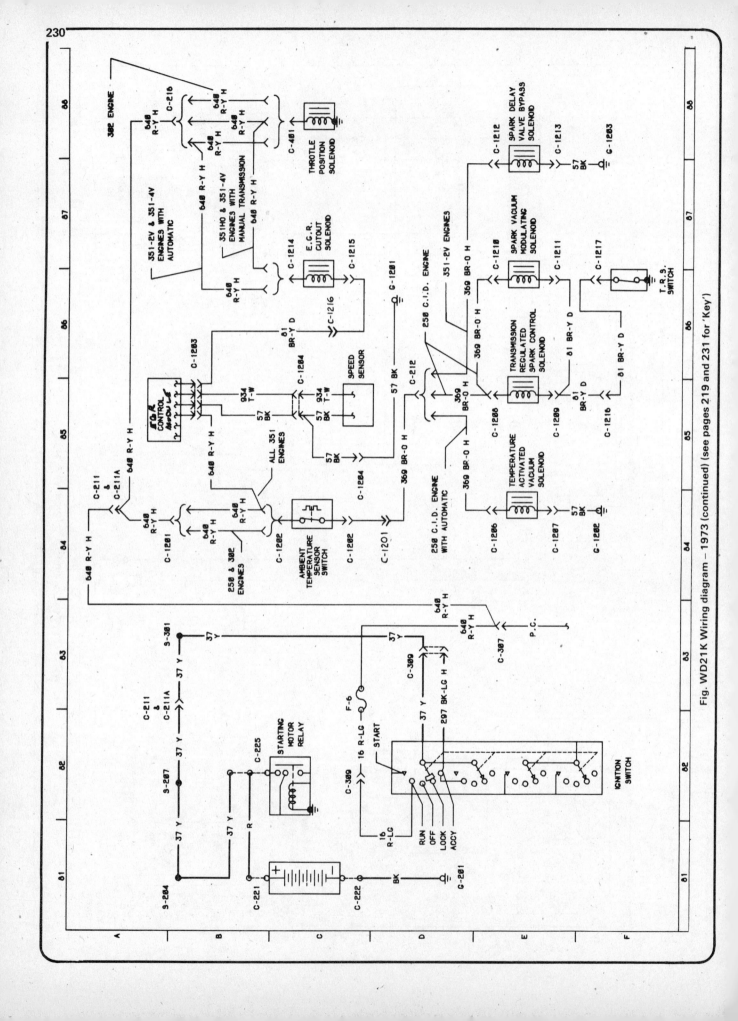

Fig. WD21K Wiring diagram — 1973 (continued) (see pages 219 and 231 for 'Key')

Wiring color key
Primary colors

Black	BK
Brown	BR
Tan	T
Red	R
Pink	PK
Orange	O
Yellow	Y
Dark green	DG
Light green	LG
Dark blue	DB
Light blue	LB
Purple	P
Gray	GY
White	W
Hash	(H)
Dot	(D)

Stripe is understood
and has no color key

Heavy solid line represents battery feed ───────────

Heavy dashed line represents accessory feed – – – – – – – – – –

Chapter 11 Suspension and steering

Contents

Specifications

Front suspension

Type .... Independent, coil springs, upper and lower arms, and double-acting shock absorbers. Stabilizer bar.

Balljoints – radial play:
  Lower balljoint .... Renew if visibly loose
  Upper balljoint .... 0.250 in (6.35 mm) maximum

Rear suspension

Type .... Semi-elliptic leaf springs with double-acting shock absorbers

Steering (manual and power-assisted steering gear)

Type	Worm and recirculating ball			
Model	SMB-D	SMB-K	SMA-R	SMA-T
Gear ratio	19.9 : 1	16 : 1	22 : 1	24 : 1
Turns lock-to-lock	$4\frac{5}{8}$	$3\frac{3}{4}$	$5\frac{3}{4}$	$6\frac{1}{2}$
Lubricant	ESW-MIC87-A	ESW-MIC87-A	ESW-MIC87-A	ESW-MIC87-A
Capacity lb (g)	0.55 ± 0.05 lb (249 ± 22g)	0.55 ± 0.05 lb (249 ± 22g)	0.87 ± 0.07 lb (349 ± 31g)	0.87 ± 0.07 lb (349 ± 31g)
Worm bearing preload	4 to 5 lbf in (4.6 to 5.75 kgf cm)	4 to 5 lbf in (4.6 to 5.75 kgf cm)	4 to 5 lbf in (4.6 to 5.75 kgf cm)	4 to 5 lbf in (4.6 to 5.75 kgf cm)
Total center meshload	9 to 10 lbf in (10.3 to 11.5 kgf cm)	9 to 10 lbf in (10.3 to 11.5 kgf cm)	9 to 10 lbf in (10.3 to 11.5 kgf cm)	9 to 10 lbf in (10.3 to 11.5 kgf cm)
Adjustments	Adjusting screw to bottom of sector shaft T-slot clearance 0 to 0.002 in (0 to 0.050 mm)			

Power steering pump

Make	Ford-Thompson
Type	Belt-driven slipper type
Rotor shaft endplay	0.003 to 0.017 in (0.076 to 0.431 mm)
Max. torque allowed to rotate rotor shaft	15 lbf in (17.25 kgf cm)
Worm bearing preload	9 lbf in (10.3 kgf cm) max
Worm-to-piston preload	0.5 to 4.5 lbf in (0.57 to 5.17 kgf cm)

Integral power steering gears

Make	Saginaw
Type	Recirculation ball torsion bar
Ratio:	
Variable	16 : 1 center to 13 : 1 at lock
Constant	17.5 : 1
Fluid capacity (including reservoir)	1.6 pt (0.75 litre) approx.
Fluid specification	D2AZ-19582-A
Total meshload over worm bearing preload	4 to 8 lbf in (4.6 to 9.2 kgf cm)
Total meshload over mechanical center	18 lbf in (20.7 kgf cm) max.

Steering wheel turning effort	lb	kg
Manual steering	37	16.7 approx.
Power steering	6.5	2.9

Front wheel alignment

	Min	Max	Optimum
Caster – 1965	$-\frac{1}{4}°$	$+\frac{3}{4}°$	$+\frac{1}{4}°$
1966	$-1°$	$+1°$	$0°$
1967	$-\frac{1}{4}°$	$+\frac{3}{4}°$	$\frac{1}{4}°$
1968	$-\frac{3}{4}°$	$+1\frac{1}{4}°$	$+\frac{1}{4}°$
1970-71	$-1°$	$+1°$	$0°$
1972-73	$-2°$	$+2°$	$0°$
Camber – 1965	$0°$	$+1°$	$+\frac{1}{2}°$
1966	$-\frac{1}{4}°$	$+1\frac{1}{4}°$	$+\frac{1}{2}°$
1967	$+\frac{1}{2}°$	$+1\frac{1}{2}°$	$+1°$
1968	$+\frac{1}{4}°$	$+1\frac{3}{4}°$	$+1°$
1969	$+\frac{1}{4}°$	$+1\frac{3}{4}°$	$+\frac{3}{4}°$
1970-71	$0°$	$+1\frac{1}{2}°$	$+1°$
1972-73	$-\frac{1}{2}°$	$+1\frac{1}{2}°$	$+\frac{1}{2}°$

Toe-in – 1965	0.25 to 0.312 in (6.3 to 7.9 mm)
1966	0.125 to 0.375 in (3.1 to 9.5 mm)
1967 and 1969	0.125 to 0.250 in (3.1 to 6.3 mm)
1968	0.187 to 0.312 in (4.7 to 7.9 mm)
1970-71	0.062 to 0.312 in (1.5 to 7.9 mm)
1972-73	0.062 to 0.375 in (1.5 to 9.5 mm)

Torque wrench settings

	lbf ft	kgf m
Front suspension		
Shock absorber upper attachment	10 to 15	1.3 to 2.0
Shock absorber upper bracket-to-body	20 to 30	2.7 to 4.1
Upper arm inner shaft-to-body	75 to 100	10.3 to 13.8
Balljoint-to-spindle	60 to 90	8.2 to 12.4
Strut-to-lower arm	70 to 105	9.6 to 14.4
Lower arm-to-underbody	75 to 100	10.3 to 13.8
Stabilizer bracket-to-underbody	17 to 30	2.3 to 4.1
Strut-to-underbody	60 to 80	8.2 to 11.0
Stabilizer bar-to-lower arm	5 to 12	0.69 to 1.65
Rear suspension		
Spring shackle bars-to-body and spring	22 to 29	3.0 to 4.0
Shock absorber-to-upper mounting bracket	45 to 65	6.2 to 8.9
Shock absorber-to-spring clip plate	15 to 25	2.0 to 3.4
Spring-to-axle U-bolt nut	35 to 50	4.8 to 6.9
Spring-to-front hanger bolt	80 to 110	11.0 to 15.1
Spring-to-front hanger nut	70 to 95	9.6 to 13.1
Steering		
Sector shaft cover bolts	15 to 22	2.0 to 3.0
Adjusting screw locknut	32 to 40	4.4 to 5.5
Ball guide clamp screw	18 to 42	20.7 to 48.3
Preload adjuster locknut	45 to 60	6.2 to 8.2
Filler Plug	3 to 9	0.4 to 1.2
Power steering pump		
Pump-to-front bracket	30 to 45	4.1 to 6.2
Pump pivot	25 to 40	3.4 to 5.5
Pump-to-rear bracket nut	20 to 30	2.7 to 4.1

11

	lbf ft	kgf m
Reservoir-to-housing nut	43 to 47	5.9 to 6.4

Integral power steering gear

	lbf ft	kgf m
Sector shaft cover bolts	30 to 35	4.1 to 4.8
Mesh load adjusting screw locknut	30 to 35	4.1 to 4.8
Ball return guide clamp screw	3 to 6	0.4 to 0.8
Preload adjusting locknut	50 to 110	6.9 to 15.1
Piston end cap	50 to 100	6.9 to 13.8
Pressure and return hoses-to-gear	25 to 34	3.4 to 4.6

Steering linkage

	lbf ft	kgf m
Power cylinder-to-bracket (power assisted steering)	18 to 24	2.4 to 3.3
Connecting rod end-to-spindle	30 to 40	4.1 to 5.5
Idler arm bracket-to-frame	28 to 35	3.8 to 4.8
Pitman arm-to-control valve (power steering)	35 to 47	4.8 to 6.4
Idler arm-to-Pitman arm-to-idler arm rod	60 to 80	8.2 to 11.0
Connecting rod adjusting sleeve clamp	10 to 14	1.3 to 1.9
Pitman arm-to-steering arm-to-idler arm rod	35 to 47	4.8 to 6.4

Steering column

	lbf ft	kgf m
Flex coupling-to-steering gear	24 to 37	3.3 to 5.1
Flex coupling-to-steering shaft flange	10 to 18	1.3 to 2.4
Steering wheel attaching nut	30 to 40	4.1 to 5.5

---

1   General description

Front suspension

1   The front wheels rotate on spindles which are mounted to the upper and lower suspension arms through balljoints. The upper arms pivot on bushing and shaft assemblies which are bolted to the frame. The lower arms pivot on bolts in the crossmember. The coil springs and shock absorbers are located between the upper arms and the top of the spring housings on the body. Struts are installed to prevent fore-and-aft movement of the suspension arms.

Rear suspension

2   The semi-elliptic leaf springs are suspended from the underbody side rail by hanger and shackle assemblies at the front and rear. The axle housing is mounted on the center of the springs and secured by U-bolts. The integral mounting stud at the upper end of each shock absorber is attached to the crossmember by a mounting plate. The lower end is attached to a stud which is integral with a bracket welded to the axle housing.

Steering

3   The manual steering is of the worm and recirculating ball type. The sector shaft is straddle-mounted with a bushing located in the cover

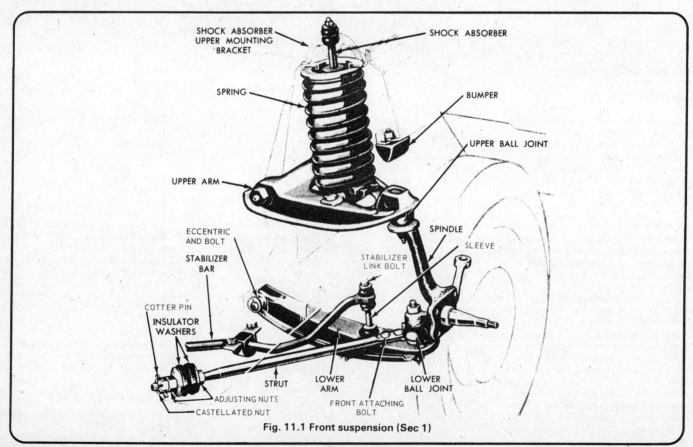

Fig. 11.1 Front suspension (Sec 1)

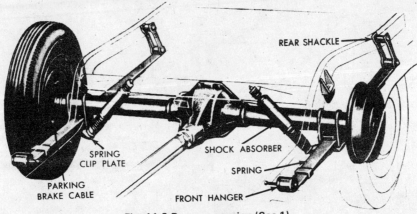

Fig. 11.2 Rear suspension (Sec 1)

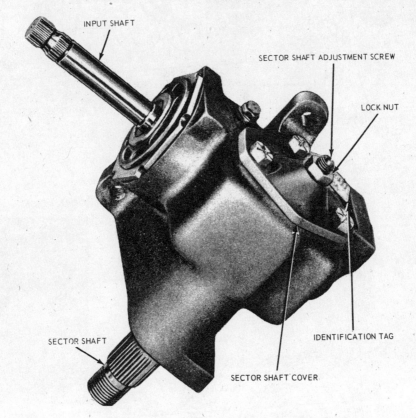

Fig. 11.3 Steering gear – manual and non-integral power steering (Sec 1)

above the gear and a roller bearing in the housing below the gear. The worm bearing preload is controlled by the large adjusting nut which is threaded into the housing, and the sector shaft mesh is controlled by an adjusting screw located in the housing cover. The steering linkage consists of a Pitman arm, steering arm-to-idler arm rod, idler arm and connecting rods.

4   Two types of power steering are available as an option. On models to 1970 a non-integral power steering system is used. It is a hydraulically controlled linkage type which includes an integral pump and fluid reservoir, a control valve, a power cylinder and fluid lines. The pump is belt-driven from the engine crank-shaft.

5   On 1971/73 models a Saginaw integral power steering gear is used. It operates by displacing fluid to provide pressure assistance only when turning. As the gear assembly is always full of fluid, all internal components of the gear are immersed in fluid making periodic lubrication unnecessary. The fluid also acts as a cushion to absorb road shocks that may be transmitted to the driver. All fluid passages are internal except the pressure and return hoses between the gear and the pump (Fig. 11.4).

6   The steering column is of the collapsible type. It will collapse by approximately six inches upon a hard impact. Once the steering column has been collapsed, a complete new steering column must be installed, together with new brackets, which also shear away during impact.

2 Front hub and bearing (drum brakes) – removal and installation

1   Apply the parking brake, chock the rear wheels, jack-up the front of the car and support it on jack stands. Remove the roadwheel.
2   Carefully pry off the grease cap. Remove the cotter pin, nut lock, adjusting nut and washer (photos).
3   Remove the outer bearing cone and roller assembly, then pull the hub assembly off the wheel spindle.
4   Remove and discard the grease retainer. Remove the inner bearing cone and roller assembly from the hub.
5   Clean the outer and inner bearing cups in the hub with solvent and

11

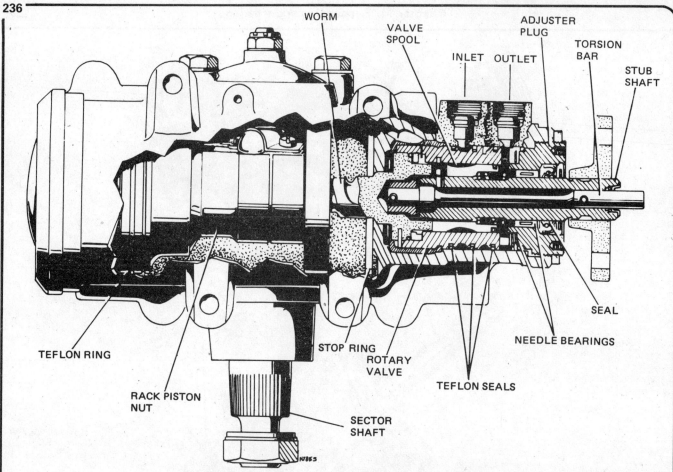

WORM
VALVE SPOOL
ADJUSTER PLUG
INLET OUTLET
TORSION BAR
STUB SHAFT
TEFLON RING
RACK PISTON NUT
STOP RING
ROTARY VALVE
SECTOR SHAFT
SEAL
NEEDLE BEARINGS
TEFLON SEALS

Fig. 11.4 Cutaway view of integral power steering gear (Sec 1)

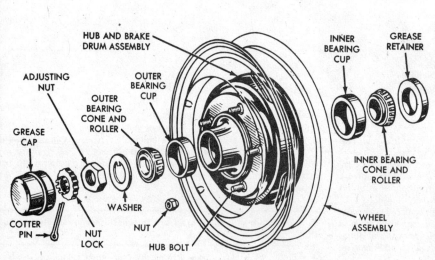

HUB AND BRAKE DRUM ASSEMBLY
INNER BEARING CUP
GREASE RETAINER
ADJUSTING NUT
OUTER BEARING CUP
OUTER BEARING CONE AND ROLLER
GREASE CAP
COTTER PIN
NUT LOCK
WASHER
NUT
HUB BOLT
INNER BEARING CONE AND ROLLER
WHEEL ASSEMBLY

Fig. 11.5 Exploded view of front wheel and bearings – drum brakes (Sec 2)

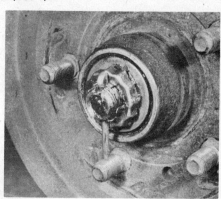

2.2A Remove the cotter pin, nut lock, adjusting nut ...

2.2B ... and washer

inspect for scoring, pitting and excessive wear. If the cups are worn or damaged, remove them from the hub with a suitable drift.

6   Clean the cone and roller assemblies, and examine them for wear and damage. If any part of the bearing assembly is defective the bearing must be renewed as a complete unit. Clean the hub and spindle to remove all old grease.

7   Install the outer and inner bearing cups in the hub, using a suitable diameter tubular drift to drive them fully home.

8   Pack the inside of the hub with the specified wheel bearing grease until the grease is flush with the inside diameter of both bearing cups. Lubricate the bearing cone and roller assemblies by working as much grease as possible between the rollers and cages (photo).

9   Insert the inner bearing cone and roller assembly in the hub then install a new grease retainer using a tubular drift. Take care not to distort the retainer, and ensure that it is properly seated.

10   Adjust the brake shoes, as described in Chapter 9, then install the hub and drum assembly on the wheel spindle. Keep the hub centered on the spindle to avoid damaging the grease retainer.

11   Install the outer bearing cone and roller assembly, the flat washer and adjusting nut.

12   Install the roadwheel.

13   While rotating the hub, torque tighten the adjusting nut to 17 to 25 lbf ft (2.4 to 3.4 kgf m) to seat the bearings. Back-off the adjusting nut one half turn, then retighten it to 10 to 15 lbf ft (1.4 to 2.0 kgf m).

14   Install the nut lock so that the castellations are aligned with the cotter pin hole on the spindle. Install a new cotter pin and bend the ends round the castellated flange of the nut lock. Install the grease cap.

15   Adjust the brakes as described in Chapter 9. Install the hub cap or wheel cover, and lower the front of the car.

3   Front hub and bearing (disc brakes) – removal and installation

1   Carry out the operations in Section 2, paragraph 1.

2   Remove the brake caliper from the rotor, as described in Chapter 9, and tie it up to prevent damage to the brake hose.

3   Carry out the operations in Section 2, paragraph 2 through 9.

4   Install the hub and rotor assembly on the spindle, taking care not to damage the grease retainer.

5   Install the outer bearing cone and roller assembly, the flat washer and adjusting nut.

6   Adjust the wheel bearings as described in Section 2, paragraphs 13 and 14.

7   Install the brake caliper (see Chapter 9)

8   Install the roadwheel and hub cap, or wheel cover, and lower the front of the car.

9   Before driving the car, pump the brake pedal several times to obtain normal pad lining-to-rotor clearance.

2.8 Hub packed with grease

4   Stabilizer bar – removal and installation

1   Raise the front of the car and support it on jack stands.

2   Remove the link bolts and insulators attaching the stabilizer bar to the lower suspension arms.

3   Disconnect both attaching brackets and remove the stabilizer bar.

4   Installation is the reverse of the removal procedure. Always use new insulators. When installing the link bolts make sure that the bolt head is at the top to prevent it fouling the brake hose.

5   Lower suspension arm strut – removal and installation

1   Position a support between the upper arm and frame side rail, as shown in Fig. 11.7, then raise the front of the car and support it on jack stands. Remove the roadwheel.

2   Remove the cotter pin, castellated nut and adjusting nut from the front of the strut.

3   Using two pry bars, one at each side and at the rear of the front washer, separate the inner sleeve from the outer sleeve and remove the front insulator.

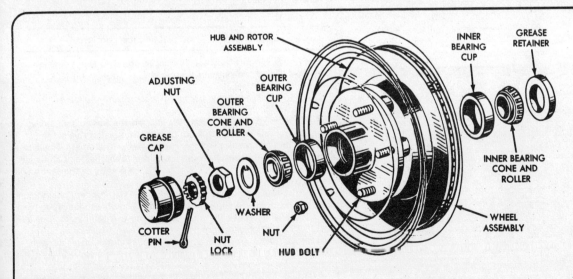

Fig. 11.6 Exploded view of front hub and bearings – disc brakes (Sec 3)

11

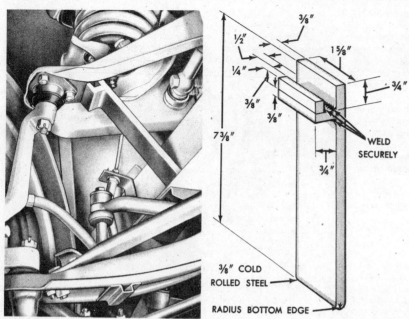

Fig. 11.7 Upper arm support in position (Secs 5 and 7)

4   Remove the strut-to-lower arm attaching bolts and lift out the strut.
5   Install a new rear washer, outer sleeve and insulator bushing on the front end of the strut.
6   Locate the strut in the crossmember and install the strut-to-arm attaching bolts. Install a new front insulator, washer, inner sleeve and adjustment nut.
7   Install the roadwheel and lower the car. Remove the upper arm support.
8   Adjust the camber and caster (see Section 42) then install the castellated nut and cotter pin.

6   Coil spring – removal and installation

1   Raise the hood. Undo the attaching nuts and remove the shock absorber and upper mounting bracket as an assembly.

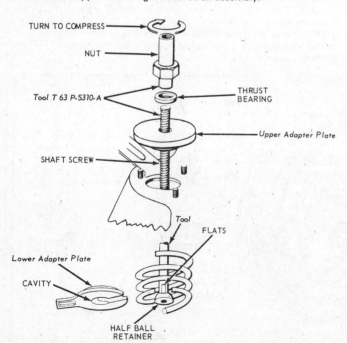

Fig. 11.8 Installing the spring compressor tool (Sec 6)

2   Raise the front of the car and support it on jack stands.
3   Remove the hub assembly as described in Section 2 or 3.
4   Install a spring compressor tool (see Fig. 11.8) and compress the spring to remove all tension from the control arms.
5   Remove the two upper arm-to-spring tower attaching nuts and swing the upper arm outward from the spring tower.
6   Release the spring compressor and remove it, then lift out the spring.
7   Position the spring upper insulator on the spring and secure it in place with tape.
8   Position the spring in the spring tower and compress the spring with the spring compressor.
9   Swing the upper arm inward and insert the bolts through the holes in the side of the spring tower. Install the nuts and tighten them to a torque of 75 to 100 lbf ft (10.4 to 13.8 kgf m).
10   Release the spring pressure and guide the spring into the upper arm spring seat. The end of the spring must not be more than 0.5 in (12.7 mm) from the tab on the spring seat. Remove the spring compressor.
11   Install the hub assembly as described in Section 2 or 3.
12   Lower the front of the car and install the shock absorber and upper bracket assembly, making sure the shock absorber lower studs are in the pivot plate holes.

7   Lower suspension arm – removal and installation

1   Position a support between the upper arm and side rail as shown in Fig.11.7. Raise the front of the car and support it on jack stands. Remove the roadwheel.
2   Disconnect the stabilizer bar and the strut from the lower arm (see Sections 4 and 5).
3   Remove the cotter pin from the nut on the lower balljoint stud, loosen the nut one or two turns but do not remove it at this stage.
4   Straighten the cotter pin on the upper balljoint stud nut. Position a balljoint remover tool between the upper and lower balljoint studs (see Fig. 11.9). Make sure the tool is seated on the ends of the studs and not on the nuts.
5   Turn the tool with a wrench until the studs are under considerable pressure, and then strike the spindle, near the lower stud, a sharp blow with a hammer to break the stud loose from the spindle. Do not free the stud with tool pressure only.
6   Remove the nut from the lower balljoint stud and lower the arm.
7   Remove the lower arm-to-underbody pivot bolt and lift out the lower arm.
8   Examine the arm for damage and the balljoint for wear. Renew the arm, if necessary, as a complete unit. Do not install new balljoints on a used suspension arm.
9   Installation is the reverse of the removal procedure. Tighten the

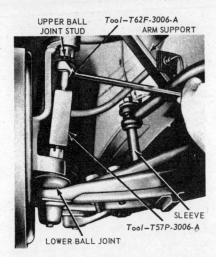

Fig. 11.9 Loosening the balljoint studs (Sec 7)

lower balljoint stud nut and the lower arm-to-underbody pivot bolt nut to the specified torque. Check caster, camber and toe-in (see Section 42).

8 Upper suspension arm – removal and installation

1 Raise the front of the car and support it on jack stands positioned under the frame. Remove the roadwheel.
2 Remove the shock absorber lower attaching nuts.
3 Undo the attaching nuts and remove the shock absorber and upper mounting bracket as an assembly.
4 Install a spring compressor tool and compress the spring, (see Section 6).
5 Position a jack stand or other suitable support under the lower arm.
6 Loosen the upper balljoint stud in the spindle, (see Section 7,

paragraph 3 through 5) then remove the nut from the upper balljoint stud and lift the stud out of the spindle.
7 Remove the upper arm inner shaft attaching nuts, from inside the engine compartment, and lift out the upper arm.
8 Examine the arm for damage and the balljoint for wear. Do not wash the balljoint in grease solvent. Renew the arm, if necessary, as a complete unit. Do not install new balljoints on a used arm.
9 Installation is the reverse of the removal procedure. Tighten the upper balljoint stud nut and the upper arm inner shaft nuts to the specified torque. If the upper arm is being renewed as a result of accident damage, check the caster, camber and toe-in (see Section 42).

9 Upper suspension arm shaft and/or bushing – renewal

1 Remove the upper arm as described in Section 8.
2 Unscrew the bushings from the shaft and arm, then remove the shaft from the arm.
3 Position the shaft in the arm, grease the new bushings and O-rings, then install the bushings loose on the shaft.
4 Center the shaft in the suspension arm. Refer to Fig. 11.11 and screw in the bushings until the dimensions A and B are equal.
5 Make a spacer from a piece of 0.75 in (19 mm) diameter steel tube. The spacer should be $6\frac{15}{16}$ in (176 mm) long for pre 1971 models, and $8\frac{1}{8}$ in (206 mm) long for models from 1971 on.
6 Force the spacer between the flanges of the upper arm, as shown in Fig. 11.12, then torque-tighten the bushings to 25 to 35 lbf ft (3.5 to 4.8 kgf m).
7 Remove the spacer and check that the shaft is free to turn without binding.
8 Install the upper arm (see Section 8).

10 Front wheel spindle – removal and installation

1 Remove the hub assembly as described in Section 2 or 3.
2 On models with drum brakes remove the brake backing plate (see Chapter 9), and support it to avoid damage to the brake hose. On

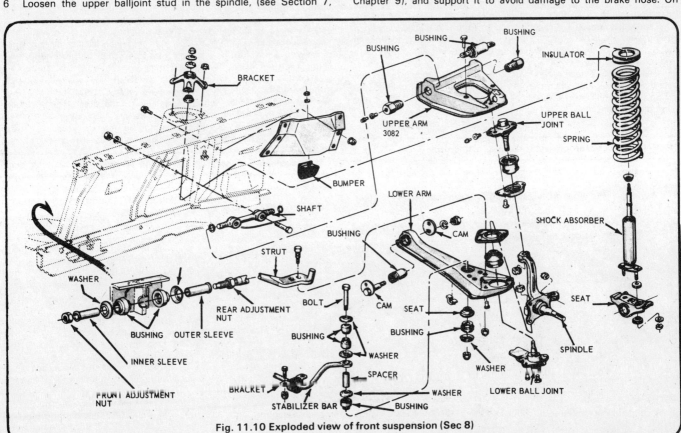

Fig. 11.10 Exploded view of front suspension (Sec 8)

11

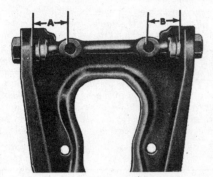

Fig. 11.11 Centering the upper arm shaft (Sec 9)

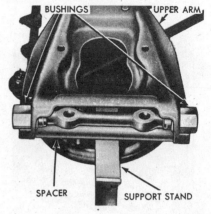

Fig. 11.12 Torque-tighten the upper arm bushings (Sec 9)

models with disc brakes remove the three caliper shield attaching bolts and lift off the shield.

3   Using a balljoint separator, disconnect the connecting rod end from the spindle arm.

4   Loosen the upper and lower suspension arm balljoints in the spindle as described in Section 7.

5   Position a jack or similar support under the lower suspension arm. Remove the upper and lower balljoint stud nuts, then lower the jack and remove the spindle.

6   Installation is the reverse of the removal procedure.

11 Front shock absorber – removal and installation

1   Raise the hood and remove the shock absorber upper mounting bracket attaching nuts (photo).

2   Raise the front of the vehicle and position jack stands under the lower arms.

3   Remove the two shock absorber lower attaching nuts and the insulators (photo).

4   Lift the shock absorber and upper bracket from the spring tower, and remove the bracket from the shock absorber.

5   Clean the exterior and inspect the shaft for signs of corrosion or distortion, and the body for damage or for signs of hydraulic fluid leaks.

6   Check the action by expanding and contracting to ascertain if equal resistance is felt on both strokes. If the resistance is very uneven the unit must be renewed. Always renew them in pairs, either both front ones or both rear ones.

7   Installation is the reverse of the removal procedure. When positioning the shock absorber and upper mounting bracket in the spring tower ensure that the shock absorber lower studs are in the pivot plate holes.

12 Rear shock absorber – removal and installation

1   Disconnect the shock absorber from the spring clip plate (see Fig. 11.15 and photo).

2   Working in the luggage compartment, remove the shock absorber

access cover, Fig. 11.13. On convertible models the rear seat and seat back must be removed.

3   Remove the shock absorber upper attaching nut.

4   The shock absorber can now be compressed and removed from the car. Remove the bushings from the studs.

5   Inspect and check the shock absorber as described in Section 11.

6   Installation is the reverse of the removal procedure.

13 Rear spring – removal and installation

1   Raise the rear of the car and support it with jack stands under the body and under the rear axle.

2   Disconnect the lower end of the shock absorber from the spring clip plate and push the shock absorber out of the way. Remove the supports from under the axle.

3   Remove the spring clip plate retaining nuts from the U-bolts and remove the plate. Jack-up the rear axle just enough to take the weight off the spring.

4   Remove the two attaching nuts, the rear shackle bar and the two shackle inner bushings. Remove the rear shackle assembly and the two outer bushings.

5   Remove the front hanger bolt from the eye at the front end of the spring and then lift out the spring.

6   If any of the shackles or bushings are worn they must be renewed. If the front eye bushing is being renewed, it can be removed and a new one installed by using a long threaded bolt, a distance piece of similar diameter as the bushing and large flat washers. Tightening the nut will draw the old bushing out of the spring eye or draw a new one into position. Fig. 11.14 shows the Ford tool being used to install a new bushing.

7   If a spring leaf is broken or the spring has weakened, then it should be renewed: in this event the other rear spring should be renewed at the same time.

8   Installation is the reverse of the removal procedure. Tighten the

11.1 Front shock absorber upper mounting

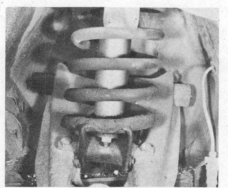

11.3 Front shock absorber lower mounting

12.1 Rear shock absorber lower mounting

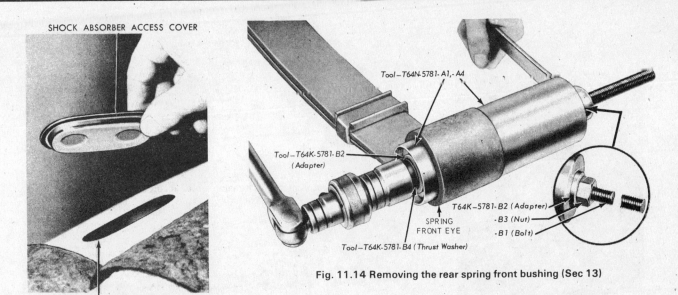

SHOCK ABSORBER ACCESS COVER

LUGGAGE COMPARTMENT
FLOOR PANEL

Fig. 11.13 Removing the rear shock absorber
access cover (Sec 12)

Tool—T64N-5781-A1,-A4
Tool—T64K-5781-B2 (Adapter)
T64K-5781-B2 (Adapter)
-B3 (Nut)
-B1 (Bolt)
SPRING FRONT EYE
Tool—T64K-5781-B4 (Thrust Washer)

Fig. 11.14 Removing the rear spring front bushing (Sec 13)

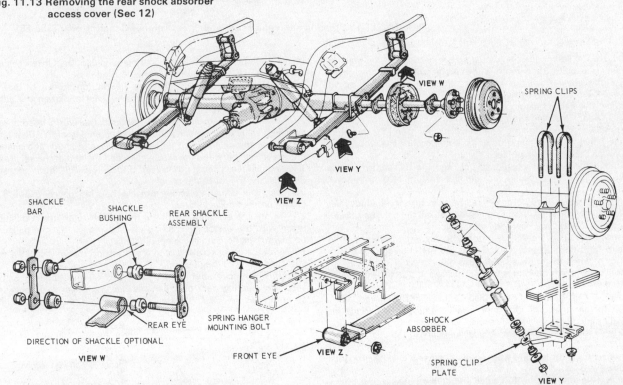

VIEW W
VIEW Y
VIEW Z
SPRING CLIPS

SHACKLE BAR
SHACKLE BUSHING
REAR SHACKLE ASSEMBLY
REAR EYE
DIRECTION OF SHACKLE OPTIONAL
VIEW W

SPRING HANGER MOUNTING BOLT
FRONT EYE
VIEW Z

SHOCK ABSORBER
SPRING CLIP PLATE
VIEW Y

Fig. 11.15 Exploded view of rear suspension (Secs 12 and 13)

front hanger bolt and the shackle locknuts to the specified torque after the car has been lowered to the ground.

14 Steering gear (manual) – removal and installation

1 Raise the front of the car and support it on jack stands.
2 Remove the bolts connecting the flexible coupling to the steering shaft.
3 Remove the nut that secures the Pitman arm to the sector shaft and, using a puller, remove the arm from the sector shaft. Do not hammer on the end of the puller as this can damage the steering gear.
4 On some models with manual transmission it may be necessary to

disconnect the clutch linkage, and on some models the exhaust system must be lowered, to provide enough clearance for removal of the arm.
5 Remove the three bolts securing the steering gear to the side rail and lift out the steering gear.
6 Installation is the reverse of the removal procedure.

15 Steering gear (manual) – dismantling, overhaul and reassembly

1 Clean the exterior of the steering gear, remove the filler plug and drain the oil.
2 Rotate the steering shaft to the center position.

11

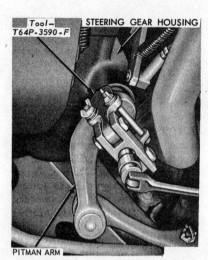

Fig. 11.16 Removing the pitman arm (Sec 14)

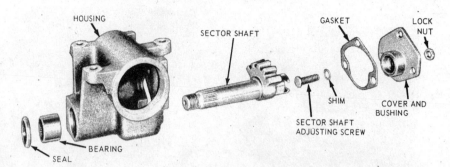

Fig. 11.17 Sector shaft and housing – manual steering gear (Sec 15)

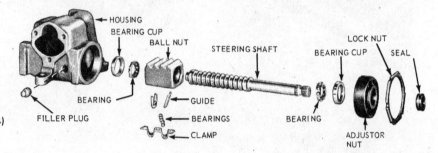

Fig. 11.18 Steering shaft and associated parts - manual steering gear (Sec 15)

3   Remove the sector shaft adjusting screw locknut and the housing cover securing bolts, then remove the sector shaft with the cover. Separate the cover from the shaft by turning the adjusting screw clockwise. Keep the shim with the screw.

4   Loosen the worm bearing adjuster nut, then remove the adjuster assembly and the steering shaft upper bearing.

5   Carefully pull the steering shaft and ballnut from the housing. Keep the ballnut from running down to either end of the worm as it may damage the ball return guides.

6   Remove the ball return guide clamp and the ball return guides from the ballnut. Keep the ballnut 'clamp side up' until ready to remove the balls.

7   Have a suitable clean container ready, then turn the ballnut over and rotate the worm shaft from side to side until all the balls have been collected. The ballnut will now slide off the worm.

8   Remove the upper bearing cup from the bearing adjuster and the lower cup from the housing. If necessary, tap the housing or adjuster on a block of wood to get the bearing cups out.

9   If the sector shaft bearing is worn or damaged press it and the oil seal out of the housing.

10 Clean all the dismantled parts. Inspect the sector shaft and steering shaft for pitting, burrs, cracks or wear. Examine the bearings for wear or damage. Renew all the oil seals.

11 During assembly apply steering gear lubricant to the bearings and seals.

12 If the sector shaft bearing was removed, press a new bearing into the housing and install a new oil seal.

13 Install a bearing cup in the lower end of the housing and in the adjuster. Install a new seal in the bearing adjuster.

14 Insert the ball guides into the holes in the ballnut, tap them lightly, if necessary, to seat them. Use the wooden handle of a screwdriver or similar.

15 Insert half of the balls into the hole in the top of each ball guide. It may be necessary to rotate the shaft slightly one way, then the other to distribute the balls.

16 Install the ball guide clamp and tighten the securing screws to the specified torque. Check that the worm shaft rotates freely.

17 Coat the threads of the steering shaft bearing adjuster, the housing cover bolts and the sector adjusting screw with an oil-resistant sealing compound. Take care not to get any sealer on the steering shaft bearings.

18 Lubricate the worm bearings, sector shaft bearings and gear teeth with steering gear oil.

19 Clamp the housing in a vise with the sector shaft horizontal and

install the steering shaft lower bearing in its cup, then insert the steering shaft and ballnut assembly in the housing.

20 Position the steering shaft upper bearing on the top of the worm and install the steering shaft bearing adjuster and then the adjuster nut. Leave the nut loose.

21 Using a lbf in torque wrench, preload the worm bearing to the specified value (see Specifications at the beginning of this Chapter).

22 Install the sector shaft adjusting screw and shim, and check the end clearance between the screw head and the end of the sector shaft. The end clearance must not exceed 0·002 in (0·050 mm); add shims, if necessary, to reduce the endplay.

23 Start the adjusting screw into the housing cover. Install a new gasket on the housing cover.

24 Rotate the steering shaft until the ballnut teeth are in position to mesh with the sector gear, tilting the housing so that the ballnut will tip toward the housing cover opening.

25 With the cover screwed onto the adjusting screw, install the sector shaft and cover to the housing.

26 Turn the cover out of the way and fill the housing with the specified steering gear oil. Push the housing cover and sector shaft assembly into place and install the two cover securing bolts. While

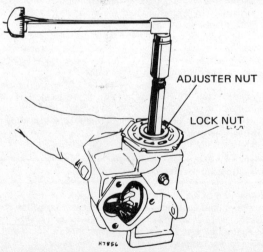

Fig. 11.19 Checking the shaft bearing preload (Sec 15)

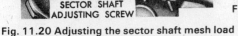

Fig. 11.20 Adjusting the sector shaft mesh load
(Sec 17)

Fig. 11.21 Checking steering gear preload
(Sec 17)

Fig. 11.22 Power steering pump
dipstick (Sec 18)

tightening the cover bolts make sure there is clearance between the ballnut and sector gear teeth.
27 Install the sector shaft adjusting screw locknut loosely on the adjusting screw, adjust the sector shaft mesh load to the specified value (see Specifications at the beginning of this Chapter) then tighten the locknut.

16 Manual steering gear – oil level check

1 Remove the filler plug and upper cover bolt.
2 Slowly turn the steering wheel to the right to the end of its travel and check that the oil rises to the cover bolt hole, then slowly turn the steering wheel to the left to the end of its travel and check that the oil rises to the filler plug hole.
3 If the oil does not rise in both the cover bolt hole and the filler plug hole, top-up with the specified steering gear oil.
4 Install the cover bolt and filler plug.

17 Manual steering gear – adjustment (in-situ)

1 Disconnect the Pitman arm from the steering Pitman arm-to-idler arm rod (see Section 14).
2 Loosen the sector shaft adjusting screw locknut and turn the adjusting screw counterclockwise.
3 Using a torque wrench on the steering wheel nut (see Fig. 11.21) and with the steering wheel off-center, check that the pull required to rotate the input shaft about $1\frac{1}{2}$ turns, either side of center, is within the limits specified (see Specifications at the beginning of this Chapter).
4 Adjustment is by loosening the steering shaft bearing adjuster locknut, and tightening or backing-off the bearing adjuster to obtain the correct preload. Tighten the bearing adjuster locknut and recheck the preload.
5 Turn the steering wheel slowly to either stop, (turn gently against the stops to avoid damaging the ball return guides) then center the ballnut.
6 Turn the sector adjusting screw clockwise until the specified torque required to rotate the worm past its center (high spot) is reached. Hold the sector adjusting screw from turning and tighten the locknut, then recheck the backlash.
7 Connect the Pitman arm to the steering arm-to-idler arm rod.

18 Power steering – checks and adjustments

Fluid level check
1 Run the engine until the fluid is at normal operating temperature, then turn the steering wheel slowly from lock-to-lock several times (do not hold against the stops).
2 Switch off the engine.
3 Check the fluid level in the power steering reservoir. The level must show on the cross-hatching between the bottom of the dipstick

and the Full mark (see Fig. 11.22). If necessary top-up with automatic transmission fluid. Take care not to overfill the reservoir.

Air bleeding
4 If there is air in the system, indicated by bubbles in the fluid, then the system must be bled.
5 Ensure that the reservoir is filled to the correct level and that the fluid is at normal operating temperature (165° to 175°F). Turn the steering wheel from lock-to-lock until the bubbles are removed. Do not hold the wheels against their stops. Recheck the fluid level.

Pump drivebelt
6 If the pump belt is broken, glazed or worn it must be renewed.
7 The pump drivebelt tension cannot be checked accurately using the thumb pressure and belt deflection method. A belt tension gauge must be used. Check and adjust the belt tension as follows:

(a) When installing a new belt the tension should be within 120 to 150 lb (54 to 68 kg) and after it has been run for 15 minutes it should be within 90 to 120 lb (40 to 54 kg)
(b) Adjust the tension by loosening the adjusting and mounting bolts on the front face of the pump cover plate (hub side) (see Fig. 11.23). Place a tension gauge in the drivebelt, insert a pry bar as shown in Fig. 11.24 and adjust the tension. CAUTION: Do not lever against the fluid reservoir as it can easily be damaged. Tighten the adjusting arm bolt first and then the mounting bolts. Recheck the tension.

Power steering hoses
8 Examine the input and output hoses for signs of leakage, cracks or deterioration. Renew defective hoses.

19 Power steering gear (non-integral) – removal, overhaul and installation

Refer to Sections 14 and 15.

20 Power steering pump drivebelt – renewal

1 If equipped with an air conditioner, loosen the idler pulley attaching bolts and remove the compressor drivebelt.
2 Loosen the three bolts and one nut attaching the pump to the pump bracket, and remove the belt.
3 Install the new belt on the pulleys and adjust the tension (see Section 18).
4 Install the compressor drivebelt (if so equipped) and adjust the tension as described in Chapter 2.

21 Power steering pump – removal and installation

1 Disconnect the fluid return hose at the reservoir and drain the fluid into a container.

11

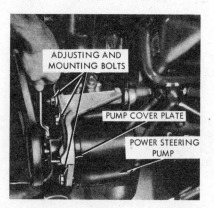
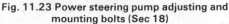

Fig. 11.23 Power steering pump adjusting and mounting bolts (Sec 18)

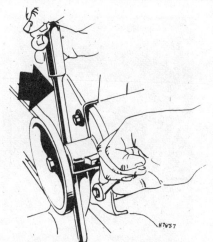

Fig. 11.24 Adjusting power steering pump drive belt tension (Sec 18)

21.3 Removing the power steering pump

2   Disconnect the pressure hose from the pump.
3   Remove the three bolts and one nut attaching the pump to the mounting bracket, and lift out the pump and drivebelt (photo).
4   Installation is the reverse of the removal procedure. Adjust the drivebelt tension (see Section 18). Fill the pump reservoir with power steering fluid and cycle the system to remove air from the system as described in Section 18.

22 Power steering pump – overhaul

1   Overhaul of the unit must be carried out in a clean area as cleanliness is of the utmost importance. Before dismantling the pump, clean the exterior with a solvent and drain as much of the fluid as possible. Wash all the parts (except seals) in a cleaning solvent.
2   It is recommended that the pump is attached to an adaptor plate, for mounting it in a vise, to prevent damage to the unit when it is being dismantled and reassembled. A suitable adaptor can be made from steel plate. The Ford adaptor is shown in the associated illustrations.
3   Remove the outlet fitting nut and the identification tag.

4   Position the pump with the pulley upwards and, using a block of wood and a plastic hammer, remove the pump reservoir and seal by tapping around the flange of the reservoir and on the underside of the filler neck.
5   Invert the pump assembly, undo the pump housing attaching bolts and remove the pump housing.
6   Remove the O-ring seal, the oil screen (if installed) and the pressure springs from the pump housing.
7   Remove and discard the pump cover gasket.
8   Remove the retainer end plate and upper pressure plate (in some pumps, the end plate and upper pressure plate are integral).
9   Remove the loose-fitting dowel pin. Take care not to bend the fixed dowel pin which remains in the housing plate assembly.
10   Remove the rotor assembly taking care to prevent the springs and slippers from falling out and getting lost.
11   Using a suitable puller remove the pump pulley. Install a $\frac{3}{8}$ – 16 in capscrew in the end of the pump shaft to prevent damaging the end of the shaft (see Fig. 11.27). **Note**: *To prevent damage to the internal thrust areas the pulley must be removed without applying in-and-out pressure on the pump shaft.*
12   Clean any rust, dirt and burrs from the end of the rotor shaft and

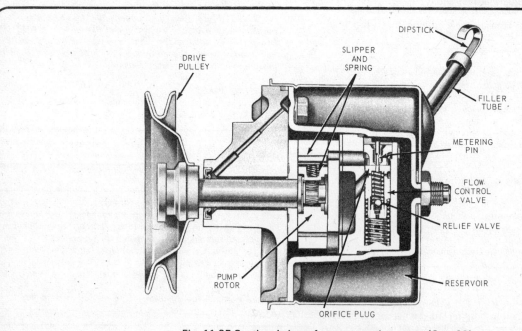

Fig. 11.25 Sectional view of power steering pump (Sec. 22)

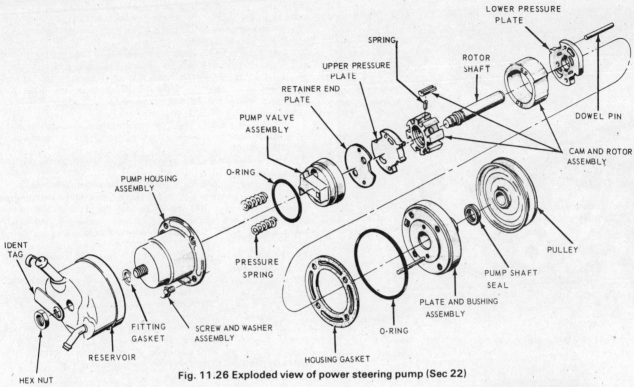

Fig. 11.26 Exploded view of power steering pump (Sec 22)

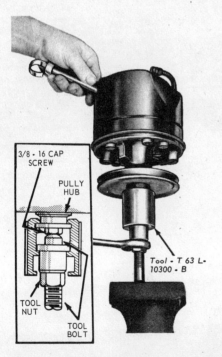

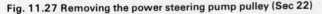

Fig. 11.27 Removing the power steering pump pulley (Sec 22)

remove it from the housing plate.

13 Remove the lower pressure plate.

14 Wash all the parts in a naptha solvent, and dry with compressed air. Clean the relief valve by depressing the tip of the relief valve pin, with a pin punch, several times to remove the oil, then submerge the valve in a container of clean solvent and repeat the procedure. The valve must move freely; if the pin is bent or damaged the valve must be renewed.

15 Renew all gaskets and seals except the rotor shaft seal which does not have to be renewed unless it is defective. Examine all the component parts for wear and damage. Do not dismantle the rotor and

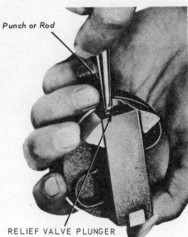

Fig. 11.28 Cleaning the power steering pump relief valve (Sec 22)

cam assembly: if the slippers are worn renew the assembly. Examine the rotor shaft front and rear thrust faces for scoring and wear, and the seal for damage. When removing the rotor shaft seal wrap a piece of 0·005 shim stock round the shaft and push it into the inside diameter of the seal until it is against the bushing, to prevent scoring of the shaft. Use a sharp tool to pierce the metal part of the seal and prise it out, see Fig. 11.29. Install a new seal, using a suitable piece of steel tubing to tap the seal in flush with the end of the seal bore.

16 Mount the pump with the pulley end facing down, and insert the lower pressure plate on the anchor pin with the wide chamfered slots at the center hole facing upward (see Fig. 11.30).

17 Dip the rotor shaft in power steering fluid, then insert the shaft through the lower pressure plate and housing.

18 Install the rotor and cam assembly onto the pump housing plate with the fixed dowel passing through the first hole to the left of the cam notch when the arrow on the cam outside diameter is pointing toward the lower pressure plate (see Fig. 11.31). If the cam and rotor assembly will not seat, turn the rotor shaft slightly until the spline teeth mesh, allowing the cam and rotor to drop down into position.

11

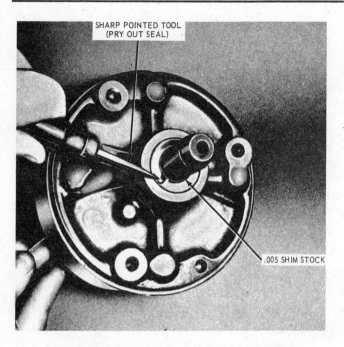

Fig. 11.29 Removing the rotor shaft seal (Sec 22)

19 Insert the loose-fitting dowel through the cam insert and lower plate, into the hole in the housing plate assembly. The height of both dowels should be equal. Lubricate the rotor, springs, slippers and cam insert with power steering fluid.

20 Install the upper pressure plate with the face having the tapered notch down against the cam insert. The fixed dowel should pass through the round dowel hole and the loose dowel through the elongated hole. The slot between the ears on the pressure plate outside diameter should match the notch on the cam insert outside diameter (see Fig. 11.32).

21 Install the retainer end plate so that the slot on the end plate outside diameter matches the notches of the upper pressure plate and cam (Fig. 11.33).

22 Install the pump valve assembly O-ring seal onto the pump valve, taking care not to twist the seal.

23 Place the pump valve assembly on top of the retainer end plate with the large exhaust slot on the pump valve in line with the outside diameter notches of the previously assembled parts. Ensure that the stack of parts are fully seated; if correctly assembled the relief valve stem will be in line with the fluid return hole in the pump housing plate.

24 Smear a little petroleum jelly on the pump housing plate and install the gasket.

25 Insert the pressure plate springs in the pockets in the pump valve assembly. Use a little petroleum jelly to hold them in position.

26 Using a clamp, blank-off the intake hole in the housing, as shown in Fig. 11.35.

27 Lubricate the inside of the housing and the housing cover seal with power steering fluid. Using two studs ($\frac{3}{8}$-16 x 1·55 in) as positioning guides, install one in the housing plate bolt hole closest to the drain hole and the other in the bolt hole diametrically opposite.

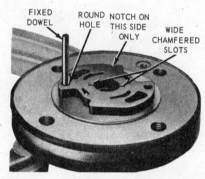

Fig. 11.30 Installing the lower pressure plate (Sec 22)

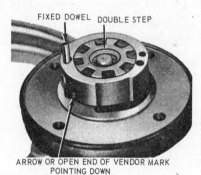

Fig. 11.31 Installing the cam and rotor assembly (Sec 22)

Fig. 11.32 Installing the upper pressure plate (Sec 22)

Fig. 11.33 Align the slot on the endplate with the notches of the upper pressure plate (Sec 22)

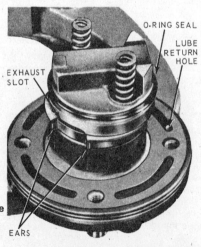

Fig. 11.34 Installing the valve and springs (Sec 22)

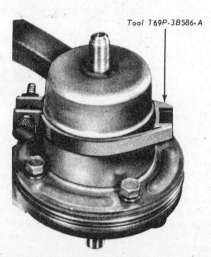

Fig. 11.35 Using a clamp to blank-off the intake hole (Sec 22)

Fig. 11.36 Checking the pump rotating torque
(Sec 22)

Tool - T 65 P - 3A733 - A

Fig. 11.37 Installing the pump pulley (Sec 22)

28 Align the small oil hole in the housing rim with the oil hole in the housing plate.

29 Install the housing, applying an even downward pressure. Take care not to move the pressure plate springs out of position. Remove the guide studs.

30 Install the housing retaining bolts finger-tight and remove the clamp.

31 Tighten the retaining bolts evenly to a torque of 28 to 32 lbf ft (3·8 to 4·4 kgf m). Install a $\frac{3}{8}$ x 16 hex head screw, finger-tight, into the end of the rotor shaft, then using a torque wrench check the input torque of the shaft (see Fig. 11.36). The torque should not exceed 15 lbf in (17·2 kgf cm). If it does, loosen the retaining bolts, rotate the rotor shaft, then re-torque the bolts evenly and again check the shaft torque. (If the input shaft torque still exceeds the limit specified it cannot be used and must be dismantled and re-examined).

32 Install the reservoir O-ring on the housing plate. Apply petroleum jelly to the seal and to the inside diameter of the reservoir flange.

33 Install the reservoir with the notch in the reservoir flange aligned with the notch in the outside diameter of the pump housing plate and bushing assembly. Tap at the rear on the outer corners of the reservoir. Use a plastic hammer to avoid damaging the reservoir. Make sure the reservoir is seated on the housing plate.

34 Install the service tag and the outlet valve fitting, then the outlet valve fitting nut and tighten it to a torque of 43 to 47 lbf ft (5·9 to 6·4 kgf m).

35 Using a suitable tool install the pulley on the shaft. Fig. 11.37 shows the special Ford tool being used. It is most important that the pulley is installed without applying in-and-out pressure on the shaft, to prevent damage to internal thrust areas.

23 Power steering pump – start-up procedure after overhaul

Upon initial start-up after a power steering pump or steering gear overhaul there is frequently excessive noise and aeration. This is due to air trapped in the overhauled unit which mixes with the surging fluid and causes aeration. The problem can be minimized if the following procedure is used:

1 Disconnect the coil wire to prevent the engine starting.

2 Fill the reservoir with power steering fluid.

3 While continuing to add fluid, have an assistant crank the engine and at the same time turn the steering wheel approximately 30 degrees each side of center.

4 Recheck the fluid level and fill as required.

5 Reconnect the coil wire, then start the engine and allow it to run for several minutes.

6 Rotate the steering wheel from stop-to-stop to remove the air from the system.

7 Shut off the engine and check the fluid level.

24 Non-integral power steering system control valve centering spring – adjustment

1 Raise the front of the car and support it on stands.

2 Remove the two spring cap attaching screws and the spring cap (photo).

3 Tighten the adjusting nut, then loosen it $\frac{1}{4}$ turn. Do not tighten the adjusting nut too tight (72 to 100 lbf in).

4 Install the spring cap to the valve housing and secure it with the two screws and lockwashers.

5 Lower the car. Start the engine and check the turning effort with a spring scale attached to the rim of the steering wheel. The effort required to turn the steering wheel in both directions should not exceed 6·5 lb (2·9 kg).

25 Non-integral power steering control valve – removal and installation

1 Disconnect the four fluid line fittings at the control valve and drain the fluid into a suitable container. Turn the front wheels to the left and right several times to force all the fluid from the system (photo).

2 Loosen the clamping nut and bolt at the right end of the sleeve. Remove the roll pin from the steering arm-to-idler arm rod through the hole in the sleeve.

3 Remove the control valve ball stud nut and using a suitable ball-joint separator disconnect the ball stud from the Pitman arm.

4 Turn the front wheels fully to the left and remove the control valve by unscrewing it from the center link steering arm-to-idler arm rod.

5 To install the valve, screw it onto the center link until about four

24.2 Non-integral power steering control valve with spring cap removed

11

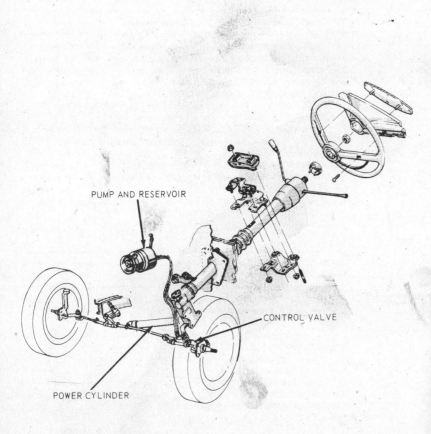

PUMP AND RESERVOIR

CONTROL VALVE

POWER CYLINDER

Fig. 11.38 Non-integral power steering system (Sec 25)

25.1 Disconnect the fluid lines from the control valve

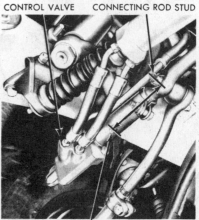

CONTROL VALVE   CONNECTING ROD STUD

LUBRICATION PLUG

Fig. 11.39 Installing the control valve (non-integral power steering) (Sec. 25)

threads are still visible on the link.

6   Position the ball stud in the Pitman arm.

7   Measure the distance between the center of the grease plug in the sleeve and the center of the stud at the inner end of the left spindle connecting rod (see Fig. 11.39). The distance should be 4·875 in (124 mm). If necessary, turn the valve on the center link to increase or decrease the distance.

8   Align the hole in the steering arm-to-idler arm rod with the slot near the end of the valve sleeve. Install the roll pin in the rod hole to lock the valve on the rod.

9   Tighten the valve sleeve clamp bolt and the ball stud nut. Install a new cotter pin.

10   Fill the reservoir with steering gear fluid. Run the engine for a few minutes then turn the steering wheel from lock-to-lock several times and check the system for leaks.

11   Check the fluid level and top-up if necessary.

12   Check the effort to turn the steering wheel in both directions (see Section 24).

26   Non-integral power steering control valve – overhaul

1   Clean all fluid and dirt from the exterior of the control valve.

2   Remove the two attaching screws and the centering spring cap from the valve housing, (see Fig. 11.41).

3   Mount the valve in a soft-jawed vise, hold it by the sleeve flange to prevent damage to the housing spool or sleeve.

4   Undo the nut on the end of the valve spool bolt and remove the washers, spacer, centering spring, adaptor and bushing.

5   Undo the two attaching bolts and separate the housing from the sleeve, then remove the plug from the sleeve.

6   Push the valve spool out of the centering spring end of the valve housing and remove the seal from the spool.

7   Remove the spacer, bushing and seal from the sleeve end of the housing.

8   Drive the stop pin out of the regulator stop with a punch (see Fig.11.40).

9   Turn the travel regulator stop counterclockwise in the sleeve and withdraw it from the sleeve.

10   Remove the valve spool bolt, spacer and rubber washer.

11   Remove the rubber boot and clamp from the valve sleeve.

12   Slide the bumper, spring and ball stud seat out and remove the ball socket from the sleeve.

13   Remove the return port hose seat and then the return port relief valve.

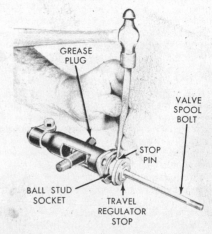

GREASE PLUG

VALVE SPOOL BOLT

STOP PIN

BALL STUD SOCKET

TRAVEL REGULATOR STOP

Fig. 11.40 Driving out the stop pin (Sec 26)

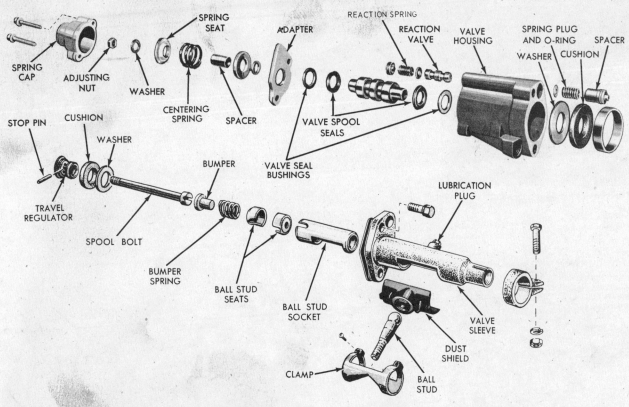

Fig. 11.41 Exploded view of control valve (non-integral power steering) (Sec 26)

Fig. 11.42 Removing the reaction valve (Sec 26)

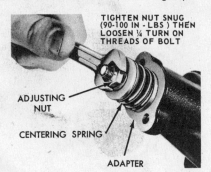

Fig. 11.43 Adjusting the control valve centering spring (Sec 26)

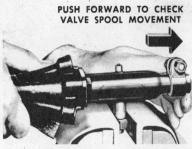

Fig. 11.44 Checking the control valve spool for friction of movement (Sec 26)

14 Remove the plug, spring, O-ring and reaction valve (see Fig. 11.42).
15 Clean all the parts and inspect for wear, scoring or other damage. Install new seals and O-rings. Before reassembling the control valve, coat all metal parts with steering gear fluid. Smear the seals with a silicone grease.
16 Reassembly is the reverse of the dismantling procedure. Adjust the control valve centering spring as described in Section 24.
17 Mount the valve in a vise, as shown in Fig. 11.44, and check the spool for freedom of movement by pushing forward on the cap end and then turning it round and pushing on the sleeve end.

27 Non-integral power steering cylinder – removal and installation

1 Disconnect the two fluid hoses from the power cylinder and allow them to drain into a container (photo).
2 Remove the nuts, washer and insulator from the end of the power cylinder rod.
3 Withdraw the cotter pin and remove the power cylinder stud-to-center link securing nut, then disconnect the cylinder from the center link, using a balljoint separator.

4 Remove the insulator sleeve and washer from the end of the power cylinder rod.
5 Installation is the reverse of the removal procedure. Fill the reservoir and bleed the air from the system as described in Section 18.

28 Power steering cylinder seal – removal and installation

1 Mount the power cylinder in a vise, taking care not to damage it, and remove the snap-ring from the end of the cylinder.
2 Pull the piston rod out all the way to remove the scraper, bushing and seals. If the seals do not come out with the piston rod use a sharp tool to pick them out taking care not to damage the shaft or seal seat.
3 Use all the parts in the repair kit. Coat the seals and the piston rod with silicone grease and then install all the parts on the piston rod in the order shown in Fig. 11.45.
4 Push the rod all the way into the cylinder then tap the assembled parts fully in, as shown in Fig. 11.46, and install the snap-ring.

29 Integral power steering gear – removal and installation

1 Disconnect the pressure and return lines from the steering gear.

11

27.1 Disconnect the fluid hoses from the power cylinder

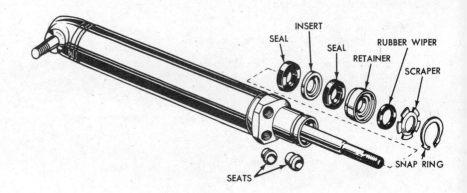

Fig. 11.45 Removing the power cylinder seals (Sec 28)

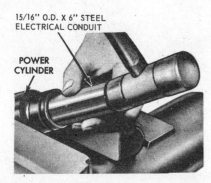

Fig. 11.46 Installing the power cylinder seals (Sec 28)

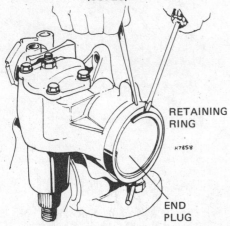

Fig. 11.47 Removing the retaining ring (Sec 29)

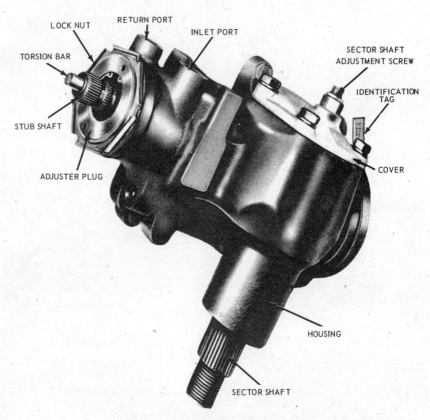

Fig. 11.48 Integral power steering gear – Saginaw (Sec 30)

Plug the lines and ports to prevent the ingress of dirt.

2   Remove the two bolts securing the flex coupling to the steering gear and to the column.

3   Raise the front of the car and support it on stands. Undo the Pitman arm securing nut and using a suitable puller remove the Pitman arm. Do not hammer on the end of the puller as the steering gear may be damaged.

4   On cars with manual transmission remove the clutch lever retracting spring.

5   Support the steering gear and remove the three attaching bolts. Work the steering gear free of the flex coupling and lift it out.

6   When installing the steering gear, set the steering wheel so that the spokes are horizontal and the roadwheels are in the straight-ahead position. Center the steering gear input shaft and then install the steering gear using the reverse of the removal procedure. Tighten the Pitman arm securing nut and the steering gear attaching bolts to the specified torque.

7   Carry out the start-up procedure described in Section 23.

30 Integral power steering gear – dismantling

Note: *Special tool no. T65P–3D517–A or an equivalent will be needed during this operation.*

1   Refer to Section 22 paragraph 1.

2   Mount the steering gear in a vise.

3   Remove the retaining ring (see Fig. 11.47).

4   Rotate the input shaft counterclockwise to force the plug out of the housing. Do not rotate the shaft more than necessary or the balls will fall out. Remove the O-ring.

5   Rotate the input shaft clockwise to draw the piston inward then remove the end plug from the piston.

6   Remove the sector shaft adjusting screw and the four cover attaching screws then rotate the adjusting screw with an Allen wrench until the cover is free of the housing. Remove the cover and O-ring.

7   Remove the sector shaft. If necessary, tap the shaft with a plastic hammer.

8 Remove the adjuster plug locknut and the adjuster plug (Fig. 11.50).

9 Insert the tool shown in Fig. 11.51 into the end of the rack piston until it contacts the wormshaft. Rotate the stub shaft counterclockwise until the worm is free of the rack piston. Withdraw the piston and keep the tool in position to prevent the balls dropping out.

10 Pull the stub shaft and valve assembly from the housing and lift out the worm, lower thrust bearing and the races.

31 Integral power steering gear housing – dismantling, renovation and reassembly

1 Refer to Fig. 11.52 and remove the snap-ring, lower spacer washer, lower seal (double lip), spacer washer and upper seal.

2 Examine the housing bearing for wear; remove it, if worn or damaged using a suitable drift. A stop ring is located in the piston bore.

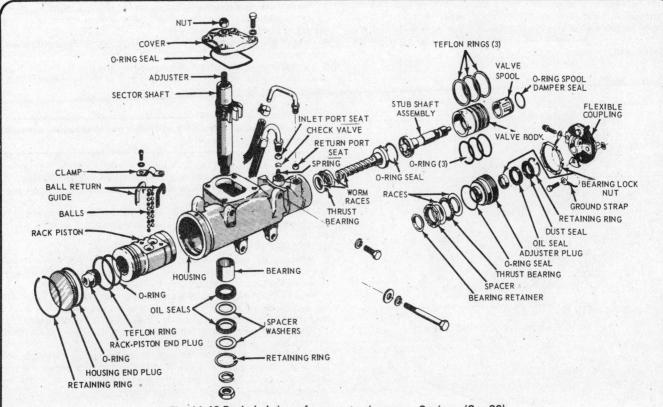

Fig. 11.49 Exploded view of power steering gear – Saginaw (Sec 30)

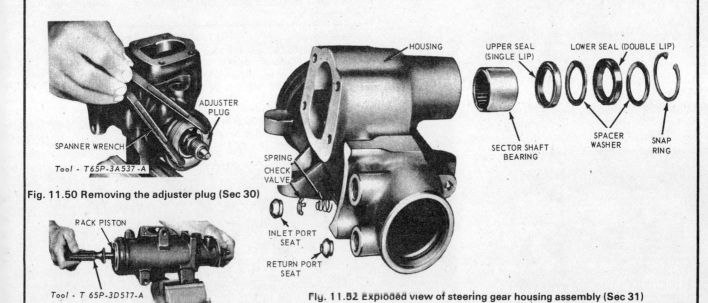

Fig. 11.50 Removing the adjuster plug (Sec 30)

Fig. 11.51 Removing the rack piston (Sec 30)

Fig. 11.52 Exploded view of steering gear housing assembly (Sec 31)

11

Do not attempt to remove it; if it is damaged the housing assembly must be renewed. To remove a damaged port seat, cut a thread in the seat and, using a bolt, nut and flat washer, withdraw the seat (see Fig. 11.53). Remove the check valve and spring from the inlet port.

3   Insert the spring, check valve and new seat in the inlet port and using a drift with a concave end to fit on the valve seat, drive the seat into place. Install the outlet port seat.

4   Press a new sector shaft bearing into the housing until the upper end is 0·030 in (0·76 mm) below the housing bore.

5   Lubricate the new seals with power steering fluid. Install the single lip seal and spacer washer, and using a suitable drift, drive them in far enough to provide clearance for the other seal. The seal must not bottom on the end of the counterbore. Fit the double lip seal and spacer washer, and drive them in only far enough to allow for the installation of the retaining snap-ring.

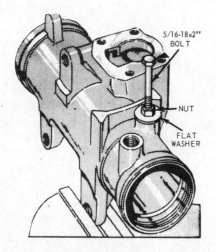

Fig. 11.53 Removing a port seat (Sec 31)

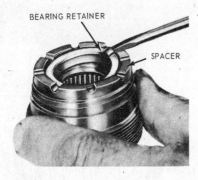

Fig. 11.54 Removing the thrust bearing retainer (Sec 32)

32 Adjuster plug (integral power steering) – dismantling and reassembly

1   Remove the thrust bearing retainer, as shown in Fig. 11.54, taking care not to score the needle bearing bore, then lift the spacer, thrust bearing, races and O-ring from the plug.

2   Remove the dust seal retaining ring, and using a drift inserted from the spacer end, remove the roller bearing, oil seal and dust seal (see Fig. 11.55).

3   Install the new bearing with the manufacturer's marking facing outwards and drive it into the plug until it is flush with the bottom surface of the stub shaft bearing bore.

4   Install the new oil seal, dust seal and snap-ring. Fit the dust seal with its smooth rubber surface facing outwards.

5   Install a new O-ring seal, then assemble the thrust bearing outer race, the thrust bearing, inner race and spacer on the adjuster plug, then install the bearing retainer.

33 Stub shaft and rotary valve assembly (integral power steering) – dismantling and reassembly

1   Invert the valve and tap on a block of wood until the torsion bar cap separates from the valve body. Discard the cap-to-body O-ring.

2   Push the stub shaft through the valve body until the drive pin hole is visible.

3   Tilt the stub shaft, so that the drive pin will disengage from the spool, and remove it from the valve body and spool assembly (Fig. 11.56).

4   Slide the spool out of the top of the valve body.

5   Clean all the parts, examine for wear or damage, and renew defective parts. Install new O-rings and Teflon seals on the valve body. Lubricate the parts with power steering fluid.

6   Install the dampener O-ring on the spool and slide the spool into the body with a turning motion. Take care not to damage the O-ring. Locate the drive pin hole opposite the deep notch in the valve body.

7   Install the stub shaft in the spool with the drive pin hole aligned with the hole in the spool.

8   Insert the drive pin into the spool hole and pull the assembly into the valve body keeping the cap slot and pin aligned. When the cap seats correctly in the valve body, the top surface of the cap should be at least 0·094 in (2·38 mm) below the notch.

9   Install a new cap-to-body O-ring.

34 Rack piston (integral power steering) – dismantling and reassembly

Note: Special tool no. T65P–3D517–A or an equivalent will be needed during this operation.

1   Cut the Teflon ring and O-ring from the piston.

2   Place the assembly on a clean lint-free cloth; remove the screws attaching the ball return guide clamp to the rack piston, and remove the clamp (Fig. 11.57).

3   Lift off the ball return guides from the rack piston.

4   Remove the tool, left in the piston when dismantling the steering gear, and remove the remaining balls.

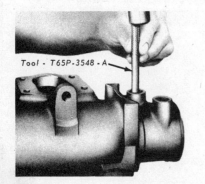

Fig. 11.55 Exploded view of adjuster plug (Sec 32)

5 Clean the parts, examining for damage or wear; renew any defective parts.

6 Lubricate a new O-ring and Teflon ring, then install the O-ring on the piston taking care not to twist it. Slide the Teflon ring into place. Do not stretch it unnecessarily.

7 Slide the worm (Fig. 11.58) fully into the rack piston. Load 16 balls into the guide hole nearest the Teflon ring, slowly rotating the worm counterclockwise, thus feeding the balls through circuit. Alternate the dark colored and polished balls through the circuit as they are loaded.

8 Apply petroleum jelly to one of the ball return guides and install the remaining balls in the guide. The constant ratio gear requires 22 balls, and the variable ratio gear 24 balls. Position the other half of the guide, and insert the balls into the holes in the rack piston. Ensure that dark and polished balls are alternated in the rack piston. Install the ball return guide clamp, and retain with the screws and lockwashers.

9 When the rack piston passes over the high point in the center of the worm groove there should be a preload of 1 to 4 lbf in (1·15 to 4·6 kgf cm). Clamp the rack piston in a soft-jawed vise, wormshaft pointing up. Avoid overtightening which might cause distortion.

10 Place the valve assembly on the worm, and engage the worm drive pins. Rotate the worm until it extends $1\frac{1}{4}$ in (32 mm) from the rack piston to the thrust bearing face to obtain the center position.

11 Place a torque wrench ($\frac{3}{4}$ in deep wall, 12-point socket) on the stub shaft, rotating the wrench through a 60° arc in both directions several times. Take a torque reading. The optimum reading with the worm rotating should be between 1 and 4 lbf in (1·15 and 4·6 kgf cm).

12 Install a new set of balls if this reading is too high or too low. See Fig. 11.59 for sizes of service replacement balls available.

13 Note the ball size stamped on the rack piston. Install the next size larger to increase preload. If the rack piston is devoid of a size-stamp, the original ball code size was No. 7.

14 Each ball size larger increases preload approximately 1 lbf in (1·15 kgf cm). Final preload on replacement balls should be 2 to 3 lbf in (2·3 to 3·45 kgf cm).

15 Remove the valve assembly from the worm and release the rack piston from the vise.

16 Insert tool T65P–3D517–A into the plug end of the rack and piston so that it contacts the wormshaft (Fig. 11.60). Apply pressure on the tool and rotate the wormshaft out of the piston and rack. Leave the tool in position until the piston is installed in the housing.

35 Integral power steering gear – reassembly

1 Mount the steering gear housing in a vise.

2 During assembly lubricate the parts with power steering fluid. Lubricate Teflon rings and O-rings with petroleum jelly.

3 See Fig. 11.49. Install the thrust bearing and races on the worm. Align the valve body drive pin on the worm with the narrow slot in the valve body.

4 Install the valve and wormshaft assembly by pushing on the outer diameter of the valve body. The assembly is correctly seated when the fluid return hole in the gear housing is fully visible.

5 Install a new O-ring in the adjuster plug groove and insert the adjuster plug over the end of the stub shaft and tighten it just enough to seat the parts. Install the locknut loosely on the adjuster plug.

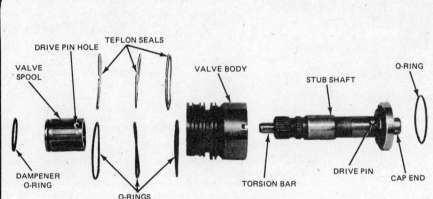

Fig. 11.56 Stub shaft and rotary valve assembly (Sec 33)

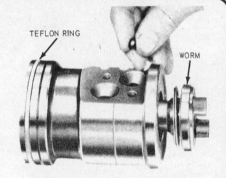

Fig. 11.58 Installing the worm and balls (Sec 34)

Code Size	Diameter Mean	Size Range of Ball (Inch)
6	0.28117	0.28112-0.28122
7	0.28125	0.28120-0.28130
8	0.28133	0.28128-0.28138
9	0.28141	0.28136-0.28146
10	0.28149	0.28144-0.28154
11	0.28157	0.28152-0.28162

Fig. 11.59 Worm ball sizes (Sec 34)

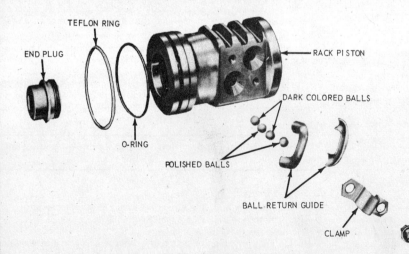

Fig. 11.57 Exploded view of rack piston assembly (Sec 34)

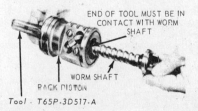

Fig. 11.60 Installing the ball retaining tool in the rack piston (Sec 35)

11

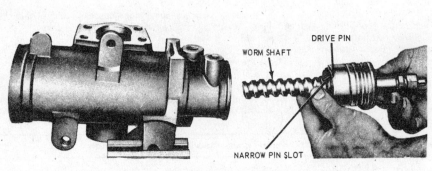

Fig. 11.61 Installing the valve and wormshaft assembly (Sec 35)

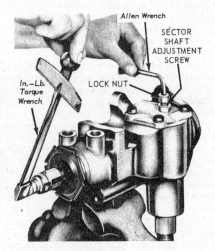

Fig. 11.63 Adjusting the sector shaft mesh load
(Sec 35)

Fig. 11.62 Installing the rack piston (Sec 35)

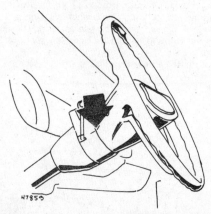

Fig. 11.64 Steering wheel alignment marks
(Sec 36)

6   Tighten the adjuster plug while turning the input shaft. As soon as additional torque is noted back-off the adjuster plug $\frac{1}{8}$ turn. Measure the input shaft turning torque with a torque wrench.

7   Tighten the adjuster plug to obtain a 1 to 3 lbf in (1·15 to 3·45 kgf cm) preload in excess of the figure noted in paragraph 6, then tighten the adjuster plug locknut. Recheck the preload; it must not exceed 8 lbf in (9·20 kgf cm).

8   Install the rack piston in the housing. Be sure the ball retaining tool is contacting the wormshaft and push the piston inward. Turn the stub shaft clockwise until the middle rack groove in the piston is aligned with the center of the sector shaft roller bearing, then remove the tool from the housing (Fig. 11.62).

9   Install a new O-ring in the sector shaft cover. Screw the cover onto the adjusting screw until it bottoms then back it off $1\frac{1}{2}$ turns.

10   Install the sector shaft so that the center gear tooth meshes with the center groove in the rack piston; push the cover down on the housing and install the securing screws. Install the locknut loosely on the adjuster screw.

11   Install the end plug in the rack piston and tighten it to 50 to 100 lbf ft (7 to 13 kgf m).

12   Install a new end plug O-ring in the housing. Insert the end plug in the housing and tap it lightly with a plastic hammer to seat it against the O-ring, then install the retainer ring.

13   Center the worm and fit a torque wrench on the input shaft (see Fig. 11.63).

14   With the gear on center and the sector shaft adjuster backed-off, measure the turning torque. Adjust the sector shaft thrust screw so that the preload is 4 to 8 lbf in (4·60 to 9·20 kgf cm) in excess of the figure previously obtained. Readings should be made through an arc not exceeding 20 degrees, with the gear on center.

15   Tighten the sector shaft adjuster screw locknut to a torque of 30 to 35 lbf ft (4·14 to 4·83 kgf m).

36 Steering wheel – removal and installation

1   Disconnect the ground cable from the negative terminal on the battery.

2   Remove the crash pad attaching screws and lift off the pad. Remove the horn ring (if so equipped) by turning it clockwise to release the locking tabs. Disconnect the horn wires.

3   Remove the steering wheel securing nut. Make alignment marks on the column shaft and wheel hub (unless already marked – Fig. 11.64).

4   Install a steering wheel puller and remove the wheel. Do not use a knock-off puller or strike the end of the steering shaft with a hammer as this will cause damage to the column bearing or the collapsible column.

5   Installing is the reverse of the removal procedure. Make sure the matching marks are aligned. Tighten the steering wheel securing nut to a torque of 30 to 40 lbf ft (4.14 to 5.52 kgf m).

37 Steering column upper shaft bearing – removal and installation

Fixed columns

1   Disconnect the horn and turn indicator wires at the connector.

2   Remove the steering wheel (see Section 36).

3   Remove the turn indicator lever.

4   Undo the turn indicator switch attaching screws and lift the switch over the end of the steering shaft and place it to one side.

5   Remove the snap-ring from the top of the steering shaft.

6   Loosen the two flange-to-steering column tube retaining nuts to

disengage them from the tube, then raise the flange upward while tapping the steering shaft lightly with a plastic hammer to free the bearing and flange from the shaft.

7 Remove the bearing and insulator from the flange.

8 Installation is the reverse of the removal procedure. When installing the new bearing, use a piece of tubing and the steering wheel nut as shown in Fig. 11.65 to press the bearing into position.

Tilt columns

9 Remove the tilt column mechanism as described in Section 39.

10 Position the flange casting with the smaller bearing facing downward. Drive lightly on the outer race at each slot with a small diameter pin punch. Invert the flange and remove the larger upper bearing in the same way.

11 Install the bearings, using a socket wrench of the same diameter as the bearing outer races, and tap the bearings into place.

12 Install the tilt column mechanism as described in Section 39.

38 Steering column – removal and installation

1 Disconnect the battery negative cable.

2 Disconnect the transmission lock rod (if installed) and the two nuts retaining the flex coupling to the steering shaft (fixed columns). On tilt columns, remove the one bolt attaching the flex coupling to the shaft.

Fig. 11.65 Installing the upper bearing – fixed steering column

(Sec 37)

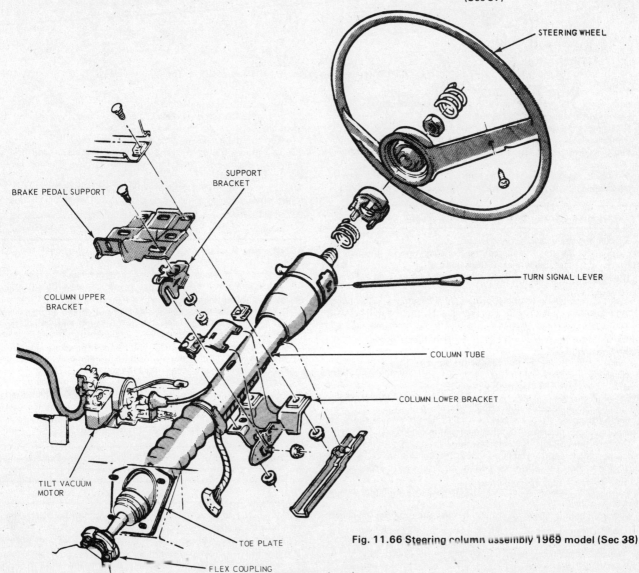

STEERING WHEEL

SUPPORT BRACKET

BRAKE PEDAL SUPPORT

COLUMN UPPER BRACKET

TURN SIGNAL LEVER

COLUMN TUBE

COLUMN LOWER BRACKET

TILT VACUUM MOTOR

TOE PLATE

FLEX COUPLING

Fig. 11.66 Steering column assembly 1969 model (Sec 38)

11

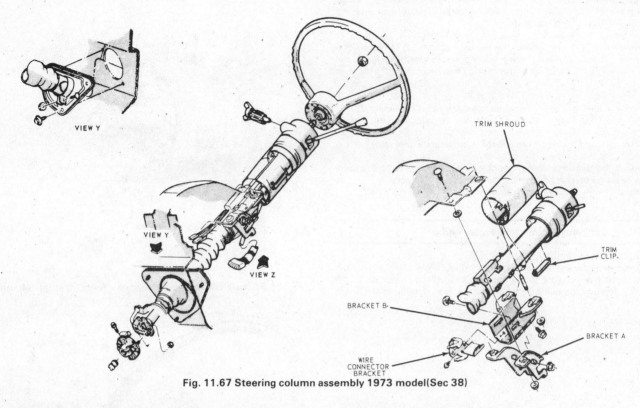

VIEW Y

VIEW Y

VIEW Z

TRIM SHROUD

TRIM CLIP.

BRACKET B

BRACKET A

WIRE CONNECTOR BRACKET

Fig. 11.67 Steering column assembly 1973 model(Sec 38)

(On early models disconnect the vacuum motor control cable).
3 Remove the four screws in the toe-plate.
4 Disconnect the electrical connectors.
5 Remove the four nuts securing the column to the brake support bracket, then drop the column from the instrument panel and remove it from the car.
6 Installation is the reverse of the removal procedure. Make sure the flex coupling is not distorted when tightening the attaching nuts.

39 Tilt steering column mechanism – removal and installation

1 Disconnect the battery ground cable.
2 Disconnect the steering shaft at the flex coupling.
3 Remove the steering wheel (see Section 36).
4 Remove the turn indicator lever and switch as described in Section 37.
5 Insert a wire pin in the hole located on the outside of the flange casting adjacent to the turn indicator warning flasher button.
6 Turn the ignition key to the *ON* position, depress the wire pin and lift out the lock cylinder. Remove the lock cylinder spring clips from the lock cylinder housing.
7 Using a flat bladed screwdriver, insert the blade into the recess in the drivegear at the bottom of the housing. Turn the drivegear three notches in a counterclockwise direction. Remove the snap-ring, washer and drivegear (see Fig. 11.70). Note the position of the drivegear to the upper actuator teeth.
8 Undo the cover attaching screws and lift the cover over the shaft. Unhook the upper actuator from the lower actuator.
9 Remove the column trim shrouds, the steering column instrument panel trim cover, and the bolts attaching the column brackets to the brake support bracket. Allow the column to drop down, exposing the ignition switch.
10 Remove the three Allen screws attaching the lower flange casting to the outer tube.
11 Loosen the ignition switch nut and remove the rod from the switch end.
12 Remove the two spring clips holding the wire bale which acts as a release lever for the locking lever and remove the wire bale (see Fig. 11.71).
13 Using a small drift, drive out the pin securing the locking lever. Remove the locking lever and spring.

14 Remove the steering shaft snap-ring.
15 Separate the upper and lower flange castings by removing the two pivot pins as shown in Fig. 11.72.
16 Remove the lower actuator and ignition switch rod.
17 To remove the socket casting, rotate the inner tube and socket casting to expose the retaining bolt, then remove the bolt and lift off the casting.
18 Installation is the reverse of the removal procedure. Use a C-clamp to press the pivot pins into place. Do not use the old pins if loose in the holes (Fig. 11.73).

40 Steering linakge connecting rod ends – removal and installation

1 The connecting rod ends, which are screwed into the adjusting sleeves, cannot be greased or serviced. When the ball-studs become worn and loose the ends must be renewed (photo).
2 Remove the cotter pin and nut from the ball-stud.
3 Disconnect the end from the spindle arm or center link using a balljoint separator.
4 Loosen the connecting rod sleeve clamp bolts and count the number of turns required to remove the rod end.
5 Screw the new rod end into the sleeve the same number of turns as was required to remove the old rod end and tighten the clamp bolts.
6 Connect the rod end to the spindle arm or center link, then tighten the retaining nut to the specified torque and install the cotter pin.
7 It will be necessary to have the front wheel alignment checked, refer to Section 42.

41 Steering linkage idler arm and bracket – removal and installation

1 When the idler arm bushings are worn the complete idler arm assembly must be renewed.
2 Remove the cotter pin and nut attaching the steering center link to the idler arm.
3 Remove the two bolts attaching the idler arm and bracket assembly to the frame and lift away the assembly (photo).
4 Installation is the reverse of the removal procedure.

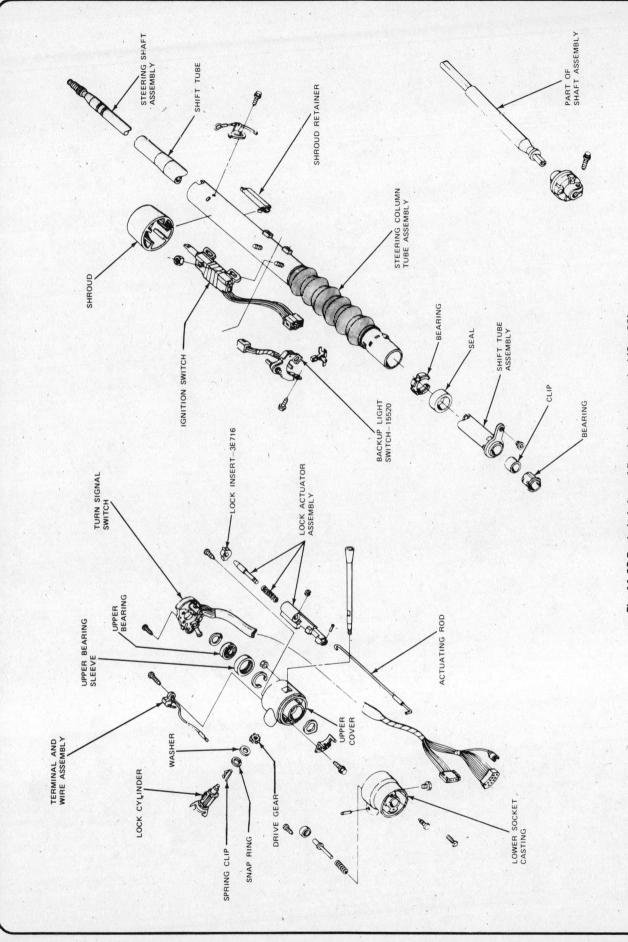

Fig. 11.68 Exploded view of fixed column – typical (Sec 38)

11

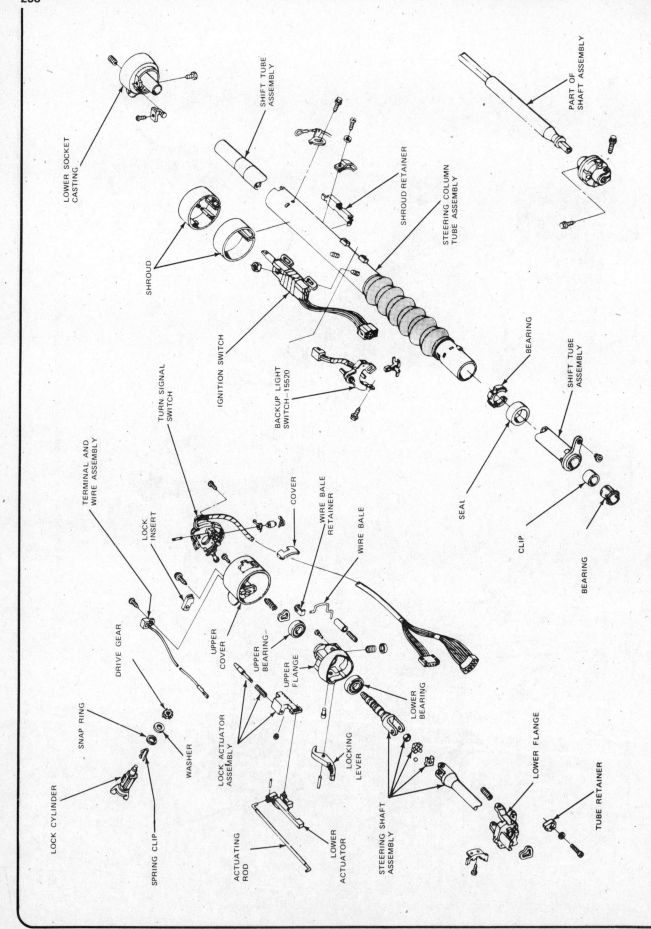

LOWER SOCKET CASTING

SHIFT TUBE ASSEMBLY

SHROUD RETAINER

STEERING COLUMN TUBE ASSEMBLY

PART OF SHAFT ASSEMBLY

SHROUD

IGNITION SWITCH

TURN SIGNAL SWITCH

BACKUP LIGHT SWITCH—15520

BEARING

SHIFT TUBE ASSEMBLY

SEAL

CLIP

BEARING

TERMINAL AND WIRE ASSEMBLY

LOCK INSERT

COVER

WIRE BALE RETAINER

WIRE BALE

DRIVE GEAR

UPPER COVER

UPPER BEARING

UPPER FLANGE

SNAP RING

WASHER

LOCK ACTUATOR ASSEMBLY

LOWER BEARING

LOCK CYLINDER

SPRING CLIP

LOCKING LEVER

STEERING SHAFT ASSEMBLY

LOWER FLANGE

TUBE RETAINER

ACTUATING ROD

LOWER ACTUATOR

Fig. 11.69 Exploded view of tilt column – typical (Sec 39)

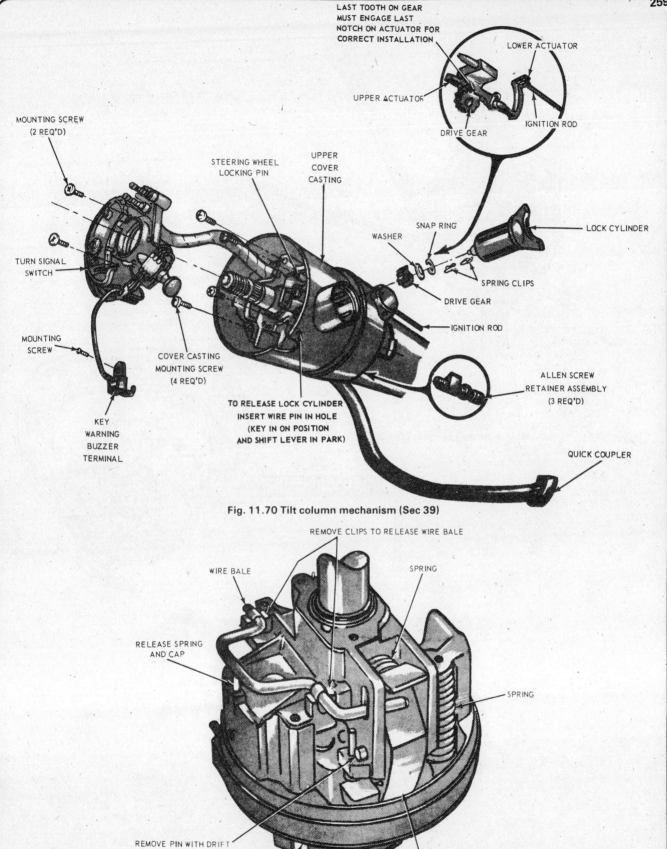

LAST TOOTH ON GEAR
MUST ENGAGE LAST
NOTCH ON ACTUATOR FOR
CORRECT INSTALLATION

LOWER ACTUATOR

UPPER ACTUATOR

IGNITION ROD

DRIVE GEAR

MOUNTING SCREW
(2 REQ'D)

STEERING WHEEL
LOCKING PIN

UPPER
COVER
CASTING

SNAP RING

WASHER

LOCK CYLINDER

TURN SIGNAL
SWITCH

SPRING CLIPS

DRIVE GEAR

MOUNTING
SCREW

COVER CASTING
MOUNTING SCREW
(4 REQ'D)

IGNITION ROD

ALLEN SCREW
RETAINER ASSEMBLY
(3 REQ'D)

KEY
WARNING
BUZZER
TERMINAL

TO RELEASE LOCK CYLINDER
INSERT WIRE PIN IN HOLE
(KEY IN ON POSITION
AND SHIFT LEVER IN PARK)

QUICK COUPLER

Fig. 11.70 Tilt column mechanism (Sec 39)

REMOVE CLIPS TO RELEASE WIRE BALE

WIRE BALE

SPRING

RELEASE SPRING
AND CAP

SPRING

REMOVE PIN WITH DRIFT

LOCKING LEVER

FLANGE ASSEMBLY

Fig. 11.71 Removing the wire bale and tilt locking lever (Sec 39)

11

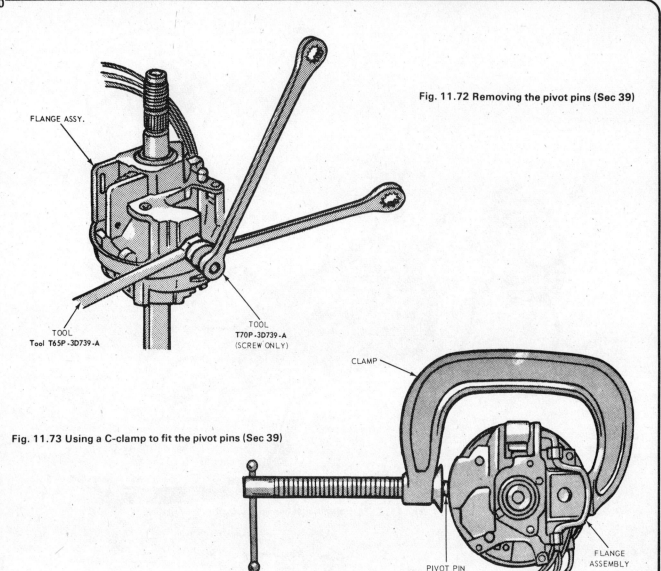

FLANGE ASSY.

Fig. 11.72 Removing the pivot pins (Sec 39)

TOOL
Tool T65P-3D739-A

TOOL
T70P-3D739-A
(SCREW ONLY)

Fig. 11.73 Using a C-clamp to fit the pivot pins (Sec 39)

CLAMP

PIVOT PIN

FLANGE
ASSEMBLY

40.1 Connecting rod adjusting sleeve

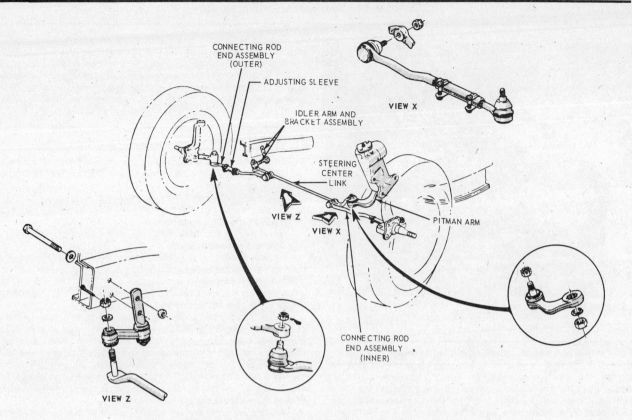

Fig. 11.74 Steering linkage – manual or integral power steering (Sec 41)

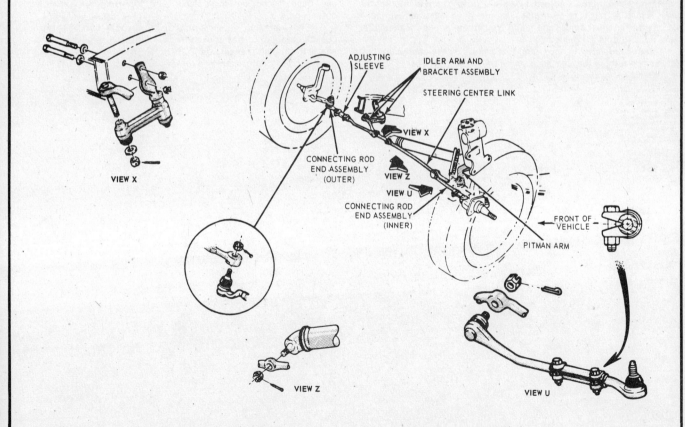

Fig 11.75 Steering linkage – non-integral power steering (Sec 41)

11

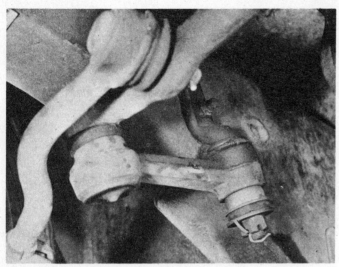

41.3 Steering linkage idler arm removal

42 Front wheel alignment – checking and adjustment

1   Unless the front suspension or steering linkage has been damaged, the castor angle, camber angle, turning angle and the toe-in will not alter, provided the suspension balljoints or suspension arm pivot bushings and steering linkages are not worn.

2   On models before 1967 castor and camber angles are adjusted by shims between the frame bracket and the upper suspension arm pivot shaft. On models from 1967 castor is adjusted by altering the length of the struts, and camber is adjusted by the eccentric cam located at the lower arm attachment to the frame. Turning angle is not adjustable; it is a result of castor, camber and toe-in adjustment and is checked after these adjustments are made.

3   Toe-in is adjusted by loosening the clamps on the connecting rod sleeves and turning the sleeves as required.

4   Indications of incorrect wheel alignment are uneven tire wear and erratic steering, particularly when turning. To check wheel alignment requires special measuring equipment so this is a job for a service station with the necessary equipment. Ensure that a complete inspection of the front suspension and steering is made before the alignment is checked.

43 Wheels and tires

1   To provide equal, and obtain maximum wear from all the tires they should be rotated on the car at intervals of 6000 miles (10 000 km) to the following pattern:
   Spare to offside rear
   Offside rear to nearside front
   Nearside front to nearside rear
   Nearside rear to offside front
   Offside front to spare
Wheels should be rebalanced when this is done. However, some owners baulk at the prospect of having to buy five new tires all at once and tend to let two run on and replace a pair only. The new pair should always be on the front wheels, as these are the most important from the safety aspect of steering and braking.

2   Never mix tires of a radial and crossply construction on the same car, as the basic design differences can cause unusual and, in certain conditions, very dangerous handling and braking characteristics. If an emergency should force the use of two different types, make sure the radials are on the rear wheels and drive particularly carefully. If three of the five wheels have radial tires then make sure that no more than two radials are in use on the car (and those at the rear). Rationalize the tires at the earliest possible opportunity.

3   Wheels are normally not subject to servicing problems, but when tires are renewed or changed the wheels should be balanced to reduce vibration and wear. If a wheel is suspected of damage – caused by hitting a curb or pothole which could distort it out of true, change it and have it checked for balance and true-running at the earliest opportunity.

4   When installing wheels do not overtighten the nuts. The maximum possible manual torque applied by the manufacturers wheel wrench is adequate. It also prevents difficulty when the same wheel wrench has to be used in an emergency to remove the wheels.

44 Fault diagnosis – Suspension and steering

Before diagnosing faults from the following chart, check that any irregularities are not caused by:
1 Binding brakes
2 Incorrect 'mix' of radial and cross-ply tires
3 Incorrect tire pressures
4 Misalignment of the body frame or rear axle

Symptom	Reason/s
Steering wheel can be moved considerably before any sign of movement of the wheels is apparent	Wear in the steering linkage, gear and column coupling
Vehicle difficult to steer in a consistent straight line (wandering)	As above Wheel alignment incorrect (indicated by excessive or uneven tire wear) Front wheel hub bearings loose or worn Worn balljoints on connecting rods or suspension arms
Steering stiff and heavy	Incorrect wheel alignment (indicated by excessive or uneven tire wear) Excessive wear or seizure in one or more of the balljoints in the steering linkage or suspension arms Excessive wear in the steering gear unit
Wheel wobble and vibration	Road wheels out of balance Road wheels buckled Wheel alignment incorrect Wear in the steering linkage, suspension arm balljoints or suspension arm pivot bushings Broken front spring
Excessive pitching and rolling on corners and during braking	Defective shock absorbers and/or broken spring

Faults which can usually be attributed to the power steering system exclusively

Symptom	Reason/s
Car wanders	Low fluid level Air in system
Steering stiff	Low fluid level Air in system Pump control valves seized Reservoir filter blocked Damaged seals in steering gear
Steering stiff on one lock only	Lack of pressure on one side of piston due to wear
Front wheels wobble	Air in system
Steering heavy if steering wheel is being turned	Slack pump drivebelt Pump control valve blocked Air in system

11

Chapter 12 Bodywork and fittings

Contents

1 General description

1 The two-door body is of a unitized, all-welded construction which makes it a very strong and torsionally rigid shell which can withstand a considerable amount of stress.

2 Three types of body are used on the different models: Hardtop, Fastback (Sportroof) and Convertible.

2 Maintenance – body exterior

1 The general condition of a car's bodywork is the one thing that significantly affects its value. Maintenance is easy but needs to be regular. Neglect, particularly after minor damage, can lead quickly to further deterioration and costly repair bills. It is important also to keep watch on those parts of the car not immediately visible, for instance the underside, inside all the wheel aprons and the lower part of the engine compartment.

2 The basic maintenance routine for the bodywork is washing – preferably with a lot of water, from a hose. This will remove all the loose solids which may have stuck to the car. It is important to flush these off in such a way as to prevent grit from scratching the finish.

3 The wheel aprons and underbody need washing in the same way to remove any accumulated mud which will retain moisture and tend to encourage rust. Paradoxically enough, the best time to clean the underbody and wheel aprons is in wet weather when the mud is thoroughly wet and soft. In very wet weather the underbody is usually cleaned of large accumulations automatically and this is a good time for inspection.

4 Periodically, it is a good idea to have the whole of the underside of the car steam cleaned, engine compartment included, so that a thorough inspection can be carried out to see what minor repairs and renovations are necessary. Steam cleaning is available at many garages and is necessary for removal of accumulation of oily grime which sometimes is allowed to cake thick in certain areas near the engine, transmission and back axle. If steam cleaning facilities are not available, there are one or two excellent grease solvents available which can be brush applied. The dirt can then be simply hosed off.

5 After washing paintwork, wipe off with a chamois leather to give an unspotted clear finish. A coat of clear protective wax polish will give added protection against chemical pollutants in the air. If the paintwork sheen has dulled or oxidised, use a cleaner/polisher combination to restore the brilliance of the shine. Always check that the door and ventilator opening drain holes and pipes are completely clear so that water can drain out.

6 Bright work should be treated in the same way as paintwork. Windshields can be kept clear of the smeary film, which often appears, if detergent is added to the water in the windshield washer reservoir. Use a mild one, such as washing-up liquid. Never use any type of wax or chromium polish on glass.

3 Maintenance – body interior

1 Mats and carpets should be brushed or vacuum cleaned regularly to keep them free from grit. If they are badly stained remove them from the car for scrubbing or sponging and make quite sure they are dry before installation. Seats and interior trim panels can be kept clean by a wipe over with a damp cloth. If they do become stained (which can be more apparent on light coloured upholstery) use a little liquid detergent and a soft nail brush to scour the grime out of the grain of the material. Do not forget to keep the headlining clean in the same way as the upholstery. When using liquid cleaners inside the car do not over-wet the surfaces being cleaned. Excessive damp could get into the seams and padded interior causing stains, offensive odors or even rot. If the inside of the car gets wet accidentally it is worthwhile taking the trouble to dry it out properly, particularly where carpets are involved. **Do not** leave oil or electric heaters inside the car for this purpose.

4 Minor body damage – repair

See photo sequences on pages 270 and 271

Repair of minor scratches in the bodywork

If the scratch is very superficial, and does not penetrate to the metal of the bodywork, repair is very simple. Lightly rub the area of the scratch with a paintwork renovator or a very fine cutting paste, to remove loose paint from the scratch and to clear the surrounding bodywork of wax polish. Rinse the area with clean water.

Apply touch-up paint to the scratch using a thin paint brush; continue to apply thin layers of paint until the surface of the paint in the scratch is level with the surrounding paintwork. Allow the new paint at least two weeks to harden, then, blend it into the surrounding paintwork by rubbing the paintwork in the scratch area with a paintwork renovator or a very fine cutting paste. Finally apply wax polish.

An alternative to painting over the scratch is to use paint patches. Use the same preparation for the affected area; then simply pick a patch of a suitable size to cover the scratch completely. Hold the patch against the scratch and burnish its backing paper; the patch will adhere to the paintwork, freeing itself from the backing paper at the same time. Polish the affected area to blend the patch into the surrounding paintwork.

Where a scratch has penetrated right through to the metal of the bodywork, causing the metal to rust, a different repair technique is required. Remove any loose rust from the bottom of the scratch with a penknife, then apply rust inhibiting paint to prevent the formation of rust in the future. Using a rubber or nylon applicator fill the scratch with bodystopper paste. If required, this paint can be mixed with cellulose thinners to provide a very thin paste which is ideal for filling narrow scratches. Before the stopper paste in the scratch hardens, wrap a piece of smooth cotton rag around the tip of the finger. Dip the finger in cellulose thinners and then quickly sweep it across the surface of the stopper paste, this will ensure that it is slightly hollowed. The scratch can now be painted over as described earlier in this Section.

Repair of dents in the bodywork

When deep denting of the bodywork has taken place, the first task is to pull the dent out, until the affected bodywork almost attains its original shape. There is little point in trying to restore the original shape completely, as the metal in the damaged area will have stretched on impact and cannot be reshaped fully to its original contour. It is better to bring the level of the dent up to a point which is about $\frac{1}{8}$ inch (3mm) below the level of the surrounding bodywork. In cases where the dent is very shallow anyway, it is not worth trying to pull it out at all.

If the underside of the dent is accessible, it can be hammered out gently from behind, using a mallet with a wooden or plastic head. Whilst doing this, hold a suitable block of wood firmly against the outside of the dent. This block will absorb the impact from the hammer blows and thus prevent a large area of bodywork from being 'belled-out'.

Should the dent be in a section of the bodywork which has double skin or some other factor making it inaccessible from behind, a different technique is called for. Drill several small holes through the metal inside the dent area – particularly in the deeper sections. Then screw long self-tapping screws into the holes just sufficiently for them to gain good purchase in the metal. Now the dent can be pulled out by pulling on the protruding heads of the screws with a pair of pliers.

The next stage of the repair is the removal of the paint from the damaged area, and from an inch or so of the surrounding 'sound' bodywork. This is accomplished most easily by using a wire brush or abrasive pad on a power drill, although it can be done just as effectively by hand, using sheets of abrasive paper. To complete the preparations for filling, score the surface of the bare metal with a screwdriver or the tang of a file, or alternatively, drill small holes in the affected area. This will provide a really good 'key' for the filler paste.

To complete the repair see the Section on filling and respraying.

Repair of rust holes or gashes in the bodywork

Remove all paint from the affected area and from an inch or so of the surrounding 'sound' bodywork, using an abrasive pad or a wire brush on a power drill. If these are not available a few sheets of abrasive paper will do the job just as effectively. With the paint removed you will be able to gauge the severity of the corrosion and therefore decide whether to renew the whole panel, (if this is possible), or to repair the affected area. Replacement body panels are not as expensive as most people think and it is often quicker and more satisfactory to fit a new panel than to attempt to repair large areas of corrosion.

Remove all the fittings from the affected area except those which will act as a guide to the original shape of the damaged bodywork (eg headlamp shells etc). Then, using tin snips or a hacksaw blade, remove all loose metal and any other metal badly affected by corrosion. Hammer the edges of the holes inwards in order to create a slight depression for the filler paste.

Wire-brush the affected area to remove the powdery rust from the surface of the remaining metal. Paint the affected area with rust inhibiting paint; if the back of the rusted area is accessible, treat this also.

Before filling can take place it will be necessary to block the hole in some way. This can be achieved by the use of one of the following materials: Zinc gauze, Aluminum tape or Polyurethane foam.

Zinc gauze is probably the best material to use for a large hole. Cut a piece to the approximate size and shape of the hole to be filled, then position it in the hole so that its edges are below the level of the surrounding bodywork. It can be retained in position by several blobs of filler paste around its periphery.

Aluminum tape should be used for small or very narrow holes. Pull a piece off the roll and trim it to the approximate size and shape required, then pull off the backing paper (if used) and stick the tape over the hole; it can be overlapped if the thickness of one piece is insufficient. Burnish down the edges of the tape with the handle of a screwdriver or similar, to ensure that the tape is securely attached to the metal underneath.

Polyurethane foam is best used where the hole is situated in a section of the bodywork of complex shape, backed by a small box section (eg where the sill panel meets the rear wheel apron on most cars). The usual mixing procedure for this foam is as follows: Put equal amounts of fluid from each of the two cans provided in the kits, into one container. Stir until the mixture begins to thicken, then quickly pour this mixture into the hole, and hold a piece of cardboard over the larger apertures. Almost immediately the polyurethane will begin to expand and be forced out of any small holes left unblocked. When the foam hardens it can be cut back to just below the level of the surrounding bodywork with a hacksaw blade.

The affected area must now be filled and sprayed – see Section on filling and respraying.

Bodywork repairs – filling and respraying

Before using this Section, see the Sections on dent, deep scratch, rust hole and gash repairs.

Many types of bodyfiller are available, but generally speaking those proprietary kits which contain a tin of filler paste and a tube of resin hardener are best for this type of repair. A wide, flexible plastic or nylon applicator will be found invaluable for imparting a smooth and well contoured finish to the surface of the filler.

Mix up a little filler on a clean piece of card or board – use the hardener sparingly (follow the maker's instructions on the pack), otherwise the filler will set very rapidly.

Using the applicator, apply the filler paste to the prepared area; draw the applicator across the surface of the filler to achieve the correct contour and to level the filler surface. As soon as a contour that approximates the correct one is achieved, stop working the paste – if you carry on too long the paste will become sticky and begin to 'pick-up' on the applicator.

Continue to add thin layers of filler paste at twenty-minute intervals until the level of the filler is just 'proud' of the surrounding bodywork.

Once the filler has hardened, excess can be removed using a coarse-cut file. From then on, progressively finer grades of abrasive paper should be used, starting with a 40 grade 'wet-and-dry' paper. Always wrap the abrasive paper around a flat rubber, cork or wooden block – otherwise the surface of the filler will not be completely flat. During the smoothing of the filler surface the 'wet-and-dry' paper should be periodically rinsed in water – this will ensure that a very smooth finish is imparted to the filler at the final stage.

At this stage the 'dent' should be surrounded by a ring of bare metal, which in turn should be encircled by the finely 'feathered' edge of the good paintwork. Rinse the repair area with clean water, until all of the dust produced by the rubbing-down operation is gone.

12

Spray the whole repair area with a light coat of grey primer – this will show up any imperfections in the surface of the filler. Repair these imperfections with fresh filler paste or bodystopper and once more smooth the surface with abrasive paper. If bodystopper is used, it can be mixed with cellulose thinners to form a really thin paste which is ideal for filling small holes. Repeat this spray and repair procedure until you are satisfied that the surface of the filler, and the feathered edge of the paintwork are perfect. Clean the repair area with clean water and allow to dry fully.

The repair area is now ready for spraying. Paint spraying must be carried out in a warm, dry, windless and dust free atmosphere. This condition can be created artificially if you have access to a large indoor working area, but if you are forced to work in the open, you will have to pick your day carefully. If you are working indoors, dousing the floor in the work area with water will 'lay' the dust which would otherwise be in the atmosphere. If the repair area is confined to one body panel,

mask off the surrounding panels; this will help to minimise the effects of a slight mis-match in paint colours. Bodywork fittings (eg chrome strips, door handles etc) will also need to be masked off. Use genuine masking tape and several thicknesses of newspaper for the masking operation.

Before commencing to spray, agitate the aerosol can thoroughly, then spray a test area (an old tin, or similar) until the technique is mastered. Cover the repair area with a thick coat of primer; the thickness should be built up using several thin layers of paint rather than one thick one. Using 400 grade 'wet-and-dry' paper, rub down the surface of the primer until it is really smooth. While doing this, the work area should be thoroughly doused with water, and the wet-and-dry paper periodically rinsed in water. Allow to dry before spraying on more paint.

Spray on the top coat, again building up the thickness by using several thin layers of paint. Start spraying in the centre of the repair

Fig. 12.1 Hood alignment – adjustment points (Sec 6)

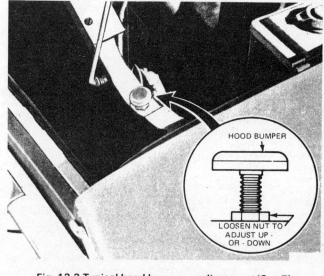

Fig. 12.3 Typical hood bumper – adjustment (Sec 7)

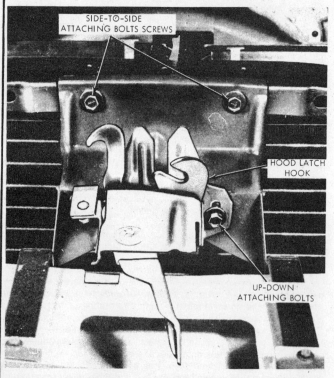

Fig. 12.2 Hood latch – adjustment (Sec 7)

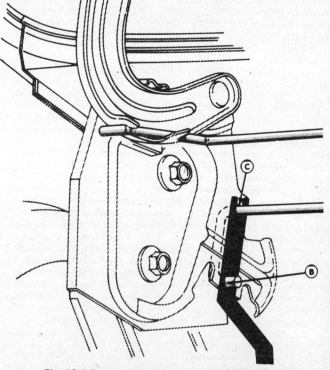

Fig. 12.4 Trunk lid torsion bar – adjustment (Sec 8)

area and then using a circular motion, work outwards until the whole repair area and about 2 inches of the surrounding original paintwork is covered. Remove all masking material 10 to 15 minutes after spraying on the final coat of paint. Allow the new paint at least 2 weeks to harden fully, then, using a paintwork renovator or a very fine cutting paste blend the edges of the new paint into the existing paintwork. Finally apply wax polish.

5 Major body damage – repair

Where serious damage has occurred or large areas need renewal due to neglect, it means that new sections will need welding in and this is best left to the professionals. If the damage is due to impact it will also be necessary to completely check the alignment of the body shell structure. Due to the principle of construction the strength and shape of the whole can be affected by damage to a part. In such cases the services of a Ford repair station with specialist checking jigs are essential.

6 Hood – alignment

1 Loosen the hinge-to-hood securing bolts and move the hood from side to side as necessary.
2 Loosen the hinge-to-fender apron securing bolts and adjust the vertical, and fore-and-aft position of the hood (Fig. 12.1).
3 The hood bumpers located on top of the radiator support can be adjusted up and down to provide a level surface alignment of the hood with the front fenders.
4 Tighten the securing bolts.

7 Hood latch – adjustment

The hood latch can be moved from side-to-side to align it with the hood latch hook and up-and-down to obtain a flush fit with the front fenders. The hood must be properly aligned before adjusting the hood latch.

1 Loosen the hood latch securing bolts until they are just loose enough to move the latch.
2 Position the latch in alignment with the hood latch hook.
3 Loosen the locknuts on the two hood bumpers and lower the bumpers.
4 Adjust the hood latch up or down, as necessary, to obtain a flush-fit between the top of the hood and the fenders when an upward pressure is applied to the front of the hood, then tighten the hood latch securing bolts.
5 Raise the two hood bumpers to eliminate any looseness when the hood is closed. Tighten the hood bumper locknuts.

8 Trunk lid hinge torsion bar – adjustment

1 Check the pop-up distance of the trunk lid when it is open. It should be approximately 3 inches.
2 If the trunk lid pops open more than 3 inches the torsion bar tension should be decreased and if it does not pop-up when the catch is released the tension should be increased. **Caution:** *Take care when adjusting the torsion bar as it is under tension and could spring out of control if not handled carefully.*
3 To adjust the torsion bar tension, place a piece of suitable steel bar over the end of the torsion bar, as shown in Fig. 12.4, then rotate the bar rearward at point C and reposition point B in another notch to increase or decrease the torsion bar tension, as necessary.
4 After adjustment, the difference of the position of the torsion bar ends between the right and left side must not be more than one notch.

9 Trunk lid – alignment

1 The trunk lid is adjusted from side-to-side by loosening the hinge-to-lid attachment screws and moving the lid as necessary.
2 To adjust the vertical alignment on pre-1971 models loosen the

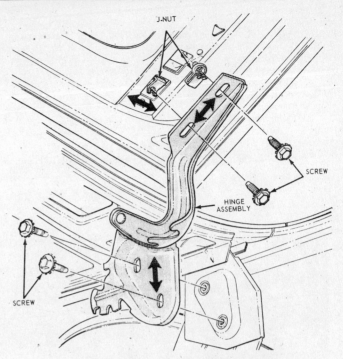

Fig. 12.5 Trunk lid hinge – 1965/70 (Sec 9)

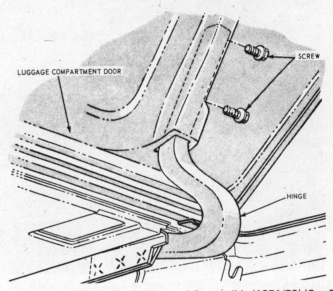

Fig. 12.6 Trunk lid hinge – Hardtop and Convertible (1971/73) (Sec 9)

hinge-to-hinge support attachment screws and move the lid up or down as necessary.
3 On models from 1971 the vertical adjustment is made by loosening the hinge-to-door attachment screws and the lid as required, or on some models by removing or adding shims between the hinge and lid.
4 After correct alignment has been achieved, tighten all the attachment screws.

10 Door trim panel – removal and installation

1965-1968 models
1 On early models remove the window regulator handle, using a handle-removing tool (available at most auto supply shops) to disengage the retaining spring clip. On later models remove the handle retaining screw and withdraw the handle (photo).
2 Remove the door-pull securing screws and the armrest (photos).
3 Undo the retaining screw and remove the door latch handle (photo).

12

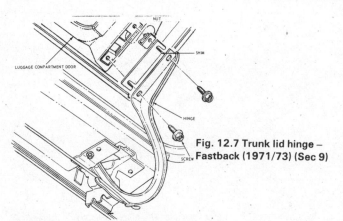

Fig. 12.7 Trunk lid hinge –
Fastback (1971/73) (Sec 9)

4   Remove all the trim panel retaining screws and then pry the panel retaining clips out of the inner panel and remove the panel. Remove the watershield (photo).
5   Installation is the reverse of the removal procedure. Apply water-resistant sealer at each panel retaining clip and around the window regulator shaft.

1969 – 73 models

6   Remove the door lock push button control knob.
7   Remove the window regulator retaining screw cover and retaining screw and pull the handle off the shaft (photos).
8   Remove the three retaining screws from the armrest assembly and withdraw the armrest.
9   Pry the two door-pull handle cover assemblies from the handle, undo the two handle retaining screws and remove the pull handle.
10   Remove the two retaining nuts and remove the door remote control handle from the door.

10.1 Removing the window regulator handle retaining screw

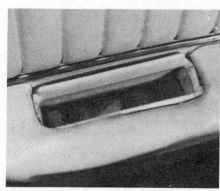

10.2A Door-pull securing screws

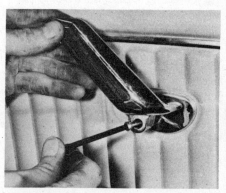

10.2B Removing the door-pull and armrest

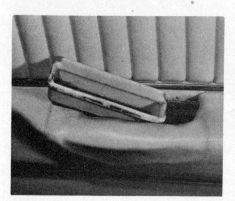

10.3 The door latch handle is secured with a screw

10.4 Door with trim panel removed and water-shield pulled back

10.7A Removing the window regulator handle retaining screw cover ...

10.7B ... and the retaining screw

10.12 Fitting the trim panel on the door

11 Using a wide-bladed knife, or similar tool, pry the trim panel retaining clips out of the inner panel of the door and remove the panel. Remove the watershield.

12 Installing the trim panel is the reverse of the removal procedure. Apply water-resistant sealer over each retaining clip hole and around the window regulator shaft hole (photo).

11 Doors – removal and installing

1 Open the door and place a support under the door to take its weight. The help of an assistant should also be enlisted to hold the door.

2 Remove the door trim panel as described in Section 10.

3 Scribe alignment marks on the hinges and door to assist when installing.

4 Remove the hinge-to-door attachment bolts and lift away the door.

5 Installing the door is the reverse of the removal procedure. Check the door alignment and, if necessary, adjust as described in Section 12.

12 Door alignment

1 The door hinges have enlarged holes to provide adjustment of the door position. Always ensure that hinges are correctly positioned before making a latch striker adjustment.

2 Refer to Fig. 12.8 to determine which hinge bolts must be loosened to move the door in the required direction.

3 Remove the door trim panel and hinge access covers. Loosen the hinge bolts just enough to allow movement of the door with a padded pry bar. Take care not to damage the paint finish when using the pry bar.

4 Move the door as necessary, then tighten the hinge bolts and check the door fit.

5 Repeat the operation until the correct alignment is obtained, and check the striker plate alignment for correct closing.

6 Install the door trim panel and hinge access covers.

13 Door latch striker – adjustment

1 The striker pin can be adjusted laterally and vertically as well as fore-and-aft. *Do not adjust the latch striker to overcome door sag.*

2 Adjust the latch striker position with shims to obtain the clearance shown in Fig. 12.9. Check the clearance by applying a thin film of grease to the striker, and then, as the door is closed and opened a measurable pattern will result.

14 Door latch – removal and installation

1 Remove the door trim panel and watershield as described in Section 10.

2 Disconnect the four rods from the latch assembly.

3 Undo the three latch attachment screws and remove the latch.

4 Remove the rod retaining clips and the 'door-open' warning switch from the latch.

5 Refitting is the reverse of the removal procedure. Adjust the warning switch and the latch actuating rod as described in Sections 15 and 16 respectively.

15 'Door open' warning switch – adjustment

1 Remove the door latch as described in Section 14.

2 Loosen the switch attachment screw and set the door latch in the closed position.

3 Position the switch contact near the latch cam, (see Fig. 12.10), but not touching it, then tighten the switch attachment screw.

4 Set the door latch for the safety and open positions. The switch contact must make electrical contact with the cam when the latch is in the safety and open positions.

5 Install the door latch (See Section 14).

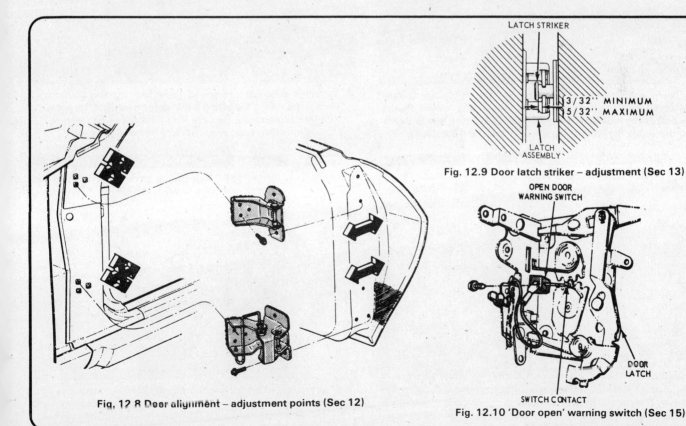

Fig. 12.8 Door alignment – adjustment points (Sec 12)

Fig. 12.9 Door latch striker – adjustment (Sec 13)

Fig. 12.10 'Door open' warning switch (Sec 15)

12

These photos illustrate a method of repairing simple dents. They are intended to supplement *Body repair - minor damage* in this Chapter and should not be used as the sole instructions for body repair on these vehicles.

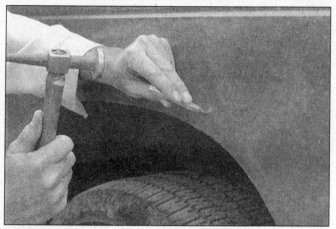

1   If you can't access the backside of the body panel to hammer out the dent, pull it out with a slide-hammer-type dent puller. In the deepest portion of the dent or along the crease line, drill or punch hole(s) at least one inch apart . . .

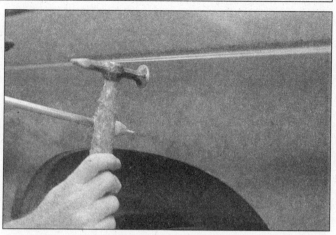

2   . . . then screw the slide-hammer into the hole and operate it. Tap with a hammer near the edge of the dent to help 'pop' the metal back to its original shape. When you're finished, the dent area should be close to its original contour and about 1/8-inch below the surface of the surrounding metal

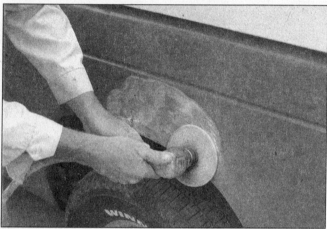

3   Using coarse-grit sandpaper, remove the paint down to the bare metal. Hand sanding works fine, but the disc sander shown here makes the job faster. Use finer (about 320-grit) sandpaper to feather-edge the paint at least one inch around the dent area

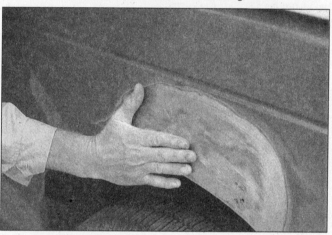

4   When the paint is removed, touch will probably be more helpful than sight for telling if the metal is straight. Hammer down the high spots or raise the low spots as necessary. Clean the repair area with wax/silicone remover

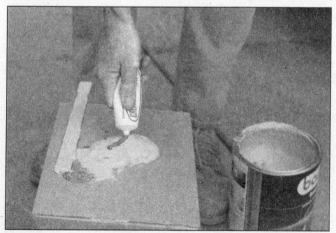

5   Following label instructions, mix up a batch of plastic filler and hardener. The ratio of filler to hardener is critical, and, if you mix it incorrectly, it will either not cure properly or cure too quickly (you won't have time to file and sand it into shape)

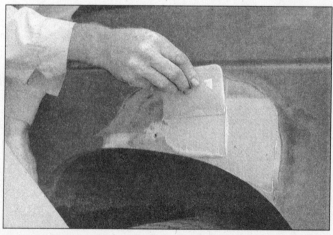

6   Working quickly so the filler doesn't harden, use a plastic applicator to press the body filler firmly into the metal, assuring it bonds completely. Work the filler until it matches the original contour and is slightly above the surrounding metal

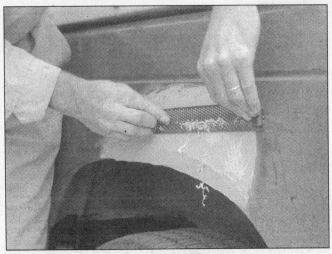

7 Let the filler harden until you can just dent it with your fingernail. Use a body file or Surform tool (shown here) to rough-shape the filler

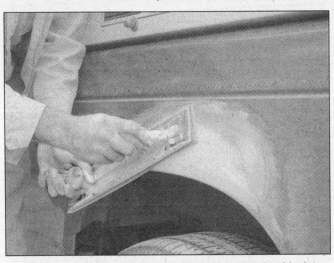

8 Use coarse-grit sandpaper and a sanding board or block to work the filler down until it's smooth and even. Work down to finer grits of sandpaper - always using a board or block - ending up with 360 or 400 grit

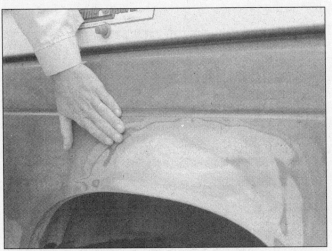

9 You shouldn't be able to feel any ridge at the transition from the filler to the bare metal or from the bare metal to the old paint. As soon as the repair is flat and uniform, remove the dust and mask off the adjacent panels or trim pieces

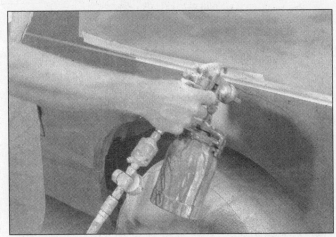

10 Apply several layers of primer to the area. Don't spray the primer on too heavy, so it sags or runs, and make sure each coat is dry before you spray on the next one. A professional-type spray gun is being used here, but aerosol spray primer is available inexpensively from auto parts stores

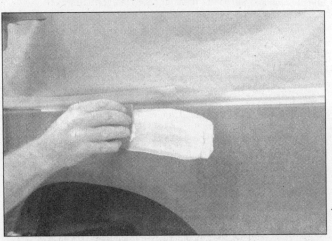

11 The primer will help reveal imperfections or scratches. Fill those with glazing compound. Follow the label instructions and sand it with 360 or 400-grit sandpaper until it's smooth. Repeat the glazing, sanding and respraying until the primer reveals a perfectly smooth surface

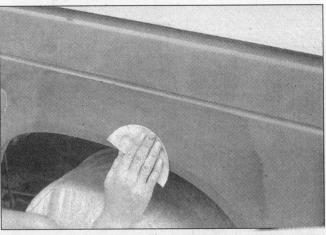

12 Finish sand the primer with very fine sandpaper (400 or 600-grit) to remove the primer overspray. Clean the area with water and allow it to dry. Use a tack rag to remove any dust, then apply the finish coat. Don't attempt to rub out or wax the repair area until the paint has dried completely (at least two weeks)

12

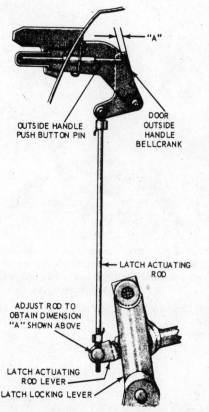

OUTSIDE HANDLE PUSH BUTTON PIN

DOOR OUTSIDE HANDLE BELLCRANK

LATCH ACTUATING ROD

ADJUST ROD TO OBTAIN DIMENSION "A" SHOWN ABOVE

LATCH ACTUATING ROD LEVER

LATCH LOCKING LEVER

Fig. 12.11 Door latch actuating rod – adjustment (Sec 16)

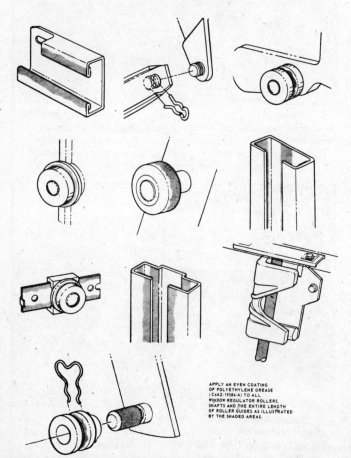

APPLY AN EVEN COATING OF POLYETHYLENE GREASE (C4AZ-19584-A) TO ALL WINDOW REGULATOR ROLLERS, SHAFTS AND THE ENTIRE LENGTH OF ROLLER GUIDES AS ILLUSTRATED BY THE SHADED AREAS.

Fig. 12.12 Window regulator mechanism lubrication points (Sec 17)

16 Door latch actuating rod – adjustment

1   Remove the door trim panel and watershield as described in Section 10.
2   Disconnect the latch actuating rod from the latch actuating rod lever.
3   Adjust the length of the rod to obtain the dimension 0.015 – 0.078 in (0.38 – 1.98 mm) at A in Fig. 12.11.
4   Install the latch actuating rod in the latch actuating rod lever and fit the retaining clip.
5   Check the operation of the door handle pushbutton and the latch assembly.
6   Install the door watershield and trim panel, (See Section 10).

17 Window regulator mechanism – lubrication

1   The door window mechanism should be lubricated whenever the glass channel or window regulator is removed or if excessive effort is required to operate the windows.
2   Apply an even coating of polyethylene grease to the window regulator rollers, shafts and roller guides, where indicated by shaded areas (Fig. 12.12).

18 Door window – removal and installation

Early models
1   Remove the door trim panel and the watershield as described in Section 10.
2   Remove the rear run retainer, undo the lower window stop retaining screws and remove the lower stop.
3   Lower the window one third of the way, and remove the screw retaining the regulator guide channel to the window frame, and move the channel forward.
4   Lower the window down in the door; tilt it ninety degrees forward and lift it up and out of the door while tilting it slightly inwards.
5   Installing is the reverse of the removal. Adjust the lower stop.

Later models
6   Remove the door trim panel and watershield.
7   Remove the front and rear guides from the glass channel.
8   Remove the rear stop from the door.
9   Disconnect the window regulator arm from the glass channel at the pivot. (See Fig. 12.13).
10   Remove the drive arm bracket from the glass channel.
11   Remove the belt weatherstrip from the door and lift out the glass and channel assembly.
12   Installing is the reverse of the removal procedure. Adjust the position of the front and rear stops.

19 Window regulator – removal and installation

Early models
1   Remove the door trim panel and watershield (refer to Section 10).
2   Wedge the glass in the fully closed position.
3   Remove the nut securing the front glass run at the base.
4   Remove the regulator attachment bolts, then disengage the regulator arms from the equalizer and window channel brackets, and remove the regulator from the door.
5   Installing is the reverse of the removal procedure.

Later models
6   Remove the door trim panel and watershield. (If fitted with power windows disconnect the wiring).
7   Disconnect the window regulator arms from the glass channel and door inner panel at the pivots (see Fig. 12.13).
8   Disconnect the glass channel bracket from the glass channel, and the remote control rod from the door latch.
9   Remove the rear weathershield cap.

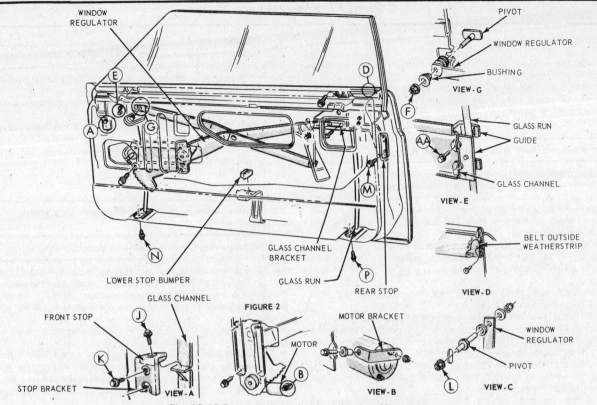

Fig. 12.13 Door window glass mechanism (Sec 19)

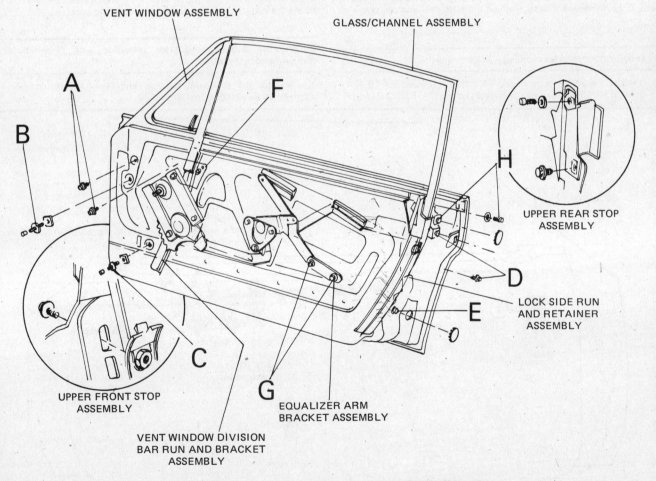

Fig. 12.14 Door window – adjustment (early models) (Sec 20)

12

10 Remove the upper rear stop and the belt weatherstrip and moulding.

11 Remove the window regulator attachment screws and withdraw the regulator from the door.

12 Installing is the reverse of the removal procedure. Align the glass and adjust the stops and guides (See Section 20) then install the watershield and trim panel.

20 Door windows (early models) – adjustment

1 Remove the door trim panel and watershield (see Section 10).

2 Close the window fully and adjust the vent window assembly backwards and forwards or up-and-down at A in Fig 12.14, so that the front edge of the door vent window is parallel with the windshield side moulding. Tighten the screw at A just enough to retain the vent window in position.

3 To align the top edge of the vent window frame with the roof rail weatherstrip, tilt the vent window assembly inwards or outwards by rotating the adjusting screw at B, as necessary. Tighten the locknut at B.

4 Adjust the screw at C until the shoulder is against the vent window division bar lower support.

5 Tighten the locknut at C and then fully tighten the screws at A.

6 To obtain the correct window-to-weatherstrip position, loosen the screws at D and E and tilt the window inwards or outwards as necessary, then tighten the screws at D and E.

7 Adjustment of the door window to the vent window frame is by loosening the screw at F and moving the front stop up or down, as necessary. Tighten the screw at F.

8 Adjust the top edge of the window parallel to the roof rail weatherstrip by loosening the screw at H and the nuts at G, then move the equalizer arm bracket and the rear stop up or down as necessary, to align the window correctly. Tighten the nuts at G and the screw at H.

21 Door windows (later models) – adjustment

1 Remove the door trim panel and watershield; see Section 10.

2 See Fig 12.15 and loosen the screws and nuts, A, B, C, D, E and F.

3 With the window closed, position the glass firmly against the belt outer weatherstrip; then position the inner stabilizers firmly against the glass and tighten the two screws A.

4 Tilt the glass in or out as necessary to install it in the roof rail weatherstrip, then tighten the nuts and screws, C and D.

5 Move the two upper stop brackets firmly downward and tighten screws E.

6 Lower the window until the top of the glass is 0.25 in (6.3 mm) above the belt weatherstrip, then move the lower stop up and tighten the screw F.

7 Check that the window operates correctly, then fit the watershield and trim panel.

22 Quarter window glass (Hardtop and Convertible) – removal and installation

1 Remove the rear seat cushion and back.

2 Pry off the regulator handle cover to gain access to the regulator handle retaining screw, and then remove the screw and handle.

3 On Convertible models remove the trim panel attachment screws. On Hardtop models remove the panel attachment screws and using a wide-bladed knife or similar tool, pry the retaining clips out of the inner panel.

4 Disengage the trim panel from the upper retainers and remove the panel. Remove the watershield.

5 Loosen the window guide bracket lower attachment nuts.

6 Lower the glass fully and disengage the regulator arm from the glass channel. Remove the upper front and rear stops (see Fig. 12.17).

7 Loosen the window guide bracket upper attachment nuts and remove the glass and channel assembly.

8 Installing is the reverse of the removal procedure. Adjust the upper stops and the window guide bracket, (refer to Section 24), before fitting the watershield, trim panel, seat back and cushion.

23 Quarter window regulator (Hardtop and Convertible) – removal and installation

1 Remove the rear seat cushion and back, the trim panel and watershield as described in Section 22.

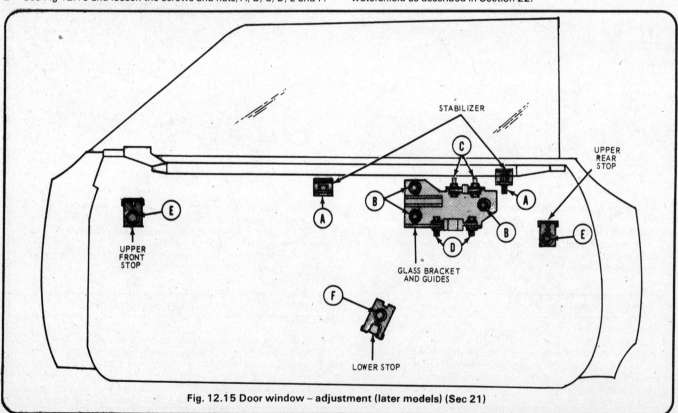

Fig. 12.15 Door window – adjustment (later models) (Sec 21)

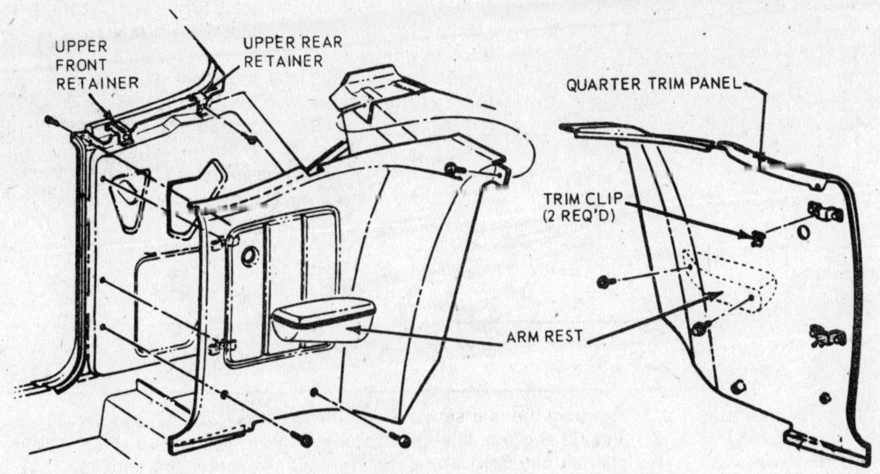

Fig. 12.16 Quarter trim panel – Hardtop (Sec 24)

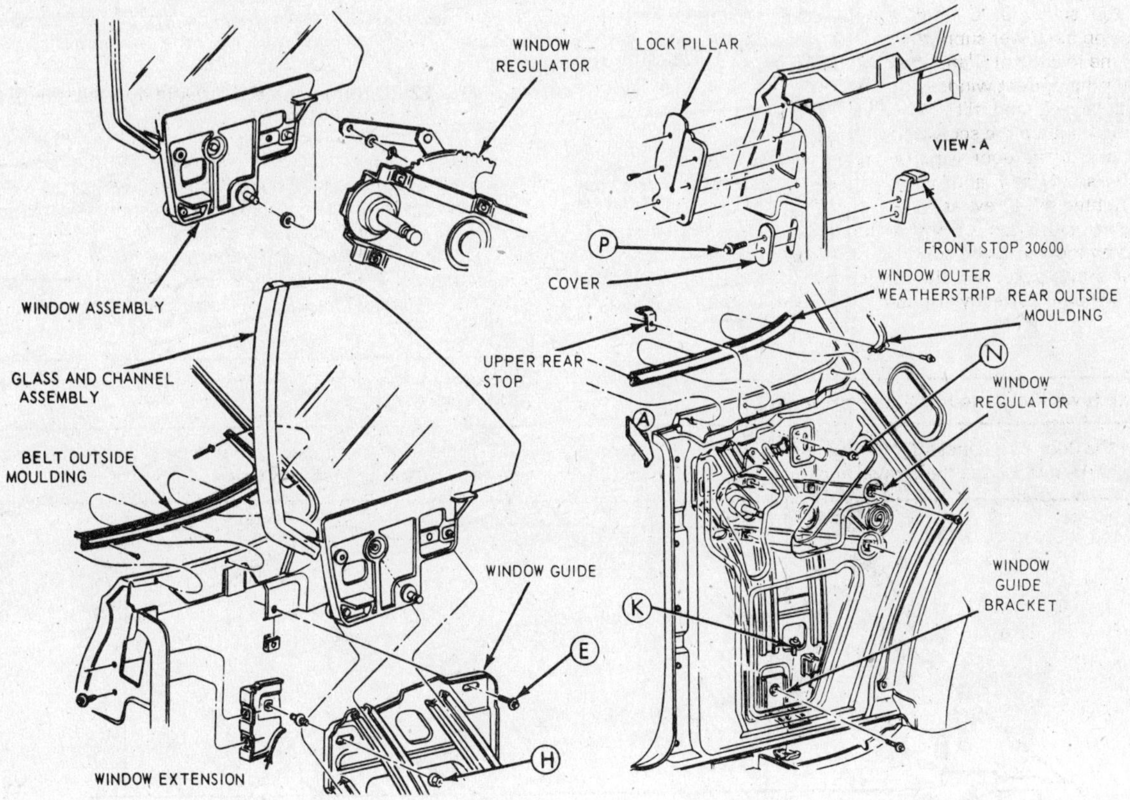

UPPER FRONT RETAINER
UPPER REAR RETAINER
QUARTER TRIM PANEL
TRIM CLIP (2 REQ'D)
ARM REST

WINDOW REGULATOR
LOCK PILLAR
VIEW - A
FRONT STOP 30600
WINDOW ASSEMBLY
GLASS AND CHANNEL ASSEMBLY
BELT OUTSIDE MOULDING
WINDOW EXTENSION
WINDOW GUIDE
UPPER REAR STOP
COVER
WINDOW OUTER WEATHERSTRIP
REAR OUTSIDE MOULDING
WINDOW REGULATOR
WINDOW GUIDE BRACKET

Fig. 12.17 Quarter window mechanism – Hardtop and Convertible (Secs 22 and 24)

2   Lower the glass and disengage the regulator arm from the glass channel.

3   Raise the glass and support it in the closed position, then remove the four window regulator attachment screws and withdraw the regulator through the lower aperture.

4   Installing is the reverse of the removal procedure.

24 Quarter window (Hardtop and Convertible) – adjustment

1   Remove the trim panel and watershield as described in Section 22.

2   Refer to Fig. 12.17, and loosen screws E, H, K, N and P.

3   Close the window fully, then position the glass to obtain a parallel fit and a flush height between the door and quarter window. Now tighten screws E and H.

4   Move the front stop down against the stop bracket on the glass channel and tighten the securing screws P, then move the upper rear stop up into position and tighten the securing screw N.

5   With the window still fully closed, move the top of the window in or out to obtain a good seal between the quarter window and the roof rail weatherstrip, then tighten screw K.

6   Check the operation of the quarter window and then install the watershield and trim panel.

25 Door latch – emergency opening procedure

1   If the door latch mechanism fails, and the door cannot be opened from either the outside or the inside of the car, get a piece of 0.125 in (3 mm) diameter rod and bend it to the dimensions in Fig. 12.18.

2   Lower the window fully and insert the rod in the glass opening at the rear edge of the door and engage the latch pawl lever, as shown in Fig. 12.19; then press down on the latch pawl lever to open the door.

3   Check the latch and actuating rod assembly; see Section 14, to ascertain the cause of the failure.

12

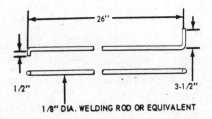

Fig. 12.18 Door latch pawl lever release tool (Sec 25)

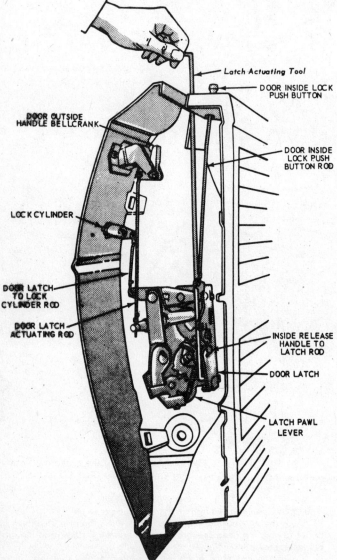

Fig. 12.19 Releasing the door latch pawl lever (Sec 25)

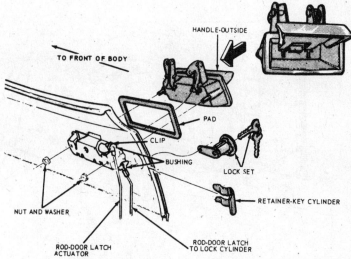

Fig. 12.20 Removing the outside door handle (Sec 26)

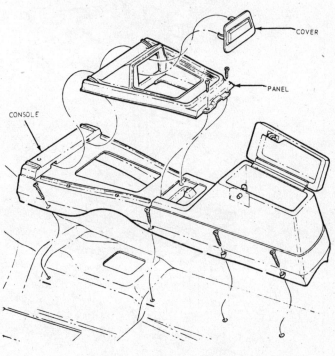

Fig. 12.21 Floor console assembly (Sec 28)

27 Windshield and back window – general

If you are unfortunate enough to have a windshield or back window shatter, fitting a replacement is one of the jobs that the average owner is advised to leave to a body repair specialist or Ford repair station, as they have the necessary tools and equipment required.

28 Floor console – removal and installation

1   Open the glove box door and remove the retaining screws and the top finish panel assembly from the console.
2   Remove the screws attaching the console to the shift assembly and to the floor.
3   Note the wire connections, then disconnect them and remove the console.

26 Outside door handle – removal and installation

1   Remove the door trim panel and watershield; see Section 10.
2   Remove the four screws attaching the door weatherstrip at the belt line.
3   Disconnect the door latch actuator rod from the outside handle, undo the two nuts and washers securing the handle to the door and then remove the handle and pad (see Fig. 12.20)
4   Installation is the reverse of the removal procedure.

4   Installation is the reverse of the removal procedure.

29 Instrument panel pad – removal and installation

1   Remove the right and left lower-end mouldings for access to the attachment screws at the lower ends of the pad (see Fig. 12.22).
2   Remove the three screws at the top inner edge of the pad to pad support, the two screws at the right and left lower pad end-to-instrument panel, and the two lower center pad-to-instrument panel screws.
3   Disconnect the clock and courtesy light wiring (if fitted) and remove the pad and retainer assembly.
4   Installation is the reverse of the removal procedure. Ensure that all the spring nuts are positioned as shown in Fig. 12.22.

30 Radiator grille – removal and installation

Early models

1   Remove the snap-in rivets from the grille attachment points, then undo the lower center attachment screw at the center support and remove the grille.

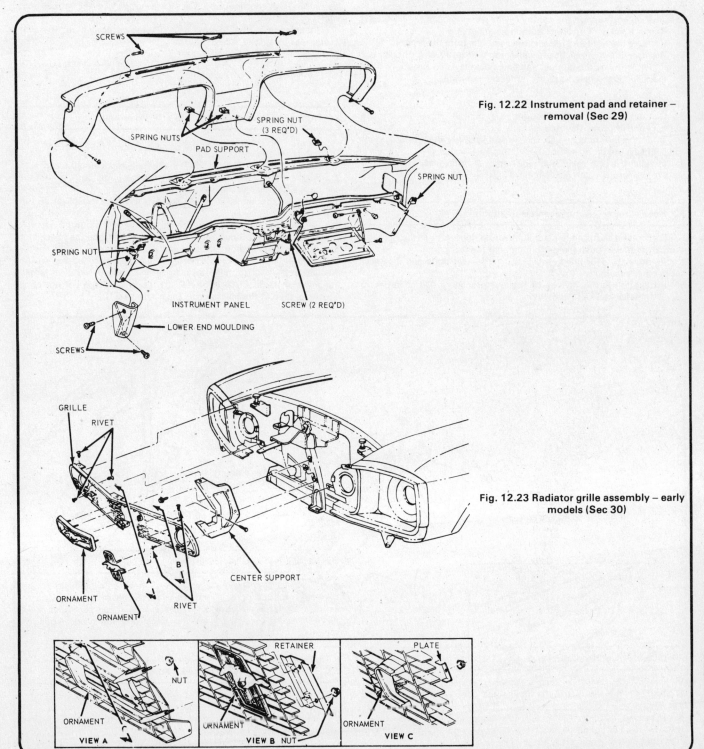

Fig. 12.22 Instrument pad and retainer – removal (Sec 29)

Fig. 12.23 Radiator grille assembly – early models (Sec 30)

12

Later models

2   Undo the four attaching screws on each side and remove both headlamp doors.
3   Open the hood and remove the parking light assemblies.
4   Remove the attachment grille attachment screws and lift away the grille.
5   Installing is the reverse of the removal procedure.

31   Front bumper – removal and installation

Early models

1   Jack up and support the car to provide working height.
2   Remove the parking lights from the bumper.
3   Remove the right and left end bracket bolts from the fender.
4   Remove the bumper bar-to-inner arm and outer arm attachment bolts, then lift away the bumper and end brackets as an assembly.
5   Installing is the reverse of the removal procedure.

Later models

6   Remove the six bolts securing the bumper assembly to the isolators and lift away the bumper.
7   Undo the four nuts and six screws and separate the reinforcement and license plate bracket from the bumper.
8   Installing is the reverse of the removal procedure. Tighten the bolts to the torque value given in Fig. 12.26.

32   Rear bumper – removal and installation

1   Disconnect the license plate light wiring connector in the luggage compartment and push the grommet out of the rear panel.
2   Remove the four bracket-to-body attachment bolts and lift away the bumper assembly.
3   Installation is the reverse of removal procedure. Don't forget to connect the license plate light wiring.

33   Motor and pump (Convertible top) – removal and installation

1   Operate the top to the fully raised position.
2   Remove the rear seat cushion and seat back.
3   Disconnect the motor leads and the ground wire.
4   Remove the filler plug and vent the reservoir, to equalize the pressure. This prevents fluid spraying on to the trim and paint finish when the hoses are disconnected.
5   Place cloths under the hose connections, disconnect the hoses and then plug the open fittings and lines.
6   Remove the attachment nuts and lift the motor and pump assembly from the floor pan. Take care not to lose the rubber grommets.
7   Installation is the reverse of the removal procedure. Bleed the system, as described in Section 35.

34   Motor and pump (Convertible top) – overhaul

A repair kit is available; use all the parts in the kit when reassembling the pump and reservoir.
)1   Remove the filler plug and drain the fluid into a suitable container.
2   Scribe matching lines on the reservoir and pump body so that they can be reassembled in their original position.
3   Unscrew the center bolt and remove the reservoir cover and the O-ring seal.
4   Remove the bolts securing the valve body to the pump body, then carefully remove the valve body, taking care not to lose the check balls. Remove the inner and outer rotors and the drive ball.
5   Reassembly is the reverse of the dismantling procedure. Position the assembly horizontally and fill the reservoir with automatic transmission fluid (CIAZ-19582-A) to the level of the bottom of the filler hole, then fit the filler plug, using a new seal.

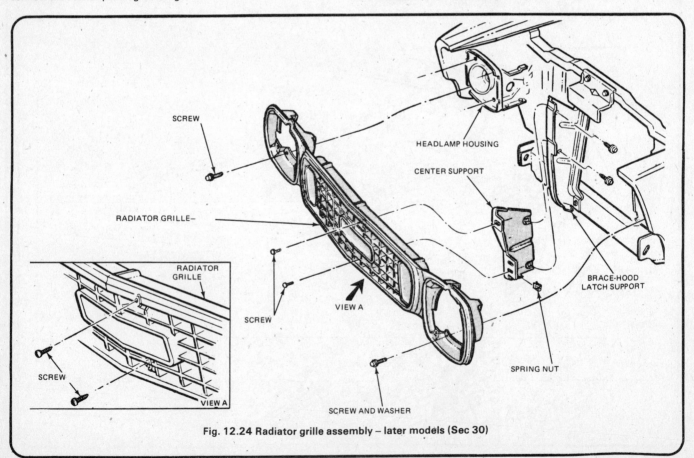

Fig. 12.24 Radiator grille assembly – later models (Sec 30)

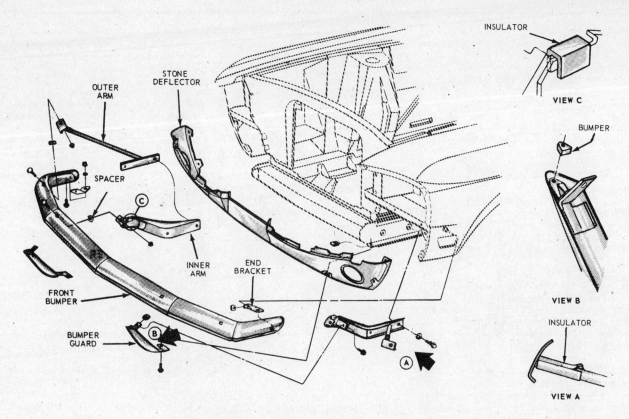

Fig. 12.25 Front bumper assembly – early models (Sec 31)

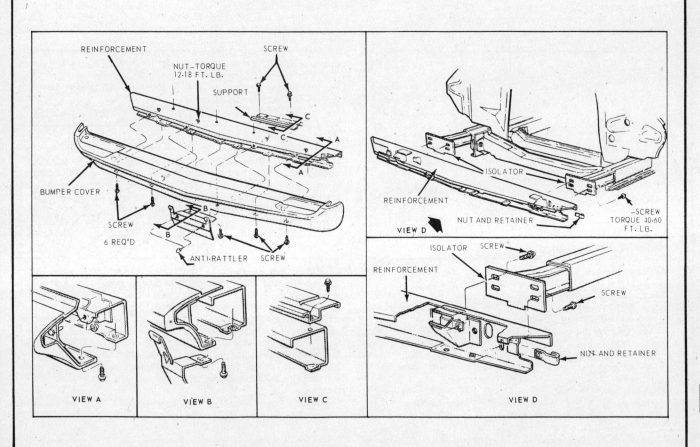

Fig. 12.26 Front bumper assembly – later models (Sec 31)

12

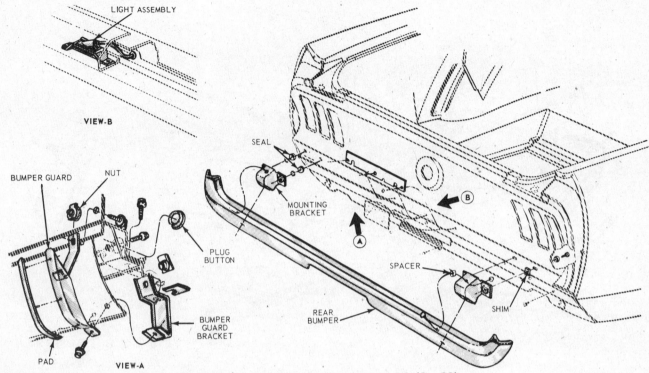

Fig. 12.27 Rear bumper assembly – later models (Sec 32)

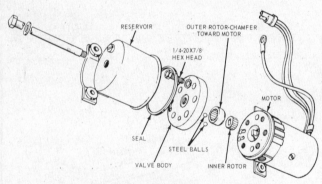

Fig. 12.28 Dismantling the motor and pump –
Convertible top (Sec 34)

of the cylinder.

3   Undo the mounting bolts and remove the bracket and bushings from the cylinder.

4   Place cloths under the hose connections to protect the paint finish then pull down the cylinder, disconnect the hydraulic lines and remove the lift cylinder. Plug the ends of the hydraulic lines.

5   Installation is the reverse of the removal procedure. Bleed the system as described in Section 35.

37 Air conditioning system – general

Should an air conditioning unit be fitted and its performance is unsatisfactory, or it has to be removed to give access to other parts, it is recommended that this be left to the local Ford repair station. This is because the unit is of a complex nature and specialist knowledge and equipment is required to service the unit.

35 Hydraulic system (Convertible top) – bleeding

1   Remove the rear seat cushion and seat back. Lower the door quarter windows.

2   Remove the reservoir filler plug and check the level and, if necessary, top-up with the specified automatic transmission fluid to the bottom of the filler plug hole.

3   Screw the filler plug in one or two threads, and with the engine running, cycle the convertible top (up, then down etc) until the system is purged of air pockets. If air is present it can be seen in the transparent lines. Check the fluid level in the reservoir during the bleeding and top-up as necessary.

4   After the air has been purged from the system top-up the reservoir, if necessary, then fit and tighten the filler plug. Note: The top must be up when the fluid level is checked.

38 Heater – general

1   On models fitted with air conditioning, the refrigerant lines have to be disconnected when removing the heater, therefore this should be left to the local Ford repair station, as explained in Section 37.

2   On models without air conditioning the heater assembly is a blend air system receiving outside air through an opening in the right-hand vent duct, which is connected directly to an opening in the upper cowl. Outside air is drawn into the system from the cowl through the right vent duct into the blower housing, forced through and/or around the heater core, mixed and then discharged through outlets in the discharge air duct to the floor area or through the defroster outlets.

The procedures described in the following Sections are in respect of heater assemblies fitted on models without air conditioning.

36 Lift cylinder (Convertible top) – removal and installation

1   Remove the rear seat and quarter trim panel.

2   Remove the hairpin clip, washer and clevis pin from the upper end

39 Heater – removal and installation

1   Disconnect the ground cable from the battery negative terminal.

2   Drain the cooling system; see Chapter 2.

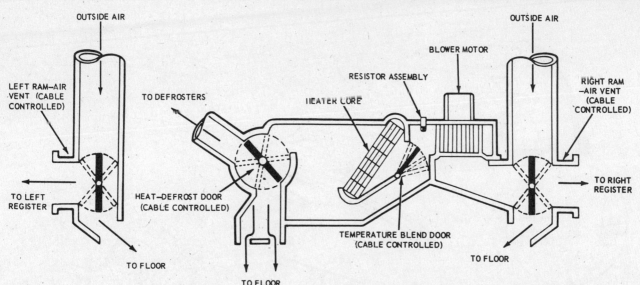

Fig. 12.29 Heater and vent system – schematic (Sec 38)

1965-66 models

3   Remove the glove box and disconnect the defroster hoses at the housing.
4   Disconnect the heater hoses at the water pump and carburetor.
5   Disconnect the wiring to the motor and the ground wire.
6   Undo the heater assembly attachment nuts, disconnect the fresh air inlet and withdraw the heater assembly.

1967-68 models

7   Disconnect the heater hoses in the engine compartment.
8   Disconnect the hose from the choke housing.
9   Remove the glove box liner and the nuts attaching the heater to the dash.

10   Disconnect the ground wire and the motor wires.
11   Disconnect the three control cables and the defroster hoses.
12   Undo the screw attaching the heater to the air intake and remove the heater assembly.

1969-70 models

13   Remove the instrument panel pad (see Section 29).
14   Remove the glove compartment liner and door.
15   Remove the air distribution duct and disconnect the control cables from the heater assembly.
16   Disconnect the wire from the blower motor resistor. Remove the

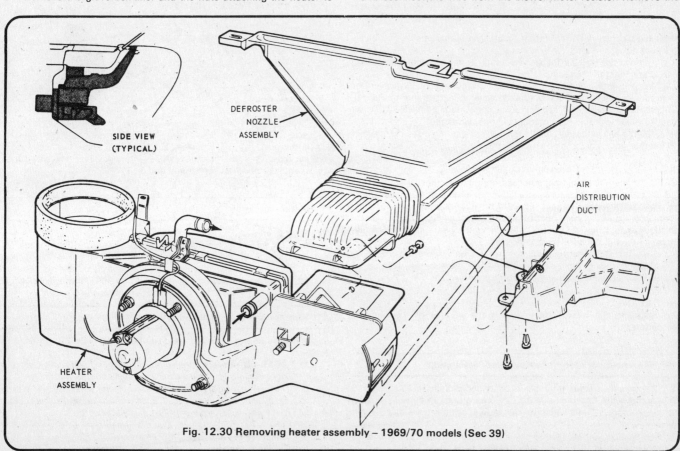

Fig. 12.30 Removing heater assembly – 1969/70 models (Sec 39)

12

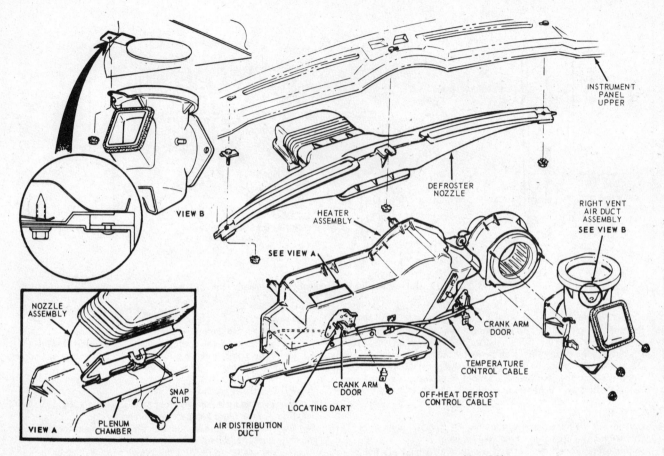

Fig. 12.31 Removing the heater assembly – 1971/73 models (Sec 39)

right-hand courtesy light (if fitted), located on the underside of the instrument panel.
17 Remove the screw attaching the heater support to the dash panel.
18 Disconnect the hoses from the heater.
19 Working in the engine compartment, disconnect the blower motor ground wire and remove the five heater assembly attachment nuts.
20 Remove the screws attaching the instrument panel to the cowl panel and remove the instrument panel right side brace.
21 Pull the heater assembly and the right side of the instrument panel to the rear and remove the heater assembly.

1971-73 models

22 Disconnect the two heater hoses from the core tubes.
23 Remove the right side vent air duct assembly. It is necessary to remove the glove box to gain access to the duct-to-upper cowl attachment screw and the three duct-to-blower nuts (see Fig. 12.31).
24 Disconnect the two control cables from the heater case assembly. Remove the defrost-to-plenum snap clip.
25 Disconnect the electrical wiring from the resistor assembly.
26 Undo the four nuts securing the heater case to the dash panel mounting studs and remove the heater assembly.

All models

27 Installing the heater assemblies is the reverse of the removal procedure.

40 Heater blower motor – removal and installation

1 Remove the heater assembly as described in Section 39.
2 Remove the four blower motor mounting plate nuts, (four screws on later models) and separate the blower motor from the heater assembly.
3 Installation is the reverse of the removal procedure (on later models match the alignment holes, see Fig. 12.33).

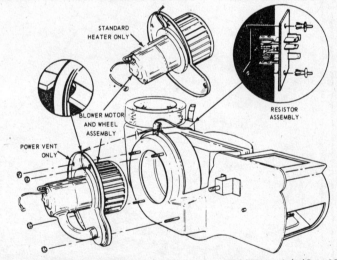

Fig. 12.32 Heater blower motor removal – 1969/70 models (Sec 40)

41 Heater core – removal and refitting

1 With the heater removed, as described in Section 39, proceed as follows:
   a) **1965-68 models** – *remove the retaining clips, separate the housing and lift the core out of the housing*
   b) **1969-70 models** – *remove the air inlet seal and the eleven retaining clips (see Fig. 12.34), then separate the heater assembly housing and lift out the heater core*
   c) **1971-73 models** – *remove the heater core cover and pad and slide the core out of the case (see Fig. 12.33)*
2 Installation is the reverse of the removal procedure.

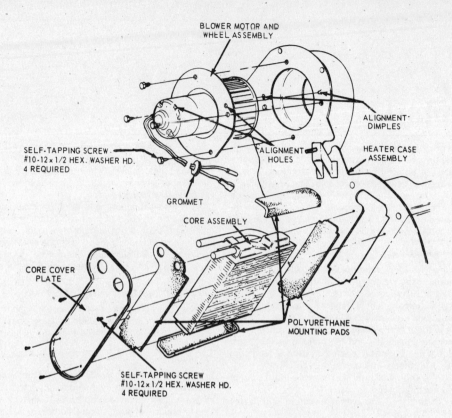

Fig. 12.33 Heater blower motor and core removal 1971/3 models (Sec 40)

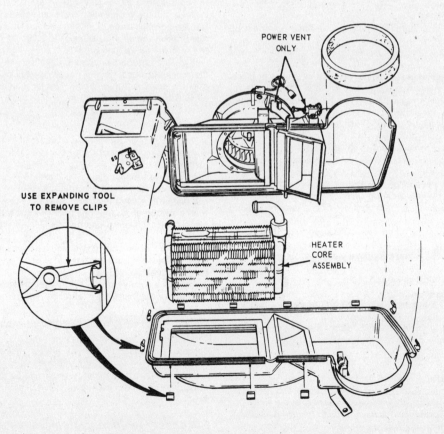

Fig. 12.34 Heater core removal – 1969/70 models (Sec 41)

Safety first!

Regardless of how enthusiastic you may be about getting on with the job at hand, take the time to ensure that your safety is not jeopardized. A moment's lack of attention can result in an accident, as can failure to observe certain simple safety precautions. The possibility of an accident will always exist, and the following points should not be considered a comprehensive list of all dangers. Rather, they are intended to make you aware of the risks and to encourage a safety conscious approach to all work you carry out on your vehicle.

Essential DOs and DON'Ts

DON'T rely on a jack when working under the vehicle. Always use approved jackstands to support the weight of the vehicle and place them under the recommended lift or support points.

DON'T attempt to loosen extremely tight fasteners (i.e. wheel lug nuts) while the vehicle is on a jack — it may fall.

DON'T start the engine without first making sure that the transmission is in Neutral (or Park where applicable) and the parking brake is set.

DON'T remove the radiator cap from a hot cooling system — let it cool or cover it with a cloth and release the pressure gradually.

DON'T attempt to drain the engine oil until you are sure it has cooled to the point that it will not burn you.

DON'T touch any part of the engine or exhaust system until it has cooled sufficiently to avoid burns.

DON'T siphon toxic liquids such as gasoline, antifreeze and brake fluid by mouth, or allow them to remain on your skin.

DON'T inhale brake lining dust — it is potentially hazardous (see *Asbestos* below)

DON'T allow spilled oil or grease to remain on the floor — wipe it up before someone slips on it.

DON'T use loose fitting wrenches or other tools which may slip and cause injury.

DON'T push on wrenches when loosening or tightening nuts or bolts. Always try to pull the wrench toward you. If the situation calls for pushing the wrench away, push with an open hand to avoid scraped knuckles if the wrench should slip.

DON'T attempt to lift a heavy component alone — get someone to help you.

DON'T rush or take unsafe shortcuts to finish a job.

DON'T allow children or animals in or around the vehicle while you are working on it.

DO wear eye protection when using power tools such as a drill, sander, bench grinder, etc. and when working under a vehicle.

DO keep loose clothing and long hair well out of the way of moving parts.

DO make sure that any hoist used has a safe working load rating adequate for the job.

DO get someone to check on you periodically when working alone on a vehicle.

DO carry out work in a logical sequence and make sure that everything is correctly assembled and tightened.

DO keep chemicals and fluids tightly capped and out of the reach of children and pets.

DO remember that your vehicle's safety affects that of yourself and others. If in doubt on any point, get professional advice.

Asbestos

Certain friction, insulating, sealing, and other products — such as brake linings, brake bands, clutch linings, torque converters, gaskets, etc. — contain asbestos. *Extreme care must be taken to avoid inhalation of dust from such products since it is hazardous to health.* If in doubt, assume that they *do* contain asbestos.

Fire

Remember at all times that gasoline is highly flammable. Never smoke or have any kind of open flame around when working on a vehicle. But the risk does not end there. A spark caused by an electrical short circuit, by two metal surfaces contacting each other, or even by static electricity built up in your body under certain conditions, can ignite gasoline vapors, which in a confined space are highly explosive. Do not, under any circumstances, use gasoline for cleaning parts. Use an approved safety solvent.

Always disconnect the battery ground (–) cable *at the battery* before working on any part of the fuel system or electrical system. Never risk spilling fuel on a hot engine or exhaust component.

It is strongly recommended that a fire extinguisher suitable for use on fuel and electrical fires be kept handy in the garage or workshop at all times. Never try to extinguish a fuel or electrical fire with water.

Torch (flashlight in the US)

Any reference to a "torch" appearing in this manual should always be taken to mean a hand-held, battery-operated electric light or flashlight. It DOES NOT mean a welding or propane torch or blowtorch.

Fumes

Certain fumes are highly toxic and can quickly cause unconsciousness and even death if inhaled to any extent. Gasoline vapor falls into this category, as do the vapors from some cleaning solvents. Any draining or pouring of such volatile fluids should be done in a well ventilated area.

When using cleaning fluids and solvents, read the instructions on the container carefully. Never use materials from unmarked containers.

Never run the engine in an enclosed space, such as a garage. Exhaust fumes contain carbon monoxide, which is extremely poisonous. If you need to run the engine, always do so in the open air, or at least have the rear of the vehicle outside the work area.

If you are fortunate enough to have the use of an inspection pit, never drain or pour gasoline and never run the engine while the vehicle is over the pit. The fumes, being heavier than air, will concentrate in the pit with possibly lethal results.

The battery

Never create a spark or allow a bare light bulb near a battery. They normally give off a certain amount of hydrogen gas, which is highly explosive.

Always disconnect the battery ground (–) cable *at the battery* before working on the fuel or electrical systems.

If possible, loosen the filler caps or cover when charging the battery from an external source (this does not apply to sealed or maintenance-free batteries). Do not charge at an excessive rate or the battery may burst.

Take care when adding water to a non maintenance-free battery and when carrying a battery. The electrolyte, even when diluted, is very corrosive and should not be allowed to contact clothing or skin.

Always wear eye protection when cleaning the battery to prevent the caustic deposits from entering your eyes.

Mains electricity (household current in the US)

When using an electric power tool, inspection light, etc., which operates on household current, always make sure that the tool is correctly connected to its plug and that, where necessary, it is properly grounded. Do not use such items in damp conditions and, again, do not create a spark or apply excessive heat in the vicinity of fuel or fuel vapor.

Secondary ignition system voltage

A severe electric shock can result from touching certain parts of the ignition system (such as the spark plug wires) when the engine is running or being cranked, particularly if components are damp or the insulation is defective. In the case of an electronic ignition system, the secondary system voltage is much higher and could prove fatal.

Index